OLIVER LANGFORD

Living Enlightenment
(Gospel of Paramahamsa Nithyananda)

Paramahamsa Nithyananda

Discourses delivered to Swamis and Ananda Samajis
of the Nithyananda order all over the world

PUBLISHED BY LIFE BLISS FOUNDATION

The meditation techniques included in this book are to be practiced only under the direct supervision of an ordained teacher of Life Bliss Foundation (LBF) and in consultation with your personal physician to determine your fitness and ability to do the techniques. They are not intended to be a substitute for medical attention, examination, diagnosis or treatment. If someone tries these techniques without prior participation in the meditation programs of LBF and without the direct supervision of an ordained teacher of LBF, they shall be doing so entirely at their own risk; neither the author nor LBF shall be responsible for the consequences of their actions.

Published by:

Life Bliss Foundation

Copyright© 2009 - 'Living Enlightenment year'

First Edition: December 2008, 1000 copies

Second edition: February 2009, 2000 copies

Third edition: March 2009, 3000 copies

Fourth edition: April 2009, 5000 copies

ISBN 13: 978-1-60607-048-2

ISBN 10: 1-60607-048-7

All proceeds from the sale of this book go towards supporting charitable activities.

Printed in India by Lovely Offset Printers Pvt. Ltd., Sivakasi.

Website : www.lovelyoffset.com

Living enlightenment is actualizing the limitless potential and experiencing the ultimate as every moment of life unfolds afresh.
Living in this divine space is living the best life and doing the greatest service to society.

CONTENTS

I. YOU ARE YOUR EMOTIONS

II. DEEPER TRUTHS OF LIFE

III. PATHS TO BLISSFUL LIVING

IV. MASTER - THE LIVING ENLIGHTENMENT

V. MEDITATIONS FOR LIVING ENLIGHTENMENT

■ Living Enlightenment is the Ultimate Meditation Technique

395

VI. THE TOUCH OF THE DIVINE ENERGY

■ Nithya Spiritual Healing - You Can Also Heal 413

VII. BLISSFUL SHARING

PREFACE

Many reputed intellectuals including scientists have recorded that there has been an elevation in human consciousness in recent times. Whether it is to do with the Age of Aquarius as rock groups foresaw or the metaphorical end of the world as the Mayans predicted is not the question here.

The question is, how do we define consciousness? As societal beings who have been guided all our lives by moral and legal commandments, our beacon of behavior has always been conscience. But conscience is not consciousness.

Consciousness is the awareness that there is something more to our life than the material pleasures that we seek. Consciousness is that tension within us that tells us there is something higher than what we see. It is the beacon of inner awareness that guides us to a state of being where we realize that we are more than what we think we are.

Human beings are far more than mere bio machines. This is why even the most powerful computer would never be able to replace the human. It can replace the mind and the body but not the energy of the human being. It might be a fact that we ascended from animals. But it is the truth that we can go further.

From time immemorial wise men of all cultures have pondered deep into this simple yet intangible issue of what lies within us. 'Who am I' has been the refrain of many sages. Many did find the answer. Their answers were experiential. The scriptures of all great religions are the expressions of these wise masters to convey their experience to us. When they live, the masters themselves are the experience that we can share.

Paramahamsa Nithyananda is such an experience.

This book is the first volume of the essence of the wisdom of Nithyananda that has so far been expressed. Nithyananda has spoken in a number of structured programs. He has commented on great scriptures like the Bhagavad Gita and spoken to large public and small private groups over the last five years. This book is an essence of these teachings.

This book takes you through an understanding of why we behave the way we do and explains how we can change the way we act so that we are in synchronicity with the energy of the cosmos. Meditation techniques provided in this book help you to experience this synchronicity.

The understanding and the experience that we are one with the energy outside us expands our consciousness. We realize that we are one with every other individual, however different the individual may be in culture, color, language, religion or tribe. We realize that we are all waves in the same cosmic ocean.

This experience is Living Enlightenment. This experience is Nithyananda.

While there is some order in the way the chapters are structured, you may move back and forth in any order to read the subject of your choice. All chapters are interconnected with the common thread of Living Enlightenment. Yet, each one is an individual pathway to the experience and not a sequential step. In this book, references of non-English words as well as of people and places have been explained as footnotes on the first three occurrences of the word, and explained in the glossary as well.

As you go deeper into the experience and feel the need to interact with others who experience a similar need, visit the Living Enlightenment section of www.lifebliss.org. You can also join one of the many hundred Life Bliss Centers around the world and interact with others who are already on this path.

This book is an amazing journey into Existential Truths and a gift from an enlightened master of this millennium.

-Nithyananda Publishers

INTRODUCTION

If you are here, it means Existence wants you to be here in this form. You are not an accident, you are an incident. You are a conscious miracle of Existence. Don't think this is positive thinking. This is the straightforward and simple Truth. If you trust this Truth, you will start experiencing life in its pinnacle.

Understand, Existence is trying to express itself through you. What you call your potential is nothing but the expression of Existence through you. When you freely allow this, you will start realizing your infinite potential. When you start becoming the fulfillment of Existence, you become flowing energy, which is what I call Living Enlightenment. Living Enlightenment is living with the flowing energy of Existence, in synchronicity with its miraculous happenings.

When you live this way, you will find there is no personal barrier, no emotional baggage, nothing that holds you back in life. Life flows continuously like a river, carrying bliss and fulfillment every moment.

In this book, you will find deeper truths and powerful techniques to tide over personal barriers and resolve emotional conflicts. You will also find truths that demystify your relevance in this vast cosmos, so you start moving in a higher plane of consciousness.

This book is for anyone who wishes to live a fulfilling life. It reveals the secrets of the self, Existence and the world. It is for every individual to start experiencing the ultimate purpose of taking human birth on planet earth. It is meant to give the experience of:

Shakti, the Energy to understand and change whatever you need to change in life

Buddhi, the Intelligence to understand and accept whatever you don't need to change in life

Yukti, the Clarity to understand and realize that however much you change, whatever you see as reality is itself a continuously changing dream

Bhakti, the Devotion, the feeling of deep connection to That which is unchanging, Eternal and Ultimate, and

Mukti, the ultimate Liberation into Living Enlightenment when all these four are integrated.

-Paramahamsa Nithyananda

You Are Your Emotions

- Flow in love
- There is nothing to worry
- Excel without stress
- Face your fears and be free
- Pain is a great teacher
- Desire is a dynamic energy
- Guilt is the original sin
- You are the best, why compare?
- You are not who you think you are!
- Gratitude is enough!

Flow in Love

Psychology explains that thoughts arise in the brain, and emotions from the heart. Irrespective of where they arise from, thoughts and emotions are inseparable. Ancient scriptures say that thoughts create us. So do emotions. We become what our emotions are. Managing our emotions is crucial to transforming our lives.

What is Love?

Whenever we look at something, the first thing we do is to calculate what we can get from it. It can be a person or an object, that doesn't matter. Our thoughts start functioning either through fear or through greed to calculate what there is in the situation for us. Our attention is centered on that object or person.

It is possible to turn our attention towards our own inner space and ask, 'What can I contribute?', 'What can I add?', 'How can I enrich others?' If the process is only to ask, 'What can I get out of it?' then it is driven by lust. If the process asks, 'How can I enrich it?' it is driven by love! Lust is an energy that demands. Love is an energy that gives.

Love is an intense experience in one's inner space. Many of us think love is a choice. We think experience and expression of love is a choice. We think that if we want to, we can handle love; otherwise we can let it go. No! It is not a choice as we think. It is a basic necessity of life.

When I say life, I don't mean just breathing and staying alive. I mean being alive at the innermost being level, as a live Consciousness. If you can express love, if you can experience love, that is the only way of being alive as a Consciousness. If you don't experience and express love, you may inhale and exhale, but you can't say you are a live being. There are so many animals, plants and other things that breathe day in and day out. You will continue to exist like them, that's all.

A small story:

A disciple asked a Zen master, 'Does an enlightened master speak?'*

Zen - Japanese Buddhist practice. Derived from *dhyana*, meditation.

> **If you try to create love, it will be like forcing open the petals of a flower to make it bloom.**

The master said, 'No, an enlightened person never speaks. Only a person who doesn't know enlightenment speaks.'

Then the disciple asked, 'So does an enlightened master keep quiet?'

The master said, 'No, an enlightened master never keeps quiet. If he keeps quiet, then he is not enlightened.'

The disciple was puzzled. He asked, 'You say he neither speaks nor keeps quiet. What does he do?'

The master replied, 'He sings! His being sings. He neither speaks, nor keeps quiet. His very being sings.'

Love is the ultimate experience of a human being. When the experience happens, we will not be able to possess the experience, only the experience will possess us! That is what the master means. When the experience possesses us, whatever we do will be like a beautiful song. Any word that comes out will be poetry. Our being will be so light. We will simply float. Our walking will be a dance. Our body language will radiate grace. All our expressions will be of great service to humanity.

All human beings are born as loving beings. A new born baby radiates causeless love. Does she know anyone around her at birth?

No! Her energy is causeless love. As we grow, society instills fear and greed in us and we orient our love based on greed and fear. Then it is no longer causeless love. It is love with a reason. It becomes suffocating. We start feeling other emotions like jealousy, fear and anger. We experience only love with a cause, a reason. But with a little awareness and awakening, it is possible to reclaim our original love.

Love cannot be created

Love can never be made to happen with just your logical decision. Our mental setup itself should be created in such a way that we become love and our actions speak love. Our logic should start radiating a love that is beyond logic!

If you try to create love, it will be like forcing open the petals of a flower to make it bloom. Can it be called flowering? No. Love is a flower that blossoms deep within your being and sends out a sweet fragrance that we share with others.

Love brings great courage

A beautiful incident happened in the life of Ramanuja*. If you study the life of Ramanuja*, you will see how he used every step of his life to move towards enlightenment.

Ramanuja - Founder of the Vishishtadvaita or modified duality principle. Along with Adi Shankara and Madhva, considered to be one of the three great teachers of Hindu philosophy.

When his teacher initiated Ramanuja*, he gave him a special chant. The teacher told him not to pass on the chant to anybody and that if he did so, he would go to hell. Ramanuja asked him what would happen to the others with whom he might share it. The teacher said that they would be led to salvation.

What would we have done? Naturally we would have kept quiet, thinking, 'Why unnecessarily go to hell?'

Ramanuja immediately stood on a platform in a temple and called out to the whole village. He loudly pronounced the chant given by his teacher and told the people, 'Let you all go to heaven! I am not bothered about me going to hell. Let you all reach heaven!'

When you are deeply in love, you feel as if your whole being is open and you are ready to go to any extreme for the sake of anybody. You are ready to go to any boundary, as there is nothing to protect within your being. Your being is totally open. You don't feel insecure when you are wild with love. That is why people who are in love always do risky things. They take the risk because they feel they have nothing to lose. There is no insecurity about anything. They feel so expansive. Love gives tremendous courage and energy. It opens you up. It makes you finally available to yourself. As of now, you are not available to yourself. Love can make you available to yourself.

When the teacher saw what Ramanuja did, he admitted that he learned a lesson from his disciple and declared that Ramanuja had reached greater heights than him. He told Ramanuja, 'You are in a different space now.'

Be Open - Not Philosophizing

The problem is that we have all practically become philosophers. We don't understand that life is not philosophy. It is spontaneous flowing energy. It is new every moment. Philosophy is all about repeating the same old things in different ways, that's all. There's nothing fresh in it. Life is fresh every moment. Philosophy robs life of the freshness.

A small story:

Ten philosophers were imprisoned in a country. They were kept together in one cell. They decided that somehow they should escape from the prison. They sat and made a big plan. They got the mold of the prison door key and made a duplicate key for the prison door.

Finally, they chose the date of escape. The whole plan was clearly laid out. They decided that on the particular night, two of them will open the prison door with the duplicate key and signal to the others. The others would escape and these two would follow after locking the door behind them.

The day of escape dawned and two of them went to open the door. The rest of them waited for the signal. They waited and

---

Ramanuja - Founder of the Vishishtadvaita or modified duality principle. Along with Adi Shankara and Madhva, considered to be one of the three great teachers of Hindu philosophy.

waited but never got any signal. Three hours passed. Suddenly the two who had gone to open the door came back and said, 'We have to drop our plan to escape. It can't happen today. We will have to do it some other day. We will have to reschedule our escape.'

The others asked, 'Why, what happened?'

They replied, 'What to do? The foolish guards forgot to lock the prison door!'

Those who philosophize cannot think of anything new! It has to be the same old mental setup. If there is some change or some new situation, they cannot think creatively to deal with it, because they are not open. They are like a closed circuit.

We have also become like philosophers when dealing with our lives. We are stuck in patterns of the past. We are never in the moment. If anything new happens, we are at a loss.

With philosophy, you have fixed ideas and you become very assertive. When you are too assertive, you can't love. Assertion is aggressiveness that does not allow love to come in. When you are too sure and filled with preconceived ideas, then where is the space for love to enter? Love needs beautiful space in order to blossom.

With philosophy, there is no room for love to settle in its existential state. It is like this: if you really want to experience the taste of nectar, can you experience it through just a set of ideas about it? No! You need to taste the nectar yourself, give it some space, allow it to fill you and settle in its existential state. Only then you will know its taste. In the same

way, to experience love, just a few ideas alone will not help. You need to allow it to grow in its existential state in your inner space. Then you will know it. Allow it to happen in your heart, not in the head. Decide to be with the heart. Then it will grow and happen.

What was once a failure within the head can become a success within the heart! Love is really a success of the heart that every individual should experience. It is easy to stay in the head. It is, after all, a mundane and familiar intellect. It requires courage to come down to the heart, because with the heart nothing is familiar, everything is fresh. At the head level you have a solid identity and familiar patterns. At the heart level there is no identity, no pattern. It is an open space. To enter into it, you need tremendous courage. That is why love is fearful for many people. It is an unfamiliar zone. With the head, there is comfortable familiarity.

Ego disconnects - Love connects

If the cosmos is a grand ocean, we are all part of it. We are one with the ocean, not individual drops in the ocean. When we think of ourselves as individual drops, we feel separate in our boundary and in our feelings. This is what is called ego. We become driven by feelings of 'I' and 'mine'. As long as this separation remains, we can never experience the energy of the ocean that is love. We never experience that causeless and surging love.

As long as we remain a drop in the ocean, we say 'no' to life. We neither love nor trust. We don't feel blissful either, because bliss is possible only for those who know how to love and trust. It happens only to those who know how to feel part of the ocean. Bliss is possible only when our heart says 'yes', when the 'no' completely disappears from our being. 'No' is darkness, 'yes' is light. 'No' is ego, 'yes' is egolessness.

'No' is the way of the unconscious person. 'Yes' is the way of the awakened one. All the conflict, all the suffering in our life is because of our saying 'no'. 'No' is a fight, a war with Existence. 'Yes' is love, peace with Existence. 'Yes' is deep accord with the totality of who we are – the ocean. Bliss is another name for that accord, that harmony.

The way to be in bliss is to dissolve into the ocean, not to be a drop but to merge with the ocean. To be a drop is to be a hindrance. To be a drop is to be with ego. The ego is the root of all misery. When the ego is absent, bliss reaches us from every nook and corner of the ocean of existence, as if it were just waiting for the ego to disappear.

Ego is a closed state of consciousness. All the windows and doors are closed. Life itself becomes insulated and encapsulated. Our ego surrounds us like a capsule. Our ego is like a sealed capsule, there is not even a small gap to allow anything to enter. It closes itself due to fear and shrinks into itself. That is how we create misery for ourselves.

Love is being in the flow with Existence, to be totally with it. Ego is like frozen ice. Love

Love is being in the flow with Existence, to be totally with it. Ego is like frozen ice.

is like liquid water. Only when we are liquid do we become part of the ocean. Then we don't have any private goal or destination. Each moment is blissful, incredibly ecstatic, just going with the plan of the cosmos.

It is such sheer joy to simply exist and flow. Just 'to be' is enough. But we need to be sensitive to feel the joy of being. We need to grow feelers. The feelers are what we call love. Love feels the joy of just being. When you grow the feelers of love, life is no longer made of independent thoughts but becomes a continuous feeling. Then the ego starts to dissolve. Once we have moved from thinking to feeling, there is only one more step and that is from feeling to being, and that is very simple.

The first step is difficult: to move from thinking to feeling. The ego has trained the mind to think so much, that's why. The second step comes almost automatically. There's nothing we need to do for it to happen. From feeling to being, the distance is nothing at all. It can happen at any moment. The poet can become the mystic at any moment. He is almost there. The real problem is how to get out of our thinking and get more and more into feeling.

Just follow the heart. Just love more, that's all! Feel more. Enjoy more so that you can feed your heart. Watch the sunrise, sunset, clouds, rainbows, birds, flowers, animals, rocks, and people, and watch them with awareness. Look into their eyes. Existence is so multidimensional. Look into every dimension like a poet. Praise it. Feel it. Be ecstatic! Expand your consciousness and experience every single detail of Existence with love. Slowly, the ego will lose its hold and disappear.

The only barrier to love is fear. When things start happening, we become fearful because with love we enter into a merger. This threatens the very basis of our ego. Ego is separateness while love is a merger. The fear we feel is nothing but the fear of the dissolving ego. Let the fear be there. It will hang around for a while. If we simply ignore it, the ego will leave us. It is a great day when fear of losing the ego leaves us. From then on growth becomes simple, easy and spontaneous. Then *we* are not, only *love* is.

Be a lover every moment

Encounter any situation in life with deep love. Soon you will become pure love. Whether it is a person or your work or a passerby or god or anything, just encounter it with deep love for love's sake. If you are a painter, just be completely in love with painting. If you are a dancer, be completely in love with dancing. If you are working with your computer, treat it with utmost love and become lost in it. Just be completely sincere and completely in love every moment.

If you are painting and at the same time thinking about which gallery to put up the painting in or how much to sell it for, then be very clear, you are not lost in love. You are in love only with some particular thing, which is money in this case. If you are dancing while calculating what you will get once you finish the dance, then be very clear you are not lost in love. You create more and more bondage by doing this.

If you become lost in every moment, you become love. Then, when you work you work with the utmost focus because you are in deep love with it. This way, your very life becomes a deep meditative love.

Then you start feeling, relating and respecting everything as a living being, just as you are. You even start feeling the other person's thoughts. You start responding and relating to the other person without him or her opening up to you. You feel the cosmos as a translucent, ever living presence. You have tremendous intelligence. You know exactly how to connect to things. Such is the power of love.

The Sufi* mystic Jalaluddin Rumi* says, 'Wherever you are, whatever your condition is, always try to be a lover!' The whole of Existence is in a deep romance with itself. You are part of it. So it is your nature to be a lover every moment. Only by being that can you experience the real fulfillment of your original nature.

Sufi - Follower of Sufism, a mystical dimension of Islam.
Rumi - 13th century Persian Sufi poet.

Love yourself first

The big problem today is that most people don't love themselves. Society never teaches that it is possible to love ourselves. Understand that unless you love yourself, you cannot possibly love another person. Only when you lose yourself to yourself can you lose yourself to others. We are taught that we can only love even ourselves if we have a reason. If we perform well, we love ourselves. If we fail, we hate ourselves. We apply the same logic to others. We love them only because of something, never without a cause, without a reason.

When you don't love yourself, you become cynical and negative towards life.

For a few minutes every day, just sit by yourself and feel overflowing love towards yourself. Feel what a wonderful being you are. Feel how much you have taken yourself for granted. Feel yourself as part of Existence and love yourself for it. Melt with the feeling of love for yourself. If you practice this everyday you will see that where you were once hard and self-centered, now you have become soft and loving.

Then, when people love you, you don't feel guilty or unworthy because just as they love you, you love yourself too. You become ready to receive love from others. Usually when others show love to you, you feel guilty or unworthy because you don't feel you are worth being loved. Once you settle within yourself with deep love, you will receive others' love with joy.

Love Existence and feel It loving you

Existence is not a thing. It is a living energy being. Every single tree, every single stalk of a plant responds to your love and hate, your every thought.

Cleve Backster*, a polygraph expert, has conducted several experiments to examine the response of plants to human emotions and thoughts. He discovered that plants would respond to human thought in a way similar to how a human being would respond. A simple thought by a person about burning the leaves of the plant would register erratic movement in the polygraph recording of the plant! Backster* called this response 'Primary Perception' - the ability of plant, animal and human cells to perceive and respond to any thought.

On one occasion, Backster* recorded graphs that registered a flat line that suggested the plants were in a state of shock. He asked the owner of the plant if she had done anything to hurt the plants. The lady told him, 'I roasted a few of its leaves to get their dry weight!'

When you start loving Existence, it begins responding to you in beautiful ways. You start rising above all of the differences around you

---

Cleve Backster - A polygraph expert who studied behavior of plants subjected to threats and affection using the lie detector equipment.

- differences between people, situations, emotions, between anything and anything. Everything merges into unity. And that is the truth. Everything is part of one Whole. And love is the only thing that can make you realize this truth.

In India, there is a tradition of spiritual wandering where people walk by foot the length and breadth of the country, visiting many temples and pilgrim centers. I used to wonder how they were able to do that, especially going through forests, sleeping with wild animals and begging for food. The secret is that they start feeling connected with nature so completely that nature protects them beautifully. Whether it rains or shines, the animals and trees, everything, takes care of them. Even though this may be logically difficult to understand, it is the truth.

If you begin to live with a little respect and love for Existence and all its creations, you will be able to recognize these things happening in your own life as well. Nature will simply reciprocate your love in many beautiful ways.

Love is different from respect

Very often, love is confused with respect. From a young age, children are brought up to always show respect but never to show love. You can hear people teach the children, 'You should respect your elders.' You will hardly hear, 'You should love your elders.' That is the problem.

Respect sows the first guilt in you that you are something inferior. It makes you feel separate from the other person to whom you show respect. On the other hand, love sows the seeds of joy and unity in you. It makes you feel connected with the other person and with everything in Existence. With respect, there is fear. With love, there is authentic respect as well as the scope for deep understanding to happen. With respect alone, not much understanding is possible. With love, there is a possibility for tremendous understanding and transformation to happen. Love by its very nature is transforming. It softens and melts you.

Respect creates distance between you and the other. Love bridges the distance between you and the other. Only because people themselves have not experienced love, do they give respect as the rule of acceptable behavior. Respect is easier but not real. Love might be difficult only because not many know how to go about it, but it is real. With love, respect is automatic and authentic. With pure respect, the appearance of love is forced and may never be authentic.

Love is the root of all religion

Love is the original religion. It is the root of all spirituality. All other religions are offshoots. Love is like the root of the tree and all religions are like leaves or branches. Even the greatest religions are only big branches compared to the religion of love!

Love has no temple or scripture. It is like the roots that lie beneath the ground but provide the nourishment for life. Without it, the whole tree dies. Through love many branches and leaves are created. But what do we do? We cling to the branches and leaves instead of clinging to the root. When we cling to the root, we get the direct nourishment. When we cling to the branches, we enjoy only one dimension of the nourishment. When you become more loving, you will enter the invisible temple of love.

A small story:

One day a master asked his disciples how they could tell when the night had ended and the day had begun.

One of them said, 'When you can look in the distance and tell whether the animal is a cow or a horse.' The master said, 'No.'

Another disciple said, 'When you can look at a tree in the distance and tell if it is a pine tree or a mango tree.' The master again said, 'No.'

They asked the master, 'Then what is it master?'

The master replied, 'When you can look into the face of any man and recognize your brother in him. When you can look into the face of any woman and recognize your sister in her. If you cannot do this, then no matter what time of the day it is, it is still only night time.'

The master can give a few hints, a little hints here and there. Then we must find our own way carefully, cautiously. Love is just a hint, but if we follow love slowly, very slowly,

we will be surprised that god becomes more and more of a reality. He is no longer just a thought, no longer simply an idea, but something that we can feel. The deeper we go into love, the closer we come to the feeling. The day we dissolve into love we merge with unity.

From time immemorial, the conclusion of many mystics has been that matter is glued together with love. An invisible force keeps atoms and molecules together. They do not fall apart because of this invisible force. Science has yet to discover this ultimate energy. It has detected a few of its manifestations such as gravitation and electricity but these are only gross manifestations. The day that science discovers love will be the day when religion and science will commune with each other in the same language.

For now, just rejoice because love *is* possible. Be joyful that love is your inner potential. You can rise to the ultimate heights with love. Nothing is impossible with love because love can transform itself into god.

Three types of Love and their integration

Many people confuse lust with love. This is one of the greatest tragedies. The person who thinks lust is love remains confined to the physical plane. He never rises higher than that. He has no idea that there is a higher plane. He remains in the basement of his house. Sex is the base-ment. It is not the place to live in. You can use it for other purposes, but it can't

You must have at least one relationship in your life that exists for no reason.

be your home. Your home is above it.

Man has three planes of being: animal, human and divine. First is the plane of lust, which is the animal plane. It is a crude form of love. It is not that love is not present there. Love is mixed or polluted by gross greed and desire, that's all.

As our being becomes more refined, we enter the second plane, ordinary human love. Human love has traces of possessiveness and jealousy. Since human love is grounded in greater understanding than animal love, one does not simply use the other person for his or her own gain. Human love is capable of seeing the other as an end unto itself.

The third type of love is divine love. It is love in its highest form, almost like a prayer. There is no possessiveness. There is nothing earthly in it. It becomes an invisible but powerful force. This is when love becomes prayer and we feel restful contentment for the first time. I say restful because the other two types of love always keep reaching for more or keep missing something. There is no restfulness in them. When the third type of love happens, even sex becomes a deep and divine act beyond mere physical pleasure.

Enter into causeless Love

The first thing we need to understand is that relationships can happen causelessly, without any reason. Only then will we understand that the experience of love is much more important than the object of love.

You must have at least one relationship in your life that exists for no reason. If you don't have such a relationship, be very clear, even if you have money, deep down you are still poor.

From today onwards start relating with someone for no reason. There should be no monetary or physical benefit from the relationship. If you experience causeless love once, after that, if the money is shared, if the body is shared, it is okay. The quality is totally different. I am not against money or against marriage. I am not against the physical relationship, but if it becomes the center of your life, you are missing something very important. That is what I want to convey here. You miss a major dimension or energy center of your being.

I always tell people, 'Do some work for half hour everyday that does not bring you money or name and fame. Just for half an hour, go to some temple or church, clean and sweep the floor, offer some service. Don't plan to become a committee member in that place! Don't think that it will fetch you good credit and a place in heaven… no. Don't look any further than that work for half an hour.'

Initially you may think, 'This half hour is a waste of time. After a few days you will realize that only in that half hour are you really alive! Only for that half hour you are not driven by fear or greed. You smile at the people around you without any calculation. You feel strangely sincere in a way that you never felt before.

If you observe yourself at other times, you will see that you even smile only after some mental calculation. Even before laughing you will see who is the person next to you. Based on that, you decide how many inches to open your mouth, how polite you should be, how you should project yourself. As of now, every action of yours is driven by fear and greed. You are fuelled by fear and greed. That's why you feel lonely and tired.

If you try this technique, you will suddenly see that your body and mind start functioning without the need for fear and greed! Once you learn this simple knack of how to move your body without fear and greed, be very clear, you can enter into love. You learn how to tap into the energy of love. You learn how to run your life on the beautiful energy of love. Only then will you know what is meant by the word 'love'.

A new center will be awakened in you. A new energy will start radiating in you. Then you will understand how loving and causeless relationships are possible.

Love, hatred and attention-need

Hatred and love are opposite sides of the same coin as long as love is conditional. Love can flip into hatred the moment we feel that our expectations are threatened. In love of this type, it remains love only as long as the conditions remain as expected. The moment the conditions change, the love also changes.

Love can flip into hatred the moment we feel that our expectations are threatened.

Often what we believe as love is actually related to time and space. So long as the distance between lovers is large and the time of contact is minimal, they feel love towards each other. However, once they get closer and spend more time together, they feel that they are not so much in love after all! That is why they say 'familiarity breeds contempt'. Familiarity can also convert love into hatred. To transcend both love and hatred, we first need to drop expectations. Expectation is the first enemy of love.

We all go through several stages of relationships in our lifetime. If you observe very closely, whichever stage we are in, when we ask for love we are actually asking only for the other person's attention. When we say a person doesn't love us, we actually mean that the other person doesn't give us enough attention. The basic need for any human being is attention from others. The attention-need, along with our dependency on others for survival, is what we experience as love.

The dependency on others might be psychological, physical or spiritual. For example, when you expect someone to lend you a shoulder to cry on, you are dependent upon that person psychologically. When you expect someone to provide you with money or fulfill your bodily pleasures, you are dependent upon them physically. In whatever way people may fulfill this dependency, what it boils down to is the attention that they give us! The whole idea of love is nothing but getting the attention of the other in some way.

In the first session of our meditation camp, I ask people to make an honest list of at least one or two persons in their lives who they really love. Usually in the beginning, people come up with a big list: husband, wife, father, mother, brother, sister and so on. They include people whom they would like to please or need to please in order to be happy themselves. As they hear me talk about real love, they start crossing out names from their list – one by one! Understand, if you cross out something, then it was not truly there in the first place.

Many people include certain people in their love list because these people give them a 'feel good' feeling. What do I mean by a 'feel good' feeling? It is a certificate saying, 'You are good. You are this, you are that' etc. We love anyone who pays us compliments, is it not? We think twice before arguing with them. We secretly nurture our good name with them in the name of love. If they go back on their approval of us, we might fall into depression, so we continue to please them and love them. Like this, there is always some hidden reason for our love.

Some people tell me, 'No *Swamiji*, I don't love my son or daughter for any of these reasons.' I ask them, 'Alright, if your son suddenly starts to make his own decisions, if he suddenly doesn't fit into your framework, if he doesn't follow your guidance, if he doesn't live according to your rules, will your love for him be the same?'

They tell me, 'No, it will not. My love will be reduced a little!'

What does this mean? We love our next generation as long as they are extensions of our life. As long as they fall into our pattern of thinking, as long as they live in accordance with our conventions, we love them. We simply fulfill our own desires through them. We fulfill our lives through them. Whatever we couldn't accomplish in our youth, we try to accomplish through them. If we wanted to be a doctor and couldn't for some reason, we inspire them to be a doctor. As long as they act and live as an extension of our life, the relationship is beautiful. But the moment they start deciding on their own, the moment they feel we are suffocating them, the moment they stand up and say 'no', the relationship takes a different turn.

Love and liberate, don't possess

As long as our love happens towards a particular object, even if the object is a person, we will try to reduce that person only to the level of an object. That is exactly what we do when we feel possessive or attached to another person. In the way that we try to possess furniture or a house or any object, we try to possess the person also. We want the person to be just how we want him or her to be, which means we are actually reducing the person to sheer matter.

So understand, whenever our love or our attention is towards something in particular, we will be only materialistic, creating suffering for ourselves and for others. We will only suffocate the object or person. Instead, if we turn our attention towards the experience of love itself, we will be liberating the object and we too will be liberated from the object. That is the beauty of love that happens just as love and not for the sake of any object.

When you start possessing someone, you bind yourself also. If you are walking holding your dog's leash, be very clear that you are also bound. Don't think only the dog is bound; you are also bound. Don't think that only the dog cannot run away, you too cannot run away! You may be thinking that you are holding the rope and the dog may be thinking that he is holding the rope. Who knows?

The next time you are with someone, when you are with your friend with whom you are completely open, remember to practice this technique.

Just sit next to him or her. Don't bother about what you are going to do or what you are going to say. Just sit, that's all! That is the technique. Actually, speaking is nothing but avoiding the other person. Because you cannot look into the other person's eyes, you go on speaking. That is the truth. The other person listens so that he can start speaking whenever you take a break! If a person is listening to you, it means that he is either thinking of something else or he is preparing for his turn. He sits there so that he can start once you finish.

Now if you try this technique, it can take you to a different space altogether. When you are with the master or your friend or your beloved, whoever you feel deeply connected with, whoever you are very open with, you can try this technique. It will straightaway lead you to enlightenment. Be very clear, I am not teaching this technique for you to have better relationships or for you to develop your personality. No! I am giving it to you to straightaway experience the pure love that can lead you to enlightenment.

This technique will take you through a quantum jump from the form to the formless, from possessive love to causeless love.

When love happens as causeless overflowing, you simply liberate yourself and the other person from your own attachment and possessiveness, because possessiveness as you know it, binds not only the other person but you as well. It tortures the other person as well as you! Real love simply liberates both of you. It gives freedom to you and the other person.

When I travel around the world, people ask me, '*Swamiji*, did you sleep well last night? It is a new place for you.' I tell them, 'Only when you have attachment to a particular house does another house become a new place for you and you struggle. When you don't have attachment to any house, you feel at home wherever you go!'

I never feel any place is mine or not mine. I feel totally at home anywhere. The comfort is always within us, never outside us. When there is no comfort within us, we look for comfort outside us. Feeling comfortable within us is the result of the causeless love energy.

> **True love is like a communion. It is a kind of resonance between two beings.**

When we don't feel attached to one home, we feel at home in the entire world. We are totally relaxed anywhere in the world.

Love in relationships

In real life, we always look to express our love towards others in some tangible way. Only if love is demonstrated in tangible form, it is considered to be love nowadays.

True love is like a communion. It is a resonance between two beings. It can be felt without any expression. It doesn't need communication because it is already happening as a communion.

If you really love a person, then your very body language will show it. It will be too much to express in words. You will feel that any words are inadequate and will only bring down the love that you feel. But if you are using words, then somewhere the love has not really happened. When you have to speak to express love, then somewhere there is a lie in it! You are using the words just to decorate the lie.

Real love liberates because it doesn't compel you to express it all the time. It just is. Real love also gives you the freedom to freely express what you want to express. You can easily express anything like disapproval or anger and it will not be mistaken for reduced love.

Not only that, with real love, there will be no domination or power play in relationships. Each person will be like a beautiful flower that has blossomed to radiate its unique fragrance, that's all.

With real love, there will be no fear or insecurity either. In normal love, physical distance between two people causes a lot of insecurity and a lack of trust.

A small story:

A young soldier went to his senior officer and said, 'Sir, my friend is not yet back from the battlefield. I request permission to go out and get him.'

The officer said, 'Permission refused. Your friend is most probably dead. I don't want you to risk your life going there.'

The young soldier went all the same and came back mortally wounded and carrying the corpse of his friend.

The officer was furious. He shouted, 'I told you he was dead. Now I have lost both of you. Tell me, was it worth going out there to bring a corpse?'

On the verge of dying, the soldier replied, 'It was, Sir. When I got there he was still alive. He said to me, I was sure you would come.'

Real love doesn't look for utility. It operates on sheer trust and is also beyond space and time.

These days I see people gifting each other with so many things to show their love. Gifting has become an expression of love. If the gifting happens as causeless overflowing, it is okay.

But if it is a condition to be fulfilled, it becomes a problem! Then it becomes a poor substitute for real love.

As long as real love is there, no relationship can become boring. One of the *ashramites* asked me one day, 'Everyday you see all of us, all our mistakes and confusions. It is the same thing for you every day. Are you not bored by us?' It was a very honest question! I told them, 'For enlightened beings, just because of their very love, they feel everybody is unique. They do not look at people as mere numbers. They see each one as unique.'

That is why, with so much patience, masters continue to work with everybody. If it were just a matter of numbers, it would be very different. When you have this love, your inner space is such that there is no logical reason behind your actions. You will just feel connected and you radiate love, that's all!

Not only that, causeless overflowing love is always total in its expression. It doesn't carry the usual dilutions of greed or fear. So any person whom you love, you will love totally without any reservations. Irrespective of the way he is, you will love him. When you love this way, even if the person leaves your life, you will not grieve. When a person passes away, you grieve only because you regret not having loved him completely. You can love him completely only when your love itself is complete. It doesn't have to do anything with the other person. It doesn't matter what kind of person he is. That is the beauty of real love.

It loves for the sake of love, not for the sake of the other person.

If you are grieving for the loss of a person, be very clear, you are grieving because you missed loving him in totality. If you had loved him in totality, you would say good-bye to him with complete restfulness, not with grief. You grieve only because you missed something somewhere. Even if it is your own father or husband or wife, it is the same. If you had radiated your causeless love to them when they were alive, then when they left there would not be any regret. But if you had loved them with rationalizations, then when they left, the incompleteness of your love towards them would create a hangover, and that hangover is what you feel as grief.

Meditation – Feel the Love overflowing in you

Sit down comfortably by yourself and close your eyes.

Focus on your heart region. Exclude everything else. Focus only on the heart.

Visualize your heart as an endless reservoir from where blessings can flow.

Feel every heartbeat deeply. Let every beat resound throughout you.

Between the heartbeats, feel the energy of love happening.

In the deepest parts of your body, mind and soul, the love energy is waiting to be acknowledged.

Invite the love energy of the heart to flow and fill these deepest parts of your body, mind and soul.

Slowly open your eyes.

There is Nothing to Worry

We talked of love so far. Love is about our relationship with others. Love is also about our relationship with us. Without loving ourselves we cannot love others. What prevents us from loving our own self is the constant worry or irritation that we generate within us. Whether things go right or wrong we worry. There is nothing more corrosive to our self-esteem than worry. What is this worry?

What is Worry?

A small story:

A man walked into a bar looking worried and upset.

The bartender asked him, 'What's the matter? You look very worried about something.'

The man said, 'My wife and I had a fight and she told me that she wouldn't talk to me for a month.'

The bartender consoled him, 'It's okay. One month isn't that long.'

The man said, 'I know. The month is up today!'

Everyone has his or her own set of worries! If I ask you what you worry about, you will tell me, 'I don't have a job, that's my worry.' Your neighbor will say, 'My job is my main worry!' Someone else will say, 'My children are my worry.' Another person will say, 'I don't have children, that's my worry!' One person's dream is another person's worry! You will not find any logic in it at all.

What is meant by 'worry'? Worry arises whenever things are not happening as you want them to happen. It is the discrepancy between your expectations and reality. For example, you feel your son should stay at home with you, whereas he feels he should be by himself - away from you. You want to finish your project by a certain time. But things are happening too slowly and it seems an impossible task. These are all causes for worry. What you want and expect does not match what others want and expect.

17

How does Worry take root?

Worry takes root from your own thoughts or words. There are two things that continuously happen in you. The first is dialogue, and the second is monologue – what I call 'inner chatter'. You either talk to people outside you or you continuously chatter within you. In any case, words and thoughts are the 'building blocks' that make up worry.

When you speak to others, what you say is strictly governed by societal rules. You automatically don't use prohibited or 'politically incorrect' words. But what you say inside yourself, no one except you knows. The thoughts that you generate inside constitute your real worries.

It is like this: there is a continuous current of chatter happening in you twenty-four hours a day, seven days a week. From this current a few spikes rise. These spikes are what you feel and express as worries. Worries are nothing but spikes in the current of thoughts constantly moving within you.

These thoughts are mostly negative. That's the problem. If I ask you to write your life story in a few pages, you will write a few incidents highlighting how and when you struggled. You will not highlight the many joyful incidents that happened in between. The mind is trained to record only negative things. Even when something joyful happens, you remember only the moment when it ended, never the moments when you felt joy. Because even when you are at the peak of joy, you are always worrying about when the

joy will end! The mind is trained from a very young age to think that life moves from one worry to the other, or from one pain to another, never from one joy to another.

In a classroom, the teacher found that one boy was sitting with a very sad face.

She asked him, 'What happened? Why do you look so worried?'

The boy said, 'It's my parents. My dad works all day to provide good clothes and an excellent education for me. He buys me anything I want. My mother cooks the best food for me and takes care of me from morning until I go to bed.'

The teacher asked, 'Then what is your problem? Why are you worried?'

The boy replied, 'I am afraid they might run away.'

The mind has a clear identity only with pain, never with joy! That is why recalling even joyful moments becomes painful.

Joy never gets recorded as thoughts, but pain does. That's why our internal recordings are always negative thoughts. Joy is like a blank recording! For example, if your entire life is like a time shaft, on that shaft the joyful moments are simply empty spaces! There won't be any recording corresponding to it. But the moments of worry and suffering will be clearly recorded as black impressions.

See what is as it IS – and move on

Buddha*, the enlightened master, used the word *tathata* - seeing what is as it IS. It is seeing what is there as it is – without any judgment.

But most of the time we see things only through our *worry*. There is a common saying, 'We don't see things as they are. We see things as *we* are.' If you feel there is something wrong with what you are seeing, then you should look back in at yourself because what you see outside is only a reflection of what is inside you. If you feel pure love inside, then you see only pure love outside. It always has to do with you, not with what you are seeing.

How can you keep thoughts away from what truly IS? How can you enjoy each moment all the time?

Try this small technique. When you see something – say a person, or a situation, or a book, or anything – normally old thoughts and familiar reactions immediately rise in you. Bring awareness that these conditioned thoughts and memories cloud your judgment and visualize shattering those thoughts. Next, see the situation, or person, or object now with a fresh eye, as though you are seeing it for the first time! Suddenly you see how much you missed, because of your own worry and thoughts.

Even when you see your husband, wife, brother, or anyone, look at them as though you are seeing them for the first time. Suddenly, you realize that not only does worry not arise, but also that you will start seeing everyone alike – whether they are strangers or familiar to you. That is the right way. No one is familiar or unchanging. Even your wife is not known to you. Everyone is constantly changing every moment along with Existence. Only your mind is trying to make them appear to be permanent.

> Once you start seeing what is as it is, all your energy will integrate within you.

Once you start seeing what is as it is, all your energy will integrate within you. There is no more worry, no more conflict.

Some one asked J. Krishnamurti*, the famous Indian philosopher, how to fall in tune with what IS. He beautifully says, 'Just don't name it, you will find you are in tune with it!'

Usually, when we see something, we either try to identify with it or we try to condemn it. For example, if you are told you are arrogant, you either accept it or you try not to be arrogant! You never understand or go beyond arrogance. You can only understand within your frame of reference, what you are familiar with. Because of this, you are caught in a limited view of possibilities. To really understand, you need to go beyond this limited point-of-view. To do that, you have to stop

---

Buddha - Enlightened master and founder of the religion of Buddhism.

J. Krishnamurti - Renowned Indian philosopher.

If you understand that everything is auspiciousness, you will drop expectation.

naming it arrogance, that's all! There will be no more arrogance. Only by naming it, you start the conflict. That is how you see what IS – by not naming it.

When you see what is as it is, you are in heaven. When you want to see what you want to see, you are in hell. If you understand that everything is auspiciousness, you will drop expectation and see things as they are, because everything is auspiciousness.

A small story:

One disciple kept asking the master, 'Master, where is paradise?'

Finally one day, the master asked him, 'Do you really want to know?'

The disciple sat up and said, 'Yes!'

The master said, 'Alright, my first disciple Hemachandra is in paradise.' After saying these words the master closed his eyes and went into meditation.

The disciple knew it would be a long time before the master opened his eyes. So, he went and asked some of the disciples if they knew where Hemachandra lived. No one seemed to know.

Finally one disciple said, 'I know how to guide you there, but I have never been there myself. It is in a deep valley beyond a range of ice covered mountains.'

The disciple wrote down the directions carefully and went back to the master. He told him, 'Master, I wish to pay a visit to Hemachandra!'

The master was absorbed deeply in some work. Without even looking up he said, 'Go ahead.'

The disciple started on his journey. He walked for many days, passing through sun, rain, snow, and what not. He became exhausted, on the verge of death. It took him one hundred days to reach the valley. When he finally reached it he looked at the valley and thought, 'This valley doesn't look all that great. I have seen many more beautiful valleys. Why did the master call this paradise?'

He looked around and walked further and finally found Hemachandra's hut. Hemachandra was very pleased to see him. He served him food and asked how the master and other disciples were doing.

All along, the disciple was thinking to himself, 'Master called this place paradise? I can't believe it.'

After a week-long stay he left and returned to his master. It took him another one hundred days to return home.

He went straight to the master and stated, 'You said that the place is paradise. But what I saw was the most ordinary place ever!'

The master said, 'Oh god! At the time of your enquiry, had you been more explicit about your intention, I would have told you the truth.'

The disciple asked, 'What is the truth?'

The master replied, 'Hemachandra is not in paradise. Paradise is in him!'

When you live close to Existence, without any expectation, seeing what is as it is and finding the blessings in it, you will carry heaven in you! Heaven is not geographical, it is psychological. It is not physical, it is mental. If you decide, you can be in heaven right now.

Worry – a legacy passed down

Worry is an unwanted legacy passed down from grandparents to parents to children. Children are like sponges. They simply absorb the body language and attitude of the parents. The parents are not even aware this is happening. For example, if a child hears the mother repeating a certain worry four or five times, the child simply internalizes the habit. He grows up repeating statements unnecessarily, which is one attribute of worry.

Ultimately he carries the worry with him into marriage and then both he and his new wife must deal with it, even though it was originally his mother's concern. They will then hand it down to their children, unless they stop naming it and learn to live with what IS.

One man was pushing his baby in a pram. The baby was screaming at the top of his voice. All the while the man kept repeating quietly, 'Keep calm George. Don't scream. It will be okay.'

His wife told him to keep quiet.

A woman who was watching this said to the wife, 'Why are you so rude to him? He is really doing his best to pacify your son!'

The wife looked at her with resentment, pointed to her husband and told her, 'He is George.'

When parents express constant worry, children grow up thinking life goes on only because of worry! Understand that life goes on not because of us, but in spite of us!

The problem is that parents expect their children to worry! If they don't worry, they brand them as uncaring. It is possible to care without worrying. Care is *doing*, worry is *chattering*. There is no use chattering. Chattering is like trying to cross a bridge before it comes.

A young boy was driving his mother to the neighboring village. They were nearing the village when they remembered a particular bridge that used to be very old and unusable.

The mother got very anxious and said, 'I will never cross that bridge by car.'

The son said, 'Let's see how it looks when we come to it.'

The mother said, 'I'm sure the bridge will break if we attempt to cross it.'

The son replied, 'Let's see how strong it is. We won't cross it without checking it carefully.'

The mother said, 'If something happens to you or me, your father will never forgive me.' She kept going on like this, becoming more and more upset.

Soon they reached the spot where the bridge stood. The bridge had been replaced with a new one!

There are two things to understand: chronological planning and psychological worry. Chronological planning is needed to set up a schedule for tasks or projects to be

Anything that we watch with awareness will dissolve. completed. For example, you decide, 'I will wake up at six a.m., do my meditation, then take a shower at seven a.m., and leave for the office by eight a.m. I'll finish work by five p.m. and return home by six p.m.'

This type of planning is perfectly alright. But before you come to each task on your list, you start creating anxiety about it. You think of the pros and cons of each, etc. This is called psychological worry! This is not needed. Chronological planning is fine, but psychological worry is not needed. It is like trying to cross a bridge before it comes.

So much energy is spent worrying and it is all of no use. In the story I just narrated, it does not mean that the son does not care. He cares without worry, that's all. Why contemplate over the bridge even before it comes?

You can clean the physical parts of your house, your carpets and floors, but what about the *space* inside your house? This space is the energy that circulates throughout your house. It captures all the thoughts you radiate. It sets the very mood of the house. Your worries rest like cobwebs in the space of your house. That is why when you enter your house, you experience a familiar pattern of worry. The patterns remaining in the space of your house grip you when you return to it. Understand that your mental setup settles into the space of your house.

The big problem is that you become so used to your patterns of worries that you end up like an island that is cut off from the fragrance of the mainland. You are cut off from the fragrance of Existence because of your worries. You miss the miracles of Existence that are continuously happening around you. You forget to appreciate and remember only to complain. You forget laughter and remember only anxiety. You forget bliss and remember only stress. Remembering these negative things becomes a mere habit.

Awareness – the benign virus!

What is the solution to this distorted software of the mind?

Deep awareness is the solution. Deep awareness is like a benign virus, if such a thing exists! Once awareness enters your system, the more you work with the mind, the more the awareness gets into the worry software and destroys it!

Awareness is nothing but bringing our focus to exactly what is happening in and around us. It is witnessing. Anything that we watch with awareness will dissolve. That is the power of awareness; whether it is physical pain, mental pain, worry, or something else. When we watch with awareness, we stop the conflict somewhere within us. We start moving with the natural flow of things.

When we watch worry with awareness, we focus light on exactly how worry is created, how it exists. Once this happens, the worry starts to dissolve and clarity starts happening.

There is a small story about Buddha* and his disciples:

One day Buddha* arrived for his usual morning discourse with his disciples. He had a knotted handkerchief in his hand. He showed the handkerchief to the disciples and asked if any of them could come up and untie the knot.

One disciple went up and tried to untie it. He pulled and pulled and the knot tightened. Another disciple went up, he looked at the knot for a few seconds and easily untied it.

All he did was look at the knot and immediately he knew how the knot was made in the first place. So, he just reversed the whole thing and untied it! The knot itself taught him how to untie it.

In life worries are the knots in the handkerchief. If we look at them with awareness, we will know how to dissolve them. We will see exactly how the worry was created and then know how to 'untie' it. The worry itself will teach us how to release it.

Work out of inspiration – not out of Worry

If you observe closely, you will see that goals always create worry in us. When we move toward any goal, we move only with the worry about the results.

Krishna*, an enlightened master from ancient India, beautifully says in the ancient Hindu* scripture, the Bhagavad Gita*, 'The person who does not expect gain or loss from anything works happily with no need even for motivation.'

When you are worried about the results, the very worry affects the results. Because when you worry, your doing is affected. Work should always be done out of inspiration, never out of worry. The motivation for any work should be inspiration, not worry. Inspiration is an overflowing energy that expands your capacity to do things. It is completely energizing. Worry, on the other hand, is something that shrinks your capacity. It limits what you are capable of really doing because it takes away your energy.

When you work out of worry, you are always bothered about the results. When you work out of inspiration, you are not bothered about the results. You are bothered only about doing the task to the fullest. Any task done

---

Buddha - Enlightened master and founder of the religion of Buddhism.

Krishna - Enlightened master from India who delivered the Truths of the Bhagavad Gita.

Hindu - Follower of Hindu religion, estimated at over a billion people.

Bhagavad Gita - Ancient Indian scripture, delivered by enlightened master Krishna, and considered the essence of the Upanishads or scriptures.

> **When you live without expectation, you are already fulfilled. There is no space for worry.**

with the energy of inspiration always turns out good results. Even if it doesn't give the expected results, you won't feel bad about it because you have received fulfillment simply by doing it. The 'doing' itself will fulfill you.

Leave no space for Worry to fill

When you live without expectation, you are already fulfilled. There is no space for worry or discontent to thrive. When you don't have worry, you see things as they are. You don't worry about what might be or might not be. Worry exists only if you give it space. The space for worry is the past or future. The present doesn't hold any space for it.

A small story:

A mother was preparing a meal for her young son. She emptied a tin of beans into a saucepan and put them on the stove to cook. Just then the phone rang. She was expecting the call and wanted to take it, but she was concerned that her son would be left alone for those few minutes while she was out of the room.

She firmly told him, 'Stay here while I answer the phone. I'll be back soon. Don't misbehave, and whatever you do, don't put those beans up your nose...'

We always worry about what is happening and what might happen, also! The boy might

not have even thought about putting beans up his nose! Now his mother has planted the idea in him. Worry infuses life into many things that never existed in the first place. Now, when the boy puts the beans in his nose, her worry turns out to be true! She concludes that her worries are always right.

Worry is only an illusion

If you look into worries, you will observe that they arise out of deep ignorance of the truth that Existence is running the whole show. If you look, you will see that all worries are mere illusion. You can understand this by observing what happens at the time of death. When you are alive, you may have one hundred worries, but suppose you are dying. At that moment, how many worries do you think will dominate you the way they did earlier? Surely only one worry will be foremost – that you are going to die. None of the earlier worries will exert any great influence. All the outer world situations remain the same, but still the worries disappear! Only loving thoughts remain for the people around you who are dear to you.

How is this possible? It is possible only because your worries were never a part of you in the first place. They were merely a part of your mind. They were nothing solid. If they were solid, they would definitely exert some amount of influence over you at the time of your death as well.

The nature of worry is such that it always goes behind something that is not present. If you have wealth, it will go after relationships, if you have relationships, it will go after education, if you have education it will go after good looks. If everything is present, it will suspect what is present!

Surrender and relax

When you clearly understand that you are part of the grand plan of Existence, no worry can take root in you. Existence is a live energy being. It has tremendous intelligence with which it runs the whole show. We are all part of it. The same intelligence that conducts Existence is available to us too. If we tune in to it, our actions will be fluid and spontaneous like the happenings of Existence. If we don't tune into it, we will harbor worry and fear and remain closed.

There is so much to learn from Existence! Take animals for example. Have you ever heard of worried sheep or cows? No! They conduct their lives like you; they are born, they reproduce, they find food, and they face death - just like human beings. You may say, 'They don't have to face the challenges that we have to face.' What about their other activities like reproduction, facing death, etc? Are they worried about all that? No! But these things happen to them too. So understand that Existence is running this whole macrocosm. It can surely take care of you as well!

Surrendering to the laws of Existence is the greatest relaxation from worry.

The Ego in disguise

If you seriously analyze every worry that arises in you, you will see that ninety nine percent of your worries are baseless. But the problem is that the ego is not willing to accept that. The ego has invested too much in worry. Worry can't be discarded just like that! Just try telling someone that his or her worries are not worth anything. They will get very offended. You would expect that a person would feel happy if you tell him his worries are not true. But it won't be so! He will feel offended. The ego feels offended whenever its worries are not acknowledged with due respect.

The ego is what sustains the worry. The worry is created out of ignorance, but sustained by ego. Worry becomes an axis around which the ego revolves. If worry is taken away, the ego suffers. The worry of work and the worry of responsibility are classic examples of this.

If you watch some people, they simply magnify their situation to prove that they have the greatest worries on planet earth! If you try to oppose them, they feel very hurt.

Even worrying about what others will say about us is a problem of the ego. The ego is constantly worried that its self-image might be spoiled by someone. It is because of the ego that we feel we want to be somebody special all the time. We spend considerable time just worrying about our self-image. Understand that the greatest blessing is being a nobody and yet being blissful. That is the greatest specialty. It is said that the most

> Our very worries become our comfort zone. We hide in them. This helps us remain lazy.

extraordinary thing about an enlightened being is that he thinks he is ordinary! So, understand that enlightenment itself is a journey to relax into yourself. You are someone special all the time, only when you drop worry and ego.

Get out of your comfort zone

If you really want to come out of your worries, you will come out right now, without trying to justify any of your worries.

The thing is, our very worries become our comfort zone. We hide in them. Hiding and merely talking about them helps us to remain lazy.

Someone asks Mahavira*, an enlightened Jain master from India, 'Who is the one who has worries?'

He beautifully replies, 'The person who is worried.'

They ask him, 'What is the cause of worry?' He replies, 'Laziness.'

Then they ask him, 'Who ends worries?' He replies, 'Man himself.'

They ask him, 'How can worry be ended?' He replies, 'By dropping laziness.'

If you drop laziness, you fall into right action. And when you fall into right action, you drop worry. Your comfort with worry can be understood even from the way you react to other people's worries. If you keenly watch, you will observe that whenever a person talks to you about his worries, you first tell them, 'What can you do... That's just the way it happens...' You never straightaway give a solution to them. When you do this, be very clear, you are not only encouraging them, but you are also encouraging yourself to remain comfortably in the worry zone.

If you really observe, we love to worry and talk about it. It makes us feel that we are shouldering a lot of problems. It makes us feel important, like the world can't make it without us to take care of it.

When you see a problem, if you want a solution, you never dwell upon the problem even for a second. You simply switch to the solution, that's all! In the same way, for every worry there is an instant solution. You have to want it; that is the key.

Most of the time, you prefer to stay in the comfort zone of your worry. It keeps you settled. For example, let's say you are visiting your child at college. You see a few students keeping their rooms all messy, or exchanging clothes and wearing them. You record the whole scene in your mind and assume that is the way of life in the dorm itself. You advise your child to keep her things neat and not to wear others' clothes. Even if she tells you her things are in order and that she doesn't wear

---

Mahavira - The 24th and last *tirthankara* or enlightened one, who established the tenets of the religion of Jainism, founded in India and now practised by millions worldwide.

Worry is that habit that keeps us from living to our full potential.

others' clothes, you will not readily erase or reprogram your recording. You stick with the earlier recording of what you observed.

There probably were many other beautiful things to record in the dorm – like the joy of the students, the campus itself, etc., but every time you think of your daughter, only this one recording comes up and you worry about her. Not only that, anyone you meet, you talk about how things are a mess in her dorm and how everyone exchanges clothes and wears them! The recording itself is not the truth. But you choose to have it as your comfort zone. You reinforce it.

Even your worry related to wealth is like this. If making money is the worry, then it clearly means, somewhere laziness is pulling you back into the comfort of worry. If you discard laziness and move, you make money. There are a million opportunities in today's world to make money.

Drop Worry, pick up health

When you create more thoughts inside you through worry, the load on the navel region increases. It is from the navel region that thoughts or worries arise. When you create more and more thoughts, you feel the heaviness in your stomach. There is an energy center in the navel area called the *manipuraka chakra**. This energy center starts shrinking with the heaviness of worry.

This energy center responds directly to worry, and affects the stomach. That is why when you worry about something your stomach starts becoming uneasy. Or when you hear shocking news you say, 'I can't digest it…' Any disturbing news causes your stomach to churn. The stomach is very sensitive to thoughts.

There was a doctor famous for his extraordinary and effective treatment of arthritis. He always had a waiting room full of people.

One day an old lady with her back badly bent walking entered the office, with the aid of a stick. When her turn came, she went into the doctor's room and amazingly, came out within five minutes, walking completely erect with her head high.

A woman in the waiting room ran to her and said, 'It's a miracle! You walked in bent in half and now you are walking erect! What did that doctor do?'

The old lady replied, 'He gave me a longer cane.'

Sometimes we are so used to living a certain way that we can't see a better way to live. Worry is that habit that keeps us from living to our full potential and invites disease into the body. Disease starts in the mind.

There are extreme forms of worry that may become habitual and slow down the

---

Manipuraka chakra - Subtle energy center located near the navel region, related to the emotion of worry.

functioning of the individual. This form of worry is diagnosed as Generalized Anxiety Disorder, called GAD. It is much more than the normal anxiety people experience day to day. According to research done by the National Institute of Mental Health in the USA, GAD affects about 6.8 million adult Americans and about twice as many women as men.

How meditation helps

Once worry happens, we visit psychiatrists. The cause of worry is in the mind, not outside. Then how will medicine alone help?

A large number of the people in the world visit psychiatrists for the treatment of worry. Medication is all right, but for psychosomatic conditions like worry, meditation is also needed.

Meditation softens you. When you soften, love and gratitude start happening in you. Then slowly, there is no room for worry. Worry is also a form of violence. It is a subtle form of violence. It is a disguised agitation in the system.

Meditation also tremendously increases awareness. When awareness increases, outwardly you might be completely involved in the outer world, but inwardly you will be untouched by anything that happens. That is the real worry-free life.

Excel without Stress

What is Stress?

Worry and stress are closely interrelated. They are like parent and child. One cannot exist without the other. What works for one works for the other as well. However, given that stress is considered the biggest destroyer of health in today's world, it is worth going into more depth on this subject.

Four hundred years ago the French philosopher Rene Descartes* declared, 'I think, therefore I exist.' This has formed the basis of modern thinking. Billions of people in this world have followed Descartes* for generations believing that unless each one outthinks the other they cannot succeed in this world.

Descartes* was right, and he was wrong. He was right in that that the human system does not know how to live without its mind, without thinking. As a result human beings become slaves to their minds. They live in bondage.

Many centuries before Descartes, a *vedic** sage declared that man does not begin to exist till he stops thinking. Adi Shankara*, at the age of eight, faced his future master across the waters of the holy Tungabhadra river. The master asked him, 'Who are you?'

In response Shankara* said, 'I am not the mind, I am not the intellect, I am not the ego and I am not the senses. I am beyond all that. I am pure consciousness.'

We are merely a bio-machine as long as we think we are mind and body. We are just a shade better than the animals we ascended from as long as we allow our senses to guide us. But the true potential of human beings is not merely to think and prove that we are superior to animals. The purpose of human life is to transcend the mind and ascend to a higher state of consciousness. In that state we

---

Rene Descartes - French philosopher scientist famous for his saying 'I think, therefore I am'.

Vedic - Referring to ancient scriptures of the Vedas.

Adi Shankara – Enlightened master from India. Greatest exponent of the doctrine of Advaita Vedanta or non-dualism, whose movement restored glory to the declining *vedic* tradition and Hinduism during his period.

You are not in tension. You are the tension. are truly in the divinity that we descended from.

Till we reach that state of unity with what we truly are, we are in turmoil. This turmoil, this confusion between our true nature and what we pretend and strive to be is what we call stress or tension.

Mind is not a machine

According to *vedic** psychology, we are not *disturbed*. We are indeed the *source* of that *disturbance*. Understand this well, you are not tensed but *you are tension*. You are not stressed but you are the source of stress. There is a big difference between the two. Let us look deeply into it. Then you will understand. You are not in tension. You are the tension. There is a very big difference between 'you are disturbed' and 'you are the disturbance'.

A group of reputed and experienced scientists, after doing research for many years, have now come up to say this. They say: We cannot make man responsible for his actions unless we teach him how to manage his emotions by managing what is happening inside him.

Whatever the *vedic** scriptures said five thousand years ago is the same thing that the modern scientists are saying now. These scriptures also provide the solution and answer for this age-old problem. They can bridge the

gap between the Western psychology and the *vedic* psychology.

Western psychology continuously gives us the hope that we can be brought back to normalcy, retaining *I* as *I*. For example, if we are feeling hot in this room, we can fix the air conditioning and make it cool to be comfortable. But we forget an important factor. The moment we bring air conditioning into this room, we need to maintain that. That brings additional tension. That brings additional problems. Now we need electricity, we need to pay the bills and for all these facilities we need money. When you go out to work, you no longer enjoy this room. The room and its air conditioning exist, but you are elsewhere working to pay the bills for the air conditioner!

We forget an important factor. *You* as *you* are, is a disease. The concept of mind, according to Western psychology, is a machine. According to *vedic* psychology, it is a process. Mind is not a machine but a process. It is constantly happening. The word *'manas'*, which is the Sanskrit word for mind, means a constant happening, something that is not passive and dead but something that is dynamic and alive.

Western psychology insists on this one idea that the mind is a biomechanical machine. We all believe unconsciously that mind is matter, a thing or a machine. That is why constantly we connect all the past happenings of the mind as a chain, and start believing our mind is a solid thing.

Vedic - Referring to ancient scriptures of the Vedas.

Connecting the unconnected

Let me give you an example. The low mood that you experienced ten years ago, the low mood that you experienced nine years ago, the low mood that you experienced eight years ago, the low mood that you experienced seven years ago and the low mood that you experienced yesterday are completely unconnected and independent incidents. All these happened for different purposes, different reasons, at different times and situations. You connect all these unconnected incidents and say, 'My life itself is a depression.'

The low mood that you experienced years ago, months ago, weeks ago or days ago are all unconnected and independent incidents. Fifteen years ago, you would have felt the low mood and felt depressed because your toys were lost. Nine years ago, you would have felt depressed because your girlfriend was lost. Few years ago you would have felt depressed or disturbed because your son was not listening to you. The reasons were different, situations were different, and the cause was totally different. However, when you connect all these low moods and decide, 'My life is full of depression,' you have created hell for yourself!

The moment you start believing that your life is depressed, your life indeed becomes depression. Please understand that it is only what you believe to be your past that you will reproduce in future. We all know that we can't fly from our past experience. How can we believe that we can start flying from tomorrow onwards? No, we can't. Whatever we believe to be our past, only that we will believe can be our future. So once we start believing that our past was filled with depression, we have created the unconscious faith that our future will also be depression.

When we believe that the mind is just a thing, a bio-machine, we have created hell for ourselves. Fortunately for us, the mind is not a thing. There is hope. The truth is that mind is not a thing as we all have been taught; it is a process. It is not a noun but a verb.

When we believe the mind is a thing, be very clear, we create problems that do not exist.

A small story:

A man goes to a psychiatric doctor and says, 'Doctor, my life is full of problems'. The doctor says, 'Everybody's life is a problem. Don't worry. Every week we will have three sessions and you will be charged hundred dollars.'

The man says, 'Doctor, three sessions per week each at hundred dollars will solve your problem. What about my problem!'

Understand, the moment we start believing that the mind is only a machine, we become helpless. No psychiatrist can help. No psychoanalyst can help. No other method can help, because the basic belief is wrong. The moment we bring a wrong belief, whatever is built on that has to go wrong. It cannot be the truth. We need to understand the basic truth that the mind is a process; we are not in tension but we are tension.

How do we decide?

Only about ten percent of what we perceive through our senses gets recorded in our conscious mind. Everything else goes directly into our unconscious mind. This is why many times we do not even remember a place that we pass every day. So long as this sensory perception does not interest us in some way it does not get recorded.

Let us now see what happens to those sensory perceptions that do get recorded in our conscious mind. These impressions are sorted out by parts of our mind and identified. Your conscious mind records whether the person you see in front of you is known to you or whether he is an unknown stranger. How you would like to interact with him is no longer a decision made at the conscious level. In case you know him, your attitude towards him and your action would be based on the engraved memories that are grooved in your mind. In case he is unknown to you also, the very appearance of that person would trigger unconscious responses. Either way the file moves into your unconscious for a decision about what you should do.

For most of us, less than ten percent of the mind is conscious. Less than ten percent of what you perceive through your senses gets recorded consciously. It is possible that less than one percent of what you decide is a rational decision!

There are two ways we can regain control. The first is to reduce the conditioning that

binds us. In our meditation programs, we work on the removal and dissolution of these *samskaras** that bind us. The second way is to be in the present moment, in total awareness and control.

Transcend time - be in the present

Your thoughts are always about your past or your future. You can only think about what happened in the past or what will happen in the future. Your thoughts of the past are usually regrets about what you did not do or guilt about what you did. Thoughts of the future are about what you wish to do.

Please understand, neither the past nor the future is real. The past is dead and gone. Most often we do not even learn from the past. All we try to do is use our past to steer the future. It is like driving a car looking only at the rear view mirror! You know for sure where you will end up!

The future is even more unreal. It has not happened. You have very little control over your future the way you are, because all your actions are steered by the unconscious mind. You are driven by the embedded memories of your past. Your thoughts are nothing but the movement of your mind between past and future. Your mind never wants to rest. If it rested you will know you can do without it!

If only you allowed the mind to rest or even persuaded your mind to rest, you will

---

Samskaras - Engrams or deeply engraved memories.

find that you reach a blissful state. That state is the present moment. All your future has to happen in this present moment. It is what you decide now in this present moment that makes your future. Once you take care of the present moment, once you live this present moment consciously, you no longer will have cause to regret your past or feel guilty about it.

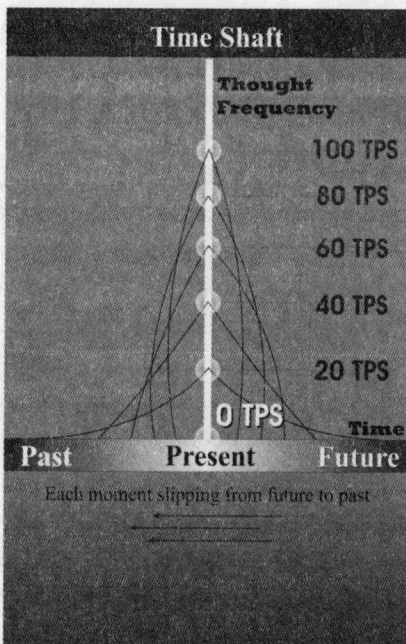

Each moment slipping from future to past

The shaft in the center represents 'time'. At any given time, the greater your TPS or Thoughts Per Second, the more far-flung you are from consciousness of the present moment. You are simply worrying about the future thus allowing it to slip into the past, without ever getting a glimpse of the present.

Meditation disengages the mind so that the mind cannot play games.

When your TPS comes down, you enter more and more into the present and when this happens, you have a clearer vision of the past and the future. You may wonder what is there to be clear about the past. One can understand that the future may not be clear, but why the past? I have lived it, so why should it be unclear! You need to understand that what you now remember of the past is your judgment of the past, not the way it happened. How many times do we talk about the golden past? How much has been written about the 'golden past'! There is nothing golden about the past. We just choose to remember the good parts, so it looks golden.

When you are in the intuitive state, be very clear: for those few moments, your TPS has dropped and you are more in the present. When your TPS is zero, you can clearly see the entire past and future.

The point where the future meets the past is the present. This is where your thought frequency is zero and you are in a no-mind state. You have not merely controlled or suppressed the mind, which is impossible. You have transcended the mind, which is possible.

Meditation brings the mind to rest. Meditation disengages the mind so that the mind cannot play games. We can also reach this state in the master's presence. The master is always in a no-mind state, which is the zero TPS state. When you are in his awareness, whether physically or otherwise, your own

> **You can reach zero TPS just by being in the master's presence.**

TPS also drops. You can reach zero TPS just by being in the master's presence. The presence of the master is meditation. Awareness of the master is meditation.

Physiological effects of Stress

We have looked at what the scriptures say and what I think about why stress is created. Let us now look at what science says.

We all have a part of our brain that controls our actions such as breathing, digestion and such activities that the body does automatically, involuntarily. Nature has designed a fail-safe system in a part of our brain called hypothalamus. This part of the brain also includes what biologists refer to as the reptilian brain.

Behavioral scientists often talk about the fight or flight response. When the body-mind perceives a danger to our survival the hypothalamus is alerted by our unconscious mind. The unconscious mind functions at speeds a million times faster than the conscious mind. So even before we consciously become aware of danger, we instinctively become alert. The hypothalamus activates the pituitary gland, the master gland, which then activates the adrenalin glands that secrete the adrenalin hormone, which is pumped into our extremities, the hands and legs. We then get ready for the

'fight or flight' reaction – either the energy prepares us to fight the threat or to run away from the threat.

The unconscious reptilian brain takes the decision to release chemicals into our body to protect us. This worked very well in the days of the caveman when he faced lions and tigers. He had to be ready even without thinking to fight or run away.

To study the effect of adrenalin on human beings today, experiments were carried out on athletes. Sprinters were lined up at the starting block and moments before the pistol was raised to signal to them to start running the umpire lowered his arm. So, the sprinters had to fall back and reposition themselves. This was repeated six times. Without even running a meter the sprinters collapsed at the starting block! The adrenalin level in their bodies had become dangerously high. The life saving adrenalin can become a killer when it is produced without reason.

The chances of our meeting a tiger or a lion are quite slim these days. Nevertheless our unconscious mind keeps sending signals of such danger. These are called 'fear strokes'. Psychologists estimate that we face at least half a dozen such fear strokes every day. These fear strokes produce large quantities of adrenalin in us. It has been established that depression is a direct result of such adrenalin production. Depression in turn is considered to be the main cause of many chronic and fatal illnesses.

Medical research has found that many young people in rich countries, even teenagers, have arteries so badly blocked that their arteries are similar to sixty-year-old people! Doctors have established that the physical condition is only one part of the problem. A much larger part is the emotional condition. It is now fairly well established that an emotional trigger causes the immediate onset of a heart attack or stroke, even though the physical condition may have been present for a long time.

Stress is a killer, but it is in the mind.

Is Stress work related?

In an IT company the Chief Executive received an enquiry for a project. He sent it down for a proposal. The team that worked on such projects did a full review and said that they could do the job in six months at a cost of a million dollars. The manager in charge of the team reviewed this and said the team can do this in 4 months at a cost of three quarter million dollars.

The proposal went up to a General Manager. The General Manager called everyone, gave them a pep talk and said, 'We should be able to do this for half a million dollars in three months.' Then he sent this as his proposal to the Chief Executive.

The Chief Executive called the client and told him that his company will deliver the product in two months at a cost of half a million dollars.

People who work in corporations can relate with this incident. People who make decisions and commitments are often out of touch with ground reality. Once such decisions are made their egos are in play. Anything can be sacrificed but not the ego! A simple study of corporate history can show how many companies have failed because of the egos of the people who led them.

Many companies have failed because of the egos of the people who led them.

I am told by some of my disciples in the corporate field about something called Level 5 Leadership. This is about those corporate leaders who put themselves behind the needs of the company and the people who work for them rather than placing their own ego needs first. Research has shown that the Chief Executives of companies that have been commercially successful consistently are hardly known to the outside world! These leaders are so humble, and focused inwards.

Stress at the workplace starts with our education system. We start ranking children from a very young age. When in a group three people are graded as heroes, the rest of the group feels useless. We are taught to compete from a very early age. This comparison continues into the workplace and converts it into a battlefield.

The so-called Human Resource programs specify that people must be categorized. I am told that in many corporations it is necessary to show that ten or fifteen percent of the people are bad performers. People are reduced to statistics! In order to survive people are forced to make others victims. This is probably why they call these offices 'concrete jungles'!

As long as people are driven by fear and greed, they cannot be inspired. They can be controlled and made to perform routine tasks but they cannot be inspired to do the impossible. This is the dilemma today's corporations face. They need people to perform but their kit of motivational techniques is not enough. It contains the whip and the carrot, nothing more.

A well known psychologist built a model of how human beings move up in their desires. This is now named after him as Maslow's[*] hierarchy of needs. At the base of this pyramid are one's survival needs of food, shelter and other material essentials. People then look for fulfillment in the society they live in, such as building a network and so on. They then seek love and attention. Then they look for respect, name and fame. After all this they are still dissatisfied. They feel that there is something still missing in their lives.

That something is within. Maslow[*] called it self-actualization. This is the zone where we flow free of stress. This is the zone of inner realization. This is the zone where you know that you are one with the universal energy. Whether you work at home, in an office or factory or you do not work at all, you still look forward to this state where you are centered.

This is what we teach in our basic Life Bliss Program courses. The five levels of the pyramid that Maslow[*] drew correspond to the seven levels of energy that we carry within us. These seven centers of energy are called *chakras*[*] in the *vedic* system. Each *chakra* represents an emotional state as well as a state of desire. As we fulfill the needs of each *chakra* we move up in energy till we reach a state of fulfillment. It is a process many thousands of people have gone through with remarkable effect. We have taught these programs in many corporations worldwide. I call this a 'Guaranteed Solution'.

Meditation technique

This is a simple and yet a powerful technique to clear stress. We teach this technique in our Life Bliss Programs for unblocking the *manipuraka chakra*[*] or navel energy center, which is the seat of stress. This technique should always be practised before a meal, when the stomach is empty and a few hours before sleep.

While standing, shout, scream, rave and rant in a language that you do not know. If anyone is listening, it should also not make any sense to them. Be aggressive in letting out all your emotions and feelings that will start

---

Maslow - American psychologist famous for his concept of the five layered hierarchy of needs.

Chakras - Energy centers in the body. Literally means 'wheel' based on the experience of mystics who perceived these energy centers as whirlpools of energy. There are seven major *chakras* along the spine: *muladhara, swadhishthana, manipuraka, anahata, vishuddhi, ajna* and *sahasrara*.

Manipuraka chakra - Subtle energy center located near the navel region, related to the emotion of worry.

pouring out of you once you start. Cry if you so wish. Roll on the floor if your emotions drive you.

This technique is a powerful meditation. It unblocks your unconscious and allows all the negativities stored inside to dissolve. Typical psychoanalytical sessions when patients talk to their analysts, or even throw things around for catharsis, are still conscious processes. Only ten percent of your stored memories will be released. Processes such as hypnosis are through the unconscious and you have no control. This technique is a superconscious process in which you retain awareness while cleansing yourself.

Practice this technique for twenty minutes. Then sit down and allow the energy to spread within you in silence for ten minutes. During this silence just be a witness to your thoughts. Do not suppress them or chase them.

Face Your Fears and Be Free

What is Fear?

Fear is a deeper dimension of worry. Worry can cause ulcers. Fear on the other hand can even destroy life. However, unlike worry without which life is possible, fear seems woven into our lives. It is possible to face fear without fear. A person who we call courageous is not one without fear, but one who has learnt to face fear without fear.

Fear is a form of energy inside us. That is why it cannot be destroyed. Energy can neither be created nor destroyed; it can only be changed from one form to another.

Understand, your fear is directly connected to your life energy. Whenever you are facing a survival threat, you will see your fear rising and the adrenalin release happening in your body. That adrenalin release gives you so much energy that you can almost fly. We call it the fight or flight response; either you face the fear and fight, or you run away. There will be so much energy in your body the moment you face a survival threat. Whenever that threat is real, the *swadhishthana chakra*[*], the seat of life, gets completely shaken!

Big Bang and Black Hole inside you

When there is pure desire or pure greed in you without any object in particular, it becomes the overflowing energy of creation, expansion, or Big Bang[*]! For no reason, you simply explode with energy. In the same way, when there is pure fear in you without any object in particular, it becomes contraction, black hole[*].

Fear is your nature, but don't direct it towards any object. Having fear is natural.

Swadhishthana chakra – Subtle energy center corresponding to the spleen.

Big Bang – Cosmological model of the universe where the universe is considered to have originated from a highly dense initial state at some time in the past, and continues to expand to this day.

Black hole - A theoretical region of space in which the gravitational field is so powerful that nothing, not even light can escape from it.

Fear is the fight between faith in oneself versus the negative idea about your future.

But connecting the fear to an object is societal. Pure fear helps in survival and it is spontaneous.

Enormous energy radiating from you for no reason is pure greed. If it is because of an object, it becomes ordinary greed. In the same way, energy settling back within you for no reason is pure fear. If it is because of an object, it becomes ordinary fear. Unless the black hole* happens, the Big Bang* cannot happen. It is part of life, part of the drama, part of the game. Pure fear means you are relaxing into yourself, settling inside you. That is what we call destruction. The birth of this cosmos is the Big Bang, and death is the black hole*. Birth of your being is big bang for you. Death of your being is black hole for you. The inhaling breath is pure desire. The exhaling breath is pure fear.

Prana – the life energy that enters along with the air - goes into you because of the Big Bang. *Prana* leaving your system with the outgoing air is the black hole. When you resist or fight with the Big Bang or black hole, you create disturbance in your system.

When fear happens, when the black hole happens, it means that you are turning towards peace or getting ready for the Big Bang. Whenever pure fear happens, you become rejuvenated with a tremendous relaxation which surges as courage and energy in you!

Fight between your potentiality and your negative approach

Whenever you are afraid of losing something that you have, or you fear you cannot achieve something that you want to have, there is a fight going on between your potentiality and your negative approach to the future.

If you are sure there is no possibility of achieving something, that you don't have the potentiality, you will not have fear. If you are sure that you can achieve something, then also, you don't have fear.

Fear is the fight between faith and belief in oneself on one hand, versus the negative idea or expectation you have about your future on the other hand. You are literally fighting with your own positive and negative energies.

If you are very sure you don't have the potentiality, that you can't achieve, then you won't have fear. If you are very confident you are going to achieve, then also you won't have fear. However, if there is something you want to achieve, but you are not sure that you can achieve it, then you will have fear. The

---

Big Bang – Cosmological model of the universe where the universe is considered to have originated from a highly dense initial state at some time in the past, and continues to expand to this day.

Black hole - A theoretical region of space in which the gravitational field is so powerful that nothing, not even light can escape from it.

fight between these two ideas, the dilemma is what we call fear.

There are two ways to escape fear. One way is to block all possibility. This means you can die, then there won't be any more fear! The second way to escape fear is to break the boundary of possibilities. If there is infinite possibility, if there is no boundary, if there is nothing that limits you, then you become fearless. Just by having this understanding, something will click in you and so many fears will disappear from your being!

There is a beautiful story:

One person wrote on the wall of a temple where the teachings are written, 'Soham' - 'I am That.' It means, 'Everything is possible by me.'

Another person came and wrote, 'Dasoham' - 'Nothing can be done by me. I am a slave.' Again that is also okay.

A third person came and wrote, 'Sadasoham' - 'Always I am That.'

If you are in tune with the idea, 'Nothing can be done by me,' you are a *bhakti yogi* * - you surrender. If you think, 'Everything can be done by me,' you are a *gnana yogi* * - you explore and experience. Whether you work in this path or in that path, going beyond fear is possible. But you should be completely connected to one ideology or the other. Either you should be ready to work with 'Everything is possible for me,' or you should be ready to work with 'Nothing is possible for me.'

Increased possibility for enlightenment

People come and say to me, 'I have too many fears. What can I do?' I tell them, 'If you have too many fears, the possibility for enlightenment is more. So many doors are available to you!'

For a person who doesn't have too many fears, the possibility, the number of doors is also fewer because he leads a dull life. A person who leads a dull life will not have much fear. He has nothing much to lose, nothing much to decide. He is not taking many risks.

All you need to do is this: every time you feel fear, do not disrespect yourself. Do not lose confidence or condemn yourself thinking, 'What kind of a being am I?' Actually people who can face their fears do not have so many problems. People who are afraid of their fears create more problems for themselves. When you brood too much about your fears, you start thinking you have problems.

Sometimes, just by switching your attention to something else, you can come out of fear. But that is not fearlessness. Fearlessness means taking a quantum jump into the consciousness where you will never experience fear of losing anything!

Be very clear: the fears that you have about your life - fear of failure, fear of losing

---

Bhakti yogi - A person who follows the path of devotion, *bhakti yoga*, as a means to enlightenment.

Gnana yogi - One who follows the path of knowledge for Self Realization.

All our fears are actually fear of death under various disguises. your near and dear ones, fear of losing your wealth, fear of the unknown - every fear can be used as a door to enlightenment.

Another important truth you should know:

There is something within you that never dies which is your source of energy. There is also something within you that dies; something that is actually never alive, even now. The fear of death exists in you because you think there is something you have now that will be taken away from you. No! Anything that you have now cannot be taken away. Anything that can be taken away, you never had in the first place. Anything that can die can never occupy your inner space.

Fearlessness is courage to face Fear

You cannot conquer fear. Fearlessness means intelligence to live the intense fear without directing it towards any object. When there is no object to be afraid of, the intense fear will give such an intense relaxation and peace.

Fear is a powerful energy which gives a deep relaxation, self-centeredness. The fear center is the rejuvenation center.

Be very clear: fearlessness does not mean non-existence of fear. It means the fear is there, but you have tremendous energy or courage to live with it and face it. Fearlessness means having the energy or the courage to

live even with the maximum fear – going beyond that fear and being neither attached to nor detached from the fear.

One more important thing you should know is fear is part of the nature of life. You can be fearless if you are already in your grave! Then there is no need to be afraid of anything because you have nothing to lose! If you have something to lose, you will have fear. That is the nature of life itself.

Fear does not exist when things are definite and known. Fear exists only when things are not definite, when they are mere possibilities and unknown in that sense. For example, death is a possibility. As an incident it is definite, but when and how it might happen, is not clear. So there is always fear associated with it.

If you can just look into the darkness, the fear, with awareness, you will live through it and get over it.

Fear of losing identity

The biggest fear human beings have is the fear of losing their identity. Even the fear of losing one's life is not as great as the fear of losing the identity. The fear of losing your identity is much worse than the fear of death.

Fear of death

All our fears – losing physical health, mental stability, wealth, name and fame, or loved ones - are actually fear of death under various disguises.

A small story:

A man had prepared thoroughly to deliver a speech at a public function. He suddenly went blank when he stepped on stage and took the microphone in hand. He was gripped by stage fright! He just stood speechless in front of the huge crowd for a few minutes.

Then suddenly, after some time, he said, 'The human mind is the most amazing thing in this world. It starts working from the moment you are born and never stops working until the moment you die – except when you have to make a speech!'

The social fear – fear of being rejected by society – makes us do things to please society, even when it is not good for us. In this process, many times, we sacrifice what our being really wants to do. That fear of not being accepted by society is just another form of the fear of death – death of the ego.

Every act of ours is unconsciously related to death and the fear of dying. Understanding death can change your entire perception of life. It can simply transform the way you handle all your fears. (*A detailed understanding of death is provided in the chapter on 'Death'.*)

Anger – the active form of Fear

Fear is what leads to anger. Fear is the passive form of the energy while anger is the active expression.

A small story:

A man rushed into the post office very angrily with a bunch of papers in hand, saying, 'How dare they send me threatening letters like this!' The official at the post office said, 'Yes, sending threatening letters is a legal offense. Do you know who has been sending you these letters?'

The man shouted back, 'Of course, I do! It is the Income Tax people!'

When you are angry, just look into the anger. At the root of it, you will find a deep fear.

Try this for yourself: if you are feeling fear, express anger at that time. Throw your hands, stamp your feet – express the energy. You will see the fear disappears. You will see for yourself how fear can simply transform to anger. Similarly, fear can also transform to hate. You just need to be aware of yourself and witness how the emotions subtly change from one form to another. When you understand this play, you can easily get out of the game.

Fear strokes

Psychologists talk about fear strokes. Say you are walking in the garden in the dark, and you see a coil of rope - you start shivering, imagining it to be a snake. That sudden shock you get before realizing it is just a rope and not a snake, is what is called a fear stroke. A fear stroke is like shaking a rose plant from its roots - if you keep shaking it long enough, it will die.

It is said that we undergo six to twelve fear strokes every day and night, in dreams and also in wakefulness. Imagine what happens to our being! Fear strokes originate from unconsciousness. When they are viewed with awareness and consciousness, they can be substantially reduced.

How to Overcome Fear

Witnessing and acceptance

When you are faced with fear, don't try to resist it or suppress it. Just look at the fear, note the fear and accept it. Acceptance of the fear dissolves the fear. Allow the fear to shake you. If your body trembles, let it tremble. If your eyes water, let the tears come. Just be like a blade of grass in the wind - bending without resistance.

A small story:

On a dark night, a man was walking on a narrow path. Suddenly, his foot hit a rock and he stumbled and slipped down. He managed to catch hold of a branch hanging over the rock. It was completely dark. The man tightly held onto the branch. He shouted for help but the only response was his voice echoing back. Hearing the echo, the man was terrified that he might be at the mouth of a huge abyss.

The night seemed endless and the man was desperately holding on, hoping he could get some help. Finally dawn arrived. The man looked down to see how deep the abyss was, but there was no abyss, just two feet down was a big rock!

Your fears are exactly like his. You think it is an abyss but it is actually just a few feet. If you can face your fears, you see they have no depth. Because you magnify the fears, you imagine them to be an abyss. It is your choice, to let go of the branch, the fear, or to keep clinging onto it and torturing yourself.

Acceptance is the only way to conquer inevitable things. When you accept, suddenly you see the fear disappear. The moment you accept, fear loses its power to frighten you. When you don't fight with it, you will see fear as deep peace. When the fear stroke happens, just live it. That is the only way.

When you have an object connected to fear, accept it. That acceptance transforms. The more you fight, the more you empower fear. Diverting your attention away from the fear is also not the way because then the fear still remains with you. It does not mean that you are out of fear.

Allow the fear to take over itself. Go into the fear two to three times. Live the fear intensely without any reservations. Suddenly you will find that it doesn't touch you anymore!

Swadhishthana Chakra - seat of life and death

Fear is associated with the *swadhishthana chakra*, the subtle energy center two inches below the navel region.

This is an incident from my life when I was young:

I used to circumambulate the Arunachala hill* every day. I would start early in the morning at around four am, and go around the hill chanting and singing keertans*.

One morning I started very early, soon after midnight. In those days there were no roads or lights on the path around the hill. It was a dense forest all the way. I was happily singing and walking with my eyes down. Suddenly, at a spot near a small river, I looked up and saw a pack of fierce-looking hyenas staring at me intensely ready to pounce on me!

In that sudden deep fear, I just let out a scream from the depths of my hara*, the swadhishthana chakra*. It was a scream of pure fear that I had never experienced before. It was so complete that never again did I feel shaken by fear again in my life!

I felt a total surrender to Arunachala* and a deep trust that Arunachala* would take care of me. Suddenly, from nowhere, an elderly sannyasi* appeared in front of me with a big stick and chased away the hyenas. As soon as the animals ran away, the old man disappeared!

With that primal scream, I found that my body had suddenly become much lighter. I was almost floating rather than walking, as if the frequency of my being had increased.

In modern psychiatric treatment, 'primal theory' is applied where patients scream as a catharsis, from the depths of their hara, to relieve fear and other suppressed negative emotions.

> **A very powerful way of overcoming fear is to visualize going through it as clearly as you can.**

Visualization

A very powerful way of overcoming fear is to visualize going through that fear as clearly as you can. The beauty with this technique is that it can be used when you are not in the fear situation, when you are calm and able to handle yourself.

You can sit by yourself and visualize the situation that causes fear. Feel clearly the fear coming up in you; face the fear with deep awareness. If you suffer, if your body feels uncomfortable, it is fine. Don't suppress the fear, just allow it to happen. When you experience something completely, you drop it.

Arunachala hill – A sacred hill located at Tiruvannamalai, in Tamil Nadu, South India. It is considered to be the embodiment of Lord Shiva, the great enlightened master.

Keertans – Devotional songs.

Hara – Seat of energy and life according to the Japanese and Chinese traditions, situated near the belly region.

Sannyasi – Monk or renunciate.

Meditation Techniques

1. Hamsa Mantra

This is a very powerful technique that can be used twenty-four hours a day. Whenever you are attacked by fear, just sit back and relax.

Put your awareness only on your exhaling breath. Repeat the word 'sah' silently as you exhale; that is, with the outgoing breath. Exhaling is like relaxing and letting go anything that can die. While inhaling you will be constantly trying to hold on to something. Exhaling is like letting go. Focus on exhaling without bothering about inhaling. When you inhale, repeat 'ham' silently.

Place more awareness and energy on the exhalation. Help yourself exhale deeper. Let the inhalation happen automatically through the body. Place your energy, attention and effort only on exhaling.

It is a silent intonation of 'ham...sah...., ham...sah'. Silent intonation of this *hamsa mantra** will suddenly take you into the awareness, the relaxation that never dies. Whatever can die will leave your system, your inner space.

This technique can also be practiced at other times when you are not faced by fear - while you are sitting, talking, walking, eating, even while you are sleeping. It is a very powerful technique. Constantly, all twenty-four hours, place your attention on exhaling and just intone the *hamsa mantra** silently – 'hamsah', 'hamsah', 'hamsah'. When you inhale, intone 'ham' and when you exhale, intone 'sah'.

Understand, when constantly intoning this *mantra*, it will become *ajapa japa** - chanting without effort. Chanting with effort is called *japa*. Chanting without effort is *ajapa**. It means that which goes on automatically in you. You just need to intone, that's all. Fall in tune, that's all. The whole day it will be resounding within you.

Whatever can die will leave your system, and you will realize whatever can die can never be part of you. If you are identifying yourself with something that can die, that identification will be disconnected and you will be unclutched. Whatever can never die, you will feel connected to that. Whatever cannot die is your very being.

Try this technique for just three days. You will suddenly see that the fear of losing your wealth, parts of your body or your health, or your near and dear ones, or the fear of unknown – all the fears will disappear. When you put your awareness on exhaling, whatever is occupying your inner space as a part of you that can die, will simply leave your inner space. You will be liberated.

Hamsa Mantra - Also called *soham mantra*, it is practised by intoning 'hmmm' while inhaling and 'sssooo' while exhaling.
Ajapa japa - Chanting a sacred chant involuntarily.

Pain is a Great Teacher

Often, fear manifests itself as pain. The most frightening thing in the world is pain.

All living beings are afraid of one thing, and that is pain. If you look deeply, you will find that people don't fear even death as much as they fear the pain and agony they will undergo at the time of death! Many are afraid of poverty, many of relationships, and many others fear disease. The root cause of all these fears is the pain that happens while going through these things. All these fears are because of the fear of pain.

What is Pain

Pain can be physical, mental or emotional.

Physical pain is a basic necessity for the body. Just imagine, if we could feel no pain in our body we might accidentally hurt ourselves or start styling our faces, hands, and legs the way we style our hair today! Actually, pain is a letter of request, written by the body to the mind, saying, 'Please pay attention to me!' because attention is energy. When attention is given to a particular area, that attention becomes energy for that area. When the body communicates pain, it is actually asking for attention or energy, which will help it heal.

Mental or emotional pain is the psychological feeling that arises when you are faced with something you don't like. Research shows that emotional pain can deeply disturb the physical body. For example, the psychological feelings that arise with sexual repression can result in lower back disorders, or the pain of shouldering too much responsibility can cause pain in the shoulders.

Whether physical or emotional pain, an important thing you need to understand is that pain is always born from resistance to the present moment.

Time Vs Understanding

If a painful incident happens in one's life – the loss of a child, the husband or wife leaving the spouse, the breakup of a close friendship – one suffers, but slowly accepts it over time. One may cry and brood many days

> **Both pleasure and pain are from the mind. The mind moves from one extreme to other.**

and nights, but then one comes to accept what happened. Time heals. It is a common saying. Understand that time is needed for healing only because you were not ready to face the pain and suffering in a conscious and aware manner at the time the incident happened .

If you can just look at the pain, if you can witness the emotion with awareness and see the play of the mind while experiencing pain, then the understanding dawns and instant healing happens. Time is needed because you are not ready to have the understanding. So you suffer a great deal. Over time, after some weeks, months, or even years, the incident fades and becomes a distant memory.

However, the pain is not completely gone from your system. If you come across a person who even distantly reminds you of your lost child or husband, it comes up. For example, if the person has a similar style of talking, walking, or laughing, the wound reopens. It hurts because you carry the memory of the past. Because of this, you feel life is too heavy a burden to bear. You choose to hold onto your entire past: when you were a child, when you were a teenager, when you first went to work. You hold onto all the stages of life with all the experiences, pains, and mistakes. That burden and load of your emotions associated with the past, is what causes you pain every time you experience it. If you decide to drop the past and look at every situation with a fresh perspective, then you will not have so much

pain. You will heal instantly. You will not need so much time.

Pain and pleasure – two sides of the same coin

A small story:

Once a disciple went to his master and said, 'Master, I am not able to meditate. My legs ache. I feel distracted.' The master just said, 'It will pass.'

After two weeks, the disciple went back to the master, this time saying, 'I am able to meditate beautifully. I feel so aware and blissful.'

The master again replied, 'It will pass.'

The root of pain and pleasure are the same. It is the same sensation with two names. It is like this: two people receive a body massage from the same person. One concludes that it was a beautiful rejuvenating process while the other decided that it hurt! The same massage will appear like pain or pleasure depending on the person receiving it.

Life has both of these opposites – pleasure and pain. Both pleasure and pain are from the mind. The mind always moves from one extreme to the other. It rarely falls into the middle path. From pleasure you move to pain, from pain you move to pleasure. As we saw earlier, pleasure and pain are completely dependent on the person feeling the pleasure or pain. Something may seem like pleasure to you while the same experience may be painful to someone else.

In the Bhagavad Gita*, the great scripture that teaches the various paths to Self-realization, the enlightened master Krishna* says beautifully, 'He who regards alike pleasure and pain, and looks on a lump of earth, a stone, and a piece of gold with an equal eye, who is wise and holds praise and blame to be the same, who is unchanged in honor and dishonor, and who treats friend and foe alike, is said to have gone beyond the modes of nature. Pleasure and pain are the same to him and he is ready for enlightenment.'

Free yourself from pleasure and pain

Buddha, an enlightened master, says, 'Free yourself from both pleasure and pain.' Craving for pleasure and nursing pain are both different aspects of the same experience. Both are chains. Pain may look like an ugly chain and pleasure a beautiful chain. Just as the day follows night and night follows day, pain and pleasure will always follow each other.

When you understand that pleasure and pain are both creations of the mind, you will realize that they are both temporary, they come and go like soap bubbles. Nobody is needed to take away your pleasure, because your mind by its very nature will move like a pendulum to the other extreme called pain!

Pain exists only in the absence of awareness.

The only way is to go beyond both pleasure and pain. This doesn't mean suppressing pleasure or forgetting about pain. It is an awareness that transforms pain to bliss – the energy that exists no matter what the external situation may be. Bliss is your very nature and cannot be lost. Just because of your resistance to what is happening, you feel pain and your natural bliss is forgotten.

Awareness in Pain

Pain, whether physical, mental, or emotional, has only a negative existence like darkness. Darkness exists only in the absence of light. As such, it has no positive existence of its own. In the same way, pain exists only in the absence of awareness. Just as darkness disappears automatically when light is brought into a room, pain dissolves automatically when the energy of your awareness is focused on it.

Any mental or emotional pain that you carry is just the tip of the iceberg. You need to go into the root where it starts. You need to work on the root cause for it and heal it. Otherwise, there is a distinct danger that you will inflict that pain on someone else or hurt yourself more with it. I always tell people, 'If you have pain, just drop everything and work on it. See that its root is healed. Only then you can be in

---

Bhagavad Gita - Ancient Indian scripture, delivered by enlightened master Krishna, and considered the essence of the Upanishads or scriptures.

Krishna - Enlightened master from India who delivered the Truths of the Bhagavad Gita.

a safe zone. Otherwise neither you nor the people living around you are in a safe zone.'

When you face any pain with awareness you become aware that you are not just the body. You become aware that no pain can touch the real 'you'. Once you realize that you are beyond pain, you rise above pain to become a *dukkha ateeta** (one who has gone beyond suffering). You experience the rare freedom that arises with non-attachment to the body. You will carry this freedom all your life. You leave mundane life behind and enter into a spiritual plane. The whole material world disappears and another world arises, one of incomparable beauty, innocence, joy and compassion.

The pain will evaporate of its own accord when you see the nature and cause of pain with intense inner clarity because the clarity evaporates the reasons for the pain to exist in you. This realization brings with it a state of absolute bliss, which is the state of enlightenment.

Pain – A phenomenon of the mind

Painless delivery

There is an interesting incident from my wandering days that I want to share with you. During the days of my spiritual journey,

I was once with some tribal people in Madhya Pradesh in India. I was living in a small temple in the center of the village. One day I noticed a pregnant lady entering a small hut. After about half an hour, she came out with a small baby in her hands! No pain, no doctor, no nurse, no medicine, no cries. In half an hour she came out walking with a baby in her arms.

I was shocked! I could not ask anything because I did not know their language. After one month, I saw another pregnant lady do the same thing. In half an hour she came out with a baby. I asked the local priest who came to the temple, 'How does this happen? Don't they have any pain?' He asked, 'Pain? Why pain?'

I was amazed. The very idea that women should have pain at the time of delivery did not exist in their society! Not only that, nobody suffered from gynecological issues like menopause problems either.

I started enquiring about their lifestyle. I understood that in their tradition, they respect women a lot. The moment a girl becomes physically mature, she is acknowledged with respect that she is now qualified to become a mother. People fall at her feet and she touches and heals them! Just because of this different conditioning, the women don't suffer the usual pains that women in other cultures do.

Dukkha ateeta - Beyond sorrow and pain.

'Phantom' Pain

There have been recorded instances of 'phantom pain' which is pain in a part of the body that does not exist. Once in the Second World War, a soldier's leg had to be amputated because it was badly damaged. The strange thing was that when he became conscious again he was still complaining about the pain in the leg. He was covered with a blanket so he had no idea that the leg had been removed. The blanket was removed and he was shown that his leg was not there anymore. He was shocked!

Further research then showed that each part of the body is related to a certain part of the brain. When a certain part of the body feels pain, the corresponding brain center shows activity. In this case, the related brain center was still vibrating in the same way it was vibrating when the leg was a part of the body. There are many such instances of people who feel pain in the empty space where their limbs were amputated. This is called 'phantom pain'.

Placebo effect

The mind has tremendous influence over the body. Even the perception of physical pain can be changed by the mind. In science they call it the 'placebo effect' when a simple sugar pill gives the same effect as a painkiller, just

because the person is made to believe that the sugar pill is a painkiller!

The perception of physical pain can be changed by the mind.

The other day, I was reading about research[*] done at the University of Michigan in the USA that appeared in the *Journal of Neuroscience*. The research was done on a group of young men who agreed to let researchers inject their jaw muscles with a concentrated saline solution, causing pain. The brain's response to the pain was studied using PET (Positron Emission Tomography) scans that showed the activity of the body's natural painkillers, called endorphins.

In one scan, the men were told they were being given a painkiller but actually what was given was just a placebo – a substance that had no painkilling properties. Then they were asked to rate the intensity of the pain they felt on a scale of 0 to 100. Also, the PET scan would indicate the brain activity related to pain. The researchers were able to study both the response of the brain and what the men actually felt.

The amazing observation was that when the men were given a placebo, meaning not a painkiller but just a neutral substance, the pain they felt was actually less. It was as if they had been given the painkiller itself! The PET scans indicated that the endorphin (natural painkiller) system in the brain was activated.

'Placebo Effects Mediated by Endogenous Opioid Activity on μ-Opioid Receptors', Journal of Neuroscience, August 24, 2005, 25(34):7754-7762

'Neurobiological Mechanisms of the Placebo Effect', Journal of Neuroscience, November 9, 2005, 25(45):10390-10402

It showed increased activity with the placebo, just because the person believed that it was a painkiller! Further studies have shown that the placebo effect was observed in more than 70% of the people, where the pain decreased by up to 22%. Science is still studying this amazing phenomenon, which so clearly shows the mind-body connection.

The cognitive shift

Pain – a path to no-mind

A small story:

Once a disciple was walking with a Zen* master when a flock of geese flew overhead. The master asked, 'What are they?' The disciple replied, 'They are wild geese, master.' The master asked, 'Where are they?' The disciple replied, 'They have flown away.'

The master suddenly caught the disciple's nose and twisted it. The disciple cried out in pain. The master said, 'You say they have flown away, but they have been here from the start.' The story says the disciple became enlightened in that moment.

This story may sound very strange, but this is the way of most Zen* masters. Pain has a tremendous value in awakening you to reality. That is why it has been used by many masters to awaken the sleeping disciple. Normally what do we do when someone is in

pain? We console. Unknowingly we enable the person to continue to sleep. But the master is not interested in consoling. His only interest is in awakening you. In the moment of great pain, the mind stops, there is only pain. In that moment, the Truth is delivered! In the story you can see that in the moment of pain, the disciple's inner space was ready to receive the Truth from the master, and the master delivered it!

The Pain of transformation

Pain can become a very creative energy. It can become a remembrance of god. It can become prayer. It can become meditation. It can become awareness. It can cause tremendous transformation in you.

An important secret of life that you need to understand is that if you become aware of something, you can get rid of it very easily. If you are not aware of it, there is no question of getting rid of it. It remains with you. The pain is a pain because it exists in your unconscious, not in your awareness. Your fear of facing the pain allows it to exist and grow more and more like a tumor. A master will simply remove this tumor through his master surgery'! When it leaves you, you transform into a new person. Once a devotee asked me, '*Swamiji*, I understand that the surgery is needed for my inner space to be cleansed. But can the master use some pain-killer while doing the 'master surgery'?'

Zen - Japanese Buddhist practice. Derived from *dhyana,* meditation.

What is the attitude needed to deal with the painful 'surgeries' of the master? Sometimes, just the awareness itself will dissolve the pain. Many times, I will just point at the pain, nothing else. It will simply disappear and it will evaporate.

Now, what is the correct attitude to deal with these painful 'surgeries'? It is having complete trust that whatever 'pain' the master causes, is only for your good and nothing else. The 'surgery' itself is because of his boundless love and compassion for you. If this is clearly understood, then even if it hurts, you will go through it with deep gratitude for what the master is doing to you. I can say that the painkiller from the master's side is the love and compassion the master showers with just a look.

One more thing is that the pain is also because you start thinking it is a pain and labeling it so. The master can teach in just two or three seconds what will ordinarily take a lifetime or a few hundred years or a few births. The master is intense life. He will simply remove the 'tumor' and throw it away. So, even if it is intense, it is better to go with the master than with life because it is a very quick process. Also, if you understand what the master is doing to you, you can enjoy it as the ultimate happening in your life.

One more thing: the pain you will experience continuing life with the 'tumors' will be much worse than the pain you experience when the master removes them. Removing a 'tumor' will take hardly a few minutes; the master just removes it, over.

Once you understand this process, you will no longer label the transformation as pain. Instead you will welcome it. You will not only welcome it, you will feel thankful that what was lurking deep down in your unconscious has been brought up and removed.

Meditation Techniques

Focus on Pain

Pain is actually the absence of attention, so the solution is 'giving your presence'. There is a simple and beautiful self-healing meditation technique that channels your presence into the diseased limb or the suffering mind. You can try it out the next time you experience pain or suffering. It is definitely a better option than painkillers, whose side-effects sometimes are worse than the original complaint.

Just try this. Suppose you have pain in your leg, or you are suffering because of some external incident. Lie down in a dark room. Make a conscious effort to forget about your whole body, focusing only on the spot which is causing you pain. If it is mental suffering, then forget your whole body and focus only on that incident that caused you suffering. As you experience the pain, deliberately drop the word 'pain' from your mind.

Your mental chatter will continue to tell you that you feel pain. Switch it off. Feel deeply; experience with an open mind. Look

Your own inner ambulance system is what you call pain! into what is happening inside your mind. You will soon see that your mind was just exaggerating the pain. Put all your awareness on the center of the pain, and it will soon shrink to become just a tiny point of pain. Concentrate completely on this point and you will discover in a sudden moment that the pain disappears, and in its place there is bliss!

Witness Pain

You can use this as a technique for dissolving physical pain in any part of your body.

When you are faced with physical pain, just witness the feeling of pain in that part of your body in a relaxed way. You will see that first, there might be a surge of pain, but soon the pain reduces to a spot and disappears. What happens is that the moment you get hurt physically, energy supplied by your own body intelligence rushes to that part to heal it. The energy rush is what you label 'pain'. If you witness the energy rushing and healing in a relaxed way, the pain disappears and healing happens. If we just understand this, we will not resist and suffer the pain, we will cooperate with the natural healing energy of the body.

I can say this from my own personal experience. Once somebody closed the door of the car on my finger. People around me got agitated and ran around to get first aid. I simply told them not to bother.

As my finger swelled, I just watched clearly what was happening inside my body. I could feel the energy rushing from my navel center to my finger. I could clearly see the body intelligence responding to the emergency on its own. It healed on its own.

Your own inner ambulance system is what you call pain!

The witnessing focus that you give the pain will make you realize that you are more than a mere body. You will touch your energy base and realize that you are more than the body-mind.

Watch the pain intensely but without attaching the word 'pain' and the meaning 'suffering' to it. For a brief moment the pain may seem to intensify, but soon it will dissolve.

Actually, the body is intelligent enough to allow energy to flow to the part of the body that is asking for energy. But you resist that energy flow by labeling it as 'pain'. Just allow the energy to flow by infusing full awareness into that part of the body. Just look at the energy flow with curiosity. Be a complete outsider; do not participate in the process. Just let the energy flow to that area and work on it. You will see it heal.

Desire is a Dynamic Energy

Fear and desire are the fundamental energies that drive our lives. We act either out of a desire to achieve something or reach somewhere, or out of a fear of not wanting to experience something. Attraction and repulsion are not merely forces of molecules, but also essential to human behavior.

Recognize Your True Desires

One of the major driving forces in human life is desire. If you look into your life, you can see most of the time we are driven by either desire or fear.

We have so many desires and many times we feel we don't have energy to fulfill them. According to the Jain tradition, the Divine sends us with enough energy and capacity to fulfill all our desires. But most of us don't feel this way. Why?

There is a difference between our true desires and 'borrowed' desires. Our true desires are called our 'needs'. Borrowed desires are called our 'wants'. We have enough energy to fulfill our true desires or needs. What are our true desires?

During the Life Bliss Program Level 2 (Nithyananda Spurana Program), we have a session where people are asked to make a list of their desires, their needs and wants. Then they meditate on these desires. At the end of the meditation, I ask them to recollect from memory their list of desires. What they can recollect is usually a fraction of what they have written! It is as if they started with a large tree full of leaves, their desires, and during this meditation the tree sheds almost all its leaves, as if the leaves were dried and dead. What leaves the tree retains glow like golden leaves. If you can understand which desire is innate and which is accumulated, spiritual growth happens automatically.

When our desires are our own true desires, when they reflect our real needs, when they express themselves in our inner energy, we don't feel any desperation about trying to achieve them. The realization comes that, as a matter of natural course of events, these desires will be fulfilled.

The true desire for fulfillment

When you have a headache, you are not comfortable with that state - because you know that it is not your true nature. Your true nature is having no headache. In the same way, when you have some desire, you immediately want to come out of it - because deep fulfillment is your very nature and desire causes an imbalance in that fulfillment.

Two important truths you need to understand:

1. Your whole life is a long chain of events performed towards the one goal that is fulfillment. Whatever you may do, whether it is eating or drinking or having relationships, wealth or joy, it is all to experience fulfillment. In different directions you seek fulfillment instead of seeking it directly.

2. Fulfillment is within you, it is your very nature. That is why you are trying to come out of non-fulfillment.

The fact that you are searching for fulfillment means that fulfillment is known to you. Otherwise you would not search for it! In the instances in your life when you have felt some fulfillment, there is also a hope that you will experience it again. That is why you extend your life.

Desire, knowledge and action

The desire that is pure and not directed towards any particular object or person is simply an overflowing energy that is called *iccha shakti* or the 'desire energy'.

From the navel, energy comes as pure energy. In the heart region, this energy gets converted to the power of desire. This further gets converted into words in the throat region. When this energy gets converted into words, it is called *vak* or the 'speech energy'. To give an analogy, the energy that comes from the navel is like loose cotton. The cotton becomes thread in the throat region. Or you can imagine it this way: the energy that comes from the navel is like molten iron. The throat is like a forge where the product is formed!

Anyhow, the speech energy moves further to the brain. There it stays as knowledge or gets converted into a command. In the brain, the energy could stay as the power of knowledge or *gnana shakti*. For example, the desire energy related to the body can become knowledge of the body.

The other option is, the words get converted to a command and get executed as well. The command goes to the entire body and moves you. This is called the power of action or *kriya shakti*. For example, the desire energy related to your body can express as the power of action like moving your body.

Pure *iccha shakti* or desire energy which comes from your being gets converted in the throat region to *gnana shakti* - power of knowledge and *kriya shakti* - power of action.

If the energy is not processed and channeled properly, the knowledge and action become disconnected from the power of the pure desire energy. The knowledge and action should be in tune with the desire energy. Then it forms a virtuous circle of desire leading to better knowledge and action, which in turn leads to clearer desires!

Let us say you have a desire to make a million dollars. If it gets converted properly as knowledge, you will have a clear plan and do the right actions to become a millionaire. If the desire energy gets converted as too much knowledge and less action, then you will end up only thinking more and more, building castles in the air.

On the other hand, if the desire energy gets converted as too much action and less knowledge, then you will end up working blindly. For example, you may work really hard like driving a truck from Los Angeles to New York, but can you become a millionaire this way? There is action but not the right knowledge. So the proper conversion of the desire to knowledge and action has to happen. The reason why this conversion doesn't happen properly is lack of awareness.

When you are honest and integrated with the desire, there is no conflict and the conversion happens properly.

The power of love

You might have even experienced some incidents like this in your life. A girl who is afraid to cross a busy street, if she sees her child run across the road will just jump onto the road to save the child without a thought about her own safety.

We should understand how she has lost her fear all of a sudden. The reason is that the love for her child has awakened the dimension of motherliness in her. It is the same thing with every relationship of love. If the feeling of love blossoms in somebody, immediately all the fear will leave the person's inner space.

Understand, love has tremendous power and so does lust. If you have a lot of energy in your *muladhara chakra**, it will override the other *chakras** immediately. There will not be any fear in your *swadhishthana chakra** and there will not be any worries in your *manipuraka chakra**. These higher *chakras** will not work when the *muladhara chakra** has the full power. Without the person's knowledge, it will unleash the latent unknown potential in him. It will spread his potential to the outer world too.

Different people activate different dimensions inside you. If you have a lover, the feeling of love will be awakened in you.

Muladhara chakra – Subtle energy center at the root of the spine, related to the emotions of greed and lust.

Chakras - Energy centers in the body. Literally means 'wheel' based on the experience of mystics who perceived these energy centers as whirlpools of energy. There are seven major *chakras* along the spine: *muladhara, swadhishthana, manipuraka, anahata, vishuddhi, ajna* and *sahasrara*.

Swadhishthana chakra – Subtle energy center located two inches below the navel region, related to the emotion of fear.

Manipuraka chakra – Subtle energy center located near the navel region, related to the emotion of worry.

If you have a son or daughter, then the dimension of motherliness will be awakened in you. If your mind is ready to receive the experience of different dimensions, those dimensions will blossom in you.

If you are completely open-minded, every person you meet in your life will cause you to blossom further. But if you are egoistic, even your spouse or your lover cannot cause you to blossom. Please understand, you have a great responsibility to create an open and non-egoistic mind before entering into a relationship such as between husband and wife or between lovers. Then the very feeling will transform you eternally. If this eternal transformation does not happen, you miss a major dimension of your life.

Why are we not able to feel true love? It is because of our *samskaras**, our emotional attachment to the past memories. Your inner space is filled with too many things related to the past. So your inner space is not available to the present moment. You can only love or feel connected to the people or objects falling in tune with the past memories you loved. If you can drop the emotional attachments to the past, suddenly you will see you have so much of inner space available to you. You can then directly open up to anybody who is in front of you without asking for his or her past.

Lust to love

Lust is a primal emotion provided by nature for continuation of the species. To go beyond lust is the first major step in realizing the ultimate potential of human life.

Humans are forever confused between love and lust. They think only animals are lustful. Actually only animals are capable of pure lust when they mate! Humans, with their rationalization, can neither be lustful nor loving. That is why they feel dissatisfied and unfulfilled.

Sex is carbon, love is diamond. Sex is mud and love is the lotus that blooms in the mud. It is the same substance – the only thing is, you should know how to process it. Just drop your expectations, and you will find a tremendous upsurge of energy.

Discover the man and woman inside you

Today, we know biologically that no man is 100% man, and no woman is 100% woman. A man may be 51% man and 49% woman. Likewise, a woman may be 51% woman, and 49% man; just a difference of 1%, may be more.

You have taken birth from the energies of your father and mother. Then, how can you be only male or only female? Whether we accept it or not, we are an embodiment of both

---

Samskaras - Engrams or deeply engraved memories.

male and female energies. We are whole, not divided.

Right from the moment of birth, society labels you as either male or female. And it expects you to start behaving accordingly. Inherent human nature is fulfillment. She starts looking to the outside world for a substitute for her own lost half. The male child starts searching for a female presence, and the female child for a male presence. This is where the whole idea of sex starts.

The search starts with the idea of how our 'would-be' should be.

A small story:

One 90-year old man used to sit every day at the beach from morning to evening, watching people going by. Another man who noticed this went up to him and asked him, 'What do you actually do sitting here everyday?'

The old man replied, 'I am searching for a woman to be my wife.' The man was simply shocked at this reply and asked him, 'Why did you not search in your youth?'

The old man replied, 'I have been searching since I was 30 years old.' The man was astonished and asked him, 'What sort of a woman are you searching for?' He replied, 'I am searching for a perfect woman.' 'The man asked, 'You haven't found one yet?'

'I found one woman who matched what I had in mind but it didn't work out well with her,' replied the old man. The man asked why.

The old man replied, 'She was searching for a perfect man!'

This is what happens when we try to get a perfect match for the image that we carry inside us.

But after a long search, we suddenly find a person who seems to match our mental image – from a distance. What happens at this point is what is called 'falling in love'. This is the science behind falling in love. Note that it is always 'falling' in love, never 'rising' in love! Because of our own strong needs and expectations, we see things as we want to see them. As long as this distance is maintained, things go on smoothly. We continue to project our imagination upon each other. But, as the person slowly comes closer we find that fantasy and reality are totally different.

We need to understand that no living person can live up to the image we carry in our minds simply because the image is not built from reality! No image can be matched with reality, because at the end of the day, it is only an image, a fantasy!

The ultimate alchemy

What is alchemy? The process of changing a lower level metal such as copper or iron into gold is alchemy. In the same way, when our being is ripe the base feeling of lust transforms to love, the highest emotion we are capable of.

In the same way, remove the impurity of your fantasies, add the purity of friendliness in your relationship and process this with your patience. In the beginning, people may not be able to understand the change in you. Just continue with belief and confidence in yourself. Your sincerity and strength has no way but to touch others around you positively.

Add friendliness to love. As of now, our lust is deep-rooted violence to possess the other person. Add friendliness to the relationship. Welcome the partner as he or she is; do not just accept him or her. Welcome and accept the mind, body and being as it is. Then you can see lust turns to love and your being is in eternal bliss.

Love adds life even to the person. With love the person is a spirit, life! Without love the person is reduced to a thing, utility! Without love, when you look at a beautiful man or woman and plan for what you can get out of that person, you reduce him or her to a thing. Only when you look at that person with love, the person is a spirit, a living being.

Celibacy is nothing but not craving for the suppressed half that is inside you, that's all. If you are a male, you need to experience such fulfillment unto yourself that you no longer miss the suppressed half or female inside you. If you are a female, you are so enough unto yourself that you don't look outside to experience this fulfillment. When you achieve this fulfillment, whether you are married or not, there will be peace in your mind. It is then that you can be celibate even in married life! This is true celibacy.

Meditation Technique

1. *Dukkha Harana* Meditation

Total duration: 30 minutes

This meditation technique will bring out all the suppressed emotions in you.

Breathing is very closely related to the mind. If your thinking is calm, your breath will be relaxed. If your thinking is aggressive, your breathing will also be aggressive.

You may practice this technique on an empty stomach, preferably in the morning. 21 days of *Dukkhaharana* will transform your being and bring a glow to your face and body.

Step 1: 10 minutes

Stand with your eyes closed. In the first part of this meditation, your mental system is made fully alive by deep breathing. This energy will melt all the repressed emotions like melting ice.

Breathe deeply and chaotically from the depths of your body, always through your nose with your mouth closed. Move your hands, flex your knees, lower yourself and then rise up. Move as if you are a bird in flight, up and down, knees moving up and down, arms moving up and down, in line with your breathing.

Do the movements gently and synchronize your inhalation with upward movement and exhalation with downward movement.

shoulders; next to your face, and finally to the top of the head. Relax each part of your entire body before you move to the next part. At the end of these ten minutes, you will become vacant inside; you will become cool, calm and composed.

Step 3: 10 minutes

Sit down keeping your eyes closed and chant the 'hoo' *kara* sound, just the word 'hoo'. There is no need to chant it deeply and loudly. Just chant it in a relaxed manner. As you chant, simply witness whatever happens inside or outside your being.

The first two parts of this technique are actually a preparation for the third part that is the actual meditation. When you come to the third part, you will see that the mind becomes silent effortlessly, by itself. Silence cannot be forced upon you; it can only happen by itself.

Remain in this relaxed state with a smiling face and blissful mood. During this time, there may be many experiences. Just watch them as you would watch the television. Watch your mind thought by thought.

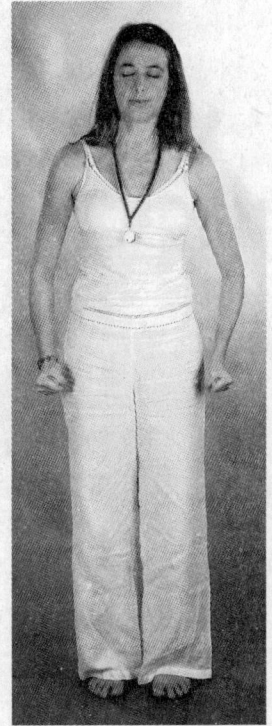

Step 2: 10 minutes

Keep your eyes closed and tense each part of your body, part by part, limb by limb, then let it relax. Tense and relax one limb and then move to the next. Start with your feet; then move to legs; then move to thighs; next to the hips; then to stomach and lower back; then to chest and upper back; then to your arms from finger tips to shoulder; next to the neck and

Guilt is The Original Sin

What is Guilt?

When you have desires you have guilt as well. Guilt is the opposite face of desire. Sometimes you feel guilty about desiring something because you feel it is not right to desire it. Other times you feel guilty when your desires are fulfilled because you feel you are not deserving of what you receive. When your desires do not come true you feel guilty because you feel you have not done what you ought to have. Desires invariably lead to guilt.

Guilt is nothing but your past decisions and actions being reviewed with your updated intelligence.

For example, when you were in school, you might have said a few mean things to one of your friends which caused a relationship to break. Now, this many years later, with the intelligence that you have, is it right to review that incident and feel guilty? No! At that time you had only that much intelligence, so you behaved in that fashion. Now, you have updated intelligence.

It doesn't make sense to review the past with your present intelligence.

The futility of the past

What is gone is gone. What has been done is done. You cannot undo it. Now if you constantly think about the past and feel guilty, you destroy your present and your future too. Nothing can be done about it, so guilt is useless. What can you do? All that you can do is not repeat the same pattern again, that's all. At that time with whatever intelligence you had, you acted, that's all.

Our past is always past, it is always dead. That is why it is called past. Yet, we always let the past affect us. How do we allow the past to affect us? In two ways:

1. If you review your past incidents or decisions using the *present* intelligence, you will create guilt in your being.

2. If you take the present decisions based on past experiences, you will be repeating the same past into the future also, maybe in a little updated fashion!

Even though you might not commit exactly the same mistake, you will be moving in the same experiential level, in the same plane.

Our mind falls into a groove, a track, a mindset that forces it to do what it has always done. So we keep making the same mistakes as well.

Three kinds of Guilt

There are three kinds of guilt that take root in us and kill our intelligence:

1. Guilt created by immediate family

2. Guilt created by social laws

3. Guilt created by ourselves

Guilt created by immediate family

Before the age of seven, guilt is created by your immediate family. If you don't do according to your parents' wishes, they instill guilt in you. They tell you that god will not approve of what you are doing. Poor god, he has to support whatever anyone says about him! Or your parents tell you that you should respect their wishes as parents. Immediately you feel guilty of making them unhappy. In this way, family sows the first guilt in you. You in turn pass it on to your child. Like a crown, it is passed on over generations.

Because you don't have the knowledge to explain why things have to be done in a certain way, you change it to a rule and impose it on the child and create guilt through it. For example, children love whirling. They love moving and flowing with the body. It is a natural way for them to center their energy. But what do we do? We stop the child and put the fear in him that he may fall. We don't stop our efforts until we make the child stiff, frozen and dull like us!

The child may want to go outside and play in the sun or collect some flowers or just jump around in the fresh air. If you think about it, it is not much the child is asking for. But the mother says 'no' - he may fall ill due to the hot sun. If you look a little deep, you can see that by saying 'no' she gets a subtle feeling of power, of being in control. She might say it is the sun but it is subtler than that.

The 'no' by the mother actually has a deep impact on the child. It creates guilt in the child. Now, the child may force himself to stay in or he may escape from his mother's eyes and step out. But either way his raw energy is being suppressed. If he forces himself to stay in, his energy is not being allowed to express. If he goes out, he will feel guilty, he will be afraid that somebody might spot him. And all this for nothing big - just for playing in the sun!

As the child grows, this deep engram of guilt will actually settle inside him. Even after he grows up into a man and becomes independent, he may be sitting in the lawn under the sun and those childhood memories may be triggered. He may feel guilty and uneasy for no reason. There is nothing to feel guilty about just sitting in the lawn but the old memories are awakened.

This is how guilt arises. Small incidents like this collect and make guilt your natural way of life.

Guilt and happiness

Why can't we enjoy and encourage the natural joy and happiness the child lives in?

If you look a little deep, you can see that happiness itself has become associated with guilt. A small child knows nothing of guilt - he is just wild and natural. That is why seeing a small child can be so captivating. He is total in whatever he does. He has not been introduced to the mask of civilization. He is still wild. That is why he is so full of energy. He is overflowing with joy and curiosity; he is just vibrating with the energy bubbling inside him.

The child wants to enjoy everything but the parents are filled with the conditionings of society – guilt, seriousness, hypocrisy. The child wants to shout and jump and dance - that is his natural expression. But the adults stop him, 'Don't shout! It is bad manners. You should be civilized. You should carry yourself well like us.' By and by, the notion of being free and happy is itself associated with feelings of guilt.

Guilt created by society

From seven to fourteen, society creates guilt in you through its rules. The guilt based on fear is created by social laws.

Till the age of fourteen, family and society create guilt for you. An important guilt in this is the guilt of sex. Parents or family never open out the topic of sex. When there is a chemical change happening in you, you feel your body is new. A lot of questions arise and clarity is needed but no one is prepared to give it.

And to add to the confusion and desire, the media around you constantly bombards you with fantasies in that vulnerable age of change.

To add to it, society instills in you the feeling that you are not enough unto yourself. It makes you feel guilty of what you are, what you do. Once it convinces you that you are a sinner, you are caught in its grips. Then you cannot enjoy the joy of life any more.

According to me, guilt is the greatest sin. At least other sins will punish you after your death. Guilt will punish you when you are alive.

The Tibetan poet-saint Milarepa* sang, 'My religion is to live - and die - without regret.'

You are called a saint or a sinner only by society. As long as society labels you a saint, you are a saint. The moment society labels you a sinner, you are a sinner. If you kill someone in society, you will be called a murderer, you will be punished. But if you kill someone on the battlefield you will be called a hero, you will be given a big award! So there is no absolute scale to decide what is right and what is wrong. It is society's own logic.

> **Guilt is the greatest sin. Guilt will punish you when you are alive.**

Milarepa - Tibetan Yogi and disciple of Tibetan Buddhist teacher Marpa.

Heaven and hell

A very subtle and cunning way of sowing guilt today is through the idea of heaven and hell. People exploit your fear and greed by showing you ideas of hell and heaven. They create in you greed for heaven and fear for hell. They create so many concepts of hell and heaven and sell them to you. They say, 'If you practice these types of things, you will be rewarded with heaven; if you practice otherwise, you will be punished with hell.' When you are given rules based on greed and fear, you automatically start creating deep guilt in you.

A small story:

Once a military general asked a Zen master, 'Master, what are heaven and hell?'

The master asked, 'What do you do for a living?'

The general replied, 'I am a general.'

The master just laughed, 'Which idiot asked you to be a general? You look more like a butcher!'

The general was furious and took out his sword shouting, 'I will cut you to pieces.'

The master just raised his hand and said, 'These are the gates of hell.'

The general realized his folly and bowed down deeply to the master for forgiveness.

The master continued, 'These are the gates of heaven.'

Be very clear, heaven and hell are not physical locations. They are psychological states of your mind. One instant the mind may be in hell and the next it may be in heaven – the gates to heaven and hell open and close at any time alternately.

Guilt created by you

Till the age of twenty one, knowledge from family and society creates guilt. After twenty one, the guilt sown in you by family and society grows roots inside you. Then you start creating guilt for yourself without any reason. Guilt becomes a permanent guest in your being!

The guilt created by family and the guilt created by society are imposed guilt; they are like a crown that is passed on from one generation to another. The third guilt is the worst - that which you create for yourself. When you internalize guilt based on greed and fear, you create new types of guilt for yourself.

The moment you start feeling guilty about something, you can be exploited. That too when you start fighting with yourself it is easier to exploit you.

If you look into your life you can see how every moment you are subtly looking for some reason to fight with yourself, to feel discontent with yourself. You cannot remain without some conflict, you want to create misery for yourself because that is what you have been taught – happiness is a sin.

The stone of guilt in the river of your mind - the block in the flow of intelligence

You are designed to move like a freely flowing river. Guilt is like the rocks in the path of the water. Society has subtly branded happiness as a sin. That is the problem. That is why you will notice, when everything is going smoothly and happily, there will be a lurking feeling of guilt in you. You are taught by society that being happy and enjoying life is being irresponsible in a way. So you feel guilty.

But when you feel sad and depressed, do you ever feel guilty? No!

You are taught that life is a chain of suffering and endurance, with happiness stepping in once in a while.

This is also why people can't take it when you are happy and smiling all the time. They try their best to bring you back to the so-called reality - by instilling guilt in you.

When you are enjoying, dancing or relaxing at the beach for example, suddenly you will observe guilt starts rising in you about all the work that is pending, about all the responsibilities that need to be fulfilled.

Guilt has no basis but it can destroy your whole life. If you can live without guilt, you will enjoy every moment without any regret and still fulfill all your responsibilities.

The prob-lem is that your being is a crowd of voices that don't belong to you. It is a totality of your mother's voice, your father's voice, your teacher's voice, your neighbor's voice and what not! All these voices are in there. If there is only one voice, you will never have any problem. Your mind will move like a river. But there are so many voices telling you so many things and creating the rocks of guilt in your path.

As long as you flow like a river, you will express extraordinary intelligence in your life.

As long as you flow like a river, you will express extraordinary intelligence in your life. You will live with an energy that is overflowing every minute. The moment you allow guilt in you, the moment you are stopped in your free flow, you create energy clots inside your being.

Lift yourself by your self

Once you become aware of how you are driven by guilt, you can start practicing to come out of it. When you start practicing anything, naturally you will slip a few times. When you practice to be without guilt, you are bound to slip back into the older patterns of greed and fear. Then suddenly you will remember, 'Oh, I started working out of fear,' 'I started working out of greed.' Then you will start afresh. When you start working, naturally you will see these things happening.

A small story:

A monk from a big spiritual organization

Nobody can hurt you unless you allow. Nobody can help you unless you allow.

was sent to a remote tribal area for doing service. Suddenly, the headquarters received a lot of complaint letters about the monk.

The president after reading the letters said, 'We have posted the right person.'

The secretary asked him, 'What is this Sir? We are getting complaints about him. How do you say we have posted the right person?'

The president replied, 'If we are getting complaints, it means he has started working, there is something happening!'

When you start something new you will have three phases - the first is resistance. The next is just avoidance – people will neither care nor resist. The third is acceptance.

In the same way, when you start doing anything inside your system, you will start growing but these three phases will be there. The first phase will be resistance. You will feel the new practice is a difficult change in your current system. Because of this, the next thing that happens is you start avoiding opportunities where you should be practicing the change. Again and again you will go back to your older ways. Your system will resist, it will try to create all kinds of complications, all possible arguments. If you allow the resistance to grow, you become your own enemy.

Krishna* says in the Bhagavad Gita*, 'Let you lift yourself by yourself. If you don't, you will be your worst enemy.' It is up to you to help yourself as your best friend or hurt yourself as your worst enemy.

Be very clear: nobody can hurt you unless you allow. Nobody can help you unless you allow.

If you have forgotten the practice, remember and again and again lift yourself. Don't fall into depression, don't have guilt. Don't think you will not be able to do it.

Even in the life of Buddha if you read, he was about to leave the body when his disciples asked him to give his ultimate message, and he said *Atma deepo bhava* – Let you be your own light, let you be guided by yourself.

The way out – looking in

To feel guilty is to be in sin. In fact that is the only sin. The hell that we talk about is not in another time and space. It is within us when we feel guilty, without doing anything to change our mindset.

All your guilt, all your pain, everything is a pure imaginary shaft you create inside your head. The mistake you did ten years ago, the mistake you did seven years ago and the mistake you did three years ago, are independent and unconnected incidents. But

---

Krishna - Enlightened master from India who delivered the Truths of the Bhagavad Gita.

Bhagavad Gita - Ancient Indian scripture, delivered by enlightened master Krishna, and considered the essence of the Upanishads or scriptures.

when you connect them and start thinking about it, naturally you start creating guilt. You start feeling like a continuous sinner. This is one approach.

There is another approach. When you commit a mistake, see objectively why you committed it, how you committed it. Watch as an observer how and why it is getting repeated. Look scientifically into the mechanism of guilt. Just this awareness will open a new door and you will never commit the same mistake again - because once you look into it, and you find the cause, it will disappear. To know a thing totally is to be free of it.

Morality

Integrity

Please understand that morality should happen out of integrity, not out of guilt.

What do I mean by integrity? Integrity is being in the present moment and being only one solid personality and not many conflicting personalities. It is seeing reality without the play of the mind. Once the mind steps in, duality also steps in. Just by being intensely aware of the present moment, you can achieve integrity where there is only one and not two or three or many personalities fighting in you. Only when the mind flits between the past and future, you become split personalities and integrity doesn't set in. If the mind is on the present, automatically you become unified and integrity sets in.

You will never make mistakes if you are deeply aware at the time of making them.

A small story:

One day, a priest knelt before god and started crying loudly, 'I am a sinner. Please have mercy on me, O god.' A man who was praying silently got inspired by this and also knelt down next to the priest and started praying. Now, another man also went down on his knees and started crying. Seeing this, the priest nudged the first man saying, 'Look who thinks he is a sinner!'

All our humility, our morality, is more or less a pretence to others and to ourselves. We pretend because we are not solidly integrated within us. We ourselves don't know which personality within us is authentic and so we get caught in such games. If we are integrated, we will be authentic in every action, and automatically we will be moral.

Be aware, be spontaneously right

Please understand, you will never make mistakes if you are deeply aware at the time of making them. When you are aware, you will be one solid personality and moral as well. When you stray from awareness, you will be many personalities and immoral also. Morality has to do with awareness, not with any other social rules. Awareness is the only way to be naturally moral.

Once you integrate yourself, you will be centered upon awareness. Awareness causes you to spontaneously take the right action in the right situation. Morality can cause you to do the wrong action in the right situation because it doesn't have the right base. Its base is not its own, it is built up by society. So you don't feel connected to it. When you don't feel connected, you cannot act with confidence. Once you integrate yourself, you will be centered upon awareness. If you remain fragmented, there will be no awareness and you will depend on morality for guidance.

Conscience Vs Consciousness

When you start internalizing the laws of society, you create a deep wound in your being. You destroy your innate intelligence. According to me, children can be given a set of rules initially so they don't move from the path of consciousness. But soon they have to be given the understanding of life and the need to operate from consciousness instead of conscience.

If you live with consciousness, you will automatically live a moral life. To start understanding the need to live with consciousness, just look into your morality. Morality is only skin deep, whereas consciousness comes from the very being. Your consciousness tries to break through your conscience. Your consciousness continuously fights with your conscience. Conscience is societal. Consciousness is natural. Conscience is a poor substitute for consciousness.

People ask me, 'Master, what is this? You are pulling down the whole social structure. Then how can we all live morally?' I tell them, 'Be very clear, it is only for kids that you need a forced morality. For them you need to say, 'Keep quiet, I will give you candy.' Of course, nowadays kids reply, 'I am happy. I don't need your candy. Who cares for your candy!' For a child you can say that you will give candy and restrict him. You can impose morality on him based on fear or greed. But for you, it is time to grow up. You are not kids anymore. Just stand up with consciousness. When I say consciousness, I mean the intelligent energy of your being.

Rules

The natural instinct to break rules

When anything is a forced rule, you always try to get around it. For example, you always speed when you don't see the policeman.

A small story:

A policeman pulls over a car on the highway for speeding. When he asks for the driver's license, the driver replies, 'But officer, I was only trying to keep a safe distance between my car and the car behind me!'

When you follow rules blindly without understanding their spirit, this is what happens – you just wait for an excuse to break them.

Honestly answer yourself: if there were no rules, no regulating authority to keep a check on what you did, would you be the same person as you are now? Would you be doing things in the same way as you do now? If your answer is no, be very clear that the rule is coming from your conscience, not from your consciousness. You have not internalized the spirit of the rule or you do not agree with the rule. That is the reason you are not doing things in a way natural to you.

The thrill of 'no'

You can see, when you tell children not to do something, they will be most tempted to do it. As long as you don't mention anything about doing it or not doing it, they may not even be bothered about it. But the moment you tell them not to do something, they will be looking to do it.

A small story:

One man says, 'I found three ways to get things done.' His friend asks, 'What are the three ways?'

The man replies, 'First, do it yourself. Second, hire someone to do it. Third, tell your kids not to do it. That's all, it will be done!'

Actually there is a taste, a thrill in doing what you are not supposed to do. Most of the time, you develop an instant urge for something if you are asked not to do it. You feel a kind of joy or satisfaction by doing it. That is the basic tendency in every human being.

There is a thrill in doing what you are not supposed to.

A small story:

Once a shopkeeper was trying hard to increase his sales. He tried various options – discounts, catchy advertisements, better customer service. Nothing worked. Then one day, he hung a black curtain on his shop window and made a small hole on it. Under the hole he put up a board, 'Peeping strictly forbidden.'

From that day, he saw crowds gathering at his shop, each one curious to peep through the hole to see what was there! His shop sales automatically increased because people now actually saw the variety of grocery items his shop carried.

When you are told not to do something, the basic human tendency is to do exactly that.

As a teenager, when you say 'no' to your parents, you feel you have proved you are independent. When you say 'no', you feel you have proved you are somebody special, somebody different. As long as you say 'yes', you feel you are only a child. When you start saying 'no', you feel you have become an adult.

You feel that you are a man only when you say 'no' to your father. Till then you feel you are a child. Just to prove that you are a man you start saying 'no' to your father. This is basic psychology. When you say 'no' you think you are somebody, until then you think you are nobody. So please be very clear, to whatever you say, your grown up son is going to say 'no', because he wants to be somebody.

Dead rules Vs Live intelligence

In the course of time, many regulations that had meaning earlier become blind rules - without any meaning.

In India, during the times before electricity was invented, tailors would sew by hand with a needle with the help of dim lanterns. So clothes would not be sewn after sunset since sewing in the dim light of the candle or lantern would cause strain on the eye. So the work was always confined to daylight hours.

But even now in India, the elderly people in the house will say, 'It is not a good thing to sew after dusk!' The very reason for not sewing at night doesn't even exist anymore! Electricity and bright lights are there. But it has become a ritual for them, with no connection to its original purpose.

A small story:

Once a paratrooper was being interviewed on television. The interviewer said, 'Your life must be really adventurous.'

The paratrooper replied, 'Yes, it does have its scary moments.'

The interviewer asked, 'What is the most anxious experience in your life?'

The paratrooper replied, 'When I was coming down on the lawn of a house and the sign read, 'Keep off the grass!'

When you don't have the right intelligence or understanding, things become dead rules in your life.

When you have understanding, any correct rule can become a friendly technique to live life happily. Rules and rituals are actually techniques for your own enlightenment. When I say enlightenment, I mean a blissful life full of clarity. Of course, when pursued deeply, it will lead to the ultimate state of enlightenment.

A small story:

A railway official reported a murder on a train, 'The murderer entered the compartment, stabbed the victim multiple times. Then he left the train through the opposite door jumping onto the railway track – thereby violating the railway regulations.'

When you don't have the right understanding, you will miss the whole thing and end up acting in a foolish way. When you are given the right understanding, you will understand that any rule was created just for you and others around you to live a happy and blissful life.

When the spirit of the rule is understood, there won't be any problem falling in line with it. By falling in tune, there will only be juice in your action; there will only be a blissful commitment to it. But if the spirit is missed, everything is missed. Life will seem dull and lifeless.

Take meditation for example. Meditation itself is done to go inwards irrespective of the outer world noise and situations. I have seen that some people, before starting their meditation routine, will first try to create a noiseless situation outside. They will go around telling everyone to keep quiet. They will practically freeze people in their normal routine just because they are going to meditate.

Only when the spirit is missed, things become dead rituals. You miss and mess!

All rules and regulations were created for a harmonious life with the understanding that you will not kill me and I will not kill you, and both of us will live happily. That was the basic understanding behind them. However in the course of time, they became laws.

All rules and regulations were created to live a harmonious and happy life, but the moment you internalize the rules without the understanding, you create guilt. As long as you follow the rules with an understanding, you will be happy. When you start following the words instead of the spirit, you will start creating guilt.

When you want to escape from the law, what do you do? You just catch on to the words of the law and drop the spirit behind them. Then you legally work around the words and escape from the law. When you catch the words, you become a bureaucrat and you miss the spirit. Only when you catch the spirit, you can be an intelligent being without guilt.

The useful guilt

There is a certain guilt that is useful for you, a guilt which if pursued intelligently can cause you to move forward in life. It is like this: when you see that you have the potential to do something, when you feel that you have so much potential which you are not using at all, then if you are intelligent, guilt will happen in you. This guilt can spur you to start doing things that will actualize your entire potential.

Sometimes we see the state of things around us and we know in one corner of our mind that we can very well help turn the situation around. But either due to laziness or due to the fear of confrontation, or due to the fear of taking responsibility, we just keep quiet and watch. This type of situation can cause deep guilt in us. This guilt is significant. If we take steps to correct the situation by doing what we really feel we should do, then the guilt will disappear and we will also move forward.

This type of guilt has the ability to drive you to do what needs to be done. Because of its very nature, you cannot harbor this guilt for long. You have to get over it. And the way to get over it is by doing what needs to be done. Once it is done, the guilt also disappears. How long you wish to harbor this guilt without taking steps, for that long you suffer from it. This is the simple logic of this guilt.

Another manifestation of this guilt happens when you can feel your ego surfacing in certain situations and you are unable to help it. When you can smell your ego but you are unable to control it, this guilt arises in you. This guilt is also good since it is a sign of the deep awareness of your own ego. It facilitates you to sincerely work towards eliminating that ego.

Guilt can result in physical disease

Guilt is the sure killer of intelligence. According to me, guilt is the worst killer of intelligence. It will never let you move in your life.

Once one of our devotees had a tumor at the base of her spinal cord. For twenty years she suffered with the tumor. She came to me complaining, 'Please help me, heal me. I am suffering with this tumor for so many years. After undergoing surgery, it has reappeared.'

I started talking to her slowly to trace the origin of the problem. I asked her a few questions at the end of which she finally opened up and started weeping. I asked her, 'Do you have any guilt related to your sex energy?' She slowly opened up.

She said she was physically abused when she was very young. One of her close relatives had abused her for many years. That guilt stayed with her. She said, 'I started hating that part of my body. I started feeling, that that part of the body should not exist in me. I felt, that part of my body was not my being. My hatred towards that person turned towards my own body.'

Her hatred was so deep. I continued speaking to her. Slowly she opened up more and more. When she brought the guilt out, she came out of the guilt. She was psychologically healed.

I gave her a small meditation technique to meditate on that area. I told her, 'Express your anger towards that man. Weep, shout, cry, hit. Close the doors, take a pillow,

imagine that it is him and show your anger on it. After that sit silently and feel that part of your body also as your own. Feel love towards that part of the body.'

You will be surprised that in just ten days the tumor disappeared! It never recurred.

Most of our ailments are due to psychological disturbances where guilt plays a major role.

Most of the time, our energy flow gets blocked because of guilt. If you look deep, wherever you are not able to move, wherever you are not able to take decisions, wherever you have fear, there will be some guilt lurking.

Acceptance – the beautiful way out

Acceptance is a wonderful tool to relieve yourself of the pull and push between the past and future. With acceptance you fall into the present straightaway. The first thing is to accept all the happenings of the outer world and all the happenings of the inner world. Whatever problems you have in the outer world and whatever problems you have in the inner world, just accept them in their entirety. Summarize all that you experience as problems and accept them in totality.

Accept all guilt, all mistakes and all failures. Even if you cannot accept, accept that you cannot accept. You will then relax and guilt will drop from your mind.

Just try this small experiment:

Just relax for three days with complete

acceptance. If you relax for three days without the pull and push in the inner and outer worlds, are you going to lose all your wealth? Surely not! So there is no problem. In three days you are not going to lose anything. Why don't you give it a try? Just for three days, sincerely, utterly, accept everything in your life one hundred percent!

If you are not able to accept one hundred percent then accept that you are not able to accept one hundred percent. Even the acceptance of 'I am not able to accept myself in the inner world and outer world' will make you drop from the pull and push between the past and future. The moment you understand, 'I am unable to free myself from the pull and push of desires and fears, I am not able to accept my reality,' that very understanding will start doing its job.

If you can fall into the present moment, relaxing from the outer world and inner world things, in three days you will have a glimpse: What is life? What does it mean to live in the present moment? If this happens to you, you will experience such ecstasy, such a different space, such a different life that you have never experienced before.

You have lived based on your philosophy for maybe the last thirty years. Just for three days, don't try to alter anybody in the outer world. You will see that when you experiment with such great techniques, they work miracles in your being. They start a great alchemy process in your being. If you are not able to be sincere, accept that you are not able to be sincere. Even that sincerity is

enough. You will start seeing a different space in you.

Meditation Techniques

From Head to Heart

Sit down and close your eyes. Take slow and deep breaths, just for a few minutes. Along with it, feel that your head is being pressed into your heart, into the chest region. Become totally headless. You have no head now. You are headless.

Feel that you are breathing from the heart. Feel that you are seeing through the heart. Feel that you are smelling through your heart. Feel very clearly that you are breathing through the heart. Listen through the heart, see through the heart, and feel through the heart.

Stand up. Have the consciousness from the heart and let your movements be as slow as possible. Don't walk. Just move your body around slowly. Remember that you are moving from the heart. Your center is the heart, not the head. Again and again, forget the head. Move from the heart. Remember you are a headless being.

Stand in one place. Now, increase the speed slowly, very slowly. Remember to move from the heart, not from the head. Forget your head. You are a headless being moving.

(After few minutes)

75

Sit down where you are. Just be without the head. Sit only with your heart. Relax.

(After few minutes)

Slowly, very slowly, open your eyes.

You Are The Best, Why Compare?

Comparison and Jealousy

Emotions of fear, desire and guilt are subjective emotions. What I mean by this is that you do not need another person or even an object to create these emotions. Imagine that you are in a sound proofed room with your eyes closed and with nothing to touch, taste or smell. You can still feel the emotions of fear or desire. But to compare yourself with another person and to feel jealous of him, you need the presence of another person. Jealousy is therefore an objective emotion. It needs an object to be activated.

A small story:

One evening a man was sitting with his wife on a park bench. Without noticing them, a young man and his girlfriend sat down next to them. The young man started talking to his girlfriend in a very loving manner.

Hearing this, the wife whispered to her husband, 'I think he is going to propose to her. Maybe you should cough or do something to warn him!'

The husband replied, 'Why should I warn him? Nobody ever warned me!'

Jealousy starts from comparison. We always compare ourselves with others in various fields – looks, wealth, knowledge, name and fame and friends to name a few. When we compare ourselves with others we feel that somebody else has something more than what we have and, we get caught in jealousy.

Comparison is the seed and jealousy is the fruit!

Why Comparison?

Why exactly do we compare ourselves with others?

First, we compare ourselves because we have never understood ourselves. We are not aware of who we are and what we have.

Second, society has conditioned us from our birth to evaluate ourselves based upon others. From childhood the comparison starts. In school, the grading system introduces a child to competition and comparison with others.

Nothing exists except in relationship. There are standard benchmarks to measure a child's qualities such as mathematical ability, scientific aptitude, artistic skill, athletic ability, musical talent and so on. But, what we don't realize is that when we try to measure a quality using a standardized benchmark, it is nothing but using comparison as the scale to measure the child himself. We are literally punishing all children with the reward systems we use in schools.

The child gets used to judging and knowing himself by looking at others and comparing himself with them. He has no understanding of himself based on what he is. He knows himself only based on others.

A small story:

Once a man was testifying in court about a road accident. Suddenly, the man noticed that the court reporter was writing while he spoke. As the man started speaking faster and faster he noticed that the reporter was writing faster and faster.

Suddenly the man said to the court reporter, 'Please don't write so fast. I am not able to keep up with you!'

Every judgment you make about yourself is based on some comparison. But why does the idea of the other enter into your mind? It is because you have not looked in and realized who you are. You have not experienced the bliss and tremendous potential you have inside you. You feel incomplete because you have not been able to express yourself as you are. So, the emptiness and lack of fulfillment inside makes you feel inferior to others.

The futility of comparison

Buddha says, 'Nothing exists except in relationship.' Suppose you were the only person on a new planet, how could you compare yourself with anyone? Could you call yourself tall or short, ugly or beautiful, rich or poor, intelligent or dumb? No! When there is no one with whom to compare ourselves, we just are!

Understand, even now, there is no scale to compare you with anybody. Each individual is unique.

Can you compare a lion and a horse? Do we ever compare ourselves with flowers or birds or mountains? Then why do we have to compare ourselves with other human beings!

A beautiful Zen story:

A king once went to a master to ask for a technique to become more powerful than his neighboring kings. He sat in front of the master and started telling him the purpose of his visit. The master listened patiently to the king.

He then told him to go into the royal garden where a rose plant and a cypress plant were growing side by side. He told the king, 'They are your teachers. They can teach you what you need to learn.'

The king went into the garden, saw the two plants but could not understand what he was meant to learn from them. He went back to the master and asked, 'What do you mean, master? I am not able to understand what and how these plants will teach me.'

The master took the king to the plants and explained, 'This cypress plant has been next to the rose plant for so many years. Never once has it even aspired to become a rose plant. Similarly, the rose plant has never ever aspired to become a cypress plant. If man had been the cypress plant, he would have compared himself with the rose and felt jealous at the attention that the rose plant was getting from people. Or if man were the rose plant, he would have looked at the cypress plant enviously thinking how peaceful the plant was without the torture of getting plucked by people all day!'

The two plants prospered because they used all of their energy for their own growth instead of using it to compare themselves with the other.

The moment you stop comparing, all jealousy disappears. Instead, you will start feeling contented in yourself and grateful to Existence for having given you so much and for making you unique.

Instead, if you feel jealous of others, you will suffer. You will constantly fight with others openly or inside yourself. If somebody laughs, you think he is laughing at you. If somebody is friendly towards another person you feel lonely and jealous of that person. Actually, you are just waiting for someone to hurt you. The jealousy you allow inside you is like a raw wound. Any action done with no intention to hurt you also touches the wound and hurts.

So when you feel hurt, understand that you have a wound. Don't throw the responsibility of the suffering on the other person. The wound needs

When you feel hurt, understand you have a wound.

to be healed and the jealousy has to be dissolved. Then nobody can hurt you. Be very clear, nobody can hurt you without your silent permission.

You compare yourself to each other because you feel that you are somehow lacking. Honestly, you have no idea of your true, unique potential! If you did, you wouldn't spend one second looking outside yourself for answers about how to live a creative, fulfilling life. All of the confidence, intelligence, and vibrant energy that you need already exist inside you. You have the potential to live like god on earth. Don't believe the limiting things that you have been made to believe about yourself. Just look in! Experiment, explore and discover the truth for yourself. Then you will simply radiate all of these qualities effortlessly.

Above and Below the Ladder

Suppose there was a huge ladder and everybody in the world was asked to stand on it in ascending order of success in any field such as beauty or intelligence. You would probably position yourself somewhere in the middle of the ladder. There are many people above you but there are also many people below you. Seeing the people above you causes you to feel jealous. So, you constantly try to become better than them in order to move further up the ladder.

Now, at some point in your life, you may realize the uselessness of this never-ending

We all function around *doing*, *having* and *being*. game. Then you want to jump off the ladder. And you look down. Now what do you see? There are so many people below you. Suddenly you start feeling happy to see so many people below you and you feel hopeful because you are not as inferior as you thought you were when you were looking at the people above you.

This is where the fight starts. When you look up, you feel miserable, but when you look down, you feel happy. Now even though you begin to realize the futility of spending your life just climbing the ladder, still you are not able to jump off the ladder because if you jump off, you will be left alone. There will be nobody above you or below you.

Doing, having and being

We all function around these three axes of *doing, having* and *being*. *Doing* for *having*, without enjoying *being*, is the sole cause of all our misery. *Doing* never catches up with *having*! Every time you work hard and fulfill one desire, suddenly that desire loses its pull over you.

As enlightened master, Ramana Maharishi[*], says beautifully, 'The mind is such that it shows a tiny mustard seed to be a huge mountain until it is attained. As soon as it has been attained, even a mountain appears as insignificant as a mustard seed!'

As soon as a desire is fulfilled, another one starts pulling at you. You don't even have time to enjoy it and feel satisfied. You may think, 'Let me get this one more thing also. Then I can relax and enjoy what I have.' Be very clear, your mind will never let it happen.

The only way to really live and enjoy life is to enjoy the very doing itself. Then automatically the doing, having and being, will be integrated and will happen.

You are unique

Nature has its own unique way of growth for each of us.

Take the Chinese bamboo for example. When it sprouts, it doesn't show much growth for the first four years. Then in the fifth year, the bamboo grows ninety feet in six weeks! It was not that the tree was not growing in the first four years. Though the growth was not visible, the roots were being strengthened to make it possible for the plant to grow fast and safely into a huge tree!

Like the bamboo's growth, there is no scale to measure yourself with anyone other than your own self. If you spend all your energy looking in and competing with yourself, you will progress in leaps and bounds.

First of all, understand that god is an artist, not an engineer. If He was an engineer, He

---

Ramana Maharishi - Enlightened master, based in Tiruvannamalai in South India. He taught the method of Self-inquiry, asking oneself, 'Who am I?', as the path to Self-realization.

would have made one perfect man and one perfect woman and then made millions of copies from that mould! No. God has made each one of us unique in every way.

It does not matter whether you are a rose or a lily or a wild flower. The important thing is that the wild flower should realize its ultimate potential as a wild flower just as the rose should actualize its inherent potential. The fragrance of you realizing your unique potential is what radiates and, without effort, touches everyone around you.

Whether it is beauty or intelligence, you are unique. It is only when you don't respect your uniqueness that you start comparing yourself with others. Even if your favorite cinema star or model is very beautiful, can you enjoy drinking even a cup of water from that body? No! You can only enjoy using your own body - your best friend. Accept and welcome it.

Peer pressure – the stick of Jealousy

There is a beautiful verse in the ancient scriptures that says the power of *maya**, the energy which runs the universe, uses jealousy as a tool to make you do whatever it wants you to do.

In India, there are people who do circus shows with monkeys in the street. They will have a small stick. Once they pick up the stick, the monkey will do whatever they say. If they just gesture to the monkey, it won't listen. Even though it knows that the man can pick up the stick at any time, unless he picks up the stick, the monkey won't listen. If he picks up the stick and tells the monkey to walk straight, it will walk straight. If the man tells the monkey to jump three times, it will jump three times.

Peer pressure is just a big ego game. Actually, it is not at all necessary for you to grow.

The man will use the stick like the ringmaster uses it in the circus. In the same way, the power of *maya** uses peer pressure and jealousy as a stick to make you do whatever it wants. Understand, peer pressure is just a big ego game. Actually, it is not at all necessary for you to grow. There is enough food, shelter, medical care and clothing in the world to satisfy all of our basic needs. There is no need to compete!

How to overcome Jealousy

Jealousy is closely related to many negative emotions such as anger, greed, possessiveness and depression. All of these emotions will dissolve when we break this cycle of jealousy.

Maya – illusion – that which does not exist but which troubles as if it exists.

1. Witnessing

Jealousy cannot be overcome either by escaping from it or hating the object of jealousy. All you need to do is just be fully aware when the feeling of jealousy arises. You will be surprised that it simply disappears.

The enlightened master, Buddha* says, 'Destroy those envying roots and enjoy lasting peace.'

Just be aware and destroy the jealousy, competition, envy and comparison that have robbed you of your very nature which is bliss. Use the light of awareness to reveal the shadow nature of these negative emotions. Otherwise, you are just caught in the rat race. I always tell people, even if you win the rat race, you are still just a rat!

Understand, the way out of jealousy is not by suppressing it or denying its existence. Expressing and encouraging it is also not the way because then you are not ready to face the jealousy with awareness.

Just watch how jealousy arises in you, how it develops into hatred for the object of jealousy, how it creates restlessness and frustration inside you and makes you lose all your peace and calm.

Be aware of the jealousy instead of hating it or the object of your jealousy. Just watch, as if you have nothing to do with it. Look at it with a scientific attitude. What do I mean by a scientific attitude?

No Prejudice – The Attitude of the Scientist

When a scientist is experimenting, he simply experiments without any judgment, without any pre-determined conclusion. If he has a conclusion already in his mind, that means he is not a scientist because his conclusion may influence the experiment.

Now, you are the scientist in the laboratory of the inner world science. Be a scientist in your inner world and let your mind be your laboratory. Just be aware and witness without any prejudice.

Don't condemn the emotion saying it is bad because that is what you have been taught. It has not become your experience. If it is your experience that jealousy is a negative emotion you will drop it automatically. It has not become your own experience. It is only something that you have picked up from others. Unless it becomes an experiential understanding in you that jealousy and comparison are negative, it will not become a part of you.

Don't condemn the object of jealousy. The object has not generated the emotion from outside. The jealousy is happening inside *you*.

Once you see your jealousy with awareness, you will realize that it does not have a basis for existence at all. When this happens, jealousy will drop automatically. You won't have to drop it.

Buddha – Founder of the religion of Buddhism now followed by millions worldwide.

A small story:

A woman once hired a professional artist to paint her portrait. The artist carefully made a large portrait and then presented it to her saying, 'How do you like it?'

The lady looked at it and said, 'Yes, very nice. But can you add a few things? I want you to add a glittering diamond necklace, a gold watch and bracelet, emerald earrings and beautiful pearl rings on the fingers. The artist was surprised and said, 'But madam, the portrait looks simple and beautiful as it is. Why do you want to add all the jewelry and clutter it?'

The woman replied, 'I want my rich neighbors to see the painting and go crazy when they see all the jewelry that they will think I have.'

The fire of jealousy can just consume you completely if you don't control it with the fire extinguisher of your awareness.

2. Infinite love

Jealousy does not allow you to experience your true nature of love and bliss. It arises out of misunderstanding life and yourself. You misunderstand love to be something outside of you that has to be acquired. Not only that, you think love is a quantity that needs to be shared. That is why you are afraid, thinking that if you share your love, your share will be reduced.

Love is a quality inside you. It is not a limited quantity. It is an unending happening overflowing from within you. It cannot be blocked by anything or anybody except you because it is your very nature.

Once love starts flowing, jealousy and possessiveness and all that simply become non-existent. If you accept yourself just as you are, you can accept others also as they are.

You Are Not Who You Think You Are!

Seriousness Vs Sincerity

All our comparison with other people begins with what we think of ourselves. Jealousy disappears when we understand our uniqueness. We may then create another problem. We may believe ourselves to be so special that we start taking ourselves far too seriously.

What is seriousness?

Seriousness is nothing but paying undue importance to something, at the cost of everything else. It arises from the inability to see that all of life is just a drama that is unfolding every minute. Seriousness is the result of over-expectation from life.

A small story:

Two boys were building sand castles on the beach. They suddenly had a quarrel and one of the boys got angry and kicked the sand castle.

The other boy went and complained to the king about his serious problem. The king began to laugh at him for getting so upset over silly sand castles. But the king's

advisor, a Zen monk, started laughing at the king.

He asked, 'When you can fight battles and lose sleep over stone castles, why do you laugh at these boys for fighting over sand castles!'

All our seriousness is just about sandcastles! For the child, at that young age, sand castles seem precious, whereas at our age, stone castles seem precious, that's all. Whether it is a sand castle or a stone castle, the seriousness behind it is the same. The object may be different, but the seriousness is the same. So, don't laugh when children fight over sand castles.

Seriousness closes your mind to the openness and freedom of life. It makes you dull and dead. It curbs your thinking and makes you stick to the familiar patterns that you know and use all the time.

A small story:

In a Zen monastery, there was a competition among disciples over who had maintained the best garden. One disciple was of a very serious nature. He took the competition quite seriously. He always kept his garden

> **Sincerity is giving the task your best without worrying excessively about the result.**

neat, clean, and well-swept. All the grass was of the same height. All the bushes were neatly trimmed. He was sure that he would get the first prize.

On the day of the competition, the master went around all the gardens. Then he came back and ranked the gardens. This disciple's garden got the lowest ranking. Everyone was shocked. The disciple could not contain himself and asked, 'Master, what is wrong with my garden? Why did you rank me the lowest?'

The master looked at him and asked, 'Where are all the dead leaves? A garden maintained in such a way is no longer alive! It is dead.'

Seriousness kills spontaneity. Seriousness destroys creativity.

Science has proved that when you perform a task in a relaxed and light manner, your thinking and decision-making capacity is automatically enhanced. The same task when performed in a serious manner dulls your mind. When you do something too seriously, when you are too concerned about the result, you are actually not allowing yourself to perform at the optimum level.

Of course, you need to make plans, and you need to think ahead. But do it with sincerity, not with seriousness. Seriousness is not the same as sincerity. Sincerity is focusing on the task with enthusiasm and youthfulness. Sincerity is giving the task your best without worrying excessively about the result! When you are serious, you don't enjoy, you don't laugh. How can you laugh when you are serious!

Perfectionism

Perfectionism always comes from your mind. It becomes a goal for you. You work towards it as a goal. When you work towards it as a goal, it becomes dead and mundane. But when you are total, when you are established in your heart, it becomes a deep experience. The outcome has to be beautiful, and it will give you joy. Then, whatever you do, you will be in tune with Existence. Whatever you do, do it wholly, totally, and it will be total. You won't have to worry about perfectionism at all.

Perfectionism never gives you joy; it only fulfills your ego. Even if you feel fulfilled at the end of it, it is only a fulfillment of your ego, never a fulfillment of your being. Be very clear, perfectionists are the biggest egoists. They miss the dimension of being total. Totality is possible when you enter into something deeply. Perfectionism is never possible because it is in your mind, and your mind keeps changing its definition of perfection!

Life is beyond your logic

Most of us unconsciously believe that life is filled with incidents that are under the control of our logic. But life again and again reminds you of the truth that life is beyond your logic. You are reminded of this fact, especially when some near and dear friend or family member dies or when something unexpected happens. If you lose your job, suddenly you see that life is not under your control. You suddenly wake up to the reality that life is beyond your logic. Then you start seeking the Truth.

Especially if you live in the city, your routine is almost fixed. From morning until night, you know exactly how your day will unfold. You know where you will go, what you will do or not do, and what and when you will eat.

Practically, your ego gives an idea, your logic gives you the feeling that your life is under the control of your logic. That is why whenever some incident happens that is beyond your logic, that is not under your control, you are totally shaken. You are not able to handle it. You don't know what to do. Either you fall into depression or you just suffer.

There is an important truth, an ultimate secret that you must understand. Never think things are going smoothly because of you. In spite of you, things are going smoothly! This is one of the important secrets. As long as you think it is because of you that things are going smoothly, you will be constantly suffering with ego.

What is Ego?

The real purpose of life cannot be understood by the ego.

According to the *Upanishads**, as long as you think that life has a purpose and you run behind that purpose, you are an egoistic person. When you realize the beauty of the purposelessness of life, you have dropped your ego. The master is the one who makes you understand the purposelessness of life. Whatever you think as being worthy now is not actually the true and worthy thing. A man with ego searches with purpose and misses reality.

Death clearly shows that whatever mind you lived with has no real existence. When you realize the purposelessness of life, a new consciousness starts blossoming in you. The moment you experience that there is nothing to be achieved, that the diamonds you are protecting are not diamonds but stones, and that all your great things in life are mere toys, you will understand the purposelessness of life.

The real purpose of life cannot be understood by the ego. When the ego is dropped, you will understand the Divine purpose of life, the *leelas* or the Divine play; you will enjoy the drama. If you keep thinking that life has a purpose and wait to achieve something, you will miss life itself.

Life itself is the path and the goal. When you have a goal, you will run. Your feet will

---

Upanishad - Scriptures that form the essence of the ancient texts of the Vedas. Literally means 'sitting with the master'. There are eleven main Upanishads that have been commented on by enlightened master Adi Shankara.

When you understand the purposelessness of life, you understand the meaning of living.

not touch the ground and you will miss the beauty of Existence or nature. When you drop the goal, the emphasis will be on the path.

When you understand the purposelessness of life, you understand the meaning of living. Until then, you are just a 'living dead' person. A person in a coma lying in the hospital bed and a normal person who has not realized the Truth, both live without proper consciousness. The master is the one who makes you realize this truth. The meaning of living is the meaning of life or Existence.

Drop the goal and enjoy life. Meditate on this teaching again and again. The Truth will dawn on you and the *nithyananda* state will flower in you, the state that is the very meaning of life.

The solid feeling of 'no'

Many times you may have seen that whenever someone says something to you, the first reaction inside you is a certain resistance, a 'no'. When you say 'no', it is ego-fulfilling. You feel solid and firm inside yourself. When you say 'yes', you feel liquid and vulnerable. Your ego feels submissive, which is uncomfortable, so you say 'no'.

This is also why you feel good when you break rules at home, school, in the workplace, or while driving. You feel boosted in ego when you say 'no' to rules. You can see this with small children. The moment you say they are not meant to have certain things, they will ask only for those things!

Ordinary Vs Extraordinary

Whenever you try to live for your ego, you make your life and others' lives miserable. Most of the time the miseries you face in your life are not created by others. They are unknowingly created by you. You may not even derive any benefits from them. But just to prove your ego, you create them.

A small story:

An enlightened master, Suzuki, lived in Japan. When his master passed away, he started weeping profusely. One person asked him, 'You are an enlightened person. Why are you crying on your master's passing away?' Suzuki replied, 'My master was the most extraordinary man on planet earth.' The person was puzzled and asked him, 'What was so extraordinary about him?'

Suzuki replied, 'I have never seen such an extraordinary person who thought he was the most ordinary man!'

In ordinary life, every average person thinks he is extraordinary. When you feel that you have undergone the maximum suffering, your ego feels good that you have been able to handle a tough life. Only when your enemy is big, you feel big. When your enemy is small, you feel small.

For the same reason, if your suffering is big, you feel good. Your ego feels satisfied. You measure life with the amount of your suffering. Unknowingly, you torture others as well as yourself. Suzuki's master was extraordinary because he thought he was the most ordinary, whereas in this world, every other person thinks he is extraordinary.

If you want to check whether you are average or not, do this experiment. If you feel extraordinary, be very clear: you are average. If you feel ordinary, you are extraordinary!

Using the right mask

You all play different roles and use different masks in your day-to-day lives. You use one mask with your mother, a different mask with your father, a different one with your boss and so on. As long as you use the right masks with the right people, it is alright. The moment you use the wrong mask with a person, be aware that your ego has stepped in.

All you have to do is switch masks efficiently and enjoy the show. Then you are a watcher. You can do this only when you know that you are something beyond the mask. Otherwise, you will get carried away by the mask and lose the whole charm of life. When you know that you are only using masks, your desires drop.

Just like when you grow up, you automatically drop your toys, in the same way, when you look at these masks intelligently, you don't have any desire for them and simply use them as needed.

Your mind exists when it hits the corners of your suffering.

Ego is born from discontentment

If you are a strong egoistic person, you don't need a separate hell because the mind can exist only in conflict and discontentment. With contentment, with satisfaction, you will lose your boundary. That is why you don't want joy or bliss. Please never think you want bliss. No! Actually you are afraid of joy and bliss. Whenever you go through a peaceful, no-worry feeling, just watch yourself. You feel you are missing something when there is nothing to think about! Unless you have something strong to brood over, you don't have a clear-cut boundary in your inner space.

Your mind exists when it hits the corners of your suffering. You don't feel your boundary or your identity unless you have enough suffering. If you look a little deeper, you will understand that many times you feel lonely if you don't have anything to worry or suffer about. That is the way you believe yourselves to be, because by its nature, the mind can record only negative things. The mind can flourish, it can create more thoughts, it can more clearly identify with suffering, dissatisfaction and discontentment. The quality of joy is boundarylessness. When you are in joy, you won't feel your boundary. Whenever you don't feel your boundary, you are in a state of joy, in a satisfied and contented mood.

Suffering leads to Ego

Your ego cannot exist without your suffering. Suffering is the root of your ego. This is an important thing you need to understand. We always think that the ego is disturbed by suffering. No! Ego is enriched by suffering. One more important thing is that if your suffering is less, your ego is less. You feel you are too small, so you increase your suffering so that you can feel you are somebody.

The less the suffering, the weaker is the ego. The more you suffer, the stronger your ego becomes. So, you always exaggerate your suffering. The problem is that after some time you forget that you exaggerated. Then you are also caught in the same net. You might disagree and say, 'No, you don't know my life; you don't know my suffering.' But be very clear, after some time you are caught in the same net that you yourself created!

Dual identities

We all have two identities, the identity that we project to the outer world, and the identity that we believe to be us in the inner world.

The identity that you believe to be you inside your mind is called *mamakar** in Sanskrit. It will always be much smaller than what you really are. You will carry or remember all your failures, past mistakes and guilt, constantly trying to work on them.

The identity that you project to the outer world is called *ahankar**. *Ahankar** is your visiting card. You print on it everything that you want others to know about yourself. This is based on the identity you show to the outer world. It will always be more than what you have, more than what you are. It will always be much more than what you are because you think you have to sell yourself. It becomes a basic need to do this, especially in the societies where you have to market yourself.

*Ahankar** will be based on a superiority complex. *Mamakar** will be based on an inferiority complex. *Ahankar* will be based on fear. *Mamakar** will be based on greed.

The basic truth is that you are much more than these two identities. When you unclutch from these two identities, you will suddenly realize that you are beyond the two identities. When that happens, these two identities can never bind you again.

Inferior Ego

An incident from the life of Ramana Maharishi*:

One of Ramana Maharishi's disciples translated one of his books into another*

Mamakar - Inner ego that constantly says you are smaller than what you think you are.

Ahankar - The false identification of the pure inner self with the outer world; a form of ego that makes you project a false identity of you to the outer world.

Ramana Maharishi – Enlightened master who encouraged Self-Realization through self-inquiry, 'Who am I?'

language. In the translation, inside the book, his name was also published as the translator.

When the disciple saw the book, he was shocked to see this. He went to the concerned authorities and scolded them for this mistake. He then went and told Ramana Maharishi, 'Bhagavan, they should not have put my name. I don't feel my name should be publicized. I am not that kind of person.'

Bhagavan said, 'The ego that asks for the name to be there and the ego that asks that the name not be there are one and the same. Relax.'

Be very clear, the inferior ego that is trying to show humbleness is also ego.

With a superiority complex, with a violent aggressive ego, at least society will teach you. This ego is very visible. With the humble ego, you will escape from society. That is more dangerous. It is the cunning ego that can nicely save itself. Ego is just the identity you carry about yourself.

Types of Ego

Active ego Vs Passive ego

The active ego is easy to recognize. People with an active ego will behave in a highhanded fashion; they will claim self-importance openly. They will be arrogant. This ego is actually easy for a master to deal with. He just needs to bang on it a few times and it will break!

A small story:

A psychiatrist asks his patient if he is suffering from fantasies of self-importance. The man replies, 'Absolutely not. In fact, I think much less of myself than I really am!'

A person with an active ego will not be willing to let go of it at any cost.

Passive ego is very subtle and cunning. People who have a passive ego will pose as being very humble, lacking courage to face people, and shying away from taking credit. The worst part of this is that they think they are like this because they are not egoistic. Actually, they are so carefully guarding their ego from getting hurt by unconsciously thinking they are humble!

People with active ego are like dried, hard twigs. They can be broken easily. People with passive ego are like fresh, green twigs. Each time their ego is hit, they bend but don't break! Their ego is so well safeguarded that it becomes difficult to deal with. Actually, they work very hard to safeguard it but in a sweet and passive way.

'I' and 'Mine'

'I' is the ego, the root of fear. 'Mine', 'this is my house', 'that is my car', 'these are my friends', is the root of greed.

'I' means continuously doing. 'Mine' means continuously having. Continuously you try to expand your boundary. Continuously you try to change the things outside. You want to expand your boundary of 'mine'. For example,

If you follow the mind, you cannot follow the master. you have a basic car now but you want to have a more luxurious car; you may want more than one car. You have a house to live in, but you want a bigger house. This kind of personality is based on having. Such people feel happy, secure and relaxed only when they continuously possess more and more things.

The deep feeling of insecurity, that fear, drives us to more greed, to continuously try to possess more things. Continuously possessing things is nothing but a feeling of deep insecurity. You can see the idea of continuously possessing more and more things is just because of fear and insecurity.

We usually feel more secure if we have more friends, more relatives, and more things around us. With more security, we feel we will not be taken away from this world.

Ego Vs Master

People ask me, 'Why do we have to follow masters?' I tell them, 'You don't *have* to follow masters. But if you don't follow masters, you will be following your ego, that's all. There are only two options. Either you listen to the master or you listen to the ego.'

Master is the being who has already achieved eternal bliss, *nithya ananda*. If you follow him you will also reach that state. As for your ego, you know what it has achieved so far and what it is heading towards! If you are happy, comfortable, contented and blissful in the path in which your ego is already leading

you, then you can follow your ego. Nothing is wrong with that. If you are a little uncomfortable, if you want to change, then follow the master's path.

There are only two to follow: master and the mind. If you follow the master, you cannot follow the mind. If you follow the mind, you cannot follow the master.

There is a beautiful word, '*na maha*'. It means, 'not mine', 'I am not' - I surrender the 'I' and 'mine' at the feet of the master or god.

Meditation Technique

1. Third Eye Meditation

Total Duration: 25 minutes

This is an extremely powerful technique, most effective when practiced in the master's presence or in front of a picture of the master's eyes.

Step 1: Duration: 5 minutes

With your eyes closed, just see through your eyes, whatever images you are seeing behind the closed eyes.

Step 2: Duration: 5 minutes

Now open your eyes and through your third eye, look intensely at the master's third eye in the picture. Look *through* your eyes.

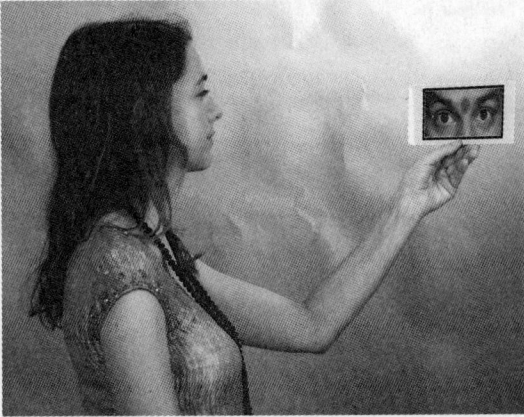

Step 3: Duration: 5 minutes

With your eyes closed, just see through your eyes, whatever images you are seeing behind the closed eyes.

Step 4: Duration: 5 minutes

Now open your eyes and through your third eye, look intensely at the master's third eye in the picture. Look *through* your eyes.

Step 5: Duration: 5 minutes

With your eyes closed, just see through your eyes, whatever images you are seeing behind the closed eyes.

During this meditation, you may see visions of your favorite deities, or you may find that the master's form is replaced by a beam of light. Sometimes you may see total emptiness where his picture was. Don't be alarmed or lose your awareness at these moments. It is not hypnosis! In fact, it is a dehypnotizing process. Your superconscious is being awakened. If you see only light or emptiness, it is a sign that you have done the meditation with deep sincerity. That is the truth of our nature - we are all nothing but energy.

Seeing through the eye, you can achieve the 'I'. Currently, you are making up your own reality. If you see through the eyes, you will wake up from it and see reality as it is!

Gratitude is Enough!

What is Gratitude

When we recognize that we are part of the total scheme of Existence, and that we are lovingly taken care of by Existence every minute, we are overcome with gratitude. We become truly thankful for what we receive every moment, even if it is as basic as the use of our very limbs and senses.

Gratitude is your response to recognizing the abundance of Existence. It is a wonderful flowering energy within you.

If there is one energy that takes care of everything in your life, it is the energy of gratitude! If you ever feel that there is something missing in your life, it is because you feel less gratitude.

Gratitude should become your very breath. Gratitude is a transforming energy. It transforms the happenings in you and around you. It is an energy that harmonizes you with the energy of the universe and brings back tremendous prosperity to you. With gratitude

you will see that Existence simply responds to you – as if it is a live being. It is the channel to commune with Existence!

When gratitude happens, it works beautifully through the law of attraction and attracts great prosperity to you. How is this possible?

A small story:

Akbar*, a great king from ancient India, and Birbal*, his advisor, were walking together on the street one day.

They passed by a sandalwood dealer and Akbar* told Birbal*, 'I don't know why but I feel like hanging this man.'

One month passed and the two of them walked past the same sandalwood dealer again.

This time Akbar* said, 'It's strange but I feel like giving this man some endowment today! How is it possible?'

Birbal* replied, 'O King! A month back, the sandalwood dealer's business was suffering

Akbar - Moghul emperor.

Birbal - One of Emperor Akbar's ministers, considered to be very intelligent. Hence a number of stories woven around him and Akbar.

> **Gratitude makes you resonate with Existence and transforms you into a beautiful human being.**

and when he saw you walking past he thought to himself, 'If the king dies, the courtiers would come to buy a lot of sandalwood from me for his funeral pyre.'

He sent out these negative vibrations which prompted you to feel hatred towards him. That is why last time you felt like hanging him without any real reason. I immediately purchased a lot of sandalwood from him to make tables and chairs for our kingdom. It made him very happy. Today, he feels very grateful to you for it. You are now struck by these positive vibrations from him and therefore you feel like giving him some endowment!'

According to the Law of Attraction, like energy attracts like energy. How does this apply to gratitude? Understand this: when you feel gratitude towards everything, it means you feel fulfilled, you feel blissful. So when you radiate gratitude, your energy of fulfillment attracts fulfillment back to you in the form of material gains, good relationships, good health and so on. This is how it works.

The main thing is that gratitude makes you resonate with Existence and transforms you into a beautiful human being.

Psychologists have studied the effects of the feeling of gratitude on people. In their first study, two researchers, Dr. Michael McCollough of Southern Methodist University in Dallas, Texas, and Dr. Robert Emmons of the University of California at Davis, California, concluded that gratitude played a major role in a person's well-being.

The results of the study indicated that daily gratitude exercises resulted in higher reported levels of alertness, enthusiasm, determination, optimism, energy, lesser depression and stress. They further suggested that anyone could increase their sense of well-being and create positive social effects just from counting their blessings.

Be grateful for just being

When I tell people to live with a sense of gratitude, they immediately start looking for reasons. Real gratitude can never have a reason. It happens as a causeless flowering within you. Does the flower bloom for a reason? No! It blooms because it is its very nature. Gratitude is our real nature. It has been covered by layers of conditioning from society.

The problem is, society doesn't know the language of gratitude. It knows only the language of utility. It straightaway instills greed and fear in you so that you will give it the needed results. Society doesn't know there is a path of gratitude that will give much better results than the paths of fear and greed.

There are endless reasons to feel gratitude. This life itself is a gift that we have received. Did any of us work for it and receive it? No. To be born with human consciousness is the first blessing we have received. Our gratitude should start right from there. Just for *being* we should feel grateful.

A young girl sat at the dinner table to eat. She started eating when her mother suddenly stopped her. She asked her, 'Did you say grace before eating?'

The girl replied, 'But there is nothing on this plate that I have not already thanked god for at least once.'

Understand, if ever you feel life is dull, that it is not as juicy as it should be, it is because gratitude has not happened in you. Gratitude is the energy that makes your life intense and exciting every moment. This is a basic secret of life.

Everything is a gift

The main reason why you miss experiencing gratitude is that you take everything for granted. You feel anything that people do for you is your birthright. Understand, people could be doing something else instead of doing things for you. So it is really a gift from them to you. You have to thank them for it.

Receive every small thing in life as a gift. When you sit down to eat, have you ever thanked your fingers? There are people who don't have fingers with which to eat! Have we ever thought about that? Never! We only look at those who have a diamond ring on their finger. We never look at those who don't have fingers.

When we start feeling grateful for small things, our whole sensitivity will increase. We will become more refined.

A small story:

A man was narrating to his friend how he got lost in a desert one day.

He told the friend, 'In sheer despair, I knelt down and prayed that I should be guided out of the desert.'

The friend was awed by the story and asked, 'So did god answer your prayer?'

The man replied, 'Oh, no! Before that an explorer appeared from nowhere and showed me the way.'

> The main reason why you miss experiencing gratitude is that you take everything for granted.

This is how insensitive we are in life! We keep taking everything for granted. If we sensitized ourselves with gratitude, we would never take anything for granted – not our fingers, not our wealth, and not the timely benevolence of Existence. When sensitivity happens, every moment passes in deep awe of the happenings in Existence.

Revere the other with Gratitude

The first thing we need to understand is that no person has taken birth only to serve us. Every other person is also on the path of life just as we are. As a kind gesture, out of love, they do things for us.

Especially between partners, a lot of things are taken for granted. Somehow, this idea has taken root very deeply in our society. Because of this, many marriages fall apart

Whenever you feel truly grateful to the people in your relationships, you will never try to possess them. today. I tell you, even during a physical relationship there can be such deep gratitude for the other person's body. It will make the whole thing a divine experience instead of mere physical pleasure. When you can derive so much pleasure because of the other, why not feel gratitude towards the other for it? If the other is deeply respected from the beginning, many marriages can be saved.

A small story:

One man prayed to god, 'Oh lord, please have mercy on me. I work so hard while my wife stays at home. She enjoys staying at home while I slog the whole day. Please grant me a boon whereby I become my wife and she becomes me. I want to teach her a lesson on how tough a man's life is.

God granted his wish.

The next morning, the man who was now the woman, woke up early in the morning, packed lunch for the children, made breakfast, got the children ready and drove them to school. She then came back and put the clothes in the washing machine, went to the bank and cashed the checks, paid the electricity and phone bills. Next she went to the market and bought some groceries, put the clothes out to dry, picked up the children from school, sorted out all their problems, helped them with their homework, watched television and ironed clothes at the same time. Then she prepared dinner, fed the children, put them to sleep,

had dinner and went to bed.

The next morning the man prayed to god again, 'Oh lord, I don't think I can handle this tomorrow. I beg you to please switch me back to a man.

God replied, 'Of course I will switch you back to yourself but you will have to wait nine months because you are now carrying a child!'

Each individual plays an equal part in life. No one should be taken for granted. There has to be some gratitude for every person on planet earth. I always tell people that even if things don't work out between you and your wife and you have to part, part with gratitude.

The problem is that somewhere we feel people are waiting to hurt us. It is not so. It is only our own insecurity which we project on others.

So many people feel ungrateful to their parents and society for conditioning them in certain ways. Please understand that with the intelligence that you have now, you are able to see that you did not receive the right kind of mental setup earlier. Those who gave us this body and mind did not have any intention to deprive us or disturb us in any way. Whatever they knew as their best, they just gave to us; that's all. We are going beyond it now because we have become more intelligent. Just feel grateful to them, that is enough.

One more thing: whenever you feel truly grateful to the people in your relationships, you will never try to possess them. You will look at them as beautiful individuals and leave it at that. Possessiveness happens only when you think of the other person as an object and not as an individual. With gratitude, you will allow the person to have his or her own space.

Decide consciously that you will respond with pure love and gratitude for the next couple of days, whatever the situation may be. Automatically you will start seeing each and every person as a unique creation of Existence, as a reflection of the Divine.

Not only that, you will find tremendous compassion towards everything around you. If you were a person who gets angry easily, you will find the anger disappearing. All the energy that was invested in other negative emotions will get released with this growing gratitude. You will be a compassionate and loving person.

Thank your body

A small story:

A middle aged woman suffered a heart attack and was taken to the hospital. While on the operating table, she had a near death experience. During the experience, she happened to see god. She asked him if this was the end of her life.

God replied that she had another thirty or forty more years to live.

Once she recovered, she decided to stay in the hospital to undergo multiple surgeries such as a face lift, jaw reconstruction, a

nose job and removal of excess fat. She also colored her hair. She thought that since she was going to live for thirty more years, she would start with a fresh look.

She finished the surgeries and was about to walk out of the hospital when she was run over by the hospital ambulance and killed. She arrived before god and asked him, 'God, I thought you told me I had another thirty years to live.'

God replied, 'Sorry, but I didn't recognize you!'

Each human being is a unique masterpiece of god. That is why no two bodies look alike. God is not an engineer. He is an artist. That is why each of us looks different. If he was an engineer he would have made us all with the same mold, like in a production line! He has uniquely created each one of us. But we never feel that we are beautiful enough. We constantly compare ourselves with others and try to look like them. We never make our body feel it is beautiful.

Our body is influenced by the thoughts we entertain about it. Every cell responds to our thoughts and feelings about it. If we feel gratitude towards our body, our body responds by improving our health. If we hate our body, the body responds by shrinking with disease. In the Sufi* tradition, body gratitude is done as an everyday meditation itself where every part of the body is felt with love and thanked.

Sufi - Mystical dimension of Islam.

Everything is auspicious, just celebrate it!

One thing has to be understood very clearly. The whole of Existence is an auspicious happening. You are part of Existence, so everything happening around you is also auspicious. This is the truth of Existence. Nothing that happens in Existence is inauspicious. Everything is only a blessing, for which we have to feel grateful.

If this is understood clearly, there is nothing to complain about in life. If this is understood clearly, your very eye becomes a grateful eye. It sees everything as extraordinary. Nothing appears mundane. Everything appears as a miracle.

A small story:

One day a duck hunter went to the market to buy a bird retriever dog. To his amazement he found a dog that could walk on water! He immediately took it home.

He invited one of his friends to hunt the next day and took the dog. When a flock of ducks came near he took aim, fired and silently watched. The dog walked on the water and retrieved the bird. He looked at his friend for a reaction but the friend remained silent.

He asked him, 'Do you see anything unusual about my dog?'

The friend replied, 'Yes, your dog is unable to swim.'

Miracles are continuously happening in front of our eyes. But we continuously miss them! Only because we miss them, life itself appears to be dull sometimes. When we start perceiving them, our entire life becomes a miracle. The truth is, there are too many miracles happening around us in our lives.

Just accept and celebrate Existence with all its different dimensions and paradoxes. Don't judge anything. You continuously judge what is going on. You feel something is right or something is wrong, something should have happened this way or something should not have happened this way.

Become aware that whatever happens in Existence is auspicious. In the whole world there are only two kinds of people. The first kind feels that whatever is happening in the world is auspicious. The second kind feels everything is happening against their will and things have to be slightly altered all the time. Such people will try to alter, judge, criticize and develop the things happening in the world according to their ideas. These people continuously suffer because of trying to change things all the time.

Understand: everything has a message for us including death and disease. Everything has something to teach us. Every incident raises our intelligence, raises our frequency of consciousness.

You need to know one important thing: there is no qualitative or quantitative difference between you and an enlightened being except that he feels contented in the outer and inner worlds while you don't feel that way. You feel something is missing all the time. Just like how Existence wants him to be here on this planet, Existence wants you too to be here. You are not an accident here; you are an incident. You are a miracle of Existence. This is the straightforward and simple truth. Don't think this is positive thinking. No. This is the plain truth. If you trust this truth, you will automatically become positive, that's all.

Understand that you are a fulfillment for Existence. If you are not here, Existence will miss you. All your wealth, relations etc are not an accident. Existence wants you to have all these; it wants to live through you, fulfill itself through you! Understand this.

A small story:

There was a certain village isolated and surrounded by acres of cornfields. The city was very far from it, so it remained very quiet.

One morning the villagers saw a sage whom they had never seen before in the village. He was seated under a banyan tree. They asked him where he came from. He told them, 'I have come to spend a few days with all of you whom I consider my own brothers.'

The villagers were happy to hear this and built a small hut for him. Soon the sage started healing and solving many problems of the villagers.

Once an epidemic struck the village and killed many birds there. The villagers reported this to the sage. He said, 'It is sad that you lost so many birds but if you have faith in Existence and pray, the loss may actually be a matter of gain.'

The villagers didn't agree fully with him but since they respected him they went away.

The next week, suddenly, all the dogs in the village ran away. The villagers got upset again because the dogs used to guard the village against burglars. They went to the sage and reported this to him. He only repeated his message, 'If you have faith in Existence and pray, even this loss may prove to be a gain.'

A few days later a very strange thing happened. In those days, there were no matchboxes. People used to rub two stones together to make fire or keep a fire alive in their ovens continuously. One day, all the fires in all of the households went out. They tried to start a fire by rubbing stones but nothing happened. They got very disturbed.

They went to the sage again and told him what was happening. The sage told them, 'It looks like some very special phenomenon is taking place.'

The villagers started doubting the sage. They started wondering in what way the sage was superior to them and whether he was in any way qualified to tell them such things. Some of the villagers proceeded to the next village to get some fire but the sage stopped them, sternly saying that they should not go.

Early next morning some of the villagers started making their way to the next village anyway. Suddenly they saw something like a sandstorm in the distance. After a few moments they could see it was actually a large invading army on horseback. They were on their way plundering the city and

Existence is not an accident. It is independent intelligence.

the villages surrounding it. The villagers hid behind trees and watched them. The army stopped ahead of the village and one of them screamed, 'Let us invade this village too!'

Another person said, 'No use will come out of it. There is no bird that chirps even so early in the morning, no dog barks, no smoke comes out of the chimney of any house. It doesn't look like a single soul lives there.'

The army turned back and went away.

The hiding villagers ran back to the village and told the villagers what had happened. They suddenly realized how true the sage was all along! They went to the sage's hut to tell him everything but the hut was empty. The sage had left.

Nobody knew where he had gone.

Existence is not an accident. It is independent intelligence. When you understand that it is an independent intelligence, when you understand that it is a profound mystery to be experienced and not solved, everything in your life will open itself and reveal to you the lesson it has brought with it.

Some people ask me, 'Swamiji, how do we express our deep gratitude to you?' I tell them that the only way to express their gratitude is to live enlightenment the way I have just described it to you. That is the best you can do for me and that I can do for you.

People ask me, 'What service can we do for the mission?' I tell them, the greatest service one can do to the world is working for the flowering of one's own consciousness. Once this happens, automatically, you will serve where required, not out of ego or to gain credit, but because you are celebrating and overflowing. Then it is not called service. It is just an overflowing. That is the way service should happen - not as a giving, but as a spontaneous sharing.

Gratitude can burn your *karmas*

Sufism* is completely a gratitude-based religion. If I have to reduce the whole of Sufism* to one word, it is gratitude. You can see it in all the poems of the great Sufi* masters like Jalaluddin Rumi* and others. You can see the flowing energy of gratitude in their words. Gratitude makes you a nobody, just flowing energy.

Gratitude is like a fire that can burn all your *karmas**. What is *karma**? It is an unfulfilled action on your part that pulls you again and again to fulfill it. In order to fulfill and exhaust all such *karmas** that we have

---

Sufism - Mystical dimension of Islam.

Sufi - Follower of Sufism.

Rumi - 13th century Persian Sufi poet.

Karma - The *vedic* concept of one's freewill actions deciding one's destiny.

accumulated, we take birth again and again on this planet. Just by being with the energy of gratitude, these *karmas* get burnt! Such is the power of gratitude.

Gratitude - the ultimate prayer and religion

When your prayer becomes gratitude, you attract more benevolence to you. Gratitude is the ultimate prayer that can bring us more than we can imagine. Real prayer is not reading prayer books, it is not offering material things to god, it is not donating money to temples, it is deep and silent gratitude to the whole of Existence for being what it is. It is the undaunted trust that Existence is taking care.

Many people think prayer and gratitude are bondage. No. They are the greatest liberators. They liberate you from the bondage of discontentment. Prayer should be an overflowing of the gratitude and fulfillment in you. Some people ask, 'Why do we go to the temple and pray?' Understand, prayer is a celebration of the benevolence of Existence. When our prayer is this way, Existence responds. When Existence responds, it comes to you as more benevolence in your life. This is the virtuous cycle of prayer and blessing!

I always tell people a wonderful story of a Sufi saint. Sufism is a religion rooted in gratitude. It is nothing but gratitude towards the whole of Existence.

One Sufi saint and his disciples were in their spiritual wandering. They went without

> **Prayer is a celebration of the benevolence of Existence.**

food for three days. On the fourth day they were even chased away by the villagers and so they slept in a graveyard that night. The next morning, the saint as usual started to say his prayer of thanksgiving to god. His disciples could not believe their eyes. They had gone without food and shelter for so many days and their master was thanking god. They refused to follow suit.

The disciples asked the saint, 'Why should we thank the lord when we were refused food and a place to stay for three days?'

The saint replied, 'You have been fed and given a place to stay for thirty years. What about thanking Him for that?'

Prayer is gratitude for the continuous showering of Existence upon us.

Expectation is the culprit - let go!

Try to sit down and make two lists. Let one be of all the things that you have and one of all the things that you don't have. The first list should include every single thing that you have, starting from your eyes, ears, hands and legs, because there are people who don't have some of these. Include all your physical and mental faculties before moving to material things. If you write very sincerely without leaving out anything, you will not be able to complete the first list! That is the truth. If you find you are unable to finish the first list, it means gratitude has started happening in you!

The problem is that there is a continuous expectation in us all the time. That is why gratitude doesn't happen easily. Working with expectation is like pouring clarified butter into the fire to quench it. Can you quench fire by pouring clarified butter into it? Never! In the same way, you can never feel fulfilled if your actions are rooted in expectation. You will only tire your senses.

You can live either in expectation or in gratitude, never in both. With expectation there is a desire to possess things. You become the owner. With gratitude, you become the enjoyer. When you are the owner you enjoy only the few things that you own. When you are the enjoyer, you enjoy everything in Existence. When you look to own, nothing will seem enough. When you enjoy, everything seems to be overflowing! That is the difference.

A small story:

In a village, the night guard was on his rounds blowing his whistle periodically.

He had an earthen pipe that he smoked. He filled it with tobacco and searched for a match box. He didn't have one.

He went to the nearby hut where an old lady lived and asked if she could give him some ember from her oven. The old lady said her stove had not been lit for the past three days and that she herself was managing with the little food they gave in the temple.

He tried in several places but it was of no use. He finally went to the village chief's house and asked the maids for fire to light his pipe.

One of the girls looked at him and asked, 'Fire to light your pipe? Why not use the lantern you are carrying?'

The guard couldn't believe his eyes. He had been carrying a lantern all along while searching for a matchbox!

When we believe that what we need is always only outside of us, we live in eternal expectation and we will continue searching like the night guard! When we believe that Existence always gives us what we need, we will find everything within us all the time.

Your very body language can change with Gratitude

When we work with expectation all the time, we carry a subtle violence in our body language; not deliberate violence, but inherent violence. If we become a little sensitive to our body language, we will be able to catch this.

Watch yourself when you type on the computer, when you handle phone calls, how you place the phone receiver back in its cradle, with what aggression you walk … everything. You will see that everything carries a subtle violence in it.

With gratitude, your entire body language changes. When you start experiencing deep gratitude, your responses to situations change. You start resonating with Existence. Your body will flow with that resonance, with a cool grace and softness. All your actions will arise out of this grace. There will be no violence. Only joy will be flowing. Then anything you do will only make life sweeter.

Nithyananda was intense in his spiritual quest right from a very young age.
As a young boy, he did various spiritual practices in the energy field of Arunachala.

Nithyananda as a young intense seeker

Addressing the Madras Management Asscoiation, Chennai, India on 'Enlightened Management - Lord Krishna's way'

Nithyananda personally conducts meditation programs from basic to advanced levels, attended by thousands worldwide

Corporate talk on 'Intuitive Management' at Microsoft Corporation, Seattle, USA

Nithyananda has delivered many breakthrough messages giving solutions for the issues faced by the corporate world. These corporate programs have been conducted in corporate organizations like Microsoft, AT&T, Qualcomm, JP Morgan, Petrobras, Pepsi, Oracle, etc

Nithyananda personally conducting a meditation program.
Ordained teachers also conduct yoga and meditation programs. These have touched over 2 million people to date including children, youth, those in rural areas, prison inmates, etc.

Nithyanandam, an advanced meditation program, at the Bidadi ashram in India, in December 2005

Life Bliss Meditation Program Level 2 attended by thousands of students at a college in South India

Kalpataru program in Malaysia, 20 November 2008

Addressing a large satsang in Tiruvannamalai, India, 21 December 2008
Satsangs are blissful gatherings of people to help them grow on the spiritual path.

Nithya Dhyaan, a 3-day meditation program in Bengaluru, India, December 20-22, 2007

Nithya Dhyaan or Life Bliss Meditation is a powerful and universal meditation working on the body-mind-spirit leading one straight to the experience of living enlightenment.

The first Inner Awakening program, a 21-day program giving the keys to live enlightenment, held in Bidadi ashram from December 1-21, 2008

First introductory talk on Nithya Yoga delivered to the yoga community in Los Angeles, USA in September 2006

Nithya Yoga is the original Patanjali Yoga re-presented for the modern man. It is not just yoga for physical exercise, but a deep science of preparing the body-mind to hold the experience of living enlightenment.

Teachers' training program, Buckhorn, USA

Nithyananda personally trains and ordains teachers who conduct meditation and yoga programs worldwide

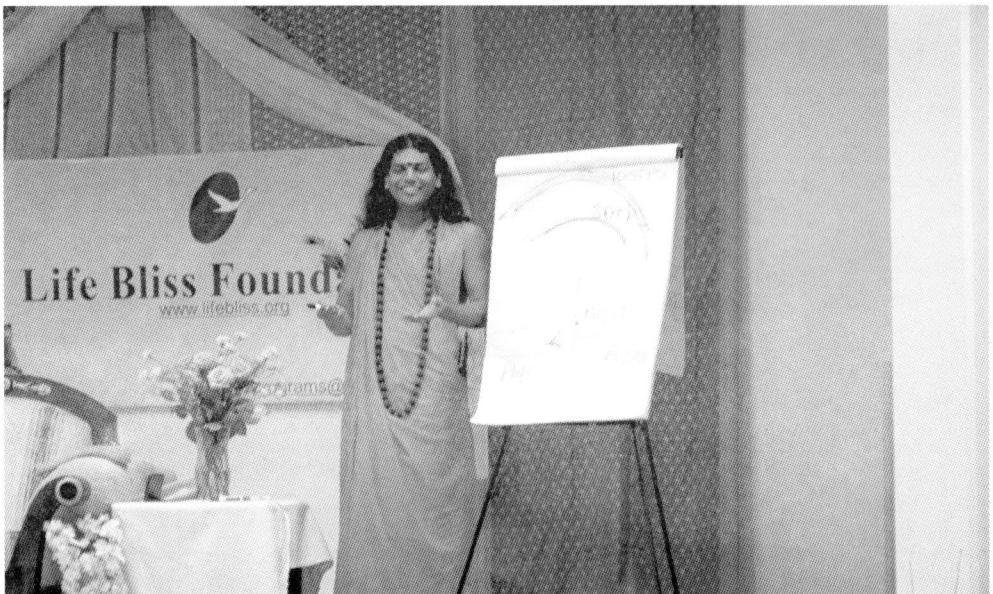

Nithyananda conducts powerful meditation programs which provide both intellectual as well as experiential understandings of the ultimate Truths.

Delivering discourses on the Bhagavad Gita at the Malibu Hindu Temple in Los Angeles, USA, from 4-21 September, 2005

Nithyananda delivered discourses on Shiva Sutras in various locations worldwide in 2007 and at the Bidadi ashram, India in March 2008

Nithyananda has delivered a wide range of discourses from life solutions to the essence of scriptures. His discourses so far include Bhagavad Gita, Shiva Sutras, Jain Sutras, Ashtavakra Gita as well as the deeper truths in the epics of Ramayana and Mahabharata.

Delivering discourses on Ashtavakra Gita in Bengaluru, India in November 2005

Delivering discourses on Jain Sutras at the Jain Temple & Cultural Center in Beuna Park, California, USA, March 6 and 7, 2007

Delivering discourses on Shiva Sutras at the Bidadi ashram, India, March 2008

Dhyana Spurana Program session in progress

Nithyananda conducts various specialized and advanced meditation programs for seekers worldwide. These programs not only offer an intellectual understanding but also an experiential understanding as well.

Participating in a book fair in Chennai, India, January 2008

Nithyananda Publishers have published over 200 books in 30 languages, which carry the timeless truths and universal messages being delivered by Nithyananda.

Nithyananda Galleria is the one stop store (also available online and in mobile vans) providing products of Nithyananda Mission – discourses in the form of books and DVDs (over 4700 hours of discourses transcribed, edited and published in-house and made available in stores), lifestyle products, ayurvedic and herbal products.

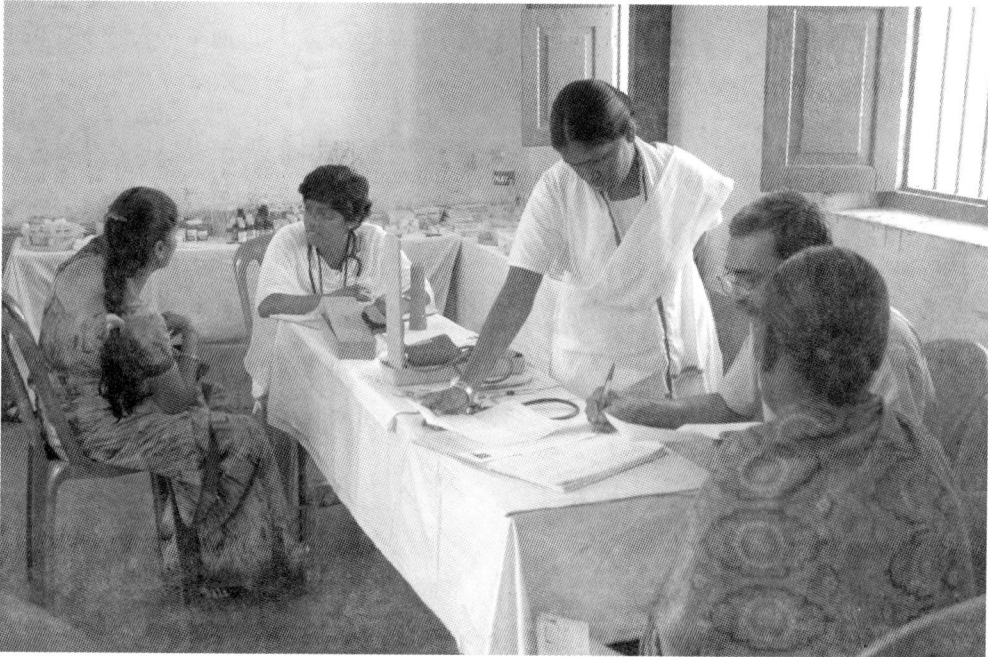

Free weekly medical camp, Bidadi, India

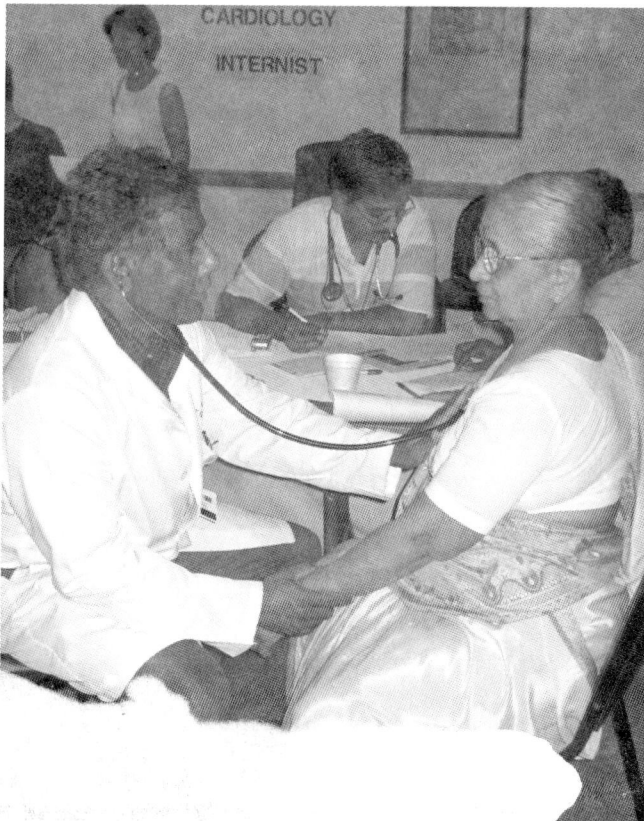

Nithyananda Mission conducts various service activities for the welfare of people like meditation programs in schools, villages, prison programs, health and awareness camps, general and specialized medical camps, in-house and mobile dispensaries, food donation camps etc.

Health fair, Ohio, 2007

LBT class in progress, Bidadi ashram, India

Life Bliss Technology (LBT) is a unique free two year residential program for youth teaching Life Engineering and the science of enlightenment, helping them grow into responsible and fulfilled individuals.

Meditation programs in prisons

Deeper Truths of Life

- You can unclutch from the mind maze

- The karmic cycle can be broken

- Death is a celebration

- You are intelligence

- Responsibility elevates you

- Leadership is a state, not a status

- Intensity is the unfailing way

- Innocence regained opens many doors to life

- You are part of the Collective Consciousness

- Global Peace begins from you

- Sannyas is the ultimate gamble

- Enlightenment is the key to your kingdom

You can Unclutch from the Mind Maze

We have thus far looked at the basic emotions that drive us. When these emotions are negatively expressed, we destroy the energy within us and block ourselves from receiving energy from without. If you have practised the techniques that have been given with each of the preceding chapters, you would also have seen how you could overcome these negative energies and unblock yourself.

Let us now look at a few other issues, which if we understand well, can change the way we live. These understandings can transform us.

Let us start with something very simple, something that we all take for granted. Let us look at the way our mind *really* works.

The Ten-Minute Experiment

Try a very simple experiment for just ten minutes.

Take a sheet of paper and a pen. Sit down alone. Write down whatever thought comes to mind – as if a transcribing software has been connected to your mind; transcribe exactly what you think. Do not edit or suppress any thoughts. It is an experiment only for you. No one else is going to look at what you have written. Just like how the transcribing software which is connected to a taped speech transcribes everything, transcribe whatever is going on in your mind verbatim. At the end of ten minutes, read what you wrote just once. You will be amazed! You can clearly see that there is no logic in the way thoughts form in your mind!

For example, you see a dog on the street. Immediately you remember the dog you were afraid of when you were young, or the one you used to play with when you were young. The next thought could be about your childhood. The third may be about the teacher and the room you used to sit in at school. The fourth may be about the house where your teacher used to live.

There is no logical connection between the dog that you recently saw on the street and the teacher who taught you in school. However, in a few seconds you simply jumped from seeing the dog to your childhood teacher.

Each thought is completely independent, completely unconnected to the previous thought.

You can see that your thoughts are just moving, drifting from one thing to another. We can't even call this 'thinking'. It is just 'association', that's all. You associate the dog with your childhood, your childhood with the teacher, and so on.

Actually, if you do this exercise just once, the very understanding that it gives you will transform the way you think about yourself, and how you treat yourself and others. Your whole life will be transformed.

How does our mind work?

How do we create thoughts and how do we give meaning to them?

How do we experience life?

The Nature of the Mind

Let me give you a simple diagram to understand how thoughts flow in the mind and how you connect them.

Each thought in your mind is shown here as a square or rectangle. Each is a different shape, size, and color. Different thoughts are continuously flowing in you. One may be related to pain or a painful experience. Another may be related to joy or a joyful experience. The next one may be related to joy, but you think of it as pain. It is referred to as JP on the chart – joyful experience, painful impression.

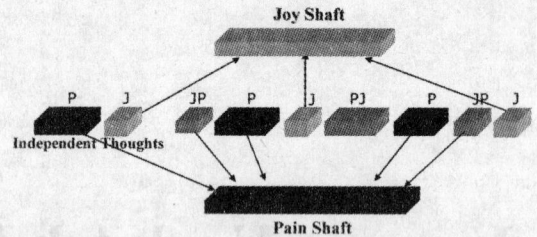

Similarly you may have a thought that is related to a painful experience, but you think of it as joy. It is referred to as PJ – painful experience, joyful impression.

Generally, all your thoughts are related to something about the past or the future. You cannot have thoughts about the present. In the present moment you can have only consciousness, no thoughts. Thoughts are either related to some joyful experiences that you had in the past and want to have in the future, or painful experiences that you had in the past and don't want to have again.

Even at the time of some serious problem, you will suddenly have a positive thought. Even in the peak of joy, you will have some unconnected negative thought. Each thought is completely independent, completely unconnected to the previous thought. That is why you are able to have a happy thought amidst sad thoughts and vice versa.

Understand that no two thoughts are logically connected. No thought is responsible for the creation of another thought. They all appear randomly, independently, and illogically.

How do you 'unclutch' from this random stream of thoughts? We will be using the word 'unclutch' again and again. Let's clearly define what is meant by 'unclutch'. When we change gears while driving a car, whether we change from first to second, or second to third, or any gear for that matter, we have to pass through neutral every time. We have to completely depress the clutch, or 'unclutch', move through neutral, and only then we can go to the next gear, right? In the same way, we experience a neutral space between any two thoughts in our mind. That neutral space, that silence that exists between two thoughts, is peace and bliss. When we no longer grab onto thoughts and connect them to the past or future, we remain 'unclutched.' As we remain 'unclutched' from our thoughts we become more aware of the neutral spaces between thoughts. The gap between the thoughts will automatically extend when we remain 'unclutched' from the stream of thoughts. We will dwell in the neutral space longer and experience more and more peace and bliss.

Awareness

The Ultimate Key

When you suddenly become aware, any thought that flows in front of you becomes your life for that moment. You start giving attention to it, either to fulfill it or to escape from it. It is like slides on a projector. Any slide that is kept in front of the projector light is seen as reality on the screen. The problem is that in your inner space, the projector light is not continuously on. When I say projector light, I mean your awareness. It just comes and goes, comes and goes – you are not fully, continuously aware.

Many times, even though your eyes are open and your body is moving, you are not aware of your existence. An example from everyday life is like when you get into your car and drive for half an hour to the office. It is only after you reach the office, park the car, and get out, do you suddenly realize, 'Oh, I have reached the office!' It means that in those moments of driving, the projector light was off most of the time.

Any slide that is placed in front of the projector during moments that the projector light, your awareness, is off is not part of your life. You don't remember it at all. When the light comes on again, when your awareness comes back again, whatever thought you have at that time becomes a part of you. Understand that this is a very subtle truth. Your life is the totality of all the thoughts you have when you are aware and unaware.

Unfortunately, many times there are thoughts, many major decisions, and life-changing incidents that happen when you are not aware. These are also part of your life, part of your biography. Unfortunately, you are not aware of these scenes, decisions, or thoughts when they come up. Without your knowledge they have contributed significantly to your life.

Be very clear, every moment that passes in your life without you being aware of it, without your presence, is suffering. You will either directly or indirectly create situations for suffering. Just like when the turn indicator

> **You do not remember your biography as it happened. You remember it only as you want it.**

light in your car blinks, your consciousness blinks also. But, because of your lack of awareness, you do not know when it is on and when it is off.

I read a joke the other day:

One man got into his car and started the engine. He flipped on the turn indicator and asked his son to see if the light blinked in the rear of the car.

His son shouted back, 'Yes, it's on...no, it's not on...yes it's on...no it's off...now it's on!'

If you just see the thought flow in front of you, suddenly you will realize, 'Oh god, all these things are actually going on in me! I don't have a clue where I am heading. I don't know what is happening in me!'

You are not aware, but constantly you believe you are aware. That is the first illusion.

If you become aware continuously, you open up to reality for the first time. It might be a bit intense initially, because until now, you have spent most of your time in unawareness. Ultimately, it will lead you to experience only joy and bliss.

You Are Not Aware of Your True Past

This is the first truth – you are not aware of all the things that are happening in front of

you. You do not remember your biography as it happened. You remember it only as you want it.

Just take a simple example. Your life is filled with different kinds of incidents relating to joy, suffering, guilt, pain, and depression. You don't look at life as it is. What do you usually do? You collect only the incidents related to suffering and create a shaft, connecting only these ideas, and you think your life is nothing but suffering. You think that your life is a long chain of suffering, a pain shaft.

Very rarely, you create a joy shaft. It is very rare that you collect joyful incidents, create a joy shaft, and feel life is joy. It is rare not only in the number of joyful shafts, but also in the quality of them. Most of the time you collect all the painful memories and incidents, and create the idea that life is only pain. The moment you believe life is continuous painful occurrences, unconsciously you try to strengthen that belief, even though consciously you try to break the pain shaft. Please understand, your belief that life is a pain shaft or a joy shaft will stay only as long as you are unconscious, not when you are aware.

Relationship Between Awareness and the Thoughts in Your Inner Space

If you normally enjoy lustful thoughts, then whenever lustful thoughts cross your system, you come to the awareness, 'I exist'. If you normally enjoy violent thoughts, whenever violent thoughts come into your system, you come to life and know that you exist. This is what I call a vicious circle: you empowering negativity and negativity bringing you back to life; you empowering more negativity, and more negativity bringing to life perceived excitement.

The Shaft That Does Not Exist

The Pain Shaft Invites Painful Incidents to Your Life

There is a very beautiful analogy by Ramana Maharishi, an enlightened master from India. A dog will chew a dry bone. As it chews, fragments of the bone will poke into its mouth making it bleed. The dog thinks the blood is coming from the bone and it enjoys the blood. It continues to chew on the bone for the pleasure of the blood! It doesn't realize that the blood is coming from its own mouth and not at all from the bone.

If violence excites you, you wait for that kind of incident in your life. If pain excites you, if you believe life is a pain shaft, you wait for that kind of incident in your life in order to strengthen and reinforce your belief. That is the general human psychology. Although people claim they want to break the violence shaft or pain shaft, they secretly nurture it.

Shaft of Pain

Let me provide a deeper understanding. The pain that you had ten years ago, the pain that you had nine years ago, the pain that you experienced seven years ago, the pain that you experienced three years ago, and the pain that you experienced yesterday are all unconnected, independent, individual incidents. But you start connecting all of them and create a shaft of pain. You connect all these thought shafts and create one big shaft. You start thinking and believing, 'My life is pain.' Is that true? No! What happened to all the sweet incidents of joy that you experienced in between? Surely, there must have been at least a few moments of joy in between? They are simply forgotten. They are never picked to form a shaft. So the shaft, any shaft, is never true, because it focuses on only a fragment of your complete biography.

First, you start archiving the painful memories for utility purpose. You archive all your pains, probably for medical history sake or to tell your doctor. By and by, you start believing that all these pains that happened in your life are connected. You decide that your life is pain; your life is suffering. The moment you come to the decision that your life is pain or your life is suffering, you create hell for yourself.

For example, until yesterday you were only walking, you were not able to fly. You know in your past you never flew, you only walked. Can you believe you can start flying from tomorrow onwards? You can't. You know tomorrow you will still only be walking. You rely solely on your remembered past experiences to predict your future, eliminating many new possibilities.

Shaft of Joy

The joy that you experienced ten years ago, the joy that you experienced nine years ago, the joy that you experienced three years ago, and the joy that you experienced one year ago are all independent, individual, unconnected thought shafts. At the present time, you connect all of those thoughts and create a big shaft of joy.

You may identify your joy with an object, a person, or a space, like a particular vacation resort. Now you will try again and again to bring that back in your life, to bring that person, that object, that space, or that same incident back in your life. Try as you might, you will not be able experience the same joy again. This puts you in further pain!

Pain Shaft or Joy Shaft – Both Lead to Suffering

In life, we constantly create either shafts of pain or joy. Once you create a shaft of pain, you try to break it. If you create the shaft of joy, you try to elongate it! But you don't understand that you can neither elongate the joy shaft nor break the pain shaft - simply because the shaft itself doesn't exist. It is just selective memory. The very shaft is your imagination.

Thoughts are like Bubbles in a Fish Tank

There is no linear connection between one thought that we have and another thought that we have. The only relationship between

thoughts is that they come from the same source. But we constantly connect one thought and the next thought in a linear manner.

Just as bubbles in a fish tank rise from the bottom, our thoughts also rise in the same manner. When one bubble comes and reaches the surface of the water, the next bubble starts and then the third bubble starts. Because the bubbles are rising at a high speed, they look like a continuous stream! Actually there is always a gap between two bubbles.

Like the bubbles, we also experience a neutral space between two thoughts. Since the gap or the neutral space between two thoughts is so small, we think all thoughts are connected and form a shaft. But there is always a gap between two thoughts.

Let me tell you about an incident that happened:

A middle aged man came to me and said, 'I am going to divorce my wife. Please bless me!' One gentleman around forty five years of age came up to me and said, 'Swamiji, I am going to divorce my wife, please bless me.' I told him, 'I only bless people for marriages. Why do you want me to bless you for a divorce?' He replied, 'No, you have to bless me, because I have suffered so much.' I told him, 'I only bless individuals for marriages. What made you come and ask me to bless you for a divorce?' He replied, 'No, no, Swamiji, you have to bless me, because I have suffered too much.'

I said, 'Suffering is always give-and-take. It is never just taking. You must have given your wife enough suffering too. So, please tell me the truth about what happened and then we will analyze the situation.'

He replied, 'How do I decide which incidents to tell you, and which ones to leave out? There are so many of them! From day one she has been torturing me. You don't know how much torture I have gone through!' Then he narrated an incident from the day of his marriage!

In Indian villages, when a wedding takes place, the newly married couple plays games after the marriage ceremony. For one of the games, a ring is dropped inside a pot filled with water. The husband and wife put their hands inside and compete to pick up the ring. Whoever grabs it first wins. These small

The only relationship between thoughts is that they come from the same source.

games were created mainly to reduce the unfamiliarity between the couple because in arranged marriages the bride and groom first meet during the wedding ceremony. They have small games to reduce the distance between the couple because they are new to each other.

This man said, 'During that game, she scratched my hand. With her nails, she scratched my hand!' And he started a big story about everything that she had done to him since that day! For all practical purposes, he had kept a file, like a police report from the first day of his marriage.

After two or three incidents, I told him, 'Please stop! If this is the case, she should be happier than you to part ways. It is very difficult to live with someone who keeps such large and detailed files in his head!' Any time she does something, this man will always be looking through the files.

Then he told me the immediate reason for the divorce. He said, 'She spilled some coffee on my clothes!' I told him, 'Spilling coffee on your clothes cannot be a reason for a divorce!'

He said, 'No, you don't know. Today she poured coffee; tomorrow she will pour acid!' He really said this. I did not understand the connection. I asked him how he could possibly connect coffee and acid. Again he said, 'No, no Swamiji, you don't know.'

He may seem extreme and you may laugh when you hear this. But just look intensely at your own life. You are doing the same thing - constantly creating illogical connections. You forget to see incidents as being independent of each other. You forget to see thoughts as independent.

If you just learn this one simple technique of unclutching, you will be able to retain a significant amount of energy in your system, in your being. As a result, you will be many times more productive and creative. Your relationships will be much friendlier because you will not clutch incidents that are not related. You will not feel suffocated by people or their expectations of you. You will have tremendous inner space available to you to fulfill your needs, as well as others' needs. You will also have tremendous compassion to know why others are suffering. It is only when you don't understand why the other person is suffering that you are harsh with them. When you unclutch, you are able to accommodate that person in your inner space. You are automatically compassionate. Your very life has a different quality and you become a different person in the world.

It is Never the 'Same'

Every single happening in our lives is unconnected, even our everyday activities like eating and drinking. Each and every experience is independent by its own right. Drinking water yesterday and drinking water today are two completely different incidents.

The food that you ate yesterday and the food that you eat today are different, even if they seem physically the same! But your mind creates the shaft between these two incidents and says, 'I eat the same food every day.'

Please be very clear, you don't eat the same food every day. You may use the same word 'eating' for both the experiences, but they are not the same experience. Do not be cheated by the words that you use. Yesterday's eating, today's eating, and tomorrow's eating are separate incidents, separate experiences. They are completely independent and unattached.

A beautiful incident from the life of an enlightened master from central India:

During the last ten years of his life, the doctors asked the master to eat a particular kind of food. He was not allowed to eat anything else. He had to eat the same kind of food three times a day, everyday.

After two years the person who cooked for him came and complained, 'Master, I am bored with cooking the same food. How are you able to eat the same food day after day?'

The master just laughed and said, 'I am not eating the same food every day. How can I eat the same food every day? I can only eat this *food today. Tomorrow's food is totally different!'*

Life is new every moment. It is the mind that makes it look repetitive, dull and mundane.

Just Let Go...And You Can Fly!

I saw this in my days of spiritual wandering. In the forests of Northern India the hunters use a trap to catch birds. They tie a rope between two trees. In the middle of the rope, they secure a wooden stick. The rope is tied at the midpoint of the stick. This is actually a hunter's trap for birds.

You may think, 'How can a bird be trapped with a small stick? How is it possible?' Actually, all they do is just hang the stick between two trees using a rope, that's all. When a bird comes and sits on the stick, the bird's own weight turns the whole stick upside down; it turns topsy-turvy. The bird is now hanging upside down, clinging to the stick.

The mom-ent it turns upside down and loses its sense of balance it feels totally shaken and tightens its grip on the stick. It simply holds onto the stick as if its life depends on it. Because it is hanging upside down, it thinks, 'If I unclutch from this stick, what will happen? I will fall and die.'

There is no record that any bird has ever fallen and broken its head! But the bird does not have the intelligence to realize this. It keeps hanging on. By not letting go, not only does it lose its freedom, it loses its life too, because ultimately the hunter traps it.

Life is new every moment. It is the mind that makes it look repetitive, dull and mundane.

Just like the bird, you don't realize that if you just drop your mind, at that moment you can become a *Paramahamsa**. That very moment you can be liberated. You can simply start flying.

The same fear that the bird clinging to the stick had, you have now. Your fear and the bird's fear are one and the same. The bird believes that it can't let go; if it does it will die. Similarly, you hold on to your mind and feel, 'I can't let go. If I start trusting that I am unconnected, unclutched, independent and illogical thoughts, I might be lost.'

Paramahamsa - Literally means Supreme Swan. Title bestowed on enlightened beings.

The hunter comes leisurely, after four or five hours, takes the bird, puts it in the cage, and leaves. Now the bird neither has the freedom to fly nor the stick to balance. The foolish bird doesn't know that if it had just let go of the stick, it could have simply flown away!

In the same way, you hold on to whatever you think is your identity and security – your education, your mind, your life, your relationships, or your bank balance. *Yama,* the god of death, ultimately comes to remove the stick – that is your identity. Then you are neither a *Paramahamsa**, a liberated soul, nor are you able to hold on to your identity. You will neither have the freedom, nor will you have the stick of your identity that you are clutching, because the stick itself is an illusion.

Let me tell you, if the bird lets go and relaxes, it may flutter to balance for a moment or two. It may take one or two moments to balance itself, but it will never fall and die. When it leaves the stick, maybe for a few seconds it will fall, but then it will adjust itself and start flying.

Be very clear, let go and you will never fall and die. You will only become a *Paramahamsa*!

This moment, trust yourself. Don't bother about losing your identity. Just trust yourself and let go of your identity. You will immediately become a *Paramahamsa* and be liberated. All you need to do is trust that you are unclutched - even if you don't trust that it is still the truth!

Safety Net of the *Sangha*

When you unclutch, there will be some revolutionary changes in your life, in your day-to-day thinking, your decision-making, and your daily routine - your lifestyle. Courageously going through that revolution, going through the transformation that happens in you, is what I call *tapas* - penance.

On rare occasions during my wanderings, I have seen a bird hanging on the stick. Another bird that was once stuck in the trap, but had the courage to let go and open up, comes back. It pokes the hanging bird and says, 'Hey, let go! Relax! I was like you. I had the same problem. When I relaxed I just started flying. All it takes is just two or three seconds to balance. When I opened up, I never fell and broke my head or died. I only became liberated. I only became a free bird. Come on...' But the hanging bird will not believe it.

Paramahamsa - Literally means Supreme Swan. Title bestowed on enlightened beings.

Understand that the responsibility of the free bird is to go about freeing other birds. It is the responsibility of the free bird to go and poke the bird trapped on the stick and say, 'Free yourself.' I am that free bird and I have created a safety net. Even if you fall, you won't hurt yourself. Relax! Let go, you will only fly! See, the *sangha*, the community of the master, is the net. Even if you fall, you will not hurt yourself.

First of all, you will *not* fall. But just to give you the deeper assurance, the *sangha*, the spiritual community, is created. So, I invite all of you to come and experience the *sangha*.

Understand that it's a free bird's responsibility to liberate all the trapped birds, to help them, to inspire them to free themselves.

The Story of the Monkey

Similar to the bird trap, hunters also have a trap to catch monkeys. They catch monkeys using a small box for a trap. They place some sweets inside a box that has a small opening. The monkey puts its hand inside the box and grabs the sweet. As long as the monkey holds onto the sweet, it will not be able to take its hand out because its fist is larger than the hole!

If the monkey lets go of the sweet, it can remove or slide its hand out immediately. But the monkey is not intelligent enough to realize that. It holds on to the sweet - and just because it is holding on, it is not able to take its hand

out. If it just lets go of the sweet, it can take its hand out and be free. If you allow the understanding of this story to happen in you, you will instantly unclutch from your shafts and be free this very moment.

All you need to do is to trust that you are unclutched - even if you don't trust that it is still the truth!

Living Intensely in the Present

By Your Very Nature You Renounce Every Moment

Fortunately, by your very nature, you can have only one thought at a time. The moment a new thought comes inside your system, it means that the old thought has lost its power or influence over you. If the new thought has entered you, it means the old thought has been renounced because you can't have two thoughts at a time. You can have only one thought at a time. If you say that the old thought is also there, it only means that for that moment, the new thought has been renounced!

There is a beautiful story by Ramakrishna Paramahamsa[*]:

A king who was inside a huge fort, was once attacked by an army that was two

---

Ramakrishna Paramahamsa - Enlightened master from West Bengal in India. His chief disciple was Swami Vivekananda.

million strong. The king only had two or three people around him and got very frightened. He told his advisor, 'Two million people, and I am all alone. They will kill me!'

The royal advisor said, 'Don't worry, King. Open only one door. Surely through one door only one person can come in at a time. As they come in, stand on this side of the door and kill them one by one. Over! Do not try to fight with the whole crowd.'

If you think all your enemies are gathered together, you will start having unnecessary fears. You cannot have two thoughts at a time. You can only have one thought at a time. This means that every thought is replaced by the next thought.

I'll repeat: the first thing is that you can have only one thought at a time.

The second thing is that unless the old thought is pushed out, the second thought cannot come.

The third thing is that if somebody can push me out and sit here, he is surely more powerful than me! Any thought that comes in and pushes the old thought out is more powerful than the old thought. This means that any thought that is coming now is rooted in the present moment. It has more power than the thought that is being renounced, whatever that thought may be about.

By your very nature you are renouncing. You don't need to learn renunciation. Every moment you *are* renouncing. What do I mean by the word 'renouncing' here? I mean that at every moment you are letting go of one

thought after another. Only then is it possible to allow new thoughts to keep entering your system. Every moment your inner space is getting cleared of the old thought.

Thoughts are constantly getting renounced by themselves. The only issue is that when you create the belief your thoughts are connected, you have the problem of linked suffering, the shaft. Your belief that you have some problem is your only problem.

Every moment your inner space is purified by the new incoming thoughts. If you allow this process to continue, it will happen by itself and clean itself also. There is no need for you to clean your mind. All you need to do is just get out - just get out of the system so that the system can proceed on its own.

One important truth you should know is that even if you want, even if you try consciously, you cannot possess or hold onto your suffering for long.

Even if you try to hold it, you cannot hold your suffering because continuously, your thought that creates suffering is also replaced by newer thoughts! In fact, to hold onto suffering will require a lot of effort on your part because thoughts are continuously flowing.

Allow Your Thoughts to Be Replaced

Be very clear, your power to bring on a new thought itself proves you have the power to drop the old thought. The problem is, instead of just watching the new thoughts flowing through you, you try to bring back old thoughts into your system. It is like picking up your trashed emails and bringing them back to the inbox. Is there any need to bring back trashed emails? No! If you constantly look to bring back the old thoughts, you will create only suffering.

Understand that if you nurture the fact that any suffering can be replaced by a stream of fresh thoughts then that becomes reality for you. And there is no suffering. If you are nurturing the thought, 'No, however much I allow replacing, the suffering comes back,' you will make *that* into reality. If you mother the thought that the suffering is going to come back, it will come back. If you mother the thought that it is going to go away, it will go away.

All you need to understand is that if even once you can replace a thought in your inner space without returning to the previous thought, you will get the confidence, 'I have replaced it once. I can do it again.' Then you can tell yourself, 'If the old thought comes back ten times, let me replace it ten times!' that's all. Soon you will see the old thought will stop coming back.

There is a very beautiful incident in Buddha's life:

Buddha says, 'Whenever I said in meditation, 'I am going to get up after a few hours', I never became enlightened. Once I decided, 'If I am not going to become enlightened, I am not going to get up from this seat. Let this body dry up in this very place. Until I become enlightened, I am not going to move.' Buddha says that the moment he created that strong clarity, the authentic sankalpa* - vow, the next second, he became enlightened!

Every moment your inner space is getting cleared of the old thought.

When you sit down to replace your suffering and think, 'Today I will replace it ten times. If it comes back the eleventh time, I can try again tomorrow,' then nothing will happen. No transformation will take place for you. Decide very clearly, 'Until it stops coming, I am going to replace the negative thoughts.' That is what I call courage.

Solutions for Physical, Mental and Emotional Problems

When we unclutch, the first thing that will happen to us will be an inner healing effect - a deep silence and peace in us.

Second, that inner healing will start radiating as physical wellbeing, which is our health.

Third, naturally it will start radiating in our relationships also.

Sankalpa - Vow or decision.

Fourth, because these three are going beautifully, we will be creative and productive!

Solution for Chronic Ailments

People come and tell me, '*Swamiji*, for the last twenty years I have had knee pain.' No, it cannot be! Please understand that in reality it cannot be. I am not disrespecting you or adding more suffering to you by saying all your problems are only in your head. I am just telling the truth: all your problems *are* in your head! I am just stating the truth.

The knee pain you experienced two years ago, the knee pain you experienced one year ago, the knee pain you experienced two months ago, and the knee pain you experienced two hours ago are independent experiences. Only because you connect all of them, you conclude that you have been having knee pain for twenty years. Is it really true that you have knee pain continuously for twenty years? What happens to the moments of 'no knee pain' in between? The important thing you need to understand is that because you connect and see all these as one continuous incident, you block the possibility of self-healing.

Solution for Depression

The depression that happened one month ago, the depression that happened one year ago, and the depression that happened three years ago are independent, individual, unconnected, and unclutched. The problem is the same as with physical pain. You start connecting them and concluding that you are having the same depression continuously. You create an idea that your life is depression. Then you start fighting with it. That only gives more life to the depressive thoughts.

When you strongly believe that your last ten years have been filled with suffering and depression, you create a strong mental setup surrounding it. Naturally you start thinking that your future is also going to be painful and filled with depression.

Suppose there is a person sitting in front of you who you think is an enemy. Suddenly if you notice that his head is separate, his legs are separate and his hands are separate, would you even feel like fighting with him? No! He is not even worth fighting! He doesn't even have a solid existence, as you imagined him to have. So what is there to fight?

In the same way, only when you imagine you have a huge problem in front of you, that a big person is in front of you, you start fighting and getting into more trouble. Your depression is not the huge enemy that you think it is. It is just like the person with disjointed body parts. It is you who joined the parts and gave it life. Your fighting with depression is the root cause of your depression.

In *Ramayana** there is a beautiful story. Whoever stands in front of the monkey king

---

Ramayana - Hindu *itihasa* or epic about prince Rama. The original version was written by poet sage Valmiki.

*Vali** and fights with him, loses half of his power to him. In the same way, whoever stands in front of the thought shaft and starts fighting with that shaft, half of their power will go away to that shaft.

The moment you unclutch from the shaft, you experience the neutral space, and inner healing starts. The moment inner healing starts, physically also you are healed.

Do not try to renounce your depression, because by your very nature it is getting renounced, flowing away from you. By your very nature just as joy disappears from your mind, depression also disappears from your mind. The moment you try to eliminate the depression, you will extend it and give it more life.

See, if you have a deep depression, will you stop going to the office? No! You may carry the depression in your mind but your body moves. You work. You may not be that productive or efficient. But your body still moves.

Instead of 'living depression', I am saying, 'live unclutched'.

When we live in depression, we don't have all these questions, 'If I am depressed, how can my body move?' We don't have such questions. The depression becomes part of our life. In the beginning you may have questions, 'How can I live unclutched? How will I even move my body?' Understand that the constant remembrance of unclutching does not interfere

with your mind or body movements. It only removes the depression because it lets the depression thoughts rise and fall without clutching to them.

Solution for Addiction

What is addiction? It is a behavior or action that if you don't do it, you will feel terrible that you are missing something. But, if you do it you won't feel any joy, it will only be mechanical. Addiction means believing that joy or ecstasy happens due to some object, person, or situation.

Understand that this is the definition of addiction: trying to elongate the joy shaft by recreating it. You bring the same persons, situations, incidents, or happenings into your life again and again, knowing that the same joy is not going to happen. Some people are addicted to partying, some to smoking, and some to drinking – there are so many addictions.

Remember that anything you bring to your life again and again will not give you the same excitement as it gave you the first time. It can only lead to addiction, not happiness. The first time you enjoy a sweet, it is a wonderful experience. The excitement is totally different. But if you keep eating more of the same sweet, the same experience is not there anymore. Eventually if you eat enough sweets you will not even like the sight of them. You

---

Vali - Monkey king in the Hindu epic Ramayana who is killed by prince Rama.

Instead of 'living depression', I am saying, 'live unclutched'. will look at them and say, 'Oh no, not more sweets. They make me feel terrible.' In the same way, when meeting a person for the first time, the excitement is totally different. Later on, the excitement falls off.

People come and ask me, 'How can I break my habits?' See, habit is a beautiful word. If you remove 'h', 'a bit' will remain. If you remove 'b', 'it' will remain. Only when you remove the 'I', the shaft 'it' will die. Only when you remove 'I', only when you throw 'I' away, will it completely die.

Be very clear, your smoking two days ago, ten years ago, and twenty years ago - all these three incidents are completely independent. They are not connected. Mentally, when you start connecting, when you start believing that you have the habit of smoking and that you are addicted to it, the belief creates a shaft. Then you start fighting with it. That is what I mean when I say the 'I' has to be dropped. It is your belief that makes it a habit. If you drop the belief, the habit drops.

If you believe it is a joyful experience, you continue to smoke more and more. If you believe it is a painful experience you start fighting with the shaft. Either way you don't win. Even if you believe that smoking is joyful, try to smoke without restraint and see for yourself how you feel. When you smoke and inhale, it can never be a pleasurable experience. It is never really joyful.

When you smoke, in that moment, just see what is happening in your inner space. You are not enjoying anything. You are just trying to escape from something. You merely believe that smoking is joyful. Even if you don't feel joyful when you are smoking, you try to squeeze joy out of it.

If you deeply scan your life and see, you will understand that whether it is smoking, or sex, or money, or any other pleasure, even if you don't feel the same joy as you felt the first time, you try to squeeze joy out of it. You try to console yourself, 'No, this *is* joy. What else is joy?' You try to cover the frustration by believing it is joy. You want to believe it is joy.

Try your best to drop some addiction. You can never be successful. Even if you drop it you may be dropping it out of some fear or greed, which is a much bigger addiction. If you drop smoking out of some fear or greed, you are not doing anything good to your consciousness, to your inner space. You are only damaging yourself more.

You might have dropped smoking, but the fear or greed that made you drop it will be added to your inner space. At least with smoking, you will destroy only this body. With fear or greed you will destroy your whole being, life after life! In the next body, you will carry over the fear and greed. The smoking habit may not carry over to the next body but the emotions of fear and greed will be carried with you to the next body. So the best way is to drop the idea that you have an addiction, and it will drop.

122

Unclutch - Work Smart, Not Hard

The moment you hear you are unclutched, the first fear that arises in you is, 'If I start living without connecting my thoughts, who will pay my bills? I could lose all my wealth. I could forget where I keep all my money. I may not be able to live successfully in society. How will I do my job? How will I take care of my things? Won't I not just lie down in my bed without doing anything? Why would I want to go to my office?'

I ask, 'Why wouldn't you go to your office?' The moment you ask that, it means that you inherently have a little hatred or a little vengeance against your office work! This is why the moment you find some excuse you want to escape from your work. By asking this question, you are only expressing your anger, your violence against your routine, nothing else! The question has nothing to do with unclutching.

If you have such questions, just unclutch and sleep for ten days. There's nothing wrong with that. Have a vacation for ten days. Decide, 'I am going to unclutch from both the identities.' How many days do you think you can sleep? How many days do you think the cessation of activity can continue in you? Only until the *tamas** energy in you is exhausted. After that you will automatically start doing something.

So, even if you feel it is a lack of responsibility or defeatist behavior, be unclutched for a few days. You will then understand and experience that when you are unclutched you will not have a lazy or passive attitude. Mentally you will be silent, but physically you will be active and alive.

> **Drop the idea that you have an addiction, and it will drop.**

When you are in that space of irresponsibility or defeatist attitude, mentally you are very active but physically you are tired. When you are unclutched, physically you are active and alive, but mentally you are silent.

You see, 33% of the body is *sattva**, pure silence. 33% of the body is *rajas**, restlessness and 33% of the body is *tamas**, deep sleep, laziness. Right now the first fear that happens in you is if you unclutch, you may become *tamasic*, a lazy person.

Unclutch. That 33% of your laziness will quickly be exhausted. It will disappear from your system within a few days. Then you will automatically start working from your innate intelligence. You don't have to be driven by fear and greed to live your day-to-day life.

I am not saying you should stop thinking completely. I am only saying, when you are unclutched, whatever thoughts have to happen will happen automatically. Initially when you are unclutched you will feel as if no thoughts are happening. Later you will understand, even

---

Tamas - One of the three *gunas* or attributes of nature. Attribute of inaction.

Sattva - One of the three *gunas* or attributes of nature. Attribute of passive action.

Rajas - One of the three *gunas* or attributes of nature. Attribute of aggression.

after unclutching, whenever thinking is necessary, the mind is clutched. Whenever thinking is not necessary, the mind is unclutched. Your mind is being used as an instrument, not as a master.

We can live purely from inspiration. But the problem is, we are never given that confidence. We are never given the courage that we can live simply by inspiration. Sometimes you can see that for no reason you radiate excitement; for no reason you radiate intelligence. That is what I call inspiration. It may last only for a few moments, but you need to realize that those few moments can become a way of life for you. If we remain unclutched, then continuous inspiration will happen in our lives. Unclutching directly kindles the energy of the being. This energy is the energy of inspiration, the energy of unclutching.

Are 'You' Needed to Run Your Life?

Understand one important thing, we have an automatic intelligence that can run our lives, that can take care of our day-to-day responsibilities. Not only can it run our lives, it can maintain, extend, and expand our lives as well.

But society conditions you from a young age. You are taught that you cannot run without planning, without fear or greed. Your self-respect is taken away from you. You are made to lose trust that you can lead your life spontaneously, without fear or greed. That is why constantly you try to infuse greed or fear into yourself. You try to use fear and greed as fuel to make your life run, to make your life alive.

Be very clear, you cannot run your life based on fear and greed. If you are driven by fear and greed, you will carry a constant irritation in you. From morning until night, from the moment you wake up until the moment you go to sleep, you will carry a constant irritation in you. You just wait for a reason to explode. Just one small touch is enough, and you are ready to jump on the other person. He does not even need to make any mistake; just coming in front of you is enough to trigger you! This happens because of the strain of running your life through fear and greed.

If you just relax, the automatic intelligence of Existence will run your life beautifully for you. Your actions will be automatically propelled by the energy of Existence.

Technique – 'I am not the Doer'

Ashtavakra[*] says,

You who have been bitten by the great black serpent of egoism 'I am the doer'

Drink the nectar of the faith, 'I am not the doer' and be happy.

Ashtavakra - An enlightened *vedic* sage who was born with eight crooked limbs. He is the author of the Ashtavakra Gita.

Ashtavakra* gives this technique to the king and seeker, Janaka*. Please understand that simply thinking that 'I am not the doer' or having faith that 'I am not the doer' will not liberate you directly. This technique by itself will not liberate you. It will just make you tired! You are not able to remember that you are not the doer continuously without a break. The moment you understand that you are not able to remember 'I am not the doer' all the time, you will be completely frustrated and you will just drop the mind. The moment you drop the mind, the truth that you are not the doer will simply become reality! That is the technique suggested here.

Unclutching – A Self-Purifying and Evolutionary Technique

This is a very simple understanding of unclutching. All you need to do is remember to unclutch whenever you start giving meaning to old thoughts or whenever you connect with old thoughts and allow them to bother you.

Do not create, maintain or destroy any thought. If you don't do any of these three things, you are the Supreme Self, *Parabrahma*!

Unclutching is like a self-purifying method. For any technique to be self-purifying and liberating, the moment you become subtle, the technique should also become subtle, by itself. Unclutching is one such technique.

The technique that does not become subtle by itself stays in the gross level. If it is not able to kill itself, if the technique is not able to commit suicide, it will kill you! The beauty with the technique of unclutching is that it will become subtler and subtler by itself as you become subtler. Finally, it will dissolve.

If you are driven by fear and greed, you will carry a constant irritation in you.

Meditation Techniques

Unclutching – Anytime Anywhere

When you sit, naturally some thoughts will come. The moment you see a thought coming, do not give meaning to it. You give it meaning only if you connect it with your past. Without giving meaning to it just remember to unclutch - and see what happens. The moment you remember, 'Let me unclutch from this thought; let me not give meaning to it,' for a few seconds there will be a small silent gap. The moment you are aware that there is a silence,

---

Ashtavakra - An enlightened *vedic* sage who was born with eight crooked limbs. He is the author of the Ashtavakra Gita.
Janaka - Indian king of the kingdom of Videha with the capital of Mithila, well-known for his righteousness.
Parabrahma - Supreme Being.

it will become one more thought. Then unclutch from that thought also. Then, again there will be a gap of a few seconds. Then, one more thought will come, 'I am in silence' or 'I am unclutching'. Unclutch from that thought also. Just the gap or the silence should become longer and longer. That is the whole idea.

Naturally it is the nature of the mind to wander somewhere after a few minutes. The moment you remember or become aware that the mind has wandered, unclutch. There is no need to have guilt or be agitated that the mind has wandered. The moment you remember, unclutch, that's all.

In the initial level it may be very gross, like a solid fight. You may have to utter the word 'unclutching' like a *mantra**. But in just a few moments, you will see it becomes a subtle process.

With unclutching…

Every moment will be new.

Every moment will be ecstasy.

Every moment will be joy.

Every moment will be excitement.

Unclutching is the source of unending excitement – *nithyananda spurana**.

Mantra - Literally means 'that which shows the way'. Sacred syllables that have a powerful positive vibrational effect.
Nithyananda spurana - Eternal flowering of bliss.

The Karmic Cycle Can Be Broken

If we are able to truly manage our mind with the understanding that it is our mind that connects thoughts to form shafts of pain and pleasure and if we stay unclutched, we can stay in what Buddha calls mindfulness. We can stay in awareness and in the present moment. It is our thought process that constantly takes us from past to future and back again and does not allow us to rest in the present moment.

Understand this clearly, when we are in the present moment we can stay out of trouble without fear and desire. We can act without fear and desire. You may ask how. How can I be motivated to do something if I do not desire it? There is no need for motivation. Do you think that it is motivation that makes you breathe or digest your food? It is the intelligence of the energy that is within and without us that makes it possible for us to live and grow. We live not because of us but in spite of us.

When we act without attachment, there is no consequence to our actions, there is no *karma* arising from our actions.

What is Karma?

There is a very beautiful verse in the *Isa Vasya Upanishad**:

Om poornamadah poornamidam

Poornaat poornamudachyate

Poornasya poornamaadaaya

Poornamevaavashishyate

From the Whole came the Whole. If you remove the Whole from the Whole, only the Whole remains. By very nature we seek the Wholeness. By very nature we seek fulfillment in anything we do.

Whether it is eating, drinking, jumping, reading, talking, sleeping, or meditating, in any activity that we engage, our being yearns to completely experience the activity and be fully involved in it. Are we fully conscious of every action we engage in? Are we aware every moment of our life?

A small story:

A man was travelling by cab to the airport. The cab driver was driving very fast even

---

Isa Vasya Upanishad - One of the major and oldest *vedic* scriptures.

The totality of all the past decisions is your present. *around corners and sharp turns. The passenger was getting terrified with his driving.*

Finally, the cab driver seeing the terrified passenger, said, 'Why don't you do what I do when I take turns? Just shut your eyes!'

When you are not completely aware and involved in the action you are engaged in, your being remains unfulfilled in that experience. The unfulfilled experience remains inside you and keeps pulling you to do the action again with intensity to fulfill it. This is *karma*.

Karma is the collection of unfulfilled experiences that stay in us and constantly pull us to fulfill them.

Anything that we do and experience intensely and deeply will always leave our system. It will liberate us. Any experience that we did not go through completely, through which we did not have complete fulfillment, that did not get our full energy, attention and awareness, remains inside us as *karma*.

Even though we carry some *karma*, basically we are complete fulfillment, Wholeness. So any *karma* that has not been fulfilled cannot rest inside us for too long. It will try its best to fulfill itself. It will drive us again and again to go through the same activity so that it can be fulfilled. Any desire, any experience, which has not become complete in our system, will remain as *karma* and push us again and again to make us go through the same experience until it is fulfilled.

We think, speak and do things without clarity, without fulfillment and with deep ignorance. All these thoughts, words and actions collectively contribute towards our *karmic* baggage because none of them gives rise to fulfillment in us. When they do not give rise to fulfillment our *karma* pushes us to somehow fulfill them.

Our own thoughts, words and deeds become our *karma* and drive us to reach fulfillment in some way.

The present is the totality of all past decisions

Understand clearly that now you are reading this book because of all your past decisions. You decided to pay attention to the book on display. You decided to buy it. You decided to sit down and read this book now. The totality of all these decisions contributes to your sitting here.

The totality of all these past decisions is your present moment. Now, applying the same logic, the totality of your present decisions will be your future.

This is the essence of *karma* theory: the totality of all your past is the present, and the totality of your present is your future.

The totality of all your past is the present. The totality of your present will be your future. The problem is that we make most of our decisions unconsciously. We take thousands of decisions unconsciously. That is the reason why we are not able to connect the cause with the effect.

Flood more awareness, more intelligence into your thinking system. Flood more awareness, more consciousness into your decision-making system.

In any given moment, the future is predestined but *conditionally*. It will be a certain future according to all the totality of events till that time - this is the predestined future. But it is conditional. There is an important factor that can and will change it – your consciousness, your will.

A small story:

Once, two brothers met a sage who was known to be able to look into the future. The brothers paid their respect to the sage and asked him if he could tell them about their future. The hermit advised them, 'It may not be good for you to know your future. Besides, your future can change later even if I tell you now.'

The brothers insisted on knowing their future. The sage looked at the elder brother and said, 'You will become a king in a year.' Looking at the younger brother, he said, 'You are destined to die in the hands of a murderer in a year's time.' The brothers started walking back home. The elder brother was overjoyed while the younger one was depressed.

Now the elder brother started creating his fantasy world dreaming of becoming a king. The younger brother, who was destined to have less than a year to live, started spending his time in spiritual activities. He used his time to serve everyone and soon came out of his depression.

Eleven months passed. One day, the elder brother

Flood more awareness, more intelligence, more consciousness into your decision-making system.

invited the younger one to his house. He wanted to look out for land for a grand palace he was planning to build since very soon he would become a king. They were walking on a huge open piece of land when the younger brother stumbled on a half-buried pot. The brothers dug the pot and removed it. It was a huge pot of gold coins.

The elder brother was thrilled and started shouting, 'This treasure is just for me! It is for me to set up my palace and kingdom!' Just then, a bandit jumped out from a bush, gave a blow on the elder brother's head and tried to snatch the pot from him. The younger brother jumped at the bandit to protect his brother. But the bandit attacked him with a dagger he had in his hand. During the struggle the bandit dropped the pot and ran away.

The elder brother was very thankful to his younger brother for saving his life and offered him half the gold coins. The younger brother politely refused saying he was not going to live much longer in any case. The elder brother with his new treasure started living a lavish life, eating, drinking and being merry.

One year passed. There was no sign of any crown in sight. The younger brother was also enjoying good health. They decided to visit the sage again. They met him and asked, 'How did your predictions go wrong?' The sage was also surprised and

Destiny depends on how you choose to respond to every situation life presents to you. went into meditation. He then explained, 'I told you your destiny can be changed.'

He looked at the elder brother and said, 'Your destiny changed because of your irresponsible actions over the past months. The crown that you were to get was reduced to a pot of gold.'

He looked at the younger brother and said, 'Your spiritual life, trust and surrender to the Divine changed your destiny also. Death in the murderer's hand was reduced to only being wounded by him.'

Understand, destiny is not something written in stone. It very much depends on how you choose to respond to every situation life presents to you. Your awareness will give you the intelligence and the courage to change the flow of events in your life.

Karma and TPS

If you don't know your past completely, you will repeat the same things in the future. If your Thoughts Per Second (TPS) can come down and you know your past as it happened, you won't repeat the same past in the future. You will then become a *karma mukta**, liberated from karma. As of now you are a *karma bandha**, bonded to karma because you have not lived your past completely.

For example, your childhood always seems golden. It is the golden past. You may feel your life in college was great, but when you were actually in college, you didn't really feel that way. Why? Because your suffering has become much more now and in comparison, the past seems very nice! Now you attribute joy to your past and if given a chance you want to repeat it. When you lived through it, did you actually experience it? No!

If you can relax in the present moment, at zero TPS, for at least 11 *kshanas**, you will penetrate the time shaft. If you can stay in zero TPS for 21 *kshanas**, you will penetrate the time shaft and can alter the future. This is in your hands.

All meditation techniques are ways to bring down your TPS so that you can penetrate the time shaft.

Kshana

It is important to understand the concept of *kshana*. There is no equivalent for this word in the English language. So, let me explain to you what *kshana* means. *Kshana* is a measure of time. It is not a second or a minute as many people believe.

Karma mukta - Free of one's actions, because they are performed without attachment.

Karma bandha - Bound by one's actions, since they are performed with vested interests.

Kshana - Interval between two thoughts.

The gap between two thoughts is one *kshana*. We are used to thinking of time in an absolute sense. But a *kshana* is absolutely relative! The thoughts of every person and the rate at which they come in a person are dependent on that person. *Kshana* varies from person to person.

If a person is restless and gets too many thoughts in a span of one second, his *kshana* is shorter because the gap between two thoughts is less.

If a person is calm and collected like a meditator is, he gets fewer thoughts in a given span of time. His *kshana* is longer because the gap between two thoughts is more.

Karma – totality of conscious choices

Your life is nothing but the totality of the conscious choices that you continuously make. Whether you want to or not, directly or indirectly, you are choosing everything. Someone else does not choose. It is you who chooses.

A small story:

An employee approached his boss, 'Sir, my wife said I should ask you for a raise.'

The boss replied, 'Oh, I will ask my wife tonight whether or not I should give you a raise!'

Understand, continuously it is your choice, your decision. You may think somebody else decides. But it is only you who is deciding.

A small example can make you understand the basic truth. If somebody criticizes you, you choose to get offended. If somebody praises you, you choose to get flattered. Because of your habit, you may choose it unconsciously. It is not someone else who chooses, it is you who choose. Because it has become your habit to think that someone else influences your decisions, you have forgotten that you are choosing.

Every time someone criticizes you, you choose to get upset. Every time someone praises you, you choose to get flattered. It is nobody else's choice but your own. You can decide either way. When someone criticizes you, you can choose not to get offended and you can choose to remain calm and relaxed. It is just your choice to feel offended or not.

All your continuous choices every minute put together decide your life. If you don't decide and if you allow incidents to decide your life you go into a mode of 'paralysis'. Our lives as of now are nothing but paralysis. It is only when you decide to live your life without any outside events, situations or decisions being forced on you, you actually decide to live.

As long as you don't understand life is your choice, your living is just paralysis.

Vasana, samskara **and** *karma*

There are three interrelated concepts, termed *vasana, samskara** and *karma,* in Sanskrit.

Vasana

Vasana is the seed of desire. For example, you are walking and you happen to see a dazzling necklace displayed outside a shop. A desire arises inside you to possess it. This is *vasana.*

Samskara

Samskara is the plant that grows when the seed of *vasana* sprouts. When you see that necklace again and again, the desire to possess it becomes stronger in you. When you feed the desire to possess the necklace, it is like supplying water and nutrition to the seed of *vasana.*

The corruption that happens to the inner space is what I call *samskara* or engraved memories. They are the memories that go and sit in your inner space and pull you to go through the same experience repeatedly. They pull you to do the same kind of actions repeatedly, pull you to run through the same kind of thought patterns, even if you don't want to. Those memories are what I call *samskaras.*

Any *samskara* that is operating in your conscious or unconscious layer is nothing but a hindrance to the fulfillment of your life. There is no such thing as good or bad *samskara.* No *samskara* is good. An inner space filled with *samskaras* is hell. An inner space without *samskaras* is heaven. Do not try to classify *samskaras* as good or bad.

A *samskara* by itself, by its very nature, is negative. By its very nature *samskara* is depressive. Anything done out of *samskaras* will reduce everything to boring emptiness. Anything that happens with a deep understanding, just out of your pure inner space, always adds value to you. Anything done out of *samskaras* adds more and more bondage to you.

From our young age we collect so many different *samskaras* in so many ways. We accumulate them and also reproduce them. *Samskaras* do reproduce themselves even without any further action from our part.

Samskaras get strengthened in different ways. There are some *samskaras* that get strengthened only by action, when you repeat the action. There are some *samskaras* that get strengthened just by receiving information with regard to them, when you receive input from the world about them. There are some other *samskaras* that need neither action nor information, just remembrance is enough, and they get strengthened!

We collect these different levels of *samskaras,* engraved memories, and store them in our system and expand them.

Samskara - Engrams or deeply engraved memories.

Karma

Finally when driven by the desire you execute the action and it becomes *karma*. The power of desire drives you into finally buying the necklace. That is the action – the *karma*.

Anything half done leaves a *samskara* (engraved memory) in your being. Anything not lived fully leaves an imprint or *samskara* in your being, which time and again pulls you, attracts you to travel the same path and fulfill it.

The cause of addiction is also related to *samskaras*. In my own experience of having worked with millions of people personally, at least a few thousand cases of addiction have been healed by meditation. The basic truth about addiction is that you have lived your life vaguely, not fully or with the whole being. Unfulfilled desires create a *samskara* in you pulling you back to fulfill the desire by re-experiencing the same desire again and again.

Any emotion lived intensely simply liberates you of that emotion - be it anger, fear, desire to eat or attachment to any object or person. You are liberated fully of anything when you live it fully. If a person keeps going back to a problem time and again, it only means that he or she has not lived out the problem fully.

When we live, half our mind is somewhere else. Patanjali* says beautifully, 'The more the quantity, the less the quality.' The moment the quality of enjoyment of any object increases, its quantity decreases in direct proportion, of its own accord. Therefore, it is the quality that needs to be increased.

Any emotion lived intensely simply liberates you of that emotion - be it anger, fear, desire to eat or attachment to any object or person.

Life is not a brief candle. It is a bright shining torch. Make it burn as brightly as possible in your life.

Three types of *karma*

There are three types of *karma* - *agamya*, *prarabdha** and *sanchita*.

Sanchita karma is like a bank, a reserve bank. Understand, this may not be the first time you have taken a body and come to planet earth. You may have taken millions of bodies before! In those millions of bodies, whatever thoughts you had, whatever you spoke, whatever you did, all those unfulfilled experiences have become your engrams – engraved memories. Put together, they are like a bank called *sanchita karma*. When I say 'bank', it is not a collection or saving, it is debt! You will have to pay back all the loans!

The next type of *karma* is *prarabdha* *karma*. *Prarabdha** means this: from the *sanchita* bank of *karma* you take some *karma* out of which you create your present body.

Patanjali - A sage of ancient India and author of Yoga Sutras, which is considered the foundation of the system of yoga.
Prarabdha - Mindset and desires that we bring into this world when we are born.

Prarabdha is just a small bit of the accumulated *sanchita karma* account that you have brought into this life.

You then decide to enjoy and exhaust all those *karmas* that you brought with you through that body. So *prarabdha* is just a small bit of the accumulated *sanchita karma* account that you have brought into this life. You have planned to enjoy or exhaust these through this body of yours.

The third type of *karma* is the worst. It is the *agamya karma*, the *karma* that you start collecting after coming down to planet earth, because of fresh thoughts, words and deeds.

Anybody who lands on planet earth has to exhaust his *prarabdha karma* before he dies. For example, let us say you have 1000 *karmas* in your *sanchita* bank. Out of these 1000 *karmas,* suppose you take only ten *karmas* with you as your *prarabdha karma* when you take up your body saying, 'Let me finish these ten *karmas* this time.' However, after coming down, instead of exhausting your own *prarabdha karmas*, you start watching others and collecting *karma* based on their desires. These are desires that you have borrowed from others around you. Because of these borrowed desires, you create certain thoughts, words and actions.

For example, if you see someone more beautiful than you, your thoughts multiply due to comparison and jealousy. You create *karma* based on thoughts. Sometimes you talk ill of others, without knowing any of the related facts. When you do this, you accumulate *karma* based on words.

The way out of the daily irritation - living your *prarabdha karma*

Let me explain the three types of *karma* from a different angle.

You see, if you take all the possibilities that you are aware of and that are available to you in the cosmos, we call that as *agamya*. There are all kinds of possibilities. You can become a fish, you can become a snake, you can become a man, or you can become a god. All these are possibilities. We call that as *agamya*.

There are also other possibilities that are available to you. These are not only within the field of your awareness like the things that you know such as fish, monkey, dog, donkey and man, but also many other possibilities that are unknown to you. Those we call *sanchita*, the whole range of known and unknown possibilities.

The whole is *sanchita* and the possibilities that lie in front of you are *agamya*. You then decide to play only with certain boundaries of these possibilities when you come into this body. That is what we call *prarabdha*. See when you came down, you decided to play inside certain boundaries. That boundary is what we can call *prarabdha*.

After coming here you see many possibilities before you that you try to accumulate, that you try to acquire. Those possibilities can be called as *agamya*.

This *prarabdha* that you brought with you has the intelligence to run your life.

One big difficulty is that you see too many *agamya*, too many possibilities in front of you. Because of that, your trust over your *prarabdha* or your own preselected possibilities reduces. You think your *prarabdha* may not be that powerful to run your life because of the *agamya*, the possibilities, which are in front of your eyes.

Let me tell you this. Trusting *prarabdha* is powerful. Fulfilling your *prarabdha* will take away one very negative aspect of your life - the continuous irritation. The constant irritation that you carry from morning till night is the gift of *agamya*.

From morning till night, from the moment you come out of your bed till the moment you fall asleep, you feel a constant irritation. We just need somebody to make some mistake and we jump on them! We are just waiting. Anybody who comes in our presence will have our 'blessing'! That constant irritation is because we are centered on *agamya*.

If our energy, our inner space is centered on *prarabdha*, we will not be carrying the constant irritation that we carry now. It is not that we will not be working or relating with the possibilities. It is not that we will stop working, no! We will continue to work but our base will be our *prarabdha*.

Moving the physical body out of fear or greed is what I call living your life based on *agamya*.

You see, the mood of constantly rejecting everything, constantly being irritated, happens because of our *agamya*, because of the possibilities we see around us. We are running behind the choices, the possibilities, the *agamya*. But we forget that the *prarabdha* is very intelligent, very powerful.

In the whole world, there are only two kinds of people, people whose inner space is centered on *agamya* and people whose inner space is centered on *prarabdha*, that's all. People whose inner space is centered on *prarabdha* live their life in restful awareness.

The mind that is based on *agamya* will be inspired only by fear or greed. You can see this when you wake up. You will come out of your dream state only if you have a desire or if you are caught by some fear. For example, you may get inspired to wake up because you wish to send your child to school so that she gets a good education and has a bright future. Or you may get up out of fear of getting late for office because you are afraid of losing your job.

Moving the physical body out of fear or greed is what I call living your life based on *agamya*.

The way out of the cycle of *karma*

All your actions are invariably driven by greed or fear and therefore end up being superficial actions, adding to your *karma*.

In this way, you end up collecting more *karmas*. By the time you go back, what will happen? Your 'karma bank balance' would have increased by the number of your *agamya karma*!

Say you came down with ten *karmas*, you did not exhaust these ten *karmas* with which you came, but you collected 200 more!

What will happen the next time you take the body? Your *sanchita* is now 1000 added to the 200 new *agamya karmas* you collected now. You now have 200 *karmas* more than in your last birth. Again you take ten out of that collection and come down with another body. But you only collect more and go back. This becomes a vicious circle. This is what we call *janma marana chakra,* life-and-death cycle, continuously taking a body and dying, again and again.

Instead, while you are living, if somebody gives you the knowledge that you are not just the body or the mind and it is *karma* that is influencing you, then the influence of that *karma* over you will begin to come down. You will then start exhausting the *prarabdha karma* that you came down with.

Let us say you brought ten *prarabdha karmas* with you when you took this body and came down. Suppose in these ten *prarabdha*

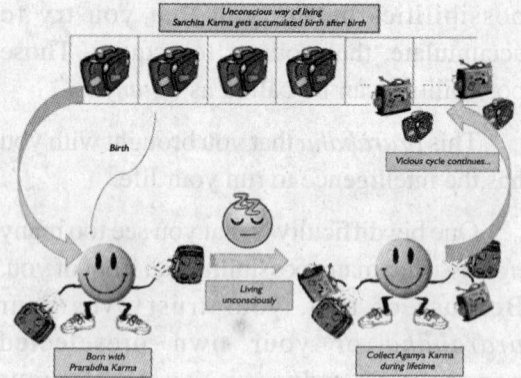

*Unconscious way of living
Sanchita Karma gets accumulated birth after birth*

karmas, you have three *samskaras* or three engrams that have the power to put you into depression. If you continue to obey those engrams and fall into depression, they will not remain just three, but will probably become ten. The additional seven *karmas* are the *agamya karmas*. If instead of exhausting your *prarabdha* you decide to remain with them, you collect *agamya*.

If on the other hand, whenever these three engrams put you in depression you have learned some technique to come out of the

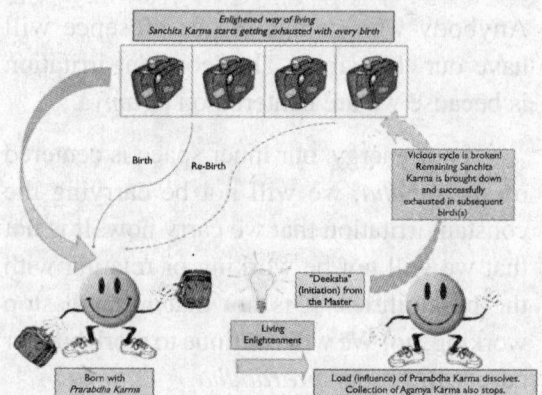

*Enlightened way of living
Sanchita Karma starts getting exhausted with every birth*

depression, then these three will start losing their power over you. So, over time, of the ten *karmas*, three will leave you. Whenever you reduce the influence of *prarabdha* on yourself, not only will the *prarabdha* get burnt, but the chances of accumulating new *karma*, the *agamya karma*, will also come down.

You stop collecting *agamya* when the *prarabdha* loses its influence over you. When the influence of these ten *prarabdha* engrams over you stops, the *agamya* collection will also stop because it is these ten engrams that are responsible for the collection of further engrams or *karma*.

Now let us come to the *sanchita karma*. Understand, you can't do anything directly with your *sanchita karma* bank. For *sanchita*

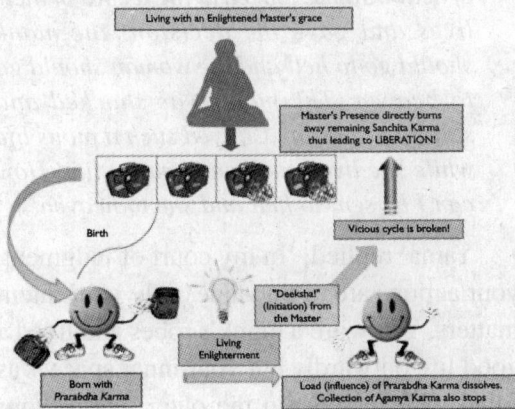

to burn out, only *Guru Krupa,* grace of the master, will work. Only the master's grace can do anything to burn out your *sanchita*.

Only intention matters

A beautiful story from the devotional *vedic* scripture *Bhagavatam**:

> *Krishna reached the banks of river Yamuna* with the gopis*, his milkmaid friends. They wanted to cross the river but there was no way to cross.*

> *Krishna declared, 'If I am true brahmachari* (celibate), then let the Yamuna* part and let us go across.'*

> *The Yamuna* parted.*

Outwardly, it may seem that Krishna was with the girls like other ordinary men. But Krishna was beyond the body-mind. His actions did not carry the intention of an ordinary man. It is the intention of any act that matters, not the act itself.

Intention is the baggage, the *karma*, not the action. If action creates intention, it becomes the baggage. Pure action with no end objective is not *karma*.

Bhagavatam - The foremost epic of Hindu religion describing the incarnations of Vishnu, especially his incarnation as Krishna. It was written by Vyasa, who was also the author of the *itihasa* or epic Mahabharata

Yamuna - A holy Indian river associated with enlightened master Krishna.

Gopis - Women who tended cows who were devotees of enlightened master Krishna.

Brahmachari - A *vedic* student, usually referring to a young celibate monk.

Action without intention is living enlightenment. **Master's presence affects the intention**

See, whatever you are doing in the presence of the master, you are doing for the master. You know it is in no way going to build your name or fame. So, the action happens without intention. There is no intention. The intention is the master's. The action is yours. Intention is in the being of the person who has no intentions!

You see, the total *sanchita karma* can be yours or mine. Mine is divine play. Yours is suffering. When it started, your total *sanchita karma* also started as a divine play. But, after gathering more and more gathered *agamya karma*, it became dirty.

Because I have no *karma*, when you flow with me you will also act without intention. Action without intention is living enlightenment.

Action without intention is free from *karma*

If a person has committed ten murders, the quantity of murders will not be recorded. But the intensity of the murderer will be recorded. It is the quality, the mindset, and the attitude, that carries the *karmic* burden.

That is why Krishna says again and again in the *Bhagavad Gita* that intention is much more important than action. That is the message of the whole Gita. He says, 'When you are without intention I will take care.'

Action does not get recorded. Only intention gets recorded.

The Mahabharata* tells us the beautiful story of a courtesan and a monk.

There was a monk who lived across a courtesan's house. He used to keep a count of the men coming to her house and used to imagine all kinds of things about her lifestyle. The woman spent all her free time praying to Krishna to redeem her from her miserable life.

One day, they both died at the same time. Both reached the court of Yama, the god of death. Yama* looked at the record of their lives and gave the decision: the monk should go to hell and the woman should go to heaven. The monk was shocked and started protesting, 'I lived such a pious life while she lived such an immoral life! How can I be sent to hell and she to heaven!'*

Yama* replied, 'In my court of judgment, your actions are of no value, only your intent matters. You wore a monk's robes and lived a good life outwardly but your inner space was filled with lust. So in the outer world, your body is now being buried with honor but you have to suffer hell. The woman's heart was forever with Krishna even while her body was

---

Mahabharata - The Hindu *itihasa* or epic whose central characters are the five Pandava princes, their hundred Kaurava cousins and enlightened master Krishna.

Yama - Hindu god of death and justice.

sold to men. So her body doesn't have anybody to even do the last rites but she is going to heaven.'

It is the intention and attitude that counts.

An enlightened being, an incarnation, is one with Existence. An enlightened being can only operate in tune with Existence. He can never be out of tune. The actions of an enlightened master can never be without awareness and compassion.

Since we do not have the consciousness or awareness, we cannot justify our actions by saying they are similar to those of an enlightened being. Be very clear, the action may look similar outwardly but the intention, the inner space, the attitude, is completely different.

A beautiful story from the life of Adi Shankara[*]:

Once while Shankara was wandering with his disciples, he suddenly felt thirsty. They were in the middle of nowhere. They traveled further and finally came across one shop. Shankara went up to the man in the shop and asked for some water to drink. The man said, 'I am sorry but I have nothing to offer you except liquor. That is all I have.'

Shankara replied, 'Alright, please give me some.' He drank a glass of liquor and thanked the man. The disciples were shocked to see their master drink liquor! The thirsty disciples decided to follow the master and they all drank liquor to their heart's content.

When they resumed the journey, Shankara continued to walk normally but the disciples under the effect of liquor were not even able to keep the next step properly. They went up further and after some distance, came across an iron forge.

Shankara went upto the man who was pouring molten iron into the cast. He asked him for a glass of water. The man apologized saying he didn't have any water to offer. Shankara said, 'Alright. Please give me the molten iron then.'

The man and Shankara's disciples were all shocked. The man gave Shankara the hot molten iron which he just poured into his mouth as if it was water!

He then turned around to his disciples and said, 'You may also drink now.' The disciples stood with their heads lowered. Shankara then explained, 'Do not follow what I do. Follow what I say. Otherwise, you just choose to follow what your mind tells you.'

An enlightened being has no personal interest because his identity is dissolved in the identity of the whole universe.

Understand, the very plane on which enlightened beings exist is different from the normal human plane of existence. So they do not need to and cannot do things according to usual logic. Their intention is what is important,

---

Adi Shankara – Enlightened master

which cannot be explained in terms of ordinary logic.

An enlightened being has no personal interest because he has no individual identity – his identity is dissolved in the identity of the whole universe.

Intention and action

If the depth of the intention is more and of the action is less, the person is lazy or in *tamas**.

If the depth of intention and of the action is the same, the person is in restless action or *rajas**.

If there is no intention but only the action, he is in purposeless action or *sattva**.

That is why Krishna says in the Bhagavad Gita, 'Fight, O Arjuna*.' It is not the act of 'killing' that will be recorded but the intention that will be recorded. The intention of Arjuna* is the intention of Krishna, who is a being with no intentions as He is one with the Cosmos!

When you act in tune with the Cosmos, the whole Cosmos blesses you. You attract all kinds of positive coincidences around you. That is why when people contribute even a little to the cause of such a person they are showered in abundance from all corners.

The power of daily intention

We have seven layers or seven bodies of energy, which are physical, *pranic**, mental, etheric, causal, pleasure and *nirvanic**. Please understand, in the causal layer our gathered or *agamya karma* is completely available for us. See, in the causal body, you may have the skills to play cricket, golf and tennis. But if you get up from deep sleep with a strong will or intention to play cricket, then you will also bring from the causal body the intelligence to play cricket. You will be naturally led into the situations, the atmosphere and the intelligence for it. If you go to sleep at night with a strong intention to play golf and you wake up in the morning with the strong intention to play golf, then you will bring with you that intelligence to play golf.

The causal layer is an exchange place. It is like monetary exchange. In the causal layer you can exchange anything. When you go to the causal layer the *karma* of this birth itself can be changed if you have that strong intention every day. This is true freedom.

Tamas - One of the three *gunas* or attributes of nature. Attribute of inaction.

Rajas - One of the three *gunas* or attributes of nature. Attribute of aggression.

Sattva - One of the three *gunas* or attributes of nature. Attribute of passive action.

Arjuna - Warrior prince and the third of the five brothers of the Pandava family in the great Indian epic Mahabharata. He was a disciple of enlightened master Krishna who received the wisdom in the Bhagavad Gita from Krishna.

Pranic - Related to *prana* or life energy.

Nirvanic - Connected to *nirvana*. The *nirvanic* layer is the seventh and final energy layer in our body mind.

Strong intention has the capacity to change the gathered *agamya karma* and the *prarabdha karma* of this birth. It cannot change the total *sanchita karma*. *Sanchita karma* can only be changed by the grace of the master – one who is without *karmas*.

Mission or machine?

Reaching out to the master, doing what the master says and acting without intention, are what the whole game of life is all about.

Action without intention is mission. If you are acting with intention, you are like a machine.

If you are acting without intention, you are the mission. Machine or mission, the choice is yours. Till you act with my intention without adding your intention, I will keep training you. Just do what I say without asking inspiration from your intention, from your greed and fear. Pure action without intention will lead to fulfillment.

Pointing the same sword inside

Karma is not a law of reward and punishment. It is not a way god uses to punish people for committing sins. It is a reflection of your own mental state giving you the experience of 'heaven' and 'hell'.

A small story:

A traffic policeman caught a man speeding. He was about to issue him a speeding ticket.

Suddenly a woman started screaming from the back seat, 'See, I told you that you will get caught! Who asked you to drive so fast? And when I tell you to be careful, slow down and watch out, you tell me to shut up. Now see you got caught!' The cop asked the driver, 'Who is she?' The driver sighed, 'My wife'.

The cop tore up the ticket and said, 'Drive on. You have been punished enough!'

When you are angry, it is not that you will incur sin and pay for it in your next life. You are suffering with your anger now. That itself is the hell you suffer! You are suffering inside in the same way that you are torturing the person you are angry with.

The fire you spit outside will burn with the same intensity inside you also. No matter whether it burns the other person or not, the fire of anger will surely burn you. The sword used to cut someone outside will cut you inside with the same intensity. Remember, it is a double edged sword.

A beautiful story from Buddha's life:

A man once came and spat on Buddha's face. Buddha wiped his face and asked the man, 'Do you want to say something more, or is this all?'

Ananda, his close disciple, was very angry. He was fuming that some man came and just spat on his master and that too for no reason at all. He said to Buddha, 'Master, if you give me permission I will handle the man.'

Meditation helps to reduce the *prarabdha karma.*

Buddha replied, 'Have you forgotten that you are a monk, a sannyasi* (renunciate)? That poor man is already suffering with his anger. See his angry face, his body shaking with that anger. And before spitting on me, do you think he would have been celebrating and dancing? He is mad with his own anger. In that state of madness, he came and spat on me.

What is a bigger punishment for him than being in such a state? And what harm has he done to me? I just had to wipe the spit off my face. Now you don't get agitated, otherwise you are building the same anger inside you. Why are you punishing yourself? That is foolishness. Feel compassion for the poor man instead.'

The man was listening and was surprised and confused to see Buddha behave in this way. He was expecting Buddha to become angry. That is what he wanted. Instead the compassion and understanding Buddha showed was just too shocking for him!

Buddha said to him, 'Go home. You look tired, you have punished yourself enough. Forget about what you did to me. You did not harm me. This body will return to the earth and people will do all kinds of things like spitting. Go home and relax.'

The man was completely shaken by Buddha's response. He went back home. He came back that evening, fell at Buddha's feet and cried, 'Please forgive me!'

Buddha calmly said, 'I was not angry in the first place. How can I forgive you? But I am happy to see you relieved from the anger and in a state of harmony. Just remember: never do such acts again, this is how you create hell for yourself.'

Karma and the next body

How do we choose the next birth?

Once the life force leaves the body, within three *kshanas**, it chooses the next body.

At the time of death the three most enjoyed experiences in that lifetime stand out as one's last thoughts. The choice of the next body arises from the mindset based on these three experiences.

These three thoughts will be based on one from each of the total *karma (sanchita)*, this birth *karma (prarabdha)* and gathered *karma (agamya)*. Based on this, the *prarabdha karma* will take shape for this birth.

Practicing spiritual life solutions in one's lifetime will reduce the gathered *sanchita karma* of that life because these understandings will help one to live with awareness.

Meditation helps to reduce the *prarabdha karma.* It acts not only upon the conscious

---

Sannyasi - One who has renounced, a monk.

Kshana - Interval between two thoughts.

and physical levels but also has the capacity to penetrate and clean the unconscious on a physical, mental and being level.

However, the largest balance in the bank of *karma*, the total *sanchita karma*, can only be dissolved through the master's grace.

The more these three *karmas* are reduced, the less the constraints of choice for the next body. Since each of the three *karmas* will dictate a corresponding intense experience to be lived, the next body will need to provide a space for these experiences to be lived.

It is like this. If I say, 'Let me meet a person who can speak English,' I have more choice than if I say, 'Let me meet a person who can speak English, Spanish and German.'

Similarly, if you have all the three types of *karma,* there are more constraints on your next birth.

For example, the desire influenced by your total sanchita *karma* may be, 'I want to be beautiful.' The desire influenced by your *karma* of this birth, *prarabdha*, may be, 'I

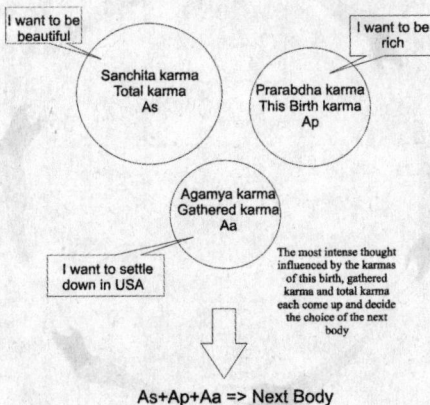

I want to be beautiful

I want to be rich

Sanchita karma
Total karma
As

Prarabdha karma
This Birth karma
Ap

Agamya karma
Gathered karma
Aa

I want to settle down in USA

The most intense thought influenced by the karmas of this birth, gathered karma and total karma each come up and decide the choice of the next body

As+Ap+Aa => Next Body

want to be rich.' The desire influenced by your gathered or *agamya karma,* may be, 'I want to settle down in USA.'

If you have all the three types of *karma,* there are more constraints on your next birth.

It is more difficult to get a body for your life energy's next birth that will lead to the satisfaction of all the three desires within the short gap of three *kshanas*. So, it ends up choosing a body that satisfies the strongest desire amongst the three desires. The combined desires, the mindset, with which the life energy leaves the previous body is the *vasana,* the seeds of desire we earlier talked about.

These three desires, these three thoughts will be seen in one glimpse in three *kshanas*, as one *vasana* . The *vasana* is like a television channel and the body that attracts the *vasana* is like the television set tuned to this channel. The depth of the *vasana* and the body that matches the *vasana* attracts the life energy. Just like a television set tuned to the satellite channel's frequency receives the corresponding electromagnetic waves, in the same way, the *vasana* is attracted by the body.

The life energy, the spirit, departing from the previous body enters the new body that it selected, as that body leaves the womb of the mother. It enters the body in the birth canal. The darkness of the causal layer that it left from the previous body corresponds to the darkness of the mother's birth canal. Since the body has been prepared by the energies of the parents, the life energy chooses the

It is the child that chooses its parents.

combined energies of the parents based on the desires, the *vasanas*, the mental attitude, with which it leaves the previous body. So the parents do not choose the child. It is the child that chooses its parents.

Having chosen a particular body, the spirit or life force has to satisfy the other two desires it had but could not choose an appropriate body for. However, during its transition through the darkness, the deep pain experienced by the spirit erases all memories of the *vasana* it carries before it enters the new body. The new entity no longer remembers the desires with which it left the previous body. Instead of fulfilling the desires with which it left the previous body, since it has forgotten them, the life energy in the new body seeks new desires and collects more *karma*.

Now, of the three types of *karma,* if one of them is gone, the choice constraints are fewer and the life force can be more focused in the choices. Cleaning the gathered *agamya karma* and this birth's *prarabdha karma* can be done by the individual by understanding about life and by meditating. The master's grace will reduce the total *sanchita karma*.

Once the total *sanchita karma* is cleansed, there is no reason to take another body. Then, if the next birth still happens, it is for no reason but out of overflowing joy and bliss. The birth is thus chosen consciously because there is no pull of *karma*. The life lived is a *leela* or reasonless play of an *avatar* or incarnation.

How did the cycle of birth and death start?

For all of us, our total *sanchita karma* initially was a divine play. For an enlightened master, it is still a divine play as he has no *karma* at all. Playing because you can play is the divine play.

We took birth out of choice. We forgot our *prarabdha* karma, started gathering *agamya karma* and expanded the total *sanchita karma*. Then, to exhaust the increased load we had to take another birth where we collected more desires and *karma*. This is how the cycle of life and death continues.

Please understand, your gathered *agamya karma* is your bondage. The total *karma* and this birth *karma* can be a divine play. The result of this play is the *karma* of that birth. After birth, if we play without gathered *karma*, it will continue to be a divine play. The bondage comes with gathered *karma*.

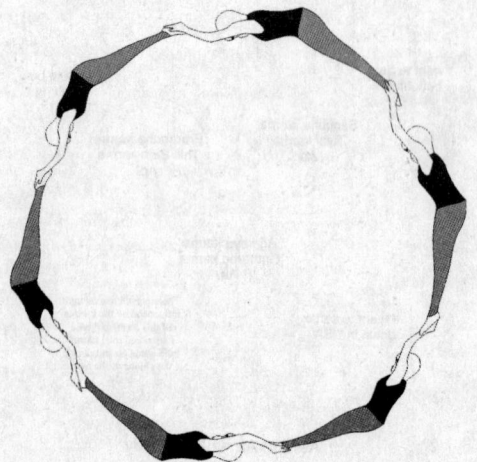

Will a human be born as an animal, bird or insect or can he be born as human being in the next birth?

This is a very good question. Let me boldly declare this truth and clear all the myths that have been surrounding this one question on the wheel of *karma*!

When a human being takes birth as human once, he will continue taking the life of a human unless he has acted against his consciousness like torturing others or committed violent acts in the physical, mental or verbal forms against Existence which is in the form of the master, nature and human consciousness. The intensity of these acts is what gets recorded in the cosmic *karmic* record. Understand, it is not the act itself but the intensity of the act that matters.

When a person spends his whole life in lower consciousness, he can be reborn as an animal. For example, if he spends his whole life in only eating or sleeping, he can be reborn as an animal.

See, if the person has not experienced the unique human qualities like falling in love, seeking enlightenment, even once in his lifetime, he will be reborn as an animal because he had a human body but the channels of human experience have not been awakened.

Do we have to wait for the next birth if we feel strongly about something but it is not our *prarabdha*?

No. You can change your *prarabdha* through a simple, strong will or *sankalpa**. The strength of the *sankalpa** can cause a rebirth in you in this birth itself. The next birth can happen now itself. For example, people, especially householder disciples who feel they are caught up in their responsibilities ask me, '*Swamiji*, please bless me that I should be with you at least in my next birth.' There are so many examples where they have been able to come and live in the ashram* just a few months later. It is just the strength of the will.

Enlightenment – Back to Home

You are like a wave in the ocean of Existence. The wave rises up from the ocean but it is still connected to the ocean. It may think it has an individual existence but that is just a myth. Whether it is rising, above the ocean or falling down, it is still a part of the ocean.

On its own, because of joy, when the wave takes the body, there will be no gathered or *agamya karma*. When *agamya karma* is

---

Sankalpa - Vow or decision.

Ashram - A monastery for Hindu or Buddhist monks.

acquired, it will corrupt the total *sanchita karma* that was pure. This *sanchita karma* has to be exhausted in the next birth. Corrupted total *sanchita karma* generates the cycle of life and birth– this is how the wheel of *karma* starts.

The new body that the life energy occupies does not remember the *prarabdha karma* that the life energy brought with it when it took the body. So, you do not remember the desires with which you left your previous body.

Reminding yourself of those desires again and fulfilling them in this birth is what doing *tapas* (penance) and becoming enlightened is all about.

So what happens when you forget at birth that you have come through divine play? When the total *karma* weight becomes excessive, you realize, 'There is some problem somewhere.' Immediately you wake up and get enlightened again. The rewinding and coming back is enlightenment.

Sometimes, if you get a really bad dream, only a thought like 'I am dreaming' will come at first. Then, you actually wake up. That thought of 'I am dreaming' coming is turning towards enlightenment. Waking up is getting enlightened.

That thought of 'I am dreaming. This whole world is a dream' and then renouncing the false world and catching the reality is enlightenment. In this world, the same experiences repeat making you tired and bored. It gives rise to the suspicion, 'I am

seeing a dream.' Then, you start doubting the world, doubting the promise the world gives.

It is like the newspaper ads about some beachside resort that show the beach, the table, the food, all looking like heaven, giving a promise of luxury. You doubt that promise, because you realize that if hundred people see this and go, not many will actually feel the ecstasy promised. Similarly in life also, you doubt the promises your mind has been making all along but never fulfilling any.

Techniques to overcome *karma*

Re-living to relieve

Till now, what we discussed was a preventive measure for incurring *karma*. As a curative for *karma*, I will give you a simple technique. Right from this moment, try and remember all the incidents in your life. Start going backwards from this moment to your childhood days. Remember what you can.

Do not bother about what you cannot. Understand: what you cannot remember is only a hangover. It has not touched you deeply. That is why it is not retained in your memory. Try this technique for a year. Re-living is a wonderful way of relieving.

Our second level Life Bliss meditation program – the *Nithyananda Spurana Program* (NSP) is focused on just this method of exhausting one's *karma*. It is like a complete spiritual bath in the presence of an enlightened master.

Deities and rnlightened masters – your paths to exhausting *karma*

There is a way to again and again remind ourselves not to collect *karma* and to live without the influence of the earlier incurred *karma*. The first step is to have a clear understanding that *karma* is powerless in the presence of an elevated consciousness.

There is an important difference between normal human beings and enlightened masters. A normal person does not have the ability to make his body alive out of his will. His body is either alive or it is dead, that's all. It is not under his control.

But for an enlightened person, it is under his control. He can either make his body alive, or relax. Because of this ability, he can also make another body alive! When an enlightened being chooses to make a stone or metal alive, that stone or metal becomes a representation of his very self.

All the deities in our major traditional temples are energized by enlightened masters. Masters like Arunagiri Yogeeshwara[*] from Tiruvannamalai[*], Patanjali[*] from Chidambaram[*], Karurar[*] from Thanjavur[*], Konganavar[*] from Tirupati[*] and Meenakshi[*] from Madurai[*] have energized the deities in these temples.

Deities are therefore considered to be the very bodies of the enlightened masters. Disciples continue serving the deities even after the masters leave their physical body. The body of the deity is considered to be the body of the master himself. That is the reason why

---

Arunagiri Yogeeshwara - The temple of Arunachaleswara in Tiruvannamalai is built on the living energy tomb of Arunagiri Yogeeshwara, who is considered an incarnation of enlightened master Shiva.

Tiruvannamalai - Temple town where Nithyananda was born and raised.

Patanjali - A sage of ancient India and author of Yoga Sutras, which is considered the foundation of the system of yoga.

Chidambaram - A place in South India famous for its ancient temple dedicated to enlightened master Shiva in his dancing form as Nataraja and where he is represented as the space energy.

Karurar - South Indian mystic saint upon whose immortal remains the temple at Thanjavur (Tanjore) is believed to have been built.

Thanjavur - Town in South India famous for its massive temple and learning and cultural heritage.

Konganavar - Hindu saint and disciple of Bogar, upon whose immortal remains, Tirupati temple is said to have been built.

Tirupati - Famous temple to Vishnu as Venkateshwara or Balaji in Andhra Pradesh, South India.

Meenakshi - The goddess at Madurai in south India. She is said to be a saint upon whose immortal remains, the temple has been built.

Madurai - Temple town in south India. A major pilgrim center with the temple to Meenakshi and her consort Sundareshwara, an aspect of enlightened master Shiva.

the deities receive the same respect offered to an enlightened master.

For example, all the disciples initiated by Arunagiri Yogeeshwara* will worship the Arunachala temple for generations together. You will see that whatever is offered to the master will be offered to the deity also.

Masters, even after they decide to leave the body, are continuously available to the disciples through the deities that they energized. For example, even during my lifetime, my physical presence is not possible everywhere at the same time. So these deities are programmed to do my work where I am physically not present! They are my representatives!

The deities possess independent intelligence. Energizing the deities is a big process. It is like giving birth to a child. These energized deities will directly respond to your prayers. They will directly relate with you if you are open in relating with them.

If you see our *puja** (offering) and our ashram* routine, you will see that in the morning, they play the wakeup song to wake up the presiding deity. Then they give a small cup of oil for His hair and a small cup of tooth powder for Him to brush His teeth! Then, they give Him a bath and offer fresh, ironed clothes,

just like how they offer to the master. They offer food and perform the evening *arati**. In the night, they put the deity to bed again in a ceremonious way.

Understand, all this does not add anything to the deity or to the master. It adds only to us! This is what is living with god. This is what is practicing the presence of god. Practicing the presence of the master is *puja**. *Puja** is done every day because it is a technique to remember the presence of god every day.

Nithyam – Dhyanam – Anandam

What is needed so as not to collect gathered *agamya karma,* is life solutions, what I call *nithyam* (eternal) because you practice them daily. To dissolve the *karma* of this birth, you need meditation or *dhyanam*. That is why you see that most of our meditations are based on breathing. Altering the breathing, making it fast, slow, silent etc is what our meditation techniques are all about. The only thing that can dissolve the total *karma* is the master's grace or *anandam* (bliss).

So understand, *karma* is simply the effects of thoughts, words and deeds that stem from

---

Arunagiri Yogeeshwara - The temple of Arunachaleswara in Tiruvannamalai is built on the living energy tomb of Arunagiri Yogeeshwara, who is considered an incarnation of enlightened master Shiva.

Puja - Hindu ritual worship.

Ashram - A monastery for Hindu or Buddhist monks.

Arati - Fire ritual performed at the end of most *vedic* worship done with lighted lamps or camphor, accompanied often by devotional songs.

deep ignorance and cause you to again and again tread familiar patterns of misery. The way to break this cycle is to tune into the clicks received from the master and live in an elevated zone of consciousness.

Myths on *karma*

Q: Can our *karma* be exhausted by doing charitable service?

You need to see the motivation for the social service. Honestly look at yourself in the face. What do you want by doing the service?

Do you feel motivated by the fear of having to go to hell if you don't do good deeds? Is it the desire for a good name and publicity? Or is it just to do something to keep yourself busy? Is it the greed of a good afterlife after death? Is it a better next birth?

If you are driven by fear or greed, you can never intensely enjoy doing the service. One part of you will be doing the act of service. Another part of you will be caught in thinking about the benefits of the service. So you are not integrated in that action. You are not completely fulfilled through it.

This action also binds. Outwardly, socially, it looks good and free from bondage. But inside your inner space, you can see it is not. The whole of mankind is swinging around result-oriented action. This is extended to service as well. At least in service, do not think of dollars or fame. Do not plan to impress. Do not plan to make your presence felt.

Do the work for the work itself! Do not plan anything. Just do any service anywhere. This kind of service will infuse tremendous power into your being. For at least half an hour a day do something selfless, without any thought of results or benefits for yourself. You can then experience the true joy of service.

Karma can be exhausted only through deep understanding, awareness and at least one glimpse of consciousness.

Q: What happens when someone has a premature death like in suicide or accident?

In the case of premature death, the soul has to wait for the time it was destined to live, before it can take a new body. In the case of suicide, the suffering is much more intense than what would have been if the spirit had continued living. It is like when you have a plate of food in front of you but you don't have hands or a body to enjoy it!

In the case of accidents, the spirit has to be without body. But there is no suffering as in the case of suicide. The spirit lives in the same consciousness it would have lived had it been alive. It just waits to get the next body.

Q: Are past life regressions useful and safe?

Past life regression should not be done except by an enlightened being. It has such a strong influence it can affect this birth. For example, if you had been a blind person in a past life, when regression happens, you can become blind in this birth!

An unenlightened being doing the regression will also suffer the *karmas* of the person he is doing the regression for.

To clear past life regression, one should know how to handle it, clear the past *samskaras* and close it.

Q: When the master clears the *karmas*, do we have to go through pain?

When the master removes the *karma*, you call that feeling pain. Actually, the master would be removing in a second the suffering of many births, what would have otherwise taken many births to dissolve. So it is practically no suffering in comparison.

Sharada Devi says, the master clearing the *samskaras* is like you facing a thorn prick instead of suffering a fracture!

Death is a Celebration

Our concern for *karma* is rooted in our fear of death. It is a primal fear, that of the unknown. Our actions in this life are for the most part driven by the desire to be in a better place after death or the fear not to be in a worse place after death. This fear of leaving the body and mind has existed through the ages.

Story of Yayati

There is a nice story in Mahabharata[*], the great Indian epic:

There was once a king by the name of Yayati. He lived extremely well for hundred years, enjoying his kingdom and all the physical and mental comforts of life. At the end of 100 years, Yama, the lord of death, came to take him away as it was time for him to leave the earth. The king was shocked to see Yama and started crying, 'Why have you come so fast and that too suddenly without any notice? I have not lived my life fully

yet. Please give me some more time to live.'

Yama replied that there is no extension possible to one's life. But Yayati pleaded with him and begged for more time. Yama finally agreed that if any one of his sons was ready to give up his life for Yayati, then the king could live for that much more time.

Yayati called one of his sons. The son agreed, 'I will give up my life, let my father live.' He gave up his life. Yama extended Yayati's life by a hundred years.

Yayati continued to enjoy all the material comforts in the same way as before and lived another hundred years. At the end of this period Yama returned to take him. This time too Yayati was shocked to see Yama again so soon. He felt he had hardly lived his life and begged Yama saying that he was not prepared to die and wanted some more time.

Yama gave him another chance; another of Yayati's sons gave up his life for his father, and Yayati got a lease of another hundred years of life.

Mahabharata - The Hindu *itihasa* or epic whose central characters are the five Pandava princes, their hundred Kaurava cousins and enlightened master Krishna.

We are afraid because instinctively we resist change and death is an abrupt change in life.

Yayati enjoyed another hundred years and again Yama came back to take him. Again as before, Yayati asked for more time but this time Yama refused to play the same game again.

Instead of agreeing to the king's plea, this time Yama asked Yayati compassionately, 'O king! Do you think you can put a fire out by pouring oil into it? Do you think that you can fulfill your desires by living them out more and more?' In just a few beautiful words Yama explained the whole purpose life to Yayati. Yayati finally realized the Truth, followed Yama and rested at the feet of the Divine.

You cannot feel fulfilled by offering sense pleasures to the senses. You cannot feel that you are ready for death if you never lived intensely. Trying to satisfy the senses, pouring pleasures into your senses, or living as you want does not mean living intensely. When you really live intensely, automatically you will be liberated.

Why are we afraid of Death?

We are afraid because instinctively we resist change and death is an abrupt change in life. The master Chuang Tzu says beautifully, 'Man's thirst for survival in the future makes him incapable of living in the present.'

We are afraid because we do not know who we are. We hold an identity of ourselves inside us, based on our family, relationships, job, wealth, social image etc. Death removes this very foundation on which our identity is built, so we feel death snatches everything that is ours.

Our understanding about death, or rather our misunderstanding about death, makes death a fearful, frightening experience. The man who resists death dies even while he lives. He dies every moment because he is tortured by the very idea of death. When I say 'death', I don't mean only physical death. Losing anything is a form of death. Losing your comfortable life is one form of death, losing your relatives is another. Please understand that loss in any form is nothing but death.

There are two issues: the incident of death that happens at the end of our lives, and psychological death. Real death happens only once, but psychological death, the fear of death, permeates our life. The idea and fear of death decides our entire life structure.

Every part of your body is connected to someone or the other. Your being is not an individual being. It is not alone, separate, as you think. We are all interlinked. That is why we undergo terrible suffering when we lose someone or something. Every missing that you experience, no matter of whom or what is what I call death. Fear of death is just the fear of continuity or discontinuity. We are afraid about the 'what next'.

In the mystery of death lies the answer to life

Once, in USA, a young lady asked the great Indian monk Vivekananda*, 'What is life?' Vivekananda* said, 'Come with me to India. I will teach you.' She asked, 'What will you teach me?'

He said, 'I will teach you how to die.'

If you know the secret of death, the quality of your life will be different. Your very understanding and attitude towards everything will change.

Death is not a mere incident at the end of your life. It is a profound knowing. If you know how to die, you know how to live. Living and leaving are two sides of the same thing. Your life will be totally different once you understand death.

Entering into Death

Almost all the traditions have tried to conquer death, to outlive death. But one group of really intelligent, intuitive people understood after much struggle that we were approaching death in a completely wrong direction. They decided to take a 180-degree turn. They started working with death in a different way.

They used meditation as a technique to take them where others had not dared to go before. Those few intelligent ones were the *rishis** of the Upanishad* age. The report they submitted on their research into the phenomenon of death is called the *Kathopanishad*.

These *rishis** researched deeply on death and finally came to the conclusion that death cannot be understood or overcome by resistance. By resisting death you cannot go beyond death. The only way to break free from the vicious cycle of birth and death is by becoming enlightened - entering into death, dropping the fear.

Please understand that death has power over you because of your belief, your faith in it, that's all. If you take a little time and look into your fear of death you will see that it has the power to transform your life in the most positive way. You will realize that it is not contradictory to life but complementary to life.

Death is a deep relaxation. It is the ultimate 'letting go'. It is the dropping of the old and starting with the new. When your being recognizes that it cannot achieve what

The only way to break free from the vicious cycle of birth and death is by becoming enlightened.

Vivekananda - Primary disciple of Ramakrishna Paramahamsa and Founder of the Ramakrishna Order. 19th century Eastern mystic considered a key figure in spreading awareness of Hinduism and Yoga in Europe and America.

Rishis - Vedic sages

Upanishad - Scriptures that form the essence of the ancient texts of the Vedas. Literally means 'sitting with the master'. There are eleven main Upanishads that have been commented on by enlightened master Adi Shankara.

> ### Your choice to start all over again is what is called death.

it wants to through this body it decides to move on. This 'moving on', this 'passing over' is what is called death.

When your brand new house becomes old after the passage of years, you either try to repair it or if that is too inconvenient and frustrating, you decide to sell the house and move into a new one. In the same way when you feel that you have not lived your life totally in the way you wanted to, you leave this body to take a new one. Your choice to start all over again is what is called death.

Mystery of mysteries

There is a beautiful story in the great Indian epic, Mahabharata[*]:

The prince Yudhishtra[*] was asked by a yaksha (demigod), 'What is the most mysterious thing on planet earth?'

Yudhishtra[*] replied, 'Every day so many lives are going to the abode of Yama, the lord of death, yet the people who stay here think they are going to live forever.'

We always think that it is someone else who will die, not us. Death is truly the mystery of all mysteries.

There are only two things that are certain about death. One is that we will die at some point in time. The other is that it is uncertain when or how we will die.

Everything that is born has to die. That is the nature of life.

A beautiful story from the life of Buddha:

Once a woman came with her dead son to Buddha. She was mad with grief at the death of her only son. She cried to Buddha, 'Master, please give me some medicine that will get my boy back to life.'

Buddha replied, 'Get me a handful of mustard seed.' The woman got up immediately and rushed to get a handful of mustard seed. Then Buddha added, 'The mustard seed must be from a house where no one has lost a dear one – child, husband, parent, friend.'

The woman went from house to house. Out of pity for the desperately crying woman, people gave her mustard seed from their house. But when she asked whether they had lost a dear one, they had someone or the other who had died in the house.

She went from house to house till sunset but found no house where a death had not happened. Slowly the truth started dawning on her – death is inevitable. She buried her son's body and returned to Buddha. She fell at the feet of Buddha and asked him, 'Master, please teach me the truth. What is death? What exists beyond death?'

She became Buddha's disciple and followed Buddha for the rest of her life.

Mahabharata - The Hindu *itihasa* or epic whose central characters are the five Pandava princes, their hundred Kaurava cousins and enlightened master Krishna.

Yudhishtra - The eldest of the five princes of the Pandava family in the Indian epic Mahabharata.

There is a beautiful saying, 'Tomorrow or the next life, which comes first, we never know.'

The topic of rebirth is not popular because it cannot be proven by science. Of course, now Near Death Experience (NDE) has become a hot subject as many doctors and psychologists have recorded their experiences. There are many people who have recorded thousands of NDEs, almost all of which fall into a similar pattern. They all relive the events of their lives. Hypnotists have regressed people into their past lives. These too fall into a pattern. They are similar to what the *rishis** said over 5000 years ago about what happens when you die, which is recorded in the Kathopanishad.

Death in my presence - before enlightenment

This incident is from the days of my spiritual journey before enlightenment.

I was near a small village in North India called Ghaziabad, a place near Varanasi, the spiritual headquarters of Hindus*. Hindus traditionally visit Varanasi at least once in their lifetime. The city has a floating population of at least two hundred thousand people every day.

I was there with an old monk who had been hospitalized and was in the Intensive Care Unit (ICU). According to the *vedic*

tradition, young monks take care of the elderly monks and *sannyasis**. As a young monk staying in that village, I started taking care of the elderly monk.

One day, while I was attending to him, suddenly it became obvious that the man in the bed next to his was about to die. He started struggling for life. I was able to see very clearly what was happening inside him. By that time I had had my deep spiritual experience or *satori* but I had not become fully enlightened; the realization of the purpose of my life had not happened. I was still seeking and my body was getting prepared for the explosion of energy that was to happen after enlightenment.

Several doctors were trying to give him critical medical care and support. The man was gasping for breath. I could see very clearly how death was happening in him. I could see very clearly how the life source was moving away from the body.

That is the strongest experience that has happened in my life outside my body. Inside my body, the strongest experience that happened was realizing the mission!

I was able to see what was happening, but I was not able to bear it. An important thing you should know is, if you see somebody in physical pain, it will affect you only about thirty to forty percent. But if you see somebody in depression and you can relate to the person and feel the depression, it will

Rishis - Vedic sages

Hindus - Followers of Hindu religion, estimated at over a billion people.

Sannyasi - One who has renounced, a monk.

affect you more - say around sixty percent. Further, if it is emotional pain and if you are able to connect and understand the pain, it will affect you much more - about eighty percent. The more subtle the pain, the more you will be affected.

I saw not only the physical, mental or emotional pains of the dying man, but I also saw the being level pain. It was almost like I was going through the pain myself. I wanted to just run away from there but the elderly monk got afraid and just held my hand begging me to stay. I had been taking care of him for two to three months, so he had got really attached to me.

Since a young age, I have loved serving monks. I used to take food and clothes from my house and give it away to the monks! Serving monks has always been my passion. I have always felt that this whole *vedic* tradition is alive even today only because of such monks. They have kept this science alive.

For doing research in any science, you need great support in many areas. For example, in the West, a lot of research happens in the outer world science because there are people and organizations to support it. If it is research on medicines, a pharmaceutical company may support the research. If it is some research related to space and astronomy, the government may sponsor and support it.

In the same way, in India, the whole country supports and sponsors spiritual science research. The whole country has taken up the responsibility to support an inner world scientist by providing him food, shelter and clothes so that he can continue his research in the inner world without spending time for basic outer world requirements. So I have always felt that it is my responsibility to take care of the monks and inner world scientists.

The elderly monk who I was taking care of in the ICU did not want me to leave because he was afraid seeing the man next to him dying. The man was going through such a hard time. It was like the whole six feet of his body was being torn apart! Imagine the pain if you have a small cut in your finger. Now imagine how painful it would be if the skin on your whole body is literally being peeled. It is something like a thousand scorpions stinging at the same time! I could clearly see the pain the man was going through.

On one side, the individual soul associated with all the unfulfilled emotions like desire, greed and guilt was undergoing terrible suffering. The individual soul wanted to stay in the body and fulfill these, but the body was tired and wanted to relax! It was a fight between the body and individual soul. It was as if the body wanted to leave but the individual soul was trying to hold onto it. If the right hand was gone, the soul was trying to hold onto the left. If the right leg was dead and gone, the individual soul was trying to hold onto the left leg. Whichever part of the body it could hold on to, the individual soul was trying to hold onto it.

Part by part the body was dying. I saw that with the lower body there was not much struggle. But when it came to the upper body, the whole body was vibrating and pulsating with pain.

Slowly the individual soul started moving out of the physical body. Understand, when the breathing stops, that is the moment when the individual soul actually leaves the physical body. There are seven layers or bodies in you. The body of flesh, bones and blood that you see is the physical body. The energy moving in you as *prana** or life energy is the *pranic** body. There are five kinds of *prana** or air movements that happen in the body: air that enters into the body, air that circulates inside the body, air that spreads all over the body as life force, air that comes out of the body, and air that cleanses. These form the second body or the *pranic** body.

The third body is the body where inner chatter continuously happens. Inner chatter is nothing but the continuous stream of words or thoughts that move within you.

The fourth body is made up of emotions like fear, anger and greed which spread as feelings all over the body without even words coming into play. An emotion by itself can simply shake you. This is the emotional layer.

The fifth layer is the body that you experience in deep sleep. This is where all the engraved memories or engrams are stored in the seed or causal level. The engrams are not active but they are not dead either. It is like a deep coma where you are neither living what you want nor are you dead. You are just stuck in this layer.

From the causal body, the individual soul moves to the cosmic body. The sixth layer is the cosmic body where you experience bliss. This is what continuously inspires you to be a seeker. If you are a seeker, understand that this layer is strong in you. If you enrich this layer, your life will be blissful. If you have any engram remaining in this layer, you will assume another body and come back.

If you continuously enjoy pleasurable experiences, then you are said to be in heaven. If you are stuck in pain, then you are said to be in hell. Depending on how much pain you experienced in life, you will stay that long in the pain body or hell at the time of death. Depending on how much pleasure you experienced in life, you will stay that long in the cosmic body or heaven. Hell and heaven are purely psychological. This is the truth. Based on what engrams you have, you experience heaven and hell. That is why different cultures visualize heaven in their own way - because heaven is not a place, it is an experience.

The seventh layer is the *nirvanic** layer which corresponds to enlightenment.

At the time of death, there is a powerful fight between the owner or the individual soul and the object or the body. The object says, 'I am tired, I can't function any more.' The owner says, 'No, I want to use you.'

Prana - Life energy or life force.

Pranic- Related to *prana* or life energy.

Nirvanic - Connected to *nirvana*. The *nirvanic* layer is the seventh and final energy layer in our body mind.

When the object wins, the physical body dies and the individual soul moves to the next layer, the *pranic* body. This is the layer you are in when you normally dream. While dreaming, your logic loses its power over you but your desires remain active. The very definition of dream is the state where logic has no power but desires and engrams remain active. Even when you are unconscious or in coma, your logic will not be active.

As long as you are in the physical body, you will have desires with the logic to analyze whether the desires are needed or not and which one of the desires should be fulfilled etc. Desires are under your control; there is a balancing mechanism. But when the desires exist without the supporting logic, the individual soul will be kicked around like a football by the desires. On one side there will be guilt and on the other side, desires that play on the individual soul.

When I saw the man dying, I could see that the individual soul was slowly moving out layer by layer. I could see the soul suffering intensely when it went through the unfulfilled desires. The soul was literally being eaten by guilt when it realized, 'I did not fulfill the purpose and mission of my life.' Understand, you will remember the purpose of your birth only during death.

When you are born, your body travels through the birth canal of the mother, and because of the intense pain that you go through, you go into coma or the deepest unconscious state, and you forget the whole purpose of taking birth. It is like this: you booked the flight ticket and sat inside the aircraft also, but during the flight you were put in coma and so when you landed, you forgot all about why you came to that particular place! Only when you leave the place and board the flight again, you suddenly remember why you had come to that place!

In the same way, when you die, you feel the strong guilt of not fulfilling the purpose of your birth or what we call the *prarabdha karma*.

After passing through this guilt, next, all the pain experiences of your life will come up. So at the time of death, you first pass through physical pain, then through all desires, next through all guilt, then through all emotional pain and finally through all the pleasures that you experienced in this birth.

Normally, as soon as you reach the cosmic body or the sixth layer itself, you return to assume the next body, the next birth. That is, the individual soul returns to assume the next body. Sometimes, rarely, you go beyond the sixth layer into the *nirvanic** body. Then you don't come back to assume another body.

When you travel through these various bodies and experience your unfulfilled desires, deep guilt and intense pain, you decide strongly, 'Let me take another body, another birth. When I do, I will not forget the purpose of my life and get caught in these illusive games. I will straightaway follow the path of Truth.' But when you actually take

---

Nirvanic - Connected to *nirvana*. The *nirvanic* layer is the seventh and final energy layer in our body mind.

birth the next time, again because of the intense pain during birth, you drop into coma and forget all about your decision!

Finally, the man died. But the experience left a strong scar in me. It left a very strong impression in my mind. The fortunate thing was that the elderly monk became alright and he was discharged from the hospital. I continued my journey, and after a few months, I had my own death experience and I became enlightened, thus realizing the mission and purpose of my life. My life as a liberated being started at the age of twelve itself when I had my deep spiritual experience. But the clarity about the mission, and what was exactly going to happen through my body, dawned when I became enlightened.

Death in my presence - after enlightenment

After my enlightenment, I came back to South India. I was in Bangalore in a devotee's house, healing people who sought me out. At that time, a devotee was admitted in the ICU and I was requested to heal him.

There again, while healing, the person in the bed next to the devotee started dying! The moment I saw that the person was about to die, the first thing I felt like doing was to move away from the suffering that was about to come! But the devotee was afraid and not ready to leave me!

Suddenly I saw that this person who was dying, was not going through any suffering like

the earlier person. I was shocked, and I became very curious. Earlier, the movement of the individual soul from layer to layer was great suffering and torture for it. But this soul was moving so smoothly from layer to layer just like how a knife moves through butter, or a snowball rolls down!

In the first layer or physical body, there was a little pain. Then suddenly the pain disappeared and the individual soul moved to the *pranic* layer. It moved from layer to layer like a royal guest! It was so empowered, that the desires, guilt and pain were not able to attack it at all. Even in the causal layer, it did not fall asleep. It was so energetic, and it finally entered the *nirvanic* layer, relaxed and just disappeared!

I thought that this person must be an evolved being. I asked his relatives whether he was a spiritual person or a meditator. The family was surprised and replied that the man had never meditated or done any spiritual practice in all his life! He had lived a completely materialistic life.

I contemplated as to why the first death I had witnessed was terrible while the second one was so wonderful. What I am about to tell you now is the honest and straight truth, and I am saying it because I have the great responsibility of telling it to you. When I meditated to know the difference between the two deaths, the revelation happened: at the time of the second death I was an enlightened person. The second person had died in the presence of an enlightened being! In the case of the first death, my presence could not help, because I could not radiate the energy of enlightenment at that time. So the first person died an ordinary death, while the second person died a wonderful death in the presence of an enlightened being who had realized the Truth.

When this revelation happened, I saw a deep compassion coming out of my being. I felt that if at all I can give this as a gift to every individual, my mission will be accomplished. A peaceful death is such a powerful and wonderful gift which nobody but an enlightened being can give. I started meditating as to how I can give this gift to everyone. Obviously I can't be in the ICU of all the hospitals and wait for people to die! I contemplated on the science behind the whole thing, and understood what really happens at the time of death.

Let me explain:

As long as you hold onto your ordinary logic and remain in the physical layer, the master is just a simple faith for you. The material world appears more solid and real. But when you travel to the deeper layers, the master becomes reality while the material world becomes vague and blurred.

It is like how during your night dream, the dream world looks real and the waking world looks vague, whereas when you are awake, that is when you are with a higher consciousness, the dream world becomes imagination while the waking world becomes reality. In the dream state, the dream world that you see appears alive, like a 4D colour film! When you come out of the dream, the whole dream appears black and white.

In the same way, if you are raised to a still higher consciousness, this waking world will become dull, while things like spiritual truths and the master will become alive and real! When you disconnect from the body and rise into higher consciousness, the master and the superconscious energy will become a gross reality.

When the second death happened, the intense enlightened presence straightaway caused him to connect strongly to it.

Understand, as you sit now and here, what is stopping you from connecting with the enlightened energy of the master and merging with it? Only your own logic and reasons.

As you sit here, there are still doubts in your unconscious like, 'If I drop my possessions and surrender, the master may take it away!' The other problem is, presently, as of now all other things in this world also appear as reality, and you think the master is also real to that same depth.

You experience me as the same frequency as the rest of the material world. In the case of the second dying person, all his outer world things became inaccessible to him at the time of death. He could not sign his checkbook or drive his car! Whatever was holding him back in the material world was automatically being taken away from him. When he looked around, only I, the enlightened energy was there! He saw the strong light energy and just held on to me! The surrender automatically happened to him because I was there at that moment. Even in his case, if he had seen me while he was alive, he may have struggled to surrender and connect to me! Only when everything was taken away from him, there was nothing to hold him back from connecting to me.

There is a beautiful story in the *Bhagavatam** which is a beautiful account of the enlightened master Krishna's life:

There was once a rich devotee. He asked Krishna, 'I want more wealth and possessions.' Krishna granted him his wish. There was also a poor lady, who had a cow and a small house. Krishna once visited her house, ate the food she served, blessed her and left. That very same day, her cow died.

Somebody asked Krishna about the strange happening of how a rich person got more wealth while the poor lady was deprived of her only source of income!

Krishna beautifully explains, 'The king was already in heavy illusion of the material world. So I gave him what he wanted so that he will ultimately get tired of material things and turn towards enlightenment. In the case of the poor lady, there was only one thing that she really wanted, and that was to connect to Me. And the only thing that was stopping her from that was the cow. I took away the cow so that she could completely merge into Me!'

In the same way, in the case of the second death, the 'cow' was taken away. In the physical layer, the man was not able to connect. But in the *pranic* layer, the consciousness entered a different space, and the man was able to clearly see me there. The master's presence is such an intense light. It is much stronger and of a higher frequency than this world, just like how this world is of a higher frequency than your dream world.

The man realized that there is something of a higher frequency and he completely surrendered to it. When he surrendered, all his other engraved memories lost their power over him. The individual consciousness became empowered. Desires, guilt, pain, pleasure, everything bowed down. Straightaway, the individual soul's frequency increased.

Understand, when the seer is strong, the seen has no power over you. This is the science of death.

In the case of the first death, the seen was stronger than the seer. In the second death, the seer was stronger than the seen.

I intensely meditated how to transmit this science to people. Suddenly, a revelation happened to me.

Understand, energy is not constrained by space and time. It is just like the satellite waves that are present in space. If you have a set-top box converter, you can see the channel that you tune into. An enlightened master's energy pervades the whole cosmos. I just need to place the set-top box in people. It is like a pacemaker, just that this is a *peacemaker*! Once it is placed, the person can connect to it while leaving the body.

Bhagavatam - The foremost epic of Hindu religion describing the incarnations of Vishnu, especially his incarnation as Krishna. It was written by Vyasa, who was also the author of the *itihasa* or epic Mahabharata.

Whatever you think in your last moment - you become *that*!

A master is a person who creates a formula to reproduce his inner world spiritual experiences in the inner world of others. Such a formula is the Life Bliss Program Level 2 also called the Nithyananda Spurana Program. It is a program that inserts the peacemaker in individuals.

Along with placing the peacemaker it is my promise that, wherever you may be, in whatever situation you may be at the time of death, I will be there and see that you beautifully relax into the *nirvanic* body. Please understand, I am responsible for what I am talking here right now. Even if I leave the body, I am responsible, because it is a promise; it is my commitment to whoever hears these words directly from me.

When I started sharing this technology, I realized that the people I shared it with, not only experienced peace at the end of their lifetime, but their life itself became intense, joyful and ecstatic once I shared it with them.

Understand, both life and death become blissful when deeply engraved memories are removed from your being. Your health becomes better, you start attracting wealth and better relationships because the frequency of being itself is different.

You will be relaxed in the *nirvanic* body when this peacemaker is placed inside you. You then have the freedom: to take one more birth as a conscious being or get enlightened and never again assume a body.

What you remember in the last moment counts

There is a beautiful story in the *Upanishads*[*], the sacred Vedic texts:

A rishi called Jadabharatha somehow became attached to a deer he had rescued. He was living the life of a renunciate but he got attached to this deer.

From morning till night, he used to spend his time taking care of that deer. When he was dying, he was not able to forget the animal. He started worrying about the deer, 'Oh! Who will take care of the deer? What will happen to it after my death?'

When he died, in the next birth, he was born as a deer.

Beautifully the verse in the Upanishad says that whatever you think in your last moment - you become *that*!

Some people think very cleverly, 'Let me live my whole life the way I want to live. In the last few moments, I will remember god and chant His name and enter heaven somehow.' Please be very clear, only that which you thought of in your whole life, will come up when you leave the body. Don't think that at that last moment you can play the game! No!

Upanishad - Scriptures that form the essence of the ancient texts of the Vedas. Literally means 'sitting with the master'. There are eleven main Upanishads that have been commented on by enlightened master Adi Shankara.

Actually, when you leave the body your whole system will be in such agony, because 80 or 90 years of your life will be run through in a fast-forward mode. All that will be seen are the scenes being fast-forwarded. Whatever experience you had intensely, only that will come up before you. Your spiritual experiences will come up in multicolor.

Please understand that 'thoughtless awareness' is the strongest experience you can have in your life. Even for a single moment, if you had that experience, it is enough. Naturally, when you leave the body that will come up. That will act as a light and you will be able to move into the Consciousness.

My own death experience

Let me narrate to you my own conscious death experience in Varanasi.

I always used to think that I should have an experience of death, that I should face death directly. But somehow, that thought never became a priority. For any experience to happen, the related thought has to become the topmost priority. It should not just be in one corner of your mind.

Usually on our 'to do' lists, we have washing, cleaning, paying the rent and phone bill, and finally if time permits, enlightenment also! No! Enlightenment will not happen if it is this way. Only when it

becomes a top priority, only when the urge becomes urgent, everything around you will start aligning itself for the experience to happen in you. This is the case not just with enlightenment. With anything, it is true.

Understand, if at all you are complaining that what you wish to happen is not happening, it is because it has not become the topmost on your priority list, nothing else. Nothing else and no one else should be blamed for it. You will see that the moment it becomes the topmost priority, there will be an energy play that comes into being and it will simply happen. Until then, it will wait for you, that's all. The death experience was not my top priority and so somehow, it was getting postponed.

In my wandering days, I had been to Varanasi, the holy city for Hindus, which has an estimated 300,000 daily floating population. Further, every day around 100 dead bodies are estimated to be burnt in a place called Manikarnika Ghat on the banks of the sacred river Ganga*. It is traditionally believed that if somebody dies or somebody's body is burnt in that area, they will be liberated. They will have direct enlightenment.

It is not just a traditional belief. The enlightened master Ramakrishna Paramahamsa* confirms it with his own experience. He says, 'I saw very clearly Shiva* himself going near every burning body, taking the soul, unclutching it from the body-mind and liberating it!' So, you

---

Ganga - The most celebrated river in India, considered holy by all Hindus.

Ramakrishna Paramahamsa - Enlightened master from West Bengal in India. His chief disciple was Swami Vivekananda.

Shiva - Enlightened master from India. The word shiva literally means 'causeless auspiciousness'.

can't say that it is a mythological belief. It is a solid experience of an enlightened master.

I had the fortune of going to Manikarnika Ghat. Traditionally, it is not only believed, but it is true that for the last 2000 years, the fire that is used to light the pyres has never been put off.

Whether it rains or shines or floods, people never bring fire when they come with the dead body to Manikarnika Ghat. The fire will already be burning there and they will just take it to light the dead body, that's all. The fire just continuously burns the bodies as they arrive. Sometimes I would see that two to three bodies are burnt at the same time, so many bodies keep coming!

Especially in the evenings, the bodies will be more in number. From the place where the person dies they will walk carrying the dead body, chanting mantras* such as, 'Ram naam satya hai, Ram naam satya hai' (Lord Rama's name is the ultimate and eternal truth). By evening they will reach Manikarnika Ghat.

The scene there, the very experience of just being there, I cannot describe to you verbally. You have to be there to experience it!

To tell you honestly, by just being there, the fear of death just disappeared from my system. You see so many bodies continuously being burned every day. You feel, 'I am also going to go like this one day...all right', that's all! You feel there are so many people giving you company! It is like one more trip that you make, that's all. You don't feel lonely about death at all.

In your life, you may see one or two bodies being burnt, so you still have the fear of death. But at Manikarnika Ghat, there will be no ritual done. They will bring the body and straightaway dip it in the river Ganga* three times while chanting, 'Ram naam satya hai, Ram naam satya hai, Ram naam satya hai'. By this time, the fire will be ready, and the wood will be arranged. They will bring the body straight from the water and burn it, that's all!

One strange thing that you see there is that none of the relatives will stay there and do any further rituals. The moment they dip the body in the Ganga* and place the body for burning, they will go away, that's all! The people who maintain the ghat will take care of the rest. You will not know how long it will take for the body that you brought to be burnt completely. There will be a queue and bodies will be burning continuously.

I thought to myself, 'Let me try to sit here and see what goes on.' I sat at the Ghat. In just an hour's time, I felt that death is no more a strange incident which happens once in a while only for some relative or friend. I was sitting there watching bodies arriving one after another. It was like any other queue, that's all. Different sizes, genders, ages, and communities of people arrived to be consumed by the same burning flame.

When you continuously see dead bodies being burnt you actually lose respect for

---

Mantra - Literally means 'that which shows the way'. Sacred syllables that have a powerful positive vibrational effect.

Ganga - The most celebrated river in India, considered holy by all Hindus.

death! As of now, you have too much of respect, too many ideas about death. That is the problem. Death is actually nothing but this. The breath that goes inside the body doesn't come out, that's all. Nothing much can be done about it. Neither can you rewind it nor fast-forward it.

As I was watching this scene continuously, initially the little fear that I had about death also disappeared and slowly it actually became interesting to watch. I went near the people who maintain the fire and started helping them. As I was helping them, I was thinking to myself, 'After all, one day this body of mine is also going to become like this dead body that is burning now.'

When you remember that death is going to happen to you, the respect that you carry for your ego will come down. Because, whenever you think that something should not leave you, it is just the ego, nothing else. When you know for sure that everything is going to leave you, then the respect for the ego just drops drastically. The respect I had for my ego just dropped from me.

Then I decided, 'After all I am going to die. Either I should have a conscious death experience now itself and live the rest of my life without the death-fear, or really die, that's all.' I decided that I have to see death happening to me one way or the other.

There was a small Shiva* temple around the corner and a small tower above the temple. I went and sat in that tower so that nobody would disturb me. I sat in that tower and from there I started seeing the dead bodies being burnt.

Whenever the fear comes out and you are not consciously facing it, it becomes a fear stroke.

I still remember the strong click, the deep understanding and instant realization that triggered the whole experience that was to follow.

An elderly lady's body was being burnt. She had a big belly. Her clothes were being consumed by the fire and then the fat that was in the belly started melting and flowing. Sorry for describing this so vividly but I have to do it to explain the strong experience! I could see clearly that because of the fat flowing, the fire was burning with even more intensity. That gave a very strong click to me and I said, 'God! Yes, the very same thing is going to happen to this body also!'

That click opened up a deep fear of death inside me. The fear spread all over the body. But I faced the fear consciously. I could see very clearly the fear spreading all over the body, and when the fear hit my awareness, that became the experience of death. I went through a conscious experience of my own death and came out of it.

Understand, whenever your fear is suppressed, it stays inside you. Whenever the fear comes out and you are not consciously facing it, it becomes a fear stroke, and shakes your whole nervous system and breaks it down. When the fear is faced consciously, it becomes the death experience, that's all!

Shiva - Enlightened master from India. The word shiva literally means 'causeless auspiciousness'.

I was able to see very clearly the fear that arose. When I faced it consciously with awareness, it became my death experience. The body was dead. It was not moving.

For two and a half days I had no food, no water, no thought, no question, no doubt. The body alone was there. Only after the experience had passed, I realized that I had been like that for two and a half days! I could see with closed eyes that the body was dead and there was no movement. Suddenly, after two and a half days, the click happened again, 'God! The body is dead but I still exist! I am there!' That clarity, when it clicked, became such an intense ecstasy in me! The fear of death had left me once and for all.

I was in such deep ecstasy, such joy, and such bliss! I slowly opened my eyes and I was able to move the body. The first thing I felt was such a surge of ecstasy and gratitude. I went down to the Ganga, sprinkled a little Ganga water on myself, took the Ganga water in the kamandalu*, took a little ash from the fire, and went straight to the Kashi Vishwanath temple. I went up to the Shiva* linga*, offered the ash I had brought and did the puja (worship) with such inexpressible gratitude. I saw that Vishwanath was simply alive there!

Understand, because I died Vishwanath became alive! Until the day before that, because I was still alive, Vishwanath was always an ordinary stone. I used to feel that to touch this stone, thousands of people are coming everyday from so far away... what foolishness! I always felt that the Vishwanath deity was an ordinary stone. I felt that way because I was still alive. When I died, I saw clearly, He became alive!

Only one can be alive, either Him or you. When you see the Truth, He will become alive. You will not be alive anymore as you now think. The fear of death left me once and for all. I can say that this is one of the very strong experiences that transformed me to search for the ultimate experience of enlightenment.

What happens at the time of Death

Only an enlightened being, a person who has gone through death consciously and come back anew, can exactly explain what happens during death.

I am going to reveal the mystery of death now. This may be surprising, even shocking to many of you. But this is the truth. Whether you believe it or not, accept it or not, this is what happens at the time of death.

We do not just have one body. The physical body is just one of the seven bodies we have. It is only the gross body that can be felt and seen in space-time. However, we actually have seven layers or bodies or planes of existence. Since these layers have a subtle

---

Kamandalu - Water pot carried by Hindu monks.

Shiva - Enlightened master from India. The word shiva literally means 'causeless auspiciousness'.

Linga - Representation of enlightened master Shiva as a symbol of rejuvenation combining male and female principles.

existence they cannot be seen or felt by the ordinary eye.

A simple representation of the seven bodies is shown below.

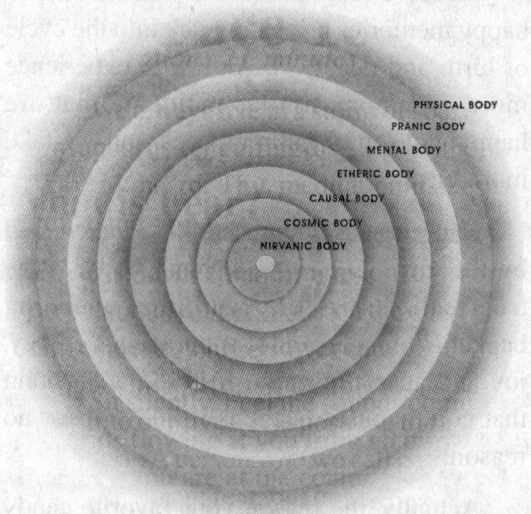

PHYSICAL BODY
PRANIC BODY
MENTAL BODY
ETHERIC BODY
CAUSAL BODY
COSMIC BODY
NIRVANIC BODY

Each of the bodies holds a corresponding emotion. For example, the *pranic* body holds all the desires that arise in life. The mental body holds all the feelings of guilt experienced in life. The etheric body holds the experiences of mental pain felt in life.

When the spirit leaves the body it crosses all the seven body layers. The physical body dies. But, the remaining six bodies do not totally die. If you are holding a lot of desires in your life, all those unfulfilled desires are held in the *pranic* body. So even though the physical body dies, the *pranic* body does not die. When the life force leaves the *pranic* body, the being experiences tremendous suffering.

When you leave the physical body, your consciousness will be torn from the body and you will immediately fall into coma. According to doctors, coma is the automatic mechanism to make you not to feel the pain. It is automatic anesthesia. If the pain becomes too much, you can't bear and you automatically fall into coma.

When you move from the first body layer to the second body layer, all the unfulfilled desires, all the ways in which you wanted to live but did not live come up. When this happens, it is almost as if ten people are standing in a room kicking a football around. What will happen? Just like how the football is kicked from corner to corner, your consciousness will be kicked from all corners. In each corner, some desire will be standing and kicking it. At the time your consciousness is trying to leave the body, all your desires will be forcing you to re-enter the body so that you can enjoy them further and fulfill them.

On one side, the desires will be forcing you to enter the body again so that you can live and enjoy, while on the other side, the body will say, 'No! I am tired. I can't host you anymore, just leave!' That is what causes the pulling and pushing at the time of death. The pulling and pushing is nothing but the fight between your desires and your body.

Somehow, you manage to move away from the *pranic* body, and enter next into the mental body. When you enter into the mental body all your guilt rises. All the guilt about the way you felt you should have lived your life but never lived, all the mistakes committed, all the regrets, everything comes up.

All the guilt that we collect over our lives rises as we pass through the mental body.

Please understand, desire is about the future and guilt is about the past. But actually, both are one and the same. The way in which we *want to live* is desire, and the way in which we *wanted to live but didn't*, is guilt. Guilt is nothing but reviewing our past decisions with updated intelligence. Like this, step by step, you move through different body layers.

The less the unfulfilled desires, the lighter is the *pranic* body and the easier it is to leave this body. Similarly, the less the guilt, the lighter is the mental body and the easier it is to leave this body.

One more thing, when the desires, guilt and pain are less intense, you not only have an easy death with less suffering but you also age gracefully. Ageing gracefully is what *vanaprastha sannyas** is all about. Being able to live in fulfillment in the latter part of life is the tremendous gift of *vanaprastha sannyas**.

All the guilt that we collect over our lives rises as we pass through the mental body. Then we come to the etheric body which is related to all our sufferings. All the suffering that we went through during our life is stored here.

The first four bodies are related to the physical body-mind system. They store all the engrams related to desires, guilt and pain experienced during that lifetime. The fifth body

is experienced during deep sleep and when leaving the body. The sixth body is associated with happy memories and the seventh body is beyond sorrows and happiness, the ultimate consciousness.

Please understand, even attachment to happy memories brings us back into the cycle of birth and death. The desire to experience more and more similar incidents that are happy and joyful pulls us back and we take more births.

Happiness is a temporary feeling created by the mind. Bliss, the seventh body, is the true reality. It is the causeless, unending happening inside you of spontaneous energy, joy and auspiciousness. It is like a fountain that continuously happens inside you for no reason.

Actually, the reason your favorite candy gives you happiness is that it acts as a trigger to put you into this space of bliss that is your true nature. But you mistake the happiness to be because of the candy, the external object. The happiness is because for those few moments, you come in touch with your inner bliss.

The cleaner the bodies, the lighter they are and the easier it is for the life force to leave the body. Just like its peel comes off a ripe banana, the life force easily moves out of the body.

Vanaprastha sannyas - The third stage of life according to the *vedic* tradition, where the wife and husband lead the rest of their married life in spiritual activities in pursuit of the Ultimate Truth.

Death happens everyday

In the seven bodies, the first four bodies - physical, *pranic*, mental and etheric, collapse into the causal body every time you go to sleep. The darkness of the causal body is associated with the deep sleep state, which is what rejuvenates you every day. So till you cross the fifth body, this 'death' happens every day. This is what happens when you fall into your daily sleep.

When the departing spirit moves beyond the fifth layer of causal body into the sixth layer, which is the cosmic body, the process of death is complete.

If the life force does not have to take another body to fulfill its remaining desires it then enters the seventh layer of *nirvanic* body, which is enlightenment. If the life force has to come back assuming another body to fulfill its desires, it is death.

Waking world Vs Dream world

One more thing: when you enter into the dream state and start dreaming, this whole world in which you live now becomes black and white because you are in the dream world. You forget this whole world of your waking state and the dream world becomes very real and seen in multicolor. If you come out of the dream, this whole world that you wake up to is again seen in four dimensions, 4D.

Now when you are in this physical body and in the waking state, you experience this world as 4D, in multi-color. When you are in the dream world, you experience that world as 4D. So, when you are here, the dream world becomes black and white, and this world becomes 4D, and when you are there, the dream becomes 4D, and this world becomes black and white.

In the same way, when you move away from the physical body to the *pranic* body at the time of death, this whole physical world will become unreal and be seen in black and white. All your achievements, your pride, your efforts, your sorrow, your happiness, everything will no longer have any meaning and will appear in black and white. You will wonder, 'Why did I do all this work? Why did I think of all this as a base for my life?'

Let me explain why this happens. When you are alive you invest in your personality. You build up your personality based upon a few pillars - money, name and fame, relationships, pride that you have a big community, support circle, and so on.

When you move from the physical body, all these pillars, all these foundations will be completely shaken. You can't sign your name on your checks any more. Your signature is not accepted. Your bank balance is no more related to you. You can't handle your bank account. Your car will not be useful to you. At the most, only the ambulance will be useful!

Only the conscious glimpse can come with you. Whatever has been the foundation for your being will be shaken. When the foundation is shaken, naturally you won't have anything to hold on to.

As of now, this whole world will appear in 4D. All this talk about spirituality, meditation, growing the inner being, consciousness etc. will appear as black and white. That is why, when I call people for meditation, they tell me, 'I don't have time to meditate. Let me finish all my work and then come. I have a few more years to think about it.'

Be very clear, never say, 'I don't have time to meditate.' Be very clear to yourself and say, 'I don't feel that it is that important in my life right now.' If you are not ready to meditate and say, 'I don't think meditation is so important in my life,' then you are honest. But if you say, 'I don't have time,' then you are just fooling yourself. Everyone has got the same 24 hours on hand to do what they feel they should. It is not that the few who are meditating are jobless. It is just a question of priority, of *what* you really want in your life. If spirituality and meditation appear as black and white to you now, you will not divert your energy in that area, that's all.

You see, now we are in two dimensions, the material world and spirituality. Right now, what is happening is that however many pillars we build our personalities and life upon, all those pillars are based on the material world which appears to be 4D. Not a single pillar is based on consciousness or our inner space. Our whole personality is built only based on the outer space - our name and fame, what society speaks about us, etc. If everyone's opinion of us is that we are great, we think we are great. If everybody says, 'You are useless', we start getting depressed.

This happens because not even a single pillar of our building, our inner core or our being, is based on spirituality. The entire structure is based on the outer space. That is the reason that when those pillars are shaken by anybody, we start suffering terribly. If we have even one pillar based on consciousness, we can depend on that to stand straight without suffering. If we build at least one pillar based on our inner space, this pillar will shine in 4D at the time of death and help us leave the body beautifully.

The art of dying

There is a beautiful Zen saying, 'Learning the art of dying is the real and the ultimate knowledge that we can learn in our life.'

A small Zen story:

One day, an enlightened master suddenly declared that he was going to die the next day morning around 6 o'clock. Of course, enlightened people always know about their death. They can declare before hand when they are going to die. He declared that he was going to die around 6 o'clock in the morning.

His disciples said, 'No, no, please wait for 2-3 hours. It will be too cold early in the morning. Why don't you wait for a few hours so that we can prepare for the last rites?' The master agreed and told the disciples that he would pass away around 12 o'clock. Exactly at 12 noon, he greeted them all and left the body!

Auspicious death

A true story:

The great master from India, Paramahamsa Yogananda*, had moved to USA in 1920 and settled there. How he left the body is very interesting. Till the last moment he was doing his routine of giving discourses and attending programs.

On the day of his passing away, he was attending a banquet in honor of the then visiting Indian Ambassador to USA, Binay Ranjan Sen, in Los Angeles. At the conclusion of his speech, he just relaxed from his body and died.

His body did not deteriorate for more than twenty days. No odor of decay came from his dead body at any time. There is a beautiful write-up about his death in his autobiography as an appendix. It was such a beautiful experience. Even his death was auspicious for him.

Reality is a dream

You are not the eyes. The eyes are just an instrument. Many times you can see, your eyes may be open but you are not seeing, not registering the scene you are seeing.

Just remember you are seeing *through* the eyes. If you look through the eyes, suddenly you will see you are witnessing everything. You are not the two 'holes' called the eyes.

You are only seeing through the two holes called eyes.

If you feel you are the two eyes, you are caught in ego. In your dream, as long as the attention is on the objects, you will continue to dream. When your attention is turned towards yourself – that is from the seen to the seer, you will be awakened.

The moment you realize you are something beyond the eyes, your attention is turned to the seer. Then you realize that this world is made of the same stuff of which your dream is made.

As long as you think you are seeing, the whole attention is on the seen. That is what I call ego. When you step back and realize you are seeing through the eyes, the whole attention is on the seer. That is what I call innocence. Innocence means having a clear understanding that whatever you see in the outer world is made of the same stuff out of which your dreams are made.

These are the steps: the first is getting the idea that what you see is a dream. The next is having the *shakti*, the energy, to change the dream. The third is the *buddhi*, the intelligence to know it is a dream and so there is no need to change it!

Paramahamsa Yogananda - An enlightened master well known for his book 'Autobiography of a Yogi'. He founded Self Realization Fellowship movement in USA in 1920.

Life and death vs Waking and sleep

Air and *prana*

To understand this powerful, life-transforming truth, we need to understand about this stuff of which the dream world and this world are made of. We need to know about *prana**, the life energy that sustains us.

Understand, the air you breathe is just a vehicle in which the *prana* comes in and goes out. *Prana* is the life force, the energy itself. Understand this one example. If a truck comes inside this campus and leaves something and goes out, the truck is like the air, the breath. The product that is delivered is *prana*.

Life or death depends on the direction of *prana*

One more thing: as long as the incoming breath is bringing in more *prana* and going out as an empty vehicle, your life will be strengthened.

If the reverse starts happening, if the air comes with less *prana* and goes out with more *prana*, it means death is nearing or the life energy is going towards death. When death nears, just the empty air will enter but when it goes out, it will go with the *prana*.

There is a beautiful concept in *Ayurveda** called as the 'peak age' which is based on this science of *prana*. Till a particular age, the person will be receiving more *prana* through the incoming breath and less *prana* will be going out through the outgoing breath. The moment the outgoing breath starts carrying more *prana* than the incoming breath, they know now the person is moving towards death.

Controlling life through awareness

Constantly, life is slipping and entering into death. Life slipping into death is what we usually call living. Please understand, actually we don't live. We are just waiting for death to happen. Ordinary human beings don't live. Life just slips into death, disappears into death. That is the reason however many years you may live, you don't feel satisfied, and you don't feel you have lived your life because you don't even know what life is.

When you become conscious of life, when you start thinking, contemplating about your life, when you bring awareness into your life, you create a new center in your being. Between this life and death, when you bring more awareness into the life, you create a new center, a new space in your life - that is what I call consciousness.

Prana - Life energy or life force.

Ayurveda - Traditional Indian system of medicine, Ayurveda literally means knowledge of life.

Whenever you are conscious, you will start deciding about your life. For example, the more you become aware, the more you start designing or choosing what type of car you should drive, what type of house you should live in, and what type of life you want. You start deciding every inch. You become conscious about everything: how you should talk, how you should behave, how you should think, every inch you start becoming aware.

The moment you start becoming aware, you start deciding, and you start controlling your life. When you become completely aware you will start controlling your death also.

These two events of life and death then happen at the conscious level. If you are consciously thinking, it is life. If your consciousness can't think, it is death.

Awareness - control dreams and deep sleep, life and death

In the unconscious level, two things happen as well, dream and deep sleep. In the unconscious level, if you are aware, it is dream. If you are able to see anything, if you are able to sense anything, if you are able to feel anything, if you are able to experience any movement, then it is called dream. If you are not aware of anything, if you are not able to feel anything, if you are not able to understand any movement, it is deep sleep.

In the waking state, when you are aware or you are in what psychology calls as conscious state, it is life. If you are not aware, it is death. When you bring more awareness into your life, you take charge of your life. In the same way, in the dream, if you start bringing in more awareness, you will take charge of your dreams and deep sleep.

> **The moment you start becoming aware, you start controlling your life and death also.**

Controlling life and death and controlling dream and deep sleep both require one important condition: awareness. Awareness is the main requirement to control life and death and to control dream and deep sleep.

Bringing awareness into your dreams can not only help you control the dream and deep sleep, it can also help you control life and death.

Prana movement in sleep and death

The moment you start moving towards the dream state, the *prana* starts coming towards the *vishuddhi**, throat center. The more you move towards the deep sleep state, it moves towards the *anahata**, heart center.

It is the same in the case of life and death as well. The more you are alive and energetic, the more the *prana* accumulates and gets centered in the forehead.

Vishuddhi chakra - *Chakra* or subtle energy center in the throat region. Locked by comparing ourselves with others.

Anahata chakra - Subtle energy center in the heart region related to love.

173

Dream and sleep, life and death can all be handled by this single key, single thread called *prana*.

When the incoming breath is bringing more *prana* and the outgoing breath is going empty, your *prana* will be centered on the forehead. If the incoming breath is getting less *prana* and the outgoing breath is taking more *prana*, slowly the *prana* will slip into *vishuddhi**, throat center. If the incoming breath is not bringing *prana* at all and only the outgoing breath is taking the *prana*, you will fall completely into the heart center.

Actually, falling from life to death, falling from the waking state to the deep sleep state, are both directly related to *prana* movement. If the *prana* movements of inhalation and exhalation are handled properly, you can handle life and death as well as dream and deep sleep. Dream and sleep, life and death can all be handled by this single key, single thread called *prana*.

Stopping the cycle of life and death

If you can be aware when you fall into the dream state, when your consciousness is slowly fading away, when you are falling asleep, you will be able to change the dream itself.

If you are able to change the dream, let you be very clear, the first thing you will do is you will stop dreaming. You will stop dreaming because you know the uselessness of dreams. You know you are wasting time and energy in dreams. Person who is aware of dreams will never dream. He will simply stop dreaming. Person who is aware of life will simply stop the cycle of birth and death. He will not take one more body.

You need to understand this: when I use the word death, I don't mean you will commit suicide. When I say that when you become aware of life you enter into death, it does not mean that you will commit suicide. You will stop living in the normal way. You will stop living with identity. You won't give importance to identity. You will be reborn.

If you can be aware when the *prana* falls into the heart center every day, you can stop, alter and manage your dreams and deep sleep. If you are aware of *prana* slipping from *ajna* to *anahata** each time you go to sleep, it means that at the end of the life you will be able to change your life and death. If you want, you can bring it a little early. If you want, you can postpone. You can play in whatever way you want.

Meditation technique

This technique has two parts: one that you do when you fall asleep, when you are lying

---

Vishuddhi chakra - Chakra or subtle energy center in the throat region. Locked by comparing ourselves with others.
Anahata chakra - Subtle energy center in the heart region related to love.

in the bed and the second one that you do whenever you can remember during the whole day.

The first one will create more energy to do the second part and vice versa. They are complementary to each other.

First part: when you lie down, before falling asleep, just remember the area near the *ajna chakra** or the third eye, the center of the forehead. Do not concentrate. If you force yourself, if you start concentrating, your sleep will be disturbed and you will have a headache. Just remember that area in a relaxed way, the way you look at a flower, just casually. Slowly, you will see that you are relaxing, you are slowly dropping into the deep sleep state.

Just be aware of this movement into deep sleep, that is enough. First day, you may feel that you are not falling asleep at all and that your sleep is getting delayed by ten or fifteen minutes. Don't bother about it. Just be aware of the *prana* movement in the *ajna chakra**.

You will be aware that you are dreaming. If you want to continue the dream, you will continue. If you don't feel like it, you will come out. There will be no intensity to the dream.

The next step, you will start having the dreamless sleep. That is the deeper level. Once you start having the dreamless sleep you will also start having the dreamless day.

Dreamless day means that your energy will be conserved without day-dreaming.

If you are aware of the *prana*, that is enough. It will automatically come back to the higher energy, and your body will heal itself as the flow of *prana* is directly related to all your diseases. Above all, when you are able to change your dream, when you are able to handle your dream, you will have the intense power and energy to handle the incidents of your life.

Life Bliss Program Level 2 – Nithyananda Spurana Program (LBP Level 2 - NSP)

Our second level meditation program, LBP Level 2-NSP journeys you through your own life, simultaneously revealing the secrets of death. It makes your inner space pure and clean by unloading the baggage of emotions that you usually carry with you. It teaches you to live blissfully and leave peacefully. It puts death in the right perspective so that your life becomes more joyful and meaningful.

It is opening up your energy layers one by one. Your pains, pleasures, guilt and desires are opened up. Once these open up and get healed, you experience a glimpse of god within you.

Ajna chakra - The sixth energy center located between the eyebrows. Means 'command' or 'will' in Sanskrit. This *chakra* is blocked by one's own ego.

You are Intelligence

To be free from the fear of death, which is really the fear of losing our identity, we need to be aware that we are something more than this body and mind. We need intelligence to understand this. We then come to these questions:

What exactly is intelligence?

Are some of us more intelligent than others?

Can we increase the level of our intelligence?

Natural intelligence

Intelligence is not something to attain; every single being is endowed with intelligence. Every one of us has intelligence. It is an inherent, inborn quality of life just as fire is hot and ice is cold.

I am reminded of a joke on 'intelligent' people:

Once there were four men travelling in a private airplane. Suddenly, there was an emergency as the tail of the aircraft caught fire. Unfortunately for the four passengers, there were only three parachutes available.

The first person in a panic took a parachute saying, 'I just got married. My wife is waiting for me.' And he jumped.

The second person declared, 'I am the most intelligent person on earth. Planet earth needs my intelligence.' He jumped as well.

One of the passengers was an old man; he told the other remaining person, 'I am old already but you have your whole life ahead of you. You take this parachute and jump.'

The young man quipped, 'You can also come, Sir. We can both go. The most intelligent person on planet earth just jumped off with my back-pack!'

Most of us have lost touch with our natural intelligence; that is why we are not able to live life to its fullest potential. We mistake our acquired knowledge for intelligence; we are like the man who jumped with the backpack as a parachute!

Every single being in nature has been endowed with inherent intelligence. Birds have a natural intelligence that enables them

Allow your complete being to simply express itself. This is what I call being integrated and fulfilled.

to fly. It is amazing to see the migratory birds travel thousands of miles in the sky - with no map or guide and retrace their paths back when the season changes!

Patanjali, an enlightened master from India and father of the ancient science of *yoga**, says that man has in him the intelligence of all the lower forms of consciousness such as the trees, birds and animals.

Man has the capacity to produce food just like trees. He has the capacity to live by himself right from the time he is born - just like animals and birds. By nature we have all the intelligence in our human body. The difficulty is we strongly believe we are limited. We have been conditioned to think that we have only limited capabilities, that 'we cannot...' so we have forgotten how to use these capabilities. And because of this, we are not tuned to the technique to tap into all the dimensions of our being.

Children are born intelligent

A small story:

One boy came back from school and told his mother, 'You said the school dentist would be painless but he was not!' His

mother became worried and asked him, 'Did he hurt you?'

The boy replied, 'No, but he screamed when I bit his finger!'

Children are born intelligent. They are so spontaneous and enthusiastic. But the family, society and conventional school destroy the natural intelligence within the child with the undue importance they pay to logic, memory and competition. The price the child pays for education is too heavy as he sacrifices his priceless creativity and uniqueness and he is not even aware of it.

The other day, I read a statement on a teenager's T-shirt, 'I was intelligent until education ruined me.'

Allow your complete being to simply express itself - and you will see your natural intelligence flowering beautifully. This is what I call being integrated and fulfilled.

The driving forces of fear and greed

We think we are very intelligent and so we try to mould our children to become intelligent like us. When we start this process, we first teach the child the logic of running in life driven by either fear or greed.

Either he has to do something to achieve more, or he has to do something to prevent what he doesn't want to happen. When you

---

Yoga - Literally means 'uniting' of body-mind-spirit.

want something to happen, it is greed. When you are afraid that something will happen, it is fear.

Either he has to study so he can get better grades and win admission in a good college - this is being driven by greed. Or he has to study so he is not left behind in his future professional life - this is being driven by fear.

The motivation for the child is greed or fear, never inner fulfillment. Naturally, the child gets into the rat race and just keeps running - with no time to even look whether he is running for what he really wants. He does not even know that he can enjoy the run! He has been taught that with any other diversion, precious time will be wasted in reaching the goal.

But how many people have felt fulfilled after reaching the 'goal'? When you reach the goal you have set, you realize the goalpost is no longer there. It has moved further and you want something else now!

Understand, if you are living your life based on just seeing what others are doing, you are just wasting your precious life. This is what they call 'herd mentality' – joining the rat race because everybody else is a part of it. You may even win the rat race but you are still a rat!

What is the measure of intelligence?

Can we measure intelligence? Is there a standard to measure intelligence?

Right from school, we use standard benchmarks to determine a person's so-called level of intelligence. In the grading system used from elementary school through college, we compare and grade all children for various skills and aptitudes.

We need to understand an important thing here: one kind of intelligence is needed to be a scientist and another kind of intelligence is needed to be a poet. To be an Olympic swimmer one needs yet another kind of intelligence! Intelligence is the ability to respond to a situation or challenge. Everyone is born intelligent; it is a question of just discovering each one's unique dimension of intelligence.

Spontaneity - straightforward intelligence

You have a natural, spontaneous intelligence inside you. You have tasted it as a child.

As a child, you looked at things in a very simple, straightforward way. That is why you were so spontaneous. What took away that spontaneity as you grew up? The societal conditioning that has been telling you right from when you were a child, 'You are not enough...' Because of this, you are constantly trying to become something else, prove something to others. By constantly thinking that you are not enough, you try to imitate others and waste the wonderful natural energy bubbling inside you.

> **The light of awareness is enough to remove the darkness created by years of living by habit.**

I read a funny one-liner on a company's notice board:

Death will be accepted as an excuse, but we would like two weeks' notice, as we feel it is your duty to teach someone your job prior to your death.

Note: this new benefit program began yesterday.

If you blindly imitate another person's performance or behavior instead of acting from your own inner spontaneity, your own intelligence, you will be cheating yourself out of wonderful possibilities.

Once there was a statistics student who, while driving, would always accelerate before coming to any junction, and then drive fast past the junction and slow down again once he passed the junction.

One day, he was travelling with his friend. They passed a junction in his usual way. The friend asked him in surprise, 'Why do you drive so fast across junctions when you are actually supposed to slow down?'

The statistics student replied, 'Well, statistically speaking, you are more likely to have an accident at a junction, so I just make sure I spend less time there!'

Knowledge is good only when applied intelligently. It is intelligence that gives the real result, not the knowledge itself. When knowledge is applied in the right place at the right time, it is intelligence. Spontaneity is when we easily express our knowledge in the right place at the right time; in other words, using our intelligence.

The key to awareness

A small story:

One boy was learning a lot of new things at school and home. One day, he told the teacher, 'Yesterday I killed three female and two male flies.' The curious teacher asked, 'How did you know which were males and which were females?'

The boy replied, 'Simple. Three of them were on the mirror and two were on the cigarette box!'

Intelligence is being aware and spontaneous. Understand an important thing: when you are deeply aware, you cannot make mistakes!

With awareness, you don't rely on what others have taught you. You don't rely on the past conditioning that has gone on inside you for many years. You act just out of the fresh intelligence that comes with awareness.

The light of awareness is enough to remove the darkness created by years of living by habit. The whole key lies in being aware so that your intelligence can function. Living every moment in total awareness is what meditation is all about.

Beyond rules to responsibility

A small story:

Once, a sergeant in his training session asked the recruits why walnut wood was used for making the rifle. The recruits thought hard and one of them answered, 'Because walnut is harder than other types of nuts.'

The sergeant brushed him off saying, 'Wrong!' Another recruit ventured, 'Because it is more durable.' The sergeant's voice boomed, 'Wrong!' A third person tried his luck, 'Because it is waterproof.'

The sergeant, tired of the answers by now, replied, 'You boys surely have a lot to learn. Simple reason: that is what is laid down in the rule book!'

In life, because it is easy to place responsibility on others, you blindly follow other people's directions instead of relying on your own intelligence.

Talking about responsibility, a small joke on how people understand responsibility:

Once, a convict was scolding his lawyer, 'You are a useless lawyer. You don't even understand your responsibility of when to raise an objection.'

The puzzled lawyer asked him, 'I don't understand. When do you think I should have raised an objection that I did not?'

The convict replied, 'When the opposing lawyer spoke, you objected. But, when the judge declared me guilty, you kept your big mouth shut. That was the time to do all the objecting!'

It is always easy to put the blame on the whole world for what happens in your life. But, if you just look a little deeper, you can see how you are completely responsible for what is happening in your life!

> **Usually, we only react like programmed machines; we do not respond to situations.**

Now and here

Being intelligent requires the effort to be yourself, which you are not used to. So you choose to react based on your past experiences.

Usually, we only react like programmed machines; we do not respond to situations. Someone insults you and you become angry even before becoming aware of what you are doing.

A beautiful story from the life of Buddha, an enlightened master from India:

Once a person insulted Buddha openly. His disciple Ananda said, 'I was getting so angry with the person. Why did you keep quiet? At least I would have given him a piece of my mind.'

Buddha calmly replied, 'You surprise me. What he was saying was completely irrelevant and you know that. Then why are you getting angry? You are punishing yourself. It is foolishness. When somebody else has made the mistake, why are you suffering for it?'

Moving with time, flowing with life, becoming a fluid process instead of being a solid ego is called intelligence.

Beyond the head is the gate to loving Intelligence

Once, a father and son checked into a cheap motel at night.

The father tucked in the son to sleep and switched off the light assuring the son, 'Don't be afraid, son. The angels are watching over you.'

'I know,' said the boy. 'Two of them just bit me!'

Operating with intelligence is the process of going back to the innocence you were born with. It is not a process of becoming. It is not attaining something new; it is discovering your very being. It is the true door to knowing you as you truly are.

When you are intellectual, you operate purely from the head, from logic.

A small story:

A man was working on his doctorate in philosophy. He was so involved in his studies and research, his wife thought he would forget her if he was not reminded of her once in a while. So one day, she casually mentioned to him, 'Honey, what is the one reason you love me so much?'

The man asked very seriously, 'When you say 'so much' are you referring to the depth, quality, quantity or mode of expression?'

When you are too caught in the head, you start thinking that your logic, your head, can understand the whole of life. You try to frame everything in this universe with your head.

Another small story:

Once, a student had freshly graduated in a course on plumbing. He went with his friends on a sight-seeing tour to Niagara Falls. He took a look at the huge Falls and said, 'I think I can fix it!'

Your knowledge gives you the false illusion of knowing everything that exists. It keeps you firmly rooted in the head.

When your intelligence awakens, you drop from the head to the heart, from logic to love. Then, you operate neither from pure intellect nor from pure sentimental love. You operate just from loving intelligence, and you automatically radiate compassion to all of those around you.

Understanding, not thinking

A small story:

Once, three wise men set out on a travel journey to the city with the hope that they would learn more about life. They entered a big city and were surprised to see a very tall building - a skyscraper - in the distance. They wondered what it might be.

They grouped and discussed what to do. They were afraid to go near and see for themselves, thinking it may have something dangerous in it. What if they did not know how to come out? So, they decided it was better to find out before they ventured inside.

They analyzed and came up with all the things it could possibly be, based on all their past experiences. Finally, they concluded it was something too big for human beings and it must belong to giants. So, it was not safe for them to be in this city of giants.

Very satisfied that they had gained this new knowledge, they picked up their bags and went back to their village!

So, you see there is not much you can understand from past knowledge. You cannot think about something in the mind and try to understand everything about it in that way. You need to see it, to experience it in order to fully understand.

One more thing: you can only think about what *you* have known, what *you* have experienced. Can you think about anything unknown? You may fantasize about what the unknown could be, but that is still based on what *you* have seen in the past.

With thinking, the energy of intelligence and truth is not there, so the answer will be based on your limited experience and it will always lead to further questions and doubts.

Not falling back on the answers rising from the past memory but functioning from your present consciousness is called understanding.

Mind – master or tool?

Thinking arises from the mind, which is actually one of the most marvelous mechanisms. But the problem arises when the mind becomes your master instead of a tool in your hands.

A small story:

There lived a king who had a very faithful servant. He was so loyal he had even risked his own life to save the life of the king on a couple of occasions.

On one such occasion, the king highly pleased with the servant asked him for anything he wanted. The servant humbly replied, 'I don't need anything, O King. You have given me everything I need.'

But the king insisted. Finally, the servant said, 'Ok. If you really want to give me something, please make me the king for one day.' The king was a bit uncomfortable but he had already promised and had to keep it up.

The morning of the day the servant became the king. He simply pointed to the king and ordered the royal guards, 'Kill him!' The king was shocked and asked the servant, 'Do you know what you are saying?' The servant calmly replied, 'I am the king today. I can do what I wish to.'

The king was killed and the servant remained king forever.

Understand: in this same way, when we give the power of attorney to our mind, it takes entire control over us.

Body Intelligence

How many of us realize the tremendous intelligence that our body possesses?

Intelligence of the digestive system

Take the example of our digestive system. The whole process of converting bread to blood is such a complex and delicate one - requiring fine intelligence to convert the different types of food into energy to run the body.

What is achieved through a few feet of coiled intestine would need a few miles, if it were an industry outside of the body!

The process of digestion starts from our mouth. We chew the food and the saliva we secrete starts the digestion. There are so many big and small body elements that perform amazing functions in the process. We swallow the food and it passes through the throat into the food pipe. Beautifully the food is blocked from going into the wind pipe instead of the food pipe - by the epiglottis. The food enters into the stomach, which is like an elastic bag and has a delicate and powerful digestive mechanism. Depending on the type of food taken in like carbohydrates, proteins or fats, the digestive mechanism varies.

The digestive fire in us, what we call *jataraagni* in Sanskrit, is related to the acid in the stomach. The stomach is such a delicate organ but it actually contains this powerful acid needed to digest the food we eat. The stomach itself is beautifully protected from this acid by a thick mucus layer around its wall which neutralizes the acid.

All the complex foods we eat take just a few hours to digest and get absorbed into our

system. Imagine not even a single process has to be consciously thought about! It is managed automatically and so precisely - adapting itself so beautifully to accommodate all our diets.

After the stomach, the food passes into the small intestine where the majority of the digestion takes place. It is actually a long structure but so efficiently fitted in a small area with many folds which increases the surface area of absorption. Most of the nutrients get absorbed in the small intestine. The main function of the small intestine is absorption of nutrients. The complex products like carbohydrates and proteins are broken down into basic elements and absorbed. The nutrients that are absorbed are carried to the liver for further processing.

Then the food moves into the large intestine where mostly water absorption occurs. Then, the food that cannot be absorbed, like fiber for example, is mixed with other waste products from the body and thrown out as waste matter. This is just a basic explanation of digestion. But in the body it is such a complex, well-organized and adaptive mechanism.

Distributed Intelligence

The human body starts from a single cell which replicates and becomes about 250 different types of cells.

Imagine, one cell transforms into so many different specialized cells that form the complex parts of the body! Not only do these cells do their specialized job, their very maintenance needs millions of things to be done in a second. And all their activities have to be coordinated for the body to function as a single organism. It is the best example of distributed intelligence.

Every cell in your body has Intelligence

We have been taught that the center of our intelligence is in our brain. We think that we control the body through our brain. Science has all along been saying that the brain controls respiration, digestion, blood circulation, and all such activities of the body.

Now, cutting-edge research has given rise to a new field called epigenetics. One of the pioneers in this field, Dr. Bruce Lipton*, an eminent biologist, has been doing research in the field of epigenetics for over ten years. In his book, 'The Biology of Belief', he states that our brain does *not* control our body. In fact, there is evidence of intelligence in every cell, even in the cell's membrane!

Recent research at Sandia Nati-onal Laboratories, USA, supports cellular intelligence theory. Scientists there studied how cells responded to a harmful substance called an antigen that attacked the cells in the body. They concluded that even the cell membrane had a beautiful and complex structure to fight the antigen, and that the cell membrane was not as simple a structure as it was earlier believed.

> You have an independent intelligence in your system which runs your life without your interference.

Our body is not a simple centralized system of intelligence controlled by the brain. The human body is a highly evolved distributed system of intelligence beautifully and seamlessly orchestrated.

'You' are not needed to run your life

An important thing to understand which may shock you:

You have an independent intelligence in your system which runs your life without your interference.

Right now, you think you need to interfere with your intelligence in order to run your life happily. But the truth is the intelligence with which you came down to planet earth, the intelligence which created your very body, can run your life beautifully for you.

The intelligence or the energy based on which you created your body at birth, is called your bio-memory. You need to understand this important truth here: it is *you* who designed your own body to enjoy specific things, to live for a particular number of years, and to do

---

Dr. Bruce Lipton - Molecular cellular biologist and author of The Biology of Belief, renowned for his seminal work in relating genetics to conditioning.

Living in harmony with our natural intelligence is living a spiritual life. particular things.

When you take birth, you decide your life, your enjoyments, whatever you want to do, based upon what you think is the 'juice' of life. That same bio-memory has enough intelligence to live, run and expand your life. That tremendous intelligence is operating every single moment whether you believe it or not, whether you accept it or not. But our limited understanding prevents us from realizing this - and we constantly feel that life has to be different from what it is at the present moment.

Trusting that intelligence and relaxing is what I call devotion. Surrendering to that higher intelligence is true surrender. Living in harmony with our natural intelligence is living a spiritual life.

Meditation technique – Nithya sutra of acceptance

Please sit straight. Close your eyes and be in a relaxed way without moving the body. Body movements will create thoughts. So if your body is stable without movement, it can take you to a deeper silence.

Very consciously and intensely, create an intention that you are accepting yourself as you are in the outer world and the inner world, this moment.

Tell yourself, 'I have enough nice things in the outer world, enough possessions. I have enough good qualities in the inner world, my inner feelings. I am accepting myself completely. There is no need to develop myself in the outer world or in the inner world. If I have ego, that is ok. If I have guilt, that is ok. If I have fear, that is ok. If I have greed, that is ok. Whatever I have been told I have, is ok. Even if I am going to die the next minute, it is ok.'

Decide consciously, 'I accept everything.' Don't bother whether it is right or wrong. Whatever objection your mind raises, accept that also.

Accept the present moment. Accept all the future moments. Whatever your mind thinks as the worst thing that can happen to your life, accept even those moments. If it happens, you cannot avoid it. It is inevitable. Understand the inevitability and accept everything.

Do this for 21 minutes.

Your intelligence will simply awaken and show you how to relate with every moment, how to relate in every situation, in every relationship.

Cosmic Intelligence responds to us

This may be a surprising revelation, but the truth is that universal or cosmic intelligence responds to every thought of ours.

Interesting research by Japanese scientist, Dr. Masaru Emoto* shows this point very clearly.

Water responds to our thoughts

Dr. Masaru Emoto* did experiments on water. He collected water samples from different sources and exposed them to various kinds of thoughts. Then he froze the samples and studied their crystalline structure through a microscope with the help of high-speed photography. Thousands of these crystals were studied under tightly regulated conditions of temperature, cooling time and lighting.

He did various experiments on these water samples – playing different types of music to the water, talking to the water, reading out from ancient life teachings, praying with a certain intention etc. He found that when the water samples were exposed to healing music, the water crystals that formed were very beautiful and graceful. The water exposed to negative feelings or thoughts did not form crystals but rather an irregular structure which reflected the emotions of the person handling them.

Our body is about seventy percent water. Planet earth is covered with over seventy percent water. After studying the effect of mental thoughts on water, just imagine the tremendous effect our thoughts, words and intentions have on the planet and us!

Another real incident from history:

When India was under British rule, the British soldiers found that when they carried water from England to India in their ships, the water got spoiled even while on the ship. But when they carried water back from India to England, the water not only stayed fresh through the voyage, but also remained fresh until they consumed all of it back in England! When scientists studied this surprising phenomenon, they found that this fresh water was from the sacred river Ganga in Calcutta which was worshipped by millions of people from around the world. It had the natural properties of neutralizing harmful bacteria and purifying itself.

Billions of people have been praying to Ganga for over thousands of years. Naturally they have left their prayerful thoughts as imprints on this water which is so energizing and self-healing.

Even in Egypt, the river Nile* has been studied by the Egyptians over thousands of years by measuring its flow, level, turbulence etc. They have found that many times these parameters reflected the calamities like earthquakes, volcanic eruptions, and tsunamis, that have happened or are about to happen in even distant parts of the world.

Dr. Masaru Emoto - Japanese scientist and author of 'The Hidden Messages in Water' showing the effects of one's thoughts and words on water and therefore on living beings.

Nile - The longest river in the world flowing through Sudan, Egypt etc in Africa.

Connection with nature

What makes us become insensitive to nature? The moment our ego comes into play we become insensitive to nature.

There was a beautiful story I was reading about a poet who in his young age used to go and play with the wild animals near his house. His father used to warn him that he should not play with the wild animals because they might harm him.

But, he still used to go and sit with the wild animals when he could. He would say, 'When I was self-conscious and afraid that there was a possibility that the animals might harm me, they would never come near me; the communication never happened, the relationship never happened.

But, whenever I had courage or I was in a very playful mood, whenever I did not have the fear or the self-consciousness, the communication and relationship used to be so strong. I could feel very clearly the animals were connecting with me and I was connecting with them.'

Understand, what I mean when I say your ego becomes strong, it means when your identity that you are a 'separate person' is felt strongly. When this happens, your connection with nature is disturbed. The innocent way of relating is lost. The feeling of being connected is lost. This is one of the big losses that can happen to a human being.

It is similar to how a person who is born blind can never be made to understand what

he is missing. In the same way, the man who has forgotten the way of relating with the heart can never be made to understand what he has lost.

Space no bar

I was reading about an experiment where some years back scientists used an electroencephalograph[*] (EEG) to measure the brain waves of two people meditating together. It was found that certain pairs of people showed a strong correlation in their brain wave patterns. These strongly bonded pairs were asked to meditate side by side for some time. Then, they were moved to different rooms.

Then one of each meditating pair was stimulated by bright lights flashing in the room. The EEG brain wave recording showed activity in the brain of that meditator as expected; but, surprisingly it also showed that the paired meditator in the other room who was not stimulated by the lights also showed the same activity in the brain automatically and instantly!

Understand: what happens in your mind affects not only you but also those around you. Space is not a criterion for thoughts. They simply travel in air. That is why in your house, if you express worry and negative thoughts a lot, the very atmosphere for your family members becomes heavy. They are affected by the negativity that you radiate.

Electroencephalograph - Machine which uses electrodes attached to the scalp to measure brain wave activity.

Intellect Vs Intelligence

Our entire educational system is based upon evaluation of information, not intelligence. It is driven by intellect and verbalization, not visualization.

When you try to move on the basis of information you lose the ability to be intelligent. In fact, if you are logically logical you will understand that logic itself is not logical. Life is not logical. It cannot be explained with the mundane logic and intellect. It happens in a plane much higher than the intellect.

The intelligent person lives moment to moment, not through logic. He does not believe in borrowed answers. He sees the challenge of the situation and directly responds to it.

The intellectual person is like a photograph; he has the imprint of the past on him. The intelligent person is like a mirror; he reflects and responds to reality and is therefore spontaneous.

The intellect is a beautiful mechanism but only as long as it remains a tool. It should not become the controlling factor. When you put your intellect aside, a deeper intelligence awakens inside you. You start functioning from your center instead of from the periphery. And your center is pure intelligent energy.

Intelligence can be rediscovered. The only way to rediscover it is meditation. Meditation destroys all the barriers, all the blocks which society has created, that prevent you from being intelligent. Like in a flowing river, it's as if meditation removes the rocks so that the water can flow smoothly.

Intelligence is creative because it is a part of the divine energy.

Intelligence requires tremendous courage; it needs a love for adventure! When you are always going into the unknown, then intelligence grows, it becomes sharpened. It grows only when it encounters the unknown every moment.

Intellect is only a mental game; it cannot be creative. Intellect is imaginative, but not creative. Intelligence is creative because it is a part of the divine energy.

Meditation technique – drop the intellect

Just try this for the next 48 hours. Consciously decide you are not going to think about your problems. Drop your intellect which continuously tells you that you do not have enough intelligence to solve your problems spontaneously, that you do not have the capacity to produce that much spontaneity.

Work on solving your problems boldly and with simple awareness and you will see that a higher intelligence comes into play. One lesson you will learn is that without your knowledge, the higher intelligence comes in to do things for you. When you become sensitive to this happening, your awareness will take a quantum jump. Then you no longer need to work to dissolve your problems. Problems will simply dissolve with the play of spontaneous intelligence in your life.

Responsibility Elevates You

With the intelligence gained about who we are and what we are doing here, comes the feeing of responsibility for others. We know then that we are not independent of others but interlinked to each other.

Some years back, there was an epidemic of tuberculosis in Tamil Nadu in South India. Finally, medicines were found and the epidemic was contained. The officials responsible for eradicating it proudly claimed that they were the ones responsible for curing it. But did they take up the responsibility for the fact that it was allowed to spread all over the town in the first place? No! They were actually responsible for allowing the tuberculosis to spread also, right? They should have prevented it to begin with and not just taken credit for managing the crisis!

Likewise, in our lives we claim responsibility for anything good that happens, but we don't take responsibility for anything bad that happens. We take up responsibility with discrimination.

Only if we take up responsibility for everything that happens in our lives will we start growing.

Vivekananda* beautifully says, 'Take as much responsibility as you can shoulder. The more responsibility you take, the more you expand. Expansion is the only growth. Without expansion, you will contract and die.'

A small story:

Once a man was giving a talk on Responsibility at the Charity Club. He gave an example of what happened a few days back. He said, 'A friend and I were walking down the street towards the park when we saw a helpless man lying unconscious on the road.' He paused and looked at the concerned faces of the audience.

Then he continued, 'Nobody had bothered to help him. Not only that, when we came back after our walk, the poor man was still lying there!'

Instead of blaming others, let us look into ourselves and see what we are doing about

---

Vivekananda – Primary disciple of Ramakrishna Paramahamsa and Founder of the Ramakrishna Order. 19th century Eastern mystic considered a key figure in spreading awareness of Hinduism and Yoga in Europe and America.

> **Only when you feel responsible for all that is happening around you, do you become a leader.**

the problem. The more responsibility you take up, the more you grow. Only when you feel responsible for all that is happening around you do you become a leader. Until then you are just a follower.

Compassion is responsibility and energy

One of my disciples once asked me, '*Swamiji*, how is it that so much energy constantly flows through you?'

When you feel compassion towards others' suffering, the whole thing takes the shape of responsibility and expresses itself as energy, that's all. For that matter, when anyone takes up the responsibility of suffering, they will immediately start radiating energy.

Be very clear, you can stand up only if you feel responsible for people's growth, only if you feel responsible for uplifting them. When you can say that you will do whatever you can for people, when you stand up with responsibility, you expand and the divine energy flows through you. Contemplate on this concept so that you can deeply understand it.

When you are free from ego and stand up with responsibility, the expansion happens and you become like the bamboo flute. Then, just as the air that enters the bamboo leaves it

as music, so too will the air that enters you flow through you as energy!

A cognitive shift

When you take up responsibility, a cognitive shift happens in you. Your mental setup changes. Many of us live life like slaves. For example, if you work eight hours in your office just following orders you will feel dull and tired. Instead, if you take up responsibility and initiative, that same eight hours will become much easier and more enjoyable.

For example, take the case of a person who is running his own business and another person who is working for a company. The owner of the business has the full responsibility of his business, but the person who is working for some other company does not really feel the full responsibility. If he does not feel the responsibility, the whole job becomes like a burden on him. There is little or no self-motivation. He keeps looking at his watch to see if it is time to leave! For him, only the first of every month is sweet, since it is payday! In a month, he sacrifices twenty nine days of his life for one day of joy. A sense of personal responsibility can help turn around any situation. A sense of personal responsibility can achieve great things.

When you stand up with responsibility, you become a solid force. Until then, you remain a burden for yourself and for others. We often think that we are in an ordinary job. We wonder why we should take up more responsibility when our higher authorities at work are not doing so.

Let me tell you, in an office, when a janitor does all his duties perfectly, he will inspire people. You see, the head of the organization has to be responsible. No credit is given to him for that! But someone in a lesser position demonstrating such responsibility is a true inspiration.

There is a greater chance of people at a lower post inspiring others through their sense of responsibility than people at a higher level doing so. So don't wait to get some authority to become responsible.

Secondly, don't think that you are in a lesser post, and therefore you need not be responsible.

Thirdly, allow the cognitive shift to happen in you.

There is a beautiful story about Buddha. It is said that when Buddha went to beg, He would appear like a king, and the kings who gave Him alms would appear like beggars! Appearing like a beggar or a king is not because of your status or the property that you own. It is because of the state inside you.

When you take up responsibility for the entire cosmos, you will expand and look like a leader, you will become a leader. Even if a leader sits on his throne and does not take responsibility, but instead points his finger at others for responsibility, he will appear small. The state is that which gets the status. The status can never get the state. The state of *Nithyananda* is different from the status of Nithyananda.

Ego Vs Responsibility

When you stand up feeling responsible, your problems will dissolve. A new intelligence will awaken in you. Don't think you are being egoistic. Ego is different from responsibility. When you feel responsible, you will take the initiative, you will not feel egoistic. Only when you think that you would have done better than the other person will ego come into play. When ego comes into play, you will not take up responsibility.

Trust and patience

I always tell people, 'Do not think you have a certain amount of energy and you will work according to that energy. No. Whatever work and responsibility you take up, the energy starts expressing accordingly. You will have energy according to the responsibilities which you take up. Whatever responsibility you take upon yourself, you will see that your inner space expands to that extent and energy flows through you!'

If you feel responsible for whatever is happening around you, you suddenly become a leader. You start transforming your life and others' lives. Responsibility is one of the ways to consciously grow.

Responsibility is a consciousness.

You only need to do two things: trust that life is good and know that you can expand to the responsibilities that you take up.

Another thing: When that expansion happens, just hold on and have patience during the transformation process. Patience during the transformation process is what I call *tapas* or penance. There is a beautiful phrase of the teachings of Shirdi Sai Baba*: '*Shraddha Saburi*' – trust and patience. This is the essence of life.

Why don't we allow big breakthroughs in our life? Because we don't trust that life leads us into a new space. Have trust and patience. The simple truth is that when you take more responsibility, you just expand and more energy starts expressing through you.

Responsibility of enlightenment

Understand, enlightenment comes with a tremendous responsibility. It comes with a tremendous 'pressured' compassion. 'Pressured' is the right word to use! Your whole being will be vibrating with an intense compassion, with a very deep compassion.

Let me tell you one incident:

Early one morning, Vivekananda suddenly got up and said, 'I have a deep pain in the right hand.' At that time he was lying down on a bed. He said, 'On this side of the ocean, some country is suffering from some natural calamity. Please find out where we are needed, and send our swamis to go and do the relief work.' The next morning they received the news that there was an earthquake on a nearby island. All the swamis rushed to do the relief work.*

Vivekananda was sensitive to and actually felt the pain felt by people so many miles away!

With enlightenment, practically the whole cosmos is felt inside your body. A deep pressured compassion lands on you along with the enlightenment experience. Understand, it is a great responsibility. It is not just freedom. It is a great responsibility too.

State, not status

Most of us wait for the status to come in order to take up the responsibility. Be very clear, it doesn't work that way. Only if you take up responsibility will the status come. Those who wait for the status will not take up responsibility even after they get the status! They will simply find another reason or excuse, that's all.

Be very clear, responsibility is a consciousness.

Many people think that if they get enlightened, they will get a golden throne. They think that somebody will give them food

---

Shirdi Sai Baba - An enlightened master worshipped by Hindus and Muslims alike. Lived in Shirdi near Nasik in India.
Swamis - A honorific term used for a *sannyasi*, a monk.

and a place to stay. They think that people will worship their photograph. If you see the status of the enlightened master and try to achieve enlightenment for that, you will feel cheated! If you see the state of the enlightened master and try to achieve it, you will be successful. You will be happy. You will enjoy it. That is the difference between state and status.

Leadership is a State, Not a Status

When we become responsible for others, we no longer are focused on us. We move towards serving other people. Serving other people is leadership. Pandering to one's own needs without a care about others is absence of leadership.

Background

There are so many books these days about leadership and how it is an important part of making an organization successful. There are so many so-called leadership *gurus* who teach and train people in organizations to 'develop' leadership. Yet when we look at all organizations, whether they are doing business to make a profit, or in government service or in the area of social services, true leaders are rare.

If you look at any organization you will find that less than 1% tends to become the so-called leaders in the organization. If you look at business organizations, we can say that there are probably only 1% of these organizations that can claim to be true leaders

in their fields who are excelling in all areas of their business – making a profit, delivering good products and services, providing service to society, providing satisfaction to their employees, etc.

So we can say, true leaders are actually 1% of the 1% of successful business organizations. It means just 0.01% of the overall working population actually has true leadership qualities in them! We can say the same about organizations in other fields. This is what I mean when I say true leaders are rare.

Let us now try and understand why this is the case. For this, we need to understand:

1. What is Leadership?

2. Can leaders be 'created' or do you have to be a born leader?

3. What are the key ingredients that make a successful leader?

4. Why do some individuals effortlessly and 'naturally' lead and most others struggle?

5. How do we start the process of our individual journey to become leaders?

Let us now understand step by step all these points.

What is Leadership?

So many books have been written on this subject of leadership by management *gurus*, professors and consultants. Most of them have spoken about how a successful leader should be. There are a lot of courses conducted by companies on leadership, team work, etc.

My disciples who have come from the corporate world have described to me how these courses are conducted and what they have been striving to achieve through these courses. They have also told me that while the courses have been helpful to them, the effect from the courses tends to wear off within a short period after the courses are completed.

I am told of weekend boot camps where team spirit is built by climbing ropes, playing games, creating a sense of friendship, etc. The gist I picked up from hearing my disciples is that these training programs tend to work on the outer attributes but do little to change or improve the 'inner software' of the individuals so that leadership can radiate from the individual. Leadership to me is not a quality, but an experience that can radiate from an individual who has experienced personal growth and transformation.

Now let me give you some explanations of how leadership is described traditionally. If you search the internet under the terms

'Leadership' and 'Leader', you will be amazed at the millions of hits that come up! Just recently when I typed the word 'Leadership' on Google it had 156 million hits and the word 'Leader' had 278 million hits!

So whatever needs to be written or said on these topics has been said! So I am here to mainly give you a few examples from the leading management gurus and their concepts of a leader and more importantly to give you the real understanding, tools and techniques on how to become a leader and how anyone can radiate leadership as a result of personal transformation!

Understand, every human being is a potential leader. Leadership is not a quality only some people have been born with as is viewed and understood currently. Everyone can become a leader and the quality of leadership arises from one's ability to take responsibility for a particular organization, a situation or a particular group.

Can leaders be 'created' or do you have to be a born leader?

A lot has been said by many people on what a leader should be. But there is very little that has been said about actually how to get there. What exactly do I mean by this?

Is leadership some quality you have to be born with or can it be cultivated? How can one develop leadership skills? Can a person truly lead an organization if he or she is caught up in personal struggles and confusions?

Before we get into these details, let me first say that leadership skills CAN be cultivated. It is all about achieving the state of consciousness of a leader and not the status that is achieved by becoming a leader.

When you read this, please do not think I am going to take you through a spiritual journey! The process I am going to take you through is a time-tested, proven science of personal transformation. It is a product of ten thousand years of research and development from the Eastern system of inner science. What do I mean by this?

Firstly, understand that every civilization has focused its energies in certain fields. In the West, they focused their efforts on the outer world science, innovation, discovery and creation of products and services to improve the quality of life and comforts. These outer world scientists have discovered so many products and services which have greatly benefitted humanity and improved the quality of life of humans all over the world.

Just as there is science of the outer world, there is a vast science of the inner world, something that lies within all of us. The scientists of the inner world or *rishis* worked on various tools and techniques to handle the different emotions we experience and our mind. Over the last ten thousand years, these scientists of the inner world have created tools and techniques that help us handle our emotions and overcome the stress and depression from emotions. They have created

techniques for us to live blissfully with ourselves. These tools and techniques are what I call meditation techniques.

So most of my discussion on leadership will be focused on giving an understanding of human emotions, the mind and how we can use these simple understandings from the inner scientists to help us lead a successful and fulfilling life.

In most organizations, those who have become leaders have achieved the status of the leader. They may not have necessarily achieved the state of the leader. What do I mean by this? To understand this, first let us understand the key ingredients that make a successful leader.

What are the key ingredients that make a successful leader?

A small story:

There was once a great war between two countries. The war had been going on for some time and the soldiers were starting to feel tired of the long battle.

On a hot afternoon, a man in civilian clothes was riding past a small group of tired soldiers digging a huge pit. The group leader was shouting orders and threatening punishment if the work was not completed within the hour.

The man riding the horse stopped and asked, 'Sir, why are you only shouting orders? Why can't you help them yourself?' asked the stranger on horseback.

The group leader looked at him and replied, 'What do you mean? I am the leader. The men do as I tell them.' He then added, 'If you feel so strongly about helping them, you are welcome to do so yourself!'

The man got down from his horse and started walking up to the soldiers at work. The group leader was simply shocked! The man took up the tools and started helping the soldiers and worked with them till the job was finished!

Before leaving the man congratulated the soldiers for their work, and approached the group leader.

He said, 'The next time your status prevents you from supporting your people, you should inform your higher authorities, and I will provide a more permanent solution.'

The group leader was now completely surprised. Only now he looked closely at the man,,and realized that the man was the army general!

We now need to ask ourselves how many so-called leaders in organizations exhibit the qualities of the group leader. And how many people do you know who exhibit the qualities of the army general?

Regardless of the status in an organization, you will agree that the majority of the so-called leaders exhibit the qualities of the group leader. They achieve the status of the leader but not the state of the leader.

There are very few people who are ready to really help get the work done.

The army general exhibited some of the key qualities that are important for a true leader:

1. Honesty and Responsibility

2. Caring genuinely about people

3. Confidence

4. Efficiency and lateral thinking skills

5. Attention to detail

6. Efficiency and Effectiveness

7. Broad-based thinking and doing

I will discuss these traits in greater detail in the following sections.

Leader Consciousness

Leadership - a result of a conscious choice made by an individual

What do I mean by this term, 'Leader Consciousness'?

Most of us achieve the status of a leader, but not the state. State is totally different from status. Status comes from society. When you are leading a group of people, if you are forced to take the responsibility of some department or if you take the responsibility out of your greed, the status comes. But the state is totally different.

When I use the word 'state' I mean your inner space or your being should be mature enough to handle what you are entering or the responsibility which you are assuming. When we just get the status without achieving the state, all the problems which exist in the corporate world start - stress and tension in the personal level, and backbiting and politics in the level of the team. All these problems start when you don't achieve the state but just achieve the status.

Here I am trying to express to you the truths from the great traditions of the East - how to achieve leader consciousness, how to achieve the state of the leader and not just the status. See, status is very easy, state is something which we really need to achieve.

Status will simply follow a man who has achieved the state of a leader. Even if the status takes its own time, he will not be bothered, he will live like a king! His very life will be totally fulfilled. The invaluable feeling of fulfillment happens to beings who achieve leader consciousness.

State of a leader Vs Status of a leader

What do I mean by the word, 'state of the leader'?

A true leader is a person who is ready to take responsibility consciously, who is ready to handle life consciously, who is not constantly dependent on the past or his memory. If you are dependent on your memory, if you are

dependent on the past to take decisions, please be very clear, you will be a follower. You cannot be a leader.

Responding spontaneously to situations is what I call responsibility.

A responsible leader is a person who is able to respond spontaneously to situations, who is fresh and continuously keeps himself alive, who is not caught in the past.

Let me try to give you a small diagram on how the mind works, how the state of a leader is achieved, how leader consciousness happens in us. Let us understand how the mind works - how we receive data, process it and make decisions.

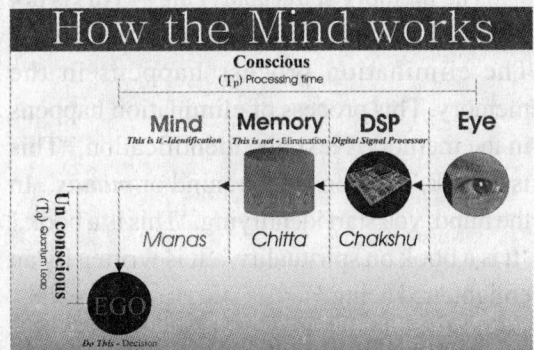

For example, you are seeing something through your eye. Of course, you receive information through all the five senses - eyes, ears, nose, tongue and touch. For now, let us take the example of the eye. When you see with your eyes, immediately the file goes to a space called the *chakshu**, it is just like a Digital Signal Processor (DSP). Whatever you

---

Chakshu - Energy behind the power of sight.

A true leader is a person who is ready to take responsibility consciously, who is not constantly dependent on the past memory.

are seeing through the eye is converted to a bio-signal, just like a digital signal file. This file moves to a space called *chitta** in Sanskrit which is just like memory in a computer. Here the process of identification starts. For example, you are now seeing this book - the whole file goes to the DSP, *chakshu**, and the whole file is converted into a bio-signal file, and then it moves to *chitta*, memory.

The memory starts analyzing - 'This is not a stone, this is not a tree, this is not an animal…' The elimination process happens in the memory. This process of elimination happens in the memory. Next, the identification, 'This is a book,' happens in the mind or *manas**. In the mind, you start identifying, 'This is a book,' 'It is a book on spirituality,' 'It is written by an enlightened being.'

After identification, the file then moves to a space which I call 'ego', the decision-making center. In the ego you start thinking, 'In what way am I connected to this situation?' If your past experiences with similar books were good, you decide to continue to read. If your past experiences were not good, if you felt 'Oh, this is not worth it, I felt very bored last time', or 'I read similar books but did not feel any benefit,' if you feel negative you will decide not to continue reading. The ego decides based on your past experiences. This is the way your mind functions.

Now, the important thing which you need to understand is, the decision is taken *unconsciously*. If the process happens like this, in a straightforward way, you will not have any problem and things will go very smoothly in your life. Everything will be clear and straight!

But this process does not always happen in a straightforward way. Sometimes things start happening in an unconscious way. For example, if you were hurt or disturbed by something that was said in a similar book you read before, the moment you see this book, unconsciously that memory will be awakened.

You see, in your life, if you are hurt or disturbed in a particular place, or by a particular situation, or by a person wearing a particular colored dress, the next time when you go to that place, or the next time you see another person wearing the same colored dress, you will go through the same low mood even if you know logically that the place or that person has nothing to do with your past experiences. You will have that same memory again in your mind. You will again have that same experience. This is what I call '*samskaras*' or 'engraved memories'.

Chitta - Memory.

Chakshu - Energy behind the power of sight.

Manas - Mind.

These engraved memories distort or disturb your decision-making capacity. You see, if the whole process of the mind map I just described happens consciously, then it is a straightforward and logical process. But due to the unconscious mind, a lot of times, the process is not straightforward. As I described earlier, we tend to get biased based on our experiences we have had with a particular person or a particular situation. This is the space where politics happens! This is the space where things move illogically. This is the space where the past memories or engrams will be sitting and you do not even know what decision you are making!

Let me give you one more example to give you more understanding of the unconscious mind. If we analyze logically or consciously, all of you know that smoking is injurious to health. If we follow through the process from eye to the mind, you know clearly that smoking is injurious to health, according to the data collected by your senses. But suddenly, even though logic tells us not to smoke, you decide to smoke, beyond your logic and consciousness. This is where the unconscious engrams are sitting.

Even though you consciously know that smoking is injurious to health, when the data moves to the ego, when the file takes a quantum leap, you just decide to smoke. Maybe some memory, or some experience which you had in the past must have made you feel relaxed when you smoked. Or maybe when you smoked during your youth, you may have felt like a hero. So these engrams have been associated with this habit, and suddenly,

because of this engram you decide to smoke, even if you consciously know that smoking is injurious to health.

In the same way, many times in your life, even if you know what is right, simply you decide unconsciously because of your engrams. Your life is under the control of unconscious engrams, it is not under your control. You may think that you are taking the decision, but your unconscious engrams are taking the decisions!

These *samskaras* or engrams are the root cause of our behavior. They are the reason why we behave in a certain way with certain people. The engrams tend to cloud our judgments when we have to take decisions. They influence how we accomplish our tasks in an organization. It is these engrams that dictate our productivity, interpersonal skills, teamwork, judgment and all our responses and behavior. But engrams are never understood and more importantly given any importance in the field of corporate training and leadership development.

The Eastern mystics and inner scientists have spent thousands of years developing tools and meditation techniques to cleanse us from these engraved memories. These *samskaras* can be effectively erased through meditation techniques.

Recently I visited one of my devotee's houses and saw a beautiful one-liner in the living room:

'I am the boss of this house, I have my wife's permission to say so!'

Similarly, you may think you are the boss, but your unconscious engrams are leading you! As long as you are caught by these unconscious *samskaras*, you can never achieve the state of a leader. You may achieve the status of a leader with a lot of suffering and struggle.

Be very clear, if you sit in the leader's chair with a lot of suffering and struggle, you will tend to create the same suffering and struggle for your subordinates!

Again and again, your mind will say, 'When I suffered and struggled so much, why not them!' You will just reproduce your old mental setup on others. This can be a very de-motivating factor in organizations.

Productivity

Definitions and understanding

A small story:

Once a boss asks his employee, 'Why did it take you six months to complete such a simple task?'

The employee replies, 'Because of your confusing directions, continuous changes and short work days!'

The boss replies, 'I was looking for something like you being lazy!'

So much has been written and said about productivity in organizations. Productivity has become the mantra in organizations for the last two or three decades. As a result of

invention of computers and new communications technologies such as the internet and cell phone, the world has become a much smaller place. While there has been an increase in productivity in companies, it has often come at a huge price on the health (physical and mental) and well being of the employees. Let us now start to understand what is productivity and how productivity can be enhanced without the side effects of stress.

In simple terms, productivity can be measured as:

Productivity = Output / Input

The measure of output may be certain number of tasks completed by a particular individual or team or revenue in the case of a manufacturing company. The measure of input may include the number of hours worked on a particular project, manufacturing costs etc.

Understanding from Eastern mysticism - impact of engrams on productivity

Billions of dollars are spent by companies globally to enhance human productivity. Most of these efforts are centered on providing new skills specific to training in a particular area of the organization's focus or improving technology such as use of computers, internet or other forms of media and communications. Some companies also invest in developing 'softer skills' such as interpersonal skills, team-building skills, etc. But most of these trainings tend to address the conscious mind - actions, behaviors and perceptions that are just on the surface. But over 90% of our emotions and behaviors reside deep under the surface of our mind. This is what the psychoanalyst, Sigmund Freud, calls the unconscious mind.

If we look at the mind, there are thoughts and perceptions which are accumulated in our mind at a conscious level. But there are deeper memories and stored knowledge that we use to help us solve problems. Then there is a whole range of emotions and experiences that are embedded in the unconscious level. This is where the *samskaras* or engraved memories reside.

Most corporate training programs focus on the conscious mind to impart knowledge or particular skills. But actually it is as though we are sitting on a volcano of emotions that is just waiting to burst and erupt any time! These hidden emotions are what make us behave inefficiently and even illogically at times!

So *samskaras* or engraved memories interfere with the decision-making process, these can be called the inefficiencies present in the mind! The more the number of engrams, the more clouded is our thought process, and the lower is the output. In other words, to produce a particular output, having more *samskaras* will require more time or people or costs. So this results in lower productivity.

Freudian representation of the unconscious mind

Most readers who have studied psychology are familiar with the Freudian interpretation of the mind. Traditional training and skills development in various organizations address only the conscious mind which is just ten percent of your potential. Ninty percent of the potential can be actualized only when we address *samskaras*. This huge potential can be experienced through meditation techniques.

To give you an example of what I just described, I would like you to take fifteen minutes of your time on a simple exercise. Take a white sheet of paper and just write down whatever comes to your mind. Please do not edit, filter or pass judgment on any of the thoughts that come to your mind. Just behave as though a 'thought recorder' (just like a voice recorder) is attached to you and you are jotting down whatever comes to your mind. Now after fifteen minutes put the pen aside and read what you have just written.

If you have honestly recorded whatever came to your mind, you will realize the kind of stray, unconnected, illogical thoughts that go through the mind. These thoughts are like friction in a machine. They make the machine very inefficient and unproductive. This is the root cause of low productivity.

Several of my disciples, who have gone through this process and consciously worked on eliminating their *samskaras,* always come and tell me that they are now finding so much time in their busy lives since they are no longer troubled by the wavering mind and illogical thoughts.

The tool for elimination of these stray thoughts arising from *samskaras* is what I call

The tool for elimination of these stray thoughts arising from *samskaras* is what I call meditation. meditation. Once these thoughts are eliminated, it is like reducing the friction in a machine and allowing the machine to be more efficient, more productive.

Thousands of people from all races, nationalities, social and economic background have gone through this process of eliminating *samskaras* in our meditation programs. Thousands of people come and tell me that in addition to improving their overall productivity, they are able to maintain better interpersonal relationships, feel less stress, and be more creative and innovative in their personal and professional lives. I have also had interesting conversations with leading corporate leaders and Nobel Laureates on this subject where they have shared amazing evidences of improved innovation and intuitive skills developed as a result of becoming free of *samskaras*.

So we can now elaborate on the equation to describe productivity. We can restate the equation as follows:

Productivity = Output/Input

Input = (Intellect + Technical Skills + *Samskaras*)

As you know, we live with our mind 24 hours a day, 365 days a year. For most people, the mind is constantly running, analyzing, passing judgment on individuals, having various emotions and responding to situations, all of which is dependent on the level of *samskaras* that may be 'haunting' us.

Without the load of these *samskaras*, you will find that your innate intellect and the skills you have developed through your education, training or life experiences will directly be used in delivering the output instead of being knocked around by your mind. You will see the productivity simply shoots up!

This is an area that has mostly not been looked at by companies and organizations. But there are simple tools and techniques from the Eastern mystics who have developed techniques to cleanse the mind of these *samskaras*.

Sometimes people ask me, 'If we are free of *samskaras*, will we stop thinking? Will we become lazy and complacent?' I tell you, it is actually the opposite. Please refer again to the experiment I gave you a while back on jotting down your thoughts on a piece of paper for fifteen minutes. If the mind is free from the effects of *samskaras,* you will see a quantum jump in intelligence and you will be creative and a whole new zone of intelligence will emerge. You will see that all of a sudden you will be able to develop skills of intuition and innovation that emerge from your being.

Understand, this is not a mystical zone you are going to enter into. Be very clear, the skills of intuition reside in all of us. They have been clouded by the impact of *samskaras*. Let me now describe how a mind-body system that is free from *samskaras* will improve intuition and innovation.

Impact of *samskaras* on intuition and innovation

Intuition is a wonderful subject. If you ask modern day CEOs how they took major decisions in their lives, what caused the turning point in their lives, again and again their answer surprises us. Again and again they tell us that their success came from something beyond their intellect that gave them the energy or the guts to take the decisions. This is not just the case with successful CEOs, it is the same with scientists also.

The other day I had a chance to have lunch with Dr Charles Townes[*], Nobel laureate in the field of Laser and maser. I asked him, 'Sir, how did your discovery happen? How were you able to do it?' He answered in a beautiful way, 'I was just sitting in a park in Washington DC and suddenly something happened. The conclusion was there in me. Suddenly the conclusion was revealed to me. I penned down what I experienced. Now I had a big difficulty. I had the conclusion but not the steps. I was not able to present this to anybody else because I knew only the conclusion but I didn't know the steps.'

This happened not only with Charles Townes[*], it had also happened with Albert Einstein[*]. He says, 'Whatever new happened to me, came through intuition and not through intellect.' He summed it up beautifully, saying, 'The intuitive mind is a sacred gift, the rational mind is a faithful servant. We have created a society that honors the servant and has forgotten the gift.'

Whether we believe it or not or accept it or not, there is something called intuition. Of course, even Einstein[*] says this is a gift, because we are not sure when it will come and whether it will come or not.

But yogis, the mystics, say again and again, you can work for it and you can be sure about it. You don't have to think that intuition is a gift. You *can* work for it. It can become a part of your life. Whatever new things have happened, have happened only through intuition, only when something has happened beyond your intellect and your whole being is integrated.

When you are at your peak, something opens. You may call it revelation or intuition, which happens beyond intellect. Mystics have again and again said that it is a science. If you can tune yourself to this intuition or this energy, which is continuously available in your being, you can use this in your regular life. Mystics again and again say it is an incident and you can make it happen. They know how to make it happen. We will see how you can awaken that power inside your being. We will see how the intuitive skills can be linked to the workings of the mind which I discussed earlier.

Before we discuss intuition in greater detail, let us first dispel the myths that intuition

---

Dr Charles Townes - Nobel laureate in physics for work related to maser and laser.

Albert Einstein - Scientist and Nobel laureate.

When you don't know the logic, you call it a coincidence. Nothing can happen without a cause on planet earth. is some kind of a 'fluke' of nature. I would like you to understand that intuition is a skill that can be developed just as any other skills that you acquire. It comes from you, from no one else! Because we have not experienced that zone, that part, that dimension of our being, we have forgotten it.

Someone asked me in a meditation program, 'I remember someone and the next moment the phone rings and he is there on the line. I remember someone at a party and next moment I see him.' I asked the people in the program if this kind of an incidence had happened to them at least once in their lifetime. More than seventy percent of the people said this had happened! If it happens in one person's life once, you can say it is a coincidence. But if it happens with seventy percent of people, it cannot be called a coincidence! There is more to it. There is some logic behind it.

We may not be able to know logically but we cannot brush it aside. When you know the logic, you call it an incident. When you don't know the logic, you call it a coincidence. Nothing can happen without a cause on planet earth. It is always cause and effect. When you know the cause and effect link, you call it an incident. When you don't know, you call it a coincidence.

In trying to understand the process of intuition, let us refer back to the mind map we discussed earlier. We talked about how the process of taking information from a sense such as the eye works through *chakshu** (Digital Signal Processor), *chitta* (memory), *manas** (mind) and then takes a quantum jump to the ego where the decisions are clouded by *samskaras* or engraved memories.

The process in the gap between the eye and mind is conscious. You are aware of this process. It happens with your awareness. But the mind to ego process – you are not aware about it. Many a time, the process happens without your awareness. You decide against your logic. You decide against your thought process. For example, according to the data that you have collected, you know that smoking is injurious to health, it is not good for your body or mind. But when the mind takes an unconscious leap to the ego, you simply take the decision to smoke!

The conscious process says, 'No, it is not good for health.' But the unconscious process says…it doesn't even say, it just takes the decision and you execute. These decisions are not under your control because the unconscious is very powerful.

The unconscious can be used in three ways – at the instinct level, intellect level and intuition level. As long as the unconscious is filled with negative memories and restlessness, it works at the instinct level. You decide just instinctively. You don't even know why you

---

Chakshu - Energy behind the power of sight.
Manas - Mind.

are angry. Suddenly you burst. Sometimes, when you see some activities or some words that you speak, you feel it is not you. You do something and then you think, 'This is not me, how did I do it? How did I allow this to happen?' This happens because the unconscious is working in the instinct level.

Many times, you just associate things without even any logical connection. For example, if you have been disturbed by somebody who was wearing a white dress, the moment you see somebody wearing a white dress, the past memory comes up and you feel the anger. This is the instinct level. Without your conscious mind, without even you understanding, just like that it happens.

If your unconscious is loaded with *samskaras*, if your unconscious is restless, you will be at the instinct level. The next is the intellect level. You are conscious but you don't have enough enthusiasm. You just go with a conscious mind but you are not creative, not innovative. You don't take big steps, you don't grow. It is just like a faithful servant as Einstein* says. The intellect is a faithful servant. You can be a servant throughout your life. You can be just a servant, but nothing more or big can happen through you. You will be collecting the data, processing it and delivering it – nothing more than a computer. If you are standing only at the intellect level, you are not using your potential to the maximum, to the extent to which it is supposed to be used.

The next is intuition. To understand intuition you need to go deep into the whole science;

only then you will be able to understand what I mean by the word 'intuition'. Intuition is something which happens to you beyond your intellect. Suddenly you know for sure that this is the right thing and you have enough energy also to do it but you don't know the step how you came to the conclusion but you know for sure this is right.

This energy is needed whenever you are faced with a situation where there is no precedence - when you are stuck with minimum data and you need to take decisions or you have a lot of choices and you are not able to decide what you are supposed to do. In these type of situations, the intuition energy can help you. The intuitive power can give you the courage or give you the right choice. Intuition again and again gives you the energy not only to decide but to execute what you have decided.

People ask me, 'How do I find out whether I am having intuition or I am just intellectual? Sometimes I am confused about whether it is intellect or intuition.' I tell them, be very clear, if you are confused, it is only intellect. The very confusion shows that it is only intellect. When you experience intuition, not only you get the intellectual clarity, the answer, but you also get enough power to execute it. The potential power which is inside your being is just unleashed. You open up and just like that you start expressing it, executing it.

Now the next question: How to awaken the intuition? How to awaken the intuitive power? If you can consciously give rest to it

---

Albert Einstein - Scientist and Nobel laureate.

> **Spontaneity has nothing to do with data which you collect; it is something to do with the way in which you process the data.**

for a while, the energy which is in that unconscious level will open up. And usually when the unconscious level energy opens up, first whatever we suppressed will come out. Next, a pure energy which we call intuition will start to express.

When pure energy starts expressing from the unconscious level, you don't use the unconscious at the instinct level or intellectual level. You use it for intuition. The higher level energy starts happening in you. And of course, above all, the mystics demonstrated to us over thousands of years that the higher level energy heals you physically, mentally and emotionally. Apart from healing, this can help reduce the stress and help decide spontaneously.

Spontaneity has nothing to do with data which you collect; it is something to do with the way in which you process the data. The same data, same information can be processed in many ways. Intuition is all about how you process and how you come to the conclusion beyond your intellect.

We can prepare ourselves, we can tune ourselves to this intuitive energy through techniques and methods which we call meditation. In the East we use the word 'meditation' to tune ourselves with the higher energy, which is in our being, which continuously invites you again and again to experience it. Whenever we find time, sit by yourself. You can always see, we give appointment to everybody, but never give appointment to ourselves. If you have given appointment to yourself, you can always see that some part of your being wants to express, wants to do something more, but we never give chance or time to that part, to that portion of our being. We are so caught up with our intellect. We think that our intellect is the ultimate, but again and again mystics prove something more than intellect is possible.

In any discovery or invention, you can see that the role of intuition is always there. Whether it is Albert Einstein or Issac Newton*, they have had something beyond intellect. Something beyond intellect has happened in them. This same energy exists in all of us. This energy can also express in all of us if we can tune ourselves to that energy. Tuning ourselves to that energy is what I call meditation.

Meditation technique

Mahamantra meditation

The *Mahamantra* meditation is an ancient Tibetan Buddhist technique to awaken the *anahata chakra**, located at the heart center.

Issac Newton - Physicist and mathematician, pioneer of classical physics.

Anahata chakra - Subtle energy center in the heart region related to love.

This meditation makes your mind firm and stable. Your mind is all the time oscillating with thoughts. This meditation makes your mind still by making it enter into the zone of no-mind. It is like a jumping board into infinity.

It should be done on an empty stomach, preferably early in the morning, or two hours after any meal. It can be done either alone or with a group. When done with a group, it effectively energizes the place where it is done.

Instructions:

Total Duration: 30 minutes

Step 1: *Duration: 20 minutes*

Sit cross-legged in a comfortable position on the floor. Your head, neck and spine should be in a straight line. If you are not able to sit on the floor, you may sit on a chair. Feel relaxed and close your eyes. Even after we close our eyes, we see forms and images from behind the eyelids. To handle this, imagine that your eyeballs have become stone-like. Just harden them with mental pressure, then the images will die. The movement of our eyes is very closely related to the movement of thoughts in our mind. That is why you are asked to arrest the movement of your eyeballs. Don't be too worried about keeping them arrested. Just proceed with the meditation.

Keep your lips together and produce the sound 'Mmmm...' from inside. If you were to put your face inside an empty aluminum vessel and make a humming sound, the sound generated would be like this. Note that this is not 'Hum...' or 'Om...', it is simply keeping your lips together and producing the sound 'Mmmm...'. This humming should be as lengthy as possible before taking the next breath. It should also be as deep as possible, from the navel center, and as loud as possible.

Don't make an effort to take in a deep breath after every 'Mmmm'. The body itself will take breaths when needed. Don't become tense. Put in your whole being and energy into creating this vibration. Just become the humming. Let your whole body be filled with the vibration of the humming. After some time, you will feel that the humming continues without your effort and that you have become simply a listener to it!

The humming is a powerful means of bringing your awareness to the present moment. If you hum intensely, you cannot have any thought at that time. So your Thoughts Per Second (TPS) automatically comes down. The energy generated by the humming cleanses the energy blocks in the mind-body system.

When you are intensely humming, all the ideas which you have about you will be completely shaken. Like an earthquake, this is a technique for a 'mind-quake'!

Step 2: *Duration: 10 minutes*

After stopping the humming, keep your eyes closed and remain silent and inactive with a smiling face and blissful mood. If any thought comes to you, let it come. Simply watch your mind as if you are watching television, without resisting your thoughts or passing any judgment on them. Remain silent and blissful. During this time, the energy created by the humming will enter all the corners of your being and cleanse it deeply. It establishes you in the awareness of the present moment. This

awareness is all that is needed to dissolve the negativities, bring clarity and enable you to experience your true potential.

Intensity is the Unfailing Way

Whether we lead or whether we follow, in order to be fulfilled in whatever we do, we need to be intense.

A small story:

A Zen master and a disciple were walking along the banks of a river. The disciple, as he had done a few times before, asked the master very longingly, 'Master, please give me enlightenment.'

Suddenly the master turned, held the disciple's head in his hand and pushed it into the river. The disciple was shocked and started struggling to get his head above water. The master continued to strongly hold his head in the water. Now the disciple started gasping for breath. The master then released the surprised and completely shaken disciple.

The master asked, 'Do you feel you want enlightenment with the same intensity that you felt you needed air to breathe when your head was in the water?'

Only when the urge becomes urgent, when the question becomes a quest, does the Ultimate happen. The key factor needed for enlightenment to happen is intensity.

What is Intensity

You see, usually we feel a terrible restlessness towards the outer world, 'I have not done this, I have not done that' and so on. The same restlessness when directed to the inner world is called intensity.

You do not know what is happening, you do not know what should be done, but the deep dissatisfaction about what is there in the inner space is what I call intensity.

You may be wondering why I am teaching dissatisfaction. I am supposed to teach satisfaction, right? I tell you, your dissatisfaction, which is now directed towards the outer world, has to turn towards the inner world, and only then it will lead to satisfaction.

First thing which needs to happen is not satisfaction but the turning of direction, the psychological revolution. Restlessness should become intensity. If it is towards the outer world, if your consciousness is constantly moving towards the outer world, it is called restlessness. If it is moving towards the inner world, it is called intensity.

Intensity does not create conflict inside or outside. It flows smoothly yet very strongly.

The meaning of intensity is that desperate feeling that something needs to be done immediately, to break free from the clutches, or to break free in the inner world.

Intensity is not emotion. When you are intense, one part of it may be emotional. But intensity cannot be called emotion. It is like heat. The part of intensity that melts and comes out can be called emotion. For example, when you integrate yourself with intensity, one part of you melts. Let us say the heart melts, then that can be called emotion. Along with your heart, your intellect will also melt, your being will also melt. The side-effect of intensity is emotion.

Do not bother about what your intensity should be about. Do not bother about 'towards what'. It should become a quality. Anything you do, whether you touch something or somebody or some object, let the intensity be there, even in that touch.

If you are talking, let the intensity be there. In your relationships, in your decisions, in your memory, in your thinking, in your desires, even in your fears, be intense without escaping from this moment. That is what I call intensity.

Intensity means radiating the energy that does not create any conflict inside and outside. Intensity is intensely being inside you.

Intensity does not create conflict inside or outside. It flows smoothly and yet very strongly.

We always think if it is flowing smoothly like a river, it will not have intensity, and if it is intense like a stone it will not be flowing freely. No. Intensity is like a flood which is intense and flowing.

I have seen some people intensely creating conflict every moment! Anything you tell them to do, they will be ready to create a conflict.

A small story:

A prisoner escaped from prison after twelve years and reached his home. The moment his wife opened the door she started shouting, 'How dare you come so late! You escaped from prison twenty four hours before. Where have you been? You should have come straight back home!'

All that the woman was bothered about was why he was not back home right after he had escaped. She certainly was intense, but only in creating conflicts.

Real intensity does not create conflicts. It is flowing but intense.

Intensity is integration. Intensity is focus. Intensity is sincerity.

Usually intensity leads to a solid feeling. You may be intense but you may have lost the ability to flow. Or you may be flowing but may have lost the intensity.

See, you may be intense but you may have lost the ability to flow - because you are driven by your ego. You are determined to achieve what you want but you have your own rigid ideas about how to get there. You fail to understand then that Existence can make events happen in a much more beautiful and effective way than you can plan.

I tell my disciples, plan in the best way to the best of your ability. Then, leave it. It may seem that all your plans are being completely trampled - don't get frustrated at that point. Something much more beautiful than what you had planned will come to life.

The other possibility is that you may be flowing but may have lost the intensity. This is the case with people who have no focus and waste their energies getting distracted by anything that comes by.

Understand, water becomes steam only at 100 degrees Celsius. Even at 99 degrees C, it is still water; it does not transform to steam. Same way, if you are not integrated in seeking, all your energies are not integrated. The total transformation cannot happen.

Take up something and follow it with full intensity. Intensity does not mean acting rigidly without scope for updating and change. Only when you are open to change you can make your way like the river flowing intensely towards the ocean.

'Being' is Intensity

What is *being*? Being complete, total, integrated, expressing your full energy, is what I call 'being'. If you are partial in your experience or expression, be very clear you are being hypocritical.

Intensity in anger

Even your anger is hypocritical.

Only when you are open to change you can make your way like the river flowing intensely towards the ocean.

You just choose whether to express your anger or not. Your anger is also directly related to your logic.

You never get angry beyond your logic. It is always managed by your logic. You analyze, 'Am I going to lose anything here in this situation?' If you are sure you are going to lose something, you just suppress your anger. If you are clear, 'I am not going to lose anything. I can shout at this person. What can he do?' then you just explode and express much more anger than what is necessary. Whatever you have stored in stock, you open up everything and give!

Not expressing, not suppressing – just be and get liberated

Be very clear, when your logic manages your anger, you will have two problems. First, you unnecessarily shout or unnecessarily show your anger when it is not necessary. Second, even when you are not expressing, you will be suppressing it.

First, if you are expressing, you will be expressing too much, much more than what is necessary. Next, if you are not expressing, you will be suppressing it. Be very clear, both are wrong.

Interest comes from the mind. Intensity comes from the being. Suppressing and expressing both are not going to help. You may ask, 'Then what are we supposed to do?' You are not asked to do anything, just be.

Modern mystic, J. Krishnamurthi, says beautifully, whenever an emotion overtakes you, if even once you can just be without moving your body, without co-operating with your emotion, you will be liberated from that emotion.

If you stay without moving your body when you are flooded or overpowered by any emotion, even once, immediately you will be liberated from that emotion. I am not saying you have to constantly practice this. No, just once, only once, and you will be liberated from that very emotion.

Intensity is independent of the nature of the work

Intensity does not depend on the nature of the work or action. It can be as complex as running a billion dollar company or as simple as cleaning the floor. It is not the 'what' that is important, but the 'how' that is important.

If you can do what you are doing with a totality and intensity that *you* are completely lost in the action, you have caught the thread of intensity.

The moment you are lost in the action, you become like a flute on the lips of Existence itself. The air that goes into the flute comes out as music because you become a channel for the energy of Existence to flow through you. Be total and intense. That is all that is needed for the arrow to hit the target, whatever it may be.

Interest Vs Intensity

What qualifies to be called as intensity? What is the difference between intensity and interest?

An interest can be lost, but never the intensity. Interest comes from the mind. Intensity comes from the being.

After a while, maybe short or long, you get fed up with your own interest. With intensity, it is a thirst of your being. It transcends the rationale of your logic. Intensity is a call from deep within. The more you have to wait for it, the more the thirst grows, the more the fire flares up.

See the difference between light and laser. Both are made up of the same light rays but the single-pointed intense focus of the laser comes from the coherence and the common frequency of the light rays.

The power of this intensity is what gives the laser the tremendous power to even burn a hole through metal. At the same time it is a controlled focus. This is what gives it the power to do even a delicate task like removing a cataract in the eye.

If in a desert your thirst for water becomes really intense, you are ready to pay with your life for a glass of water. When your thirst for realization becomes that intense, you are ready to pay with your life for the Truth.

A beautiful Zen story:

A student approached a Zen teacher to learn Zen. The teacher told him, 'Hear the sound of one hand clapping.'

The student tried for three years and did not succeed. He was depressed that he could not do what his teacher had told him. He came in tears to the teacher saying he had to leave because he could not do what he had been told.

The teacher said, 'Wait for one more week. Meditate constantly.' The student stayed for one more week and meditated. Nothing happened. The teacher said, 'Try for five more days.'

The student stayed further, yet nothing happened. The student came in despair begging to be released. Then the teacher said, 'Meditate for three more days. If you don't get enlightened, you had better kill yourself.'

The second day, the student was enlightened.

When your whole being is burning with the single intense desire to realize the Ultimate, you will simply absorb the master's instructions. The magic of transformation is bound to happen. Only then will you be open to receive him. Till then it is just an interest.

Be intense in whatever you do

When you eat, intensely eat. Let your whole attention and energy be on food.

Tantra*, the mystical science of meditation techniques, says that to know the truth one needs only one condition – intensity. Be total in what you are, what you do.

Live intensely in the moment and taste the real life. Otherwise, you are not living. You are just waiting for death.

When you eat, intensely eat. Let your whole attention and energy be on the food. Do not divert your attention and thoughts to what you need to get done at work tomorrow or where you want to go for your next vacation.

Enjoy the food with all your senses. Taste the food in your mouth, enjoy the feast in front of your eyes, touch the food with love, and smell the aroma of the food. When you eat this way totally, you will enjoy every morsel and you will actually feed into your system the living energy the food is meant to give.

If you are drinking water, drink it intensely. Become the thirst. Feel the coolness of the water going into your mouth, throat and down your food pipe. Let each drop of water that goes into your mouth give you the feeling of fulfillment.

Tantra - Ancient *vedic* tradition of achieving enlightenment through spiritual techniques or practices, meditations and ritual worship.

The Tamil classic, *Periya Puranam**, describes the stories of the Nayanmars*, the ardent devotees of Lord Shiva*. There are so many instances of the devotees realizing the Ultimate by simple activities like making garlands for the Lord. An example is Gananaatha Nayanaar, a devotee of the Lord, engaged in simple services like plucking flowers for worship, making garlands for the Lord, sweeping and washing the floor of the temple and keeping the lamps in the temple burning. Just this simple life led him to reaching the Ultimate and brought him his name 'Gananaatha' meaning the chief of the *ganas* (attendants) of Lord Shiva.

When you pray, be real and spontaneous. Whatever you feel, feel totally and offer it to the Divine. Don't cheat yourself and be hypocritical by not admitting what you feel. You cannot hide anything from the Divine. He knows you better than you know yourself.

Your intensity is the only thing that decides when your object of seeking will happen. If the intensity is total, it will happen that moment. If the intensity is not integrated and total, it will take more time because the intensity has to gain strength in that time.

If you are intense enough, it does not need time to reach the Ultimate. Where you are, who are you is irrelevant. You *can* reach here and now.

A beautiful story:

There was a dreaded bandit who was a terror in the kingdom. After looting a large number of people, he started feeling restless and uncomfortable with his actions. He approached a master and asked him, 'Master, I am a sinner. Is there any way out for me? Can I be liberated?'

The master looked at the bandit and asked him what he was good at. The bandit replied, 'Nothing.' The master asked, 'Nothing? You must be good at something!' The bandit thought for a long time and then said, 'Master, I only know stealing, that is what I have done all my life.'

The master smiled and said, 'Good! Then you will use exactly that now. Go to a quiet place and rob all your perceptions and ideas and opinions. Steal all the trees and rocks and rivers on planet earth. Steal all the planets and stars in the sky. And dissolve them in the vast emptiness inside you.'

The bandit sincerely followed exactly the instructions of the master. Within 21 days, the bandit realized his true nature – he became enlightened.

Periya Puranam - A Tamil classic by Sekkizhar on the lives of the 63 Nayanmars, the devotee saints of enlightened master Shiva.

Nayanmars - Tamil devotee saints of enlightened master Shiva, 63 in number, whose life stories are told in the book Periya Puranam.

Shiva – Enlightened master

Intensity and the four states of consciousness

Four states of consciousness

There are four states of consciousness.

Various States of Consciousness		
	With Thoughts	**Without Thoughts**
With "I" Consciousness	**Jagrat** **Wakeful State** Thinking	**Turiya** **Blissful State** State of Full Awareness
Without "I" Consciousness	**Swapna** **Dream State** Dreaming	**Sushupti** **Unconscious State** Deep Sleep

When you have 'I' Consciousness and thoughts, you are in the waking state, the state in which you are right now. In this state, 'I' has more frequency than your thoughts. So you can control your thoughts.

When you are without 'I' consciousness but having thoughts, you are in the dream state. In the dream state, your thoughts are at a higher frequency than your 'I' consciousness. That is why you have thoughts in your dreams but you are not able to control them.

When you are without 'I' Consciousness and not having any thoughts, you are in the deep sleep state. Normally, we are aware of only these three states – waking, dream and deep sleep. The fourth state is where you have I consciousness but no thoughts - *turiya*.

Intense seeking - awareness in the three states

Intensity means being intense every moment in whatever you do. So first you need to be aware of yourself in all the states. Then only you can be intense throughout.

Now you experience who you are with awareness only during the waking state. You feel, 'I am a doctor', 'I am a lawyer', 'I am an engineer' and so on. Only if we are aware of the identities that we carry and enjoy in all the three states, we have caught the thread, the center line of all the three states of waking, dream and deep sleep. When we catch the thread of all these three states, suddenly we realize our identity in all the three states.

Somebody asked me, 'I don't think that in the deep sleep state I am aware.' Then who is the person who comes back and says it was deep peace during my deep sleep? Who is the person who is reminiscing about it saying, 'It was filled with darkness. It was as if I was not there at all'? Who is coming back and remembering even this idea, 'I was not there at all'?

If the person is not there in that state, then who is coming back to connect all these three states? No, we cannot say we were not there in the deep sleep state. We were there, but we were not aware of the identity that we had in that state.

Understand, a person who is aware of all these three states is conscious. If we are aware of the identity in all these three states, then we are conscious enough, our seeking is

> **Man is like a mirror. He has the choice to face and reflect the Divine or to turn away.**

intense enough to be answered, we are intense enough to be initiated and blessed.

If we are not already aware of all these three states, if we have not experienced all these three states with the same identity, then naturally we need to now intensify our seeking.

An intense seeker will carry the identity about himself throughout all these three states. If even once or twice you have experienced your waking identity in the dream state then you are intense.

In the dream state suddenly sometimes you remember that you are beyond the identity which you think as you in the dream state. I have seen seekers going through this experience in the dream state. They will be dreaming and suddenly they will identify themselves with their identity of the waking state. Then they will think about the dream state, 'Hey, this is too small. This is nothing.'

If you have had the experience of your waking state identity in the dream state, understand, then you have the intensity. Your seeking is intense.

How to get enlightened? I want to…real bad and urgently

Understand: Question is a word. Quest is a feeling.

Man is born as a quest. The rest of Existence cannot reflect the Divine like man can. Man is like a mirror. He has the choice to face and reflect the Divine or to turn away. Man can make a conscious choice, which is why he can grow. Man can choose to realize the Divine through his human form. No other being in Existence has this choice.

If these words, 'How do I get enlightenment? I want to… real bad and urgently,' have come out, if this question has come out as a deep quest, then you don't need anything.

Just boil, let the whole being burn with this quest. That is enough. Nothing else needs to be done. Let this boiling be intense.

Allow this boiling. Allow this burning. Allow this intensity. Allow this urgency.

Let the urge become urgent. Let the question become your quest. Let it just eat your ego, eat your inner space.

People ask me, 'Have you been enlightened by the divine grace or by your effort or by your quest?'

I tell them, your having the quest is the first sign that you are having the divine grace. Unless you have the divine grace, you will not have the quest.

Understand, this quest or seeking is like a seed. It is like a seed feeling suffocated inside the shell. See, the life that is inside the seed, unless it feels suffocated inside the shell, it won't open up and become a tree.

The moment the seed starts feeling that it should open up, the moment it starts feeling the seeking, the urgency and the quest to open up to become a tree, it means that already the tree inside the seed has started expressing itself.

If you have the feeling that you should get enlightened, the Buddha in you has opened his eyes. The Buddha in you has started waking up. All you need to do is open your eyes!

Allow this seeking. From morning till night let it boil, let it create a deep dissatisfaction in you. Let every pore in your skin, every nerve in your body, every cell in you vibrate with that intensity. Let it swallow all your depressions you may have in life. In life you may have so many other depressions and sufferings of not having so many things. Let all those sufferings be swallowed by this one suffering.

A beautiful Zen story:

A Zen student was intensely studying under her master but she was not able to experience true meditation for a very long time.

One full moon night, she was carrying a bucket of water suspended on a bamboo stick. She saw the reflection of the moon in the bucket. Suddenly, the bamboo broke.

The water fell out of the bucket. The reflection of the moon disappeared and so did her ego.

When the seeking is intense, it will remove the juice from your ego. The green grass becomes like a haystack. Just a match is enough to burn the whole haystack down. The Ultimate can happen in a split second through a simple happening.

So understand, let this seeking, let this quest, your saying, 'How to get enlightened? I want to…real bad and urgently', let this seeking burn all your other sufferings, all your other depressions, all your other desires, all your other concerns about life.

Let it happen and suddenly you will see that the seeking suddenly disappears, it is not there. When the seeking disappears, you are enlightened. You have achieved what you are seeking.

If you have the feeling that you should get enlightened, the Buddha in you has started waking up.

Intensity prepares you for the ultimate

Initiation

The Upanishads, the ancient *vedic* texts by the sages and mystics that happened as revelations, say that for the person who is initiated the whole world is heaven. Understand the word 'initiation'. It does not mean doing some ceremony or ritual.

For the spiritual experience to happen, you must be completely open and be in the intense energy field.

Initiation means that 'click' happening in you. When a master expresses the truth, if the click, the realization, happens in you and if you suddenly feel, 'O god! What he says is right. I was always thinking exactly this. He put it in the right way,' that is what initiation is. If you feel whatever I am speaking is what you always thought about but I am verbalizing it and properly putting it in words, the initiation has happened.

Please understand, only after all the preparation is done and only when you are in the state of high intensity, the truth uttered by the master just clicks.

When the master says there is no need for any seeking any more and just liberate yourself right now, you will be able to do so only if you have done enough of seeking and created the intensity. That is the paradox!

The technique is to get the right attitude of intensity. Actually, if you have high intense energy, you will automatically have the right listening. You will be just waiting to catch one glimpse. You will be just waiting to listen. You will be just waiting to imbibe.

That is why masters speak again and again and again for years over years. I started speaking only a few years ago. Buddha spoke for over forty years. But, the message was the same. His first sermon and the last sermon are almost the same.

You may then think why thousands of disciples sat everyday and heard the same sermon again and again. Because, the click happens only when you are in intense energy. Only with intensity it clicks. You just catch the flame and the awakening happens.

The deep spiritual experience

Requirements for spiritual experience

For the spiritual experience to happen, two conditions need to be fulfilled. One is that you must be completely open and available to the surroundings. The other is the intense energy field.

Sometimes even if you are open, if you are not in the intense energy field, the first cracking of the coconut of your ego does not happen. The first spiritual experience is just like breaking open a coconut. Once the first opening happens, it is not difficult to break the rest of the coconut. The first opening needs an intense spiritual energy field.

These two factors are what resulted in my first spiritual experience. I was open and available to the surroundings, and I was in the intense energy field of Arunachala. Fortunately, I was attracted to the beauty of that hill. Normally, if you see a hill or a river or an ocean every day, you will take it for granted. Somehow I never took that hill for granted. I never thought I know about it. I was continuously open, available.

Understand, being open and available every time, seeing it every morning with the eyes of freshness or with the mind of openness is what I am calling 'being open and available'. Many times, we completely close ourselves to the society.

We just come to some conclusion, some understanding and after that we never update our understanding or our effort with the result.

Every day, the Arunachala hill was living for me. Everyday it was never the same old hill that I saw yesterday. I had a very funny routine. In the morning when I got up I would not open my eyes. I would slowly walk from my room to outside the house holding the parapet wall. I would come out and stand in a place from where I knew the hill could be seen. Only then I would open my eyes so that the first thing that I saw in the morning would be that hill.

Somehow my brothers knew that the first thing that I wanted to see was the hill. They would want to have fun teasing me. When they knew that I was out from my bed and slowly walking, they would come and stand in front of me.

If I opened my eyes and did not see the hill and instead saw their faces, I would go back and lie down again. I would lie down again, sleep for half an hour, then again get up and slowly walk back to see the hill and open

my eyes. Only if I saw the hill the first thing in the morning, I would carry on with my routine.

It may look funny and superstitious but I always felt I took birth, I took this body, because of that attraction and pull that hill has got for enlightened beings.

There is a very beautiful verse in Tamil that describes the hill as 'the hill that attracts enlightened beings around it'. The hill is especially respected for attracting enlightened beings not only from this planet earth, but also from other planets and spaces, towards planet earth. I never took the hill for granted. It was an ever-living presence.

Encounter with the Divine

One day I was trying to sit and meditate. It was a full moon day (Poornima) and the moon was rising as the sun was setting. I was just sitting on a rock on Arunachala hill, trying the meditation technique that the disciple of Ramana Maharishi and enlightened master, Annamalai Swamigal*, had initiated me into.

I was sitting on the rock trying to find the source from where the feeling of 'I' was rising. On that day I was sitting for a particularly long time trying to find the source in a deep way.

Suddenly something happened and I felt like I was being sucked inside, pulled inside. I was sitting with closed eyes but I saw very

Annamalai Swamigal - Disciple of Ramana Maharishi in the temple town of Tiruvannamalai, whose teachings led to Nithyananda's deep spiritual experience as a young boy.

clearly that something opened inside. The moment that opened inside, I was able to see whole 360 degrees around me. My eyes were closed but I was able to see complete 360 degrees, whatever was happening in all the directions - front, side, back, up, and down.

Not only was I able to see, but I was also able to feel very clearly with the same intensity how we all feel alive inside our skin, that I was alive in everything I was able to see.

I was able to see whatever was around me – the plants, rocks, trees and everything. I was able to feel that I am alive in everything. In the same way you all feel you are alive inside your body I felt alive with the whole cosmos, with the whole Existence.

Till then I was just a mere body. After that, I realized I am body also*. Understand, 'I am body also'.*

It was a very deep experience. If it was just a word or imagination, it won't have that much impact on the inner space. It was an intense conscious experience.

You see, now you know you are inside your skin. Now you will listen to anything as long as it does not disturb you. Naturally you know how to protect yourself because you are alive inside your body and that is your conscious experience.

No matter however many people teach you that you are not just your body you will only listen but you will not allow them to work on you! Because *your* conscious experience is your body.

My experience that 'I am this whole Existence' became my truth. That is why I started living according to that.

People are surprised that I lived such a strong intense life in such a young age. They feel that it is very difficult and unimaginable. It is unimaginable for you because it is not your conscious experience. It is easy for me because feeling the whole cosmos is me became a very solid experience.

The Intensity of Buddha

Look at the biography of enlightened master and founder of Buddhism, Gautam Buddha. He searched for six long years. He tried various paths but the beauty is that in every attempt he put in his whole being.

Whatever he decided to follow, he did with complete, unwavering intensity. He tried various techniques such as fasting, continuous penance, chanting and many such methods. He tried all possible techniques but nothing worked.

During his seeking, a teacher told him to eat only one grain of rice per day for three months. Buddha sincerely followed his instructions. He was reduced to skin and bones and became extremely weak.

One day, he stepped into the river to bathe. He had become so weak that he couldn't even move his legs and was being swept away by the current. He caught hold of a tree branch and while hanging onto it he suddenly realized the fruitlessness of all his efforts. He had been mortifying the body but in the process he had only lost his bodily strength.

He felt a deep depression that he could not achieve anything in the inner world and he had nothing meaningful in the outer world.

He came out of the river and sat under the tree. He was frustrated but the difference between ordinary frustration and Buddha's frustration was he was complete and intense in his frustration as well.

There was not even a grain of hope he had. He completely gave up. There was nothing to achieve, nothing to look forward to.

It is said that on that night as he looked at the sky ready to sleep, he attained nirvana*.

The one factor that resulted in Buddha achieving It is intensity. So many of us claim we are doing everything but nothing is happening. Look little deeper and see how integrated you are in your thirst and seeking. Whatever you may seek, integrate your energies completely and go for it. You will then see the universe open up to you completely.

Intensity for my deep spiritual experience

I had mentioned about my deep spiritual experience where I felt one with Existence and had a 360 degree vision of everything around me. There are so many people practicing so many different meditation techniques. What is the difference, what is the reason why the experience happened to a small boy?

I can say that one important reason is that my whole inner space was ripe, ready for this small technique to awaken and open it. Constantly I used to be in that high frequency of the masters without even my conscious awareness.

See, especially in the young age, whoever inspires or impresses you becomes the hero of your inner space. These great masters impressed me so much that in every situation I would think, 'How would these great masters behave?' For example, if I had some fear, I would remember, 'How will Annamalai Swamigal* face this fear? He won't bother. He is enlightened. Let me also be like that.'

The inner space was so inspired and impressed by these great masters, that before every step I took in my life I would think, 'How will he behave? Let me also do that.' The inner space was so pure also at the young age and I had no heroes other than the masters. At every step I used to think, 'How will he behave? Let me behave like that. How he will do? Let me do like that.'

Nirvana - Liberation through Self Realization.

Annamalai Swamigal - Disciple of Ramana Maharishi in the temple town of Tiruvannamalai, whose teachings led to Nithyananda's deep spiritual experience as a young boy.

When you live the Master's body language you live enlightenment.

Walking in burial grounds

I used to go for a circumambulation of the Arunachala hill. It is more than 12 kilometers around the hill. I used to go late at night. When I had a little fear I used to say, 'How will Annamalai Swamigal* behave? He won't bother about fear. Then let me also be like that.'

Let me tell you about one incident.

It was raining heavily that night as I went around the hill. I had some fear seeing the heavy rain, thunder and lightning. Immediately I thought, 'How will Annamalai Swamigal behave? He won't bother. He will just walk. Let me also do the same way.'

I was walking through the traditional crematorium. In India both cremation and burial are done in the same place. I was walking in that place because when you go around the hill the path goes through that crematorium.

Suddenly I saw a dog biting something and eating. When I went near, the dog started barking at me. At first when the fear came up I thought, 'How will Annamalai Swamigal behave? He won't bother. Let me just go.' I started moving. Anyhow when I started moving the dog got scared and ran away.

When I got nearer I saw that it was a dead body which was not completely buried. It

had come out in the rain and it was lying on the road. Just imagine a twelve or thirteen year old boy, alone at midnight, seeing a dead body without a head, since the dog had the head in its mouth.

The fear started but it did not even reach my being completely. The shock, the fear stroke did not even happen completely. As soon as the first thought started coming up, with intense awareness I thought, 'How will Annamalai Swamigal react now? He will just walk around and go. Just walk around and go.'

I continued to walk. That's all. I took a detour and walked away. I did not even turn back and see. The fear stroke, which was like a bubble, which was about to start, did not even open up, did not even reach my body. The heat or the shivering from fear was not even there in the body. It just died.

Intensely, the whole conscious inner space was ready. That is the reason, just a punch, just a small inspiration was able to put me into that experience. That is what I call 'Living Enlightenment'.

Intense, innocent inner space

When you live the master's body language you live enlightenment.

Whenever any thought came into my inner space, whether it was related to clothes or food or anything, the first thing I would think was, 'How will Annamalai Swamigal behave?

Annamalai Swamigal - Disciple of Ramana Maharishi in the temple town of Tiruvannamalai, whose teachings led to Nithyananda's deep spiritual experience as a young boy.

226

Naturally he won't have any desire. Then forget about it!'

If I felt a little lazy to meditate or to circumambulate the hill, I would think, 'How will Annamalai Swamigal think? How will he handle this situation? Naturally he will not bother about this laziness. He will just get up and meditate, that's all! So just do that!' So constantly, from morning until night, these masters became the reference. They became my life center.

I asked Annamalai Swamigal once, 'I saw Devi* in my dream. Do you also see her in the dream?' Annamalai Swamigal replied, 'No, I don't have dreams.' I was shocked, 'You don't have dream! Then how can I have dream!'

That night I said to myself, 'Now, no dream. Annamalai Swamigal said 'no dream' so I cannot have dream.' You will be surprised, that night when some dream started happening, I said clearly from inside the dream, 'No! Annamalai Swamigal doesn't have dreams. How can I have dreams?'

The dream disappeared. Just the dream disappeared. The inner space was so thorough, so innocent, so direct, it just happened.

Even if I felt cold or anything, I would remember, 'How will Annamalai Swamigal behave? He won't bother. Then don't bother. That's all.' There were no further questions or arguments inside.

Message of living enlightenment – 'How will master behave?'

You can also use this simple, powerful technique. It is so simple your mind cannot find any excuse to escape.

In any situation, ask yourself, 'How will master respond? How will master face this situation?' Do the same. You will see that a new door opens. This is what I call 'Living Enlightenment'. You don't need anything else. This one thing is enough.

Even if you are sitting, if thoughts come up, ask your mind, 'If master is sitting what will be coming up? Naturally silence. Then why are you thinking? Silent!' That's all. Nothing else.

If your mind says, 'No, no, I know it is true. I know this but it is too much.' Then think, 'If master's mind says this, how he will behave?' He would have finished the mind that moment! That's all. Just be very clear.

Take this one message and let this message become life in you, the message of Living Enlightenment. Understand, from the age of ten when I was inspired and impressed by Annamalai Swamigal, I started doing this technique. I didn't even know then that it was a meditation technique.

It just started, 'How will Annamalai Swamigal behave in this situation?' As a boy,

---

Devi - Supreme goddess in Hinduism, Cosmic Mother.

> **Relationship happens when you are thoroughly impressed by the master.**

many times in my home I have seen my brothers or family start fighting for some share in something and I would think, 'How will Annamalai Swamigal behave? He won't even bother! Forget about it. Let them have.' That's all.

True relationship with the master

Actually this is what I call relationship with the master. Relationship with the master is not just doing some worship or putting some flowers or worshipping him once in a while. No!

Relationship happens when you are thoroughly impressed by the master. Whenever anything comes up, say fear or insecurity or greed or anger, just see, 'How will master behave?' Simply it will disappear. It will just disappear.

Many times I tell people, just feeling strongly connected with the master is enough. You don't need anything else. It is not just your ordinary relationship. In an ordinary relationship, you neither try to understand nor imbibe the master. Just some feeling is there. I can't even call that as a relationship. It is an ordinary, regular interaction.

Feeling connected to the master means just living him. When you live the master, then you feel intensely connected to him. Only then

you are expanding. Only then something is happening to you. This has not happened in most of us because of so many other relationships. So many other persons occupy your inner space and so many others have inspired you or impressed you or given the idea that they are heroes. Just fill your inner space with the master and watch your problems simply dissolve.

Intensity - the ultimate technique

Be intense in whatever you do. Whether you eat, sing, dance, pray or work, be completely into that, in the moment.

Intensity is enlightenment. As of now, some part of you is intense while some part of you is lazy. Being hundred percent intense is enlightenment.

The first thing you need for living enlightenment is intensity. Intensity is the sword with which you can break the mind.

It is just like awakening from the dream. The first thing you need is the intention, the idea that you should wake up. So now you need to have the intense idea to wake up.

Understand, the intensity with which you work towards wealth, relations etc., if you just turn a little towards enlightenment, you will awaken.

Intensely decide, 'I will wake up from this life that I call life.' Create an intense will or prayer. When you create a will and direct it towards you, it is called a will. When you create a will and direct it towards the Divine, it is called a prayer.

Intensity is a strong intention to wake up, the strong intention for fulfillment, for living enlightenment, for eternal bliss. The only gap between you and enlightenment is intensity.

How to get Intensity

Remember how intensely and anxiously you run behind things that give you joy. Suppose I tell now that whoever prays intensely will get a ten million dollar prize, you will show the intensity of your life, is it not? Just because you think there is some product that will fulfill you, you are intense. With money you know it is going to add something to your life. In the same way, enlightenment is also going to add something to your life.

In order to have intensity towards enlightenment, you can start by creating intensity towards things that you have experienced a desire towards. For example, if you desire health or wealth, be intense about that. That yearning will become integrated and will get directed to the unknown, to enlightenment. Not only that, your unfulfilled desires can be simply burnt with the intensity.

Whatever you experience as fulfillment, yearn for that. The intense yearning is enough,

it will evaporate you. And the fulfillment you experience will be many times more than the fulfillment you may have ever experienced before.

Meditation techniques to be intense

This is a very powerful technique from the Shiva Sutras*.

The aphorism or *sutra* says,

Die into the infinite void where you are no more

Moving beyond the senses into Shiva Consciousness

This technique is called the *Shanmukhi Mudra**. As it will be difficult to maintain this posture for a long time, you may sit on the ground and support your hands on a chair to maintain comfort. You can put a chair in front of you and turn it facing towards your side to support your hand. Alternatively, you may sit in a chair and support your hands using the chair in front of you. By supporting your hands on a chair, you will avoid shoulder ache.

This technique closes the doorways to your senses. This should only be practised by people who have some experience in meditation. As in all meditations sit comfortably cross legged or in a chair with back, neck and head in one vertical line.

Shiva Sutras - A collection of teachings of Shiva in epigram form as techniques. Includes Vignana Bhairava Tantra, Guru Gita, Tiru Mandiram etc.

Shanmukhi Mudra - A *mudra* in which eyes, ears, nose and mouth are covered while meditating.

When you are in *Shanmukhi Mudra**, the energy flow to the outside world through the seven openings of the face (two ears, two eyes, two nostrils and one mouth) is blocked and turned inwards. Your hands are very powerful. The energy centers in the hands are so powerful that they can stop the energy flow, turn it into a concentrated beam of energy and direct it towards the *ajna chakra** or third eye.

Normally our breath goes in and out chaotically. By closing the nostrils partially with your fingers, you can reduce the air flow and balance it.

The *Shanmukhi Mudra** firstly stops the energy flow towards outside.

Secondly, we are turning the senses inwards.

Thirdly, we concentrate them towards the third eye.

Instructions:

If you wear spectacles, remove them. Place your fingers as follows:

Thumbs pressing down on the short ear lobes till you hear a humming sound.

Index fingers lightly on both the eyes.

Middle fingers on the bridge of nose.

Ring fingers lightly under nostrils.

Little fingers on lips.

For the next 21 minutes, follow the steps given below:

Close the nose partially. Just reduce the *prana* flow. When your mind settles down by itself, the *prana* flow will reduce. Be in the *Shanmukhi Mudra* and inhale and exhale as slowly as possible and as deeply as possible. Keep your mouth shut tightly. Visualize that both your eyeballs have become stones and let them not move.

Intensify your awareness. Do not create stress – try to penetrate with deep awareness. Don't create pressure, create only awareness. Visualize intensely as if you are penetrating your third eye. Visualize deeply as if you are penetrating your third eye with a drill bit.

Relax. Open your eyes slowly.

It is important to make yourself comfortable by supporting yourself properly to be in *Shanmukhi Mudra*. You will see tremendous energy created in your third eye, to awaken your intuition. When you are comfortable, you will see that you are entering into deeper energies or higher consciousness.

Shanmukhi Mudra - A *mudra* in which eyes, ears, nose and mouth are covered while meditating.

Ajna chakra – Subtle energy center located between the eyebrows.

Innocence Regained Opens Many Doors to Life

It may seem strange to speak of innocence after talking about intensity, but in the truest sense, you cannot be intense in anything you do unless you are innocent of other agenda. The innocence I speak of may not be what your own dictionary defines as innocence. What I speak about is the innocence of a child. A child is intense about anything that it does. Adults have lost that power, but it can be regained.

What is Innocence?

Innocence means purity of the inner space, not being affected by the thoughts or the engraved memories. Let you be very clear, even if you are not expressing your emotions like anger, greed and lust, if they are present in your inner space, you are not as yet a total and innocent person. Socially you may be pure, that's all. On the other hand if you express your anger, lust and greed but nothing touches your inner space and you live like an innocent child, then be very clear, you are a pure being.

You can see children get angry. Children are greedy also. They build their personality mostly on greed. That is why they are so aware and conscious of 'mine' attitude. Try to take away a toy from a child. The child will behave as if his life is taken away. He will scream and shout. This is because his whole personality is built upon 'mine' attitude. Children have greed and anger, but you cannot call them impure. This is because whatever you may think as impurity does not affect their inner space. They will sit and play with their toys and after a few hours they will throw them and go away. They don't carry anything in them. Their inner space is beautiful and pure.

Innocence is directly related to the inner space. It is in no way related to the outer world. In the Shiva Sutras*, Shiva gives us techniques to achieve this innocence. If you follow Shiva's life as is described in the Hindu mythological stories, you will not be able to

---

Shiva Sutras - A collection of teachings of Shiva in epigram form as techniques. Includes Vignana Bhairava Tantra, Guru Gita, Tiru Mandiram etc.

'Shiva' in Sanskrit means causeless auspiciousness.

see any social or traditional innocence in him. But there will be the pure and ultimate innocence. The place where he lives or the way in which he lives is not directly related to his purity or innocence. Shiva lives in a cemetery where bodies are cremated, surrounded by spirits and ghosts.

The word Shiva in Sanskrit means causeless auspiciousness. This causeless auspiciousness, the energy to create bliss wherever he is, wherever he happens, arises out of his innocent inner space.

In the *vedic* tradition, there are scriptural writings called *Upanishads*. The word *upanishad* in Sanskrit refers to teachings of a master to his disciples as they sat with him. There are 108 such *Upanishads*. They are the essence of the enlightenment science handed down by the great masters of the *vedic* times. One of these, the Chandogya Upanishad* describes a beautiful story:

A boy by name Satyakama goes to a master seeking enlightenment. The master gives him four hundred cows telling him, 'Take these cows. Go live in the forest and look after them. When these multiply into a thousand cows bring them back to me.'

Satyakama goes to the forest and lives with the cows, waiting for them to multiply. It takes many years for the cows to multiply to one thousand. For all those years he sits not talking to anybody, just being with the cows. Soon, he forgets the human language. In deep silence, not relating with any human being, he slowly loses his outer world identity.

By the time one thousand cows happen, he forgets how to count. He simply sits waiting, with a beautiful feeling of ecstasy.

Finally a cow comes to him and says, 'Sir, we have become one thousand now. We can go back to master.'

He replies, 'Is that so? Alright.'

Satyakama is in ecstasy. He has forgotten the way back. The cows lead the way. On the way back, animals, birds and even the fire that he kindles to cook his food instruct him on the nature of the Brahman, the ultimate Truth.*

When Satyakama returns to the master, the master looks at him and smiles. He says, 'You look so radiant like the knower of the Truth, Satyakama. Who taught you?'

Satyakama tells him how he had understood the Truth through animals and birds and requests the master to teach him the Truth in his own words.

The master says, 'You already know the Truth,' and blesses him.

The story says that just by being, just by listening to what nature has to say, Satyakama established himself in the Truth. He became enlightened.

Total innocence leads to enlightenment.

Chandogya Upanishad - One of the oldest and primary *Upanishads* or scriptures.

Brahman - Absolute, Cosmic Consciousness, formless god etc all referring to the universal energy source of which the individual energy of the soul is a holographic part.

Satyakama asks the master for enlightenment and the master asks him to multiply cows! Many of you will ask, what do cows have to do with enlightenment? Fortunately Satyakama was not so intellectual. Fortunately he did not receive formal intellectual education. So he did not ask this question! He was simple, innocent and humble, ready for the transformation to happen. He had no logic to use.

Understand, unless you are without logic, or tired of logic, you cannot be ready for the transformation. Logic cannot help you understand even your own life. Logic cannot help you look even into your own mind. How can it help you change?

People ask me, 'Swamiji, why are you against logic?' I am not against logic. I am only telling you that all your suffering is because of logic without intelligence. Your logic creates so much politics inside you from morning till evening.

What is politics? It is nothing but differing opinions on the same subject, is it not? Now watch your mind. It says one thing in the morning and a different thing in the evening on the same subject. This creates the dilemma in your mind. Your mind itself is such dilemma.

People say that in all spiritual organizations there is so much politics. I ask them, 'What do you mean?' There is politics inside the very persons who make this statement! To create politics, you don't even need two people. One person is more than enough. One single person with logic is

Unless you are tired of logic, you cannot be ready for the transformation.

enough because in the morning his logic will say something and in the evening it will say something else! And naturally the fight between you and you is politics! Am I right? Then why are you making the statement that even spiritual organizations have politics?

If you place the decisions that you make in the morning and the decisions that you make in the evening together in front of you, you will see a politician sitting inside you!

Logic does not allow you to be simple and innocent. It does not allow the transformation to happen easily. Logic has to be overcome for the transformation to happen. Only when there is no logic there can be innocence. Innocence is the space for transformation to happen.

In the case of Satyakama, fortunately he was not bitten by logic. The disciple goes to the master for enlightenment and the master tells him, 'Alright, take these cows, go to the forest and stay there till they become one thousand cows. Then come back!'

If today's seeker was in that disciple's place he would have said, 'I think the master is trying to exploit me. He wants a thousand cows, which is why he is telling me to do this work. He is using me to get his work done.' Innocence is lost to logic! That is why no modern day seeker receives such amazing techniques.

Understand, this is not a mere story. It has got a great truth behind it. With innocence, Satyakama simply followed what the master said. Further, he lost his logic of counting. He was completely lost in ecstasy and joy. The mind stopped functioning. He didn't care about one thousand or two thousand. Just the innocence and acceptance caused the greatest happening in him – enlightenment! When you completely accept, you don't need the mind. The mind is necessary only when you live with struggles, only when you are fighting. Just this moment accept yourself in the outer world and the inner world. You will go out enlightened.

For so many years, completely accepting what the master said, Satyakama just *was*. What else can happen to him but enlightenment?

You may think, 'How can simple acceptance do such a big job?' The problem is that even spiritual knowledge is approached by us with the space of an intellectual mind. It is from that intellectual space that we ask the 'how'. Intellect always questions. Innocence straightaway starts practicing what the master says. That is the difference.

When you are utterly innocent and open, initiation is enlightenment. Just a word is enough to enlighten. Shiva says in the Shiva Sutras*, 'Just listen while the master is expressing the truth, and become enlightened!'

How can mere listening lead to enlightenment? Why did it happen to

Satyakama when it is not happening to us? First thing: he was innocent and therefore intelligent to receive the master's instruction. Second: he was courageous enough to live with it. He had complete trust in the master. Innocence always comes with trust.

I am not asking you to get me a thousand cows. No! I am asking you to come with the same mood as Satyakama. Come with the same innocence. You don't have to do exactly what Satyakama did. But you have to *be* like Satyakama. If your being is like that, in this moment the transformation can happen. Just in this moment the transmission of light can happen.

Remain empty

The word *upanishad* means 'sitting at the feet of the master'. In ancient India, there was the *gurukul** tradition of masters and disciples. Children were left with the master at the age of seven and they grew up centering beautifully in their consciousness. Masters are living embodiments of the scriptural truths. Their thoughts, words and deeds stem from the ultimate Truth. Disciples pick up the truth just by living around them.

Swami Sri Yukteshwar Giri*, an enlightened master from India says, 'Sitting with the master is not merely being in his

---

Shiva Sutras - A collection of teachings of Shiva in epigram form as techniques. Includes Vignana Bhairava Tantra, Guru Gita, Tiru Mandiram etc.

Gurukul - *Vedic* educational institution.

Swami Sri Yukteshwar Giri - Master of enlightened master Paramahamsa Yogananda.

physical presence, but keeping him in your heart, being one with him in principle and tuning yourself to him.' This is the whole technique of *upanishad*. The master is superconscious energy. When you tune to him, you tune to that energy. You can tune only through innocence, openness.

Openness is emptiness. Let not knowledge fill you. Knowledge is but a mere tool, not your substance. Reject all knowledge as 'not this', 'not this'. When I say reject, I mean don't settle for any intermediate knowledge except the ultimate Truth. Because when you drop everything that continuously arises in you, then you have no other go. You are thrown back into yourself and it is there you will find the ultimate Truth. It is then you are ready to be filled with the Truth. That alone can make *upanishad* happen.

If you watch children, their eyes will be filled with wonder and freshness all the time. They are so empty inside. They don't hold any opinion about anything. They are ready to receive. Their readiness is expressed in their eyes. Have you ever seen an adult with such eyes? The eyes lose their glow as we grow older because we become dulled by what we start knowing. Knowledge makes us dull. We may know many things, but the knowing should not dull us in any way. We should remain empty in spirit always.

If you just look at life without any opinions, without any words of description, without any fixed ideas, then you are like an empty teacup into which the brewed tea can be poured. You receive because you hold nothing, because you are empty. Then you never lose your enthusiasm. You are never bored. You are like a child, innocent and fresh.

There is so much freshness behind innocence. Life is an unfolding mystery.

A young girl was writing something on a piece of paper. Her father asked her what it was.

She said, 'I am writing a letter.'

He asked, 'To whom?'

'To me,' she replied.

'What does the letter say?' He asked.

She replied, 'How do I know? I have not mailed it and I have not received it yet.'

There is so much freshness behind innocence. Life becomes an unfolding mystery every moment with it. That is the truth. Life *is* an ever unfolding mystery. It is the mind that typecasts it. The mind always wants life on its own specific terms. Innocence embraces life with life's own terms.

If you play hide and seek with children, you will see that they will hide in the same place as you hid the last time! Not just once but most of the time! How is this possible? Because of one thing: they move with innocence. They don't have any idea in their head. They simply follow their heart. They have great trust in you, so they simply hide where you hid, not even suspecting you will look there! That is the beauty.

Innocence trusts. Innocence does not worry about being exploited. Neuroscientists

The unknown can be known only by surrendering to it.

have explanations for this now. They say that till about the age of five or six, a child's brain wave patterns are in the theta and delta states. These are extremely impressionable states of mind in which we dream and sleep. These are states of no identity. Till the age of twelve they say that brain waves are in alpha state, still very impressionable. This is why children believe most of what adults say to them. In their innocence they trust.

When you see with empty eyes, everything you see goes deep and causes fresh insight. Life becomes an eternally unfolding mystery. The very nature of your questioning changes. The nature of the questioning reveals the depth of innocence of the questioner.

There are three ways to ask a question: you can ask out of innocence, or you can ask out of knowledge to show that you too know, and third, you can ask to confirm that what you know is correct. When you ask out of innocence, you are completely ready to receive the answer. When you ask out of knowledge, you completely miss the answer. When you ask for confirmation, you simply resist the answer. The fundamental secret of proper learning and knowing is to function from a state of innocence.

The problem is that those who are not empty never recognize that they are not empty. You cannot tell them they are full. They will neither understand nor accept it. But a man of innocence can say, 'Because of my knowing I missed it. I actually don't know. I am now eager to know.' The moment this space is created, the learning continues to happen. In this space there is no ego of knowing. The resistance is dropped and there is pure receptivity.

J. Krishnamurti[*], the great philosopher, beautifully says, 'There can be freedom from knowledge only when the motivation for gathering of knowledge is understood.'

What is generally the motivation for knowledge? You see: the present is an unfolding miracle and mystery of Existence. We try to grasp it with the net of knowledge. That is the motivation for knowledge. But it can never happen! The unknown can never be trapped with the known. The unknown can be known only by surrendering to it. That surrender is what is called intelligence! Intelligence recognizes the mystery of the present moment and surrenders to it joyfully. That joy is the joy of innocence.

Knowledge on the other hand denies the mystery of the present moment. It tries to ascertain it every minute and the present can never be ascertained. So you continuously remain with what is called 'fear of the unknown'. It is through the process of trying to ascertain the present moment that the fear of the unknown takes root. Otherwise, you have no fear! You are very clear that the present moment is a mystery!

J. Krishnamurti - Renowned Indian philosopher.

Through knowledge, you somehow try to escape from the 'not-knowing' of the moment. To the ego, not-knowing means being nothing. It cannot handle being nothing. But innocence is being nothing and enjoying the present! The present is an unopened gift. But knowledge robs it of its suspense. When knowledge understands that the ways of the Self are yet to be discovered, then it doesn't hinder the process of the ultimate Knowing. Then it behaves as a tool that comes into play when actually required and does not stand in the way of embracing the mysteries of life.

Once knowledge solidifies in the being there is no space left for experiencing. There is scope only for replay of knowledge. Everything becomes a reflection of some past knowledge or some past conclusion. The future becomes a continuation of the past patterns and experiences. You already know the fragrance of a flower. You already know the sound of the waves.

Existence is not a continuation of anything. It is fresh every minute. So it is not possible to know anything. What do you know of what will happen the next second? If this is understood, all knowing can be dropped. Then there is only wisdom and wisdom is innocent intelligence. It allows the experience to happen without knowledge hindering. Then the great discoveries of the Self and that which is around the Self as well as the mysteries that link both happen.

J. Krishnamurti* rightly says that belief discards so many possibilities and urges you

Activity causes fatigue while action creates energy and inspiration.

into one particular activity. Since the mind is constantly looking for activity you go behind belief. We base our whole life on beliefs. Because of this we are immersed in activity, but not action. Activity needs constant fuelling through beliefs. Activity cannot afford to stop. If it stops, the mind falls into depression. Action happens as and when required and stops. Activity happens out of belief. Action happens out of understanding. Activity causes fatigue while action creates energy and inspiration. What you need is action, not activity.

Just understand that belief is nothing but your own understanding of something and not the truth. In any given situation, four different people can conclude differently with four different beliefs. There is no absolute reality in belief. It is merely an individual perception. But innocence keeps the perception open. That is the beauty of it. It doesn't conclude and close the doors on anything.

There are innumerable interpretations to anything. Not holding onto any one interpretation is the essence of innocence. Then the spirit is kept alive.

Grasp with Innocence

When you are with innocence you simply enjoy the moment. If you watch innocent people, they will never appear to be with any

---

J. Krishnamurti - Renowned Indian philosopher.

Innocence knows the beauty of purposelessness.

great purpose. They will simply revel in the moment with a totality, with simplicity. Innocence grasps the moment while knowledge misses it. Knowledge knows only purpose while innocence knows the beauty of purposelessness.

If you set aside your knowledge, you are ready to grasp the moment and the Truth. The *present* holds the truth in it. The problem is that today education teaches only knowledge and how to be clever. It doesn't educate on innocence. Where in the universities do they teach innocence?

There is such a pressure to be clever today. Children lose their innocence to the conditioning that they receive in the name of 'how to be clever'. Over time, like this small boy, even innocence is used only to make up for cleverness!

A father introduced his son proudly to his colleagues at office for the first time.

All his colleagues were standing around the boy and the father said, 'Son, why don't you tell them how old you are?'

The child promptly said, 'When I am at home I am seven. But when I am on a bus, I am five.'

This is how children are trained today. They are trained to see utility in everything. Education evaluates you by your own utility. But you are not your utility. You are your being. The being can never be evaluated. Only the mind can be, and mind itself is a myth! Society creates a myth, which is your mind, and holds it as the yardstick to evaluate you.

That is the reason why knowledge is so popular today.

A small story:

Four friends lived in a town. They spent a lot of time together. Three of them were very learned. The fourth was not as learned but he was wise.

One day, they decided to travel to other lands to exhibit their learning to men and earn money.

The fourth friend had nothing to boast of, but expressed his wish to accompany them.

The first friend said, 'You don't know much. If you accompany us, we will have to unnecessarily share our money with you.'

The second friend said, 'Yes, that is true. It is better you stay back.'

The third friend was more kind. He said, 'We grew up together all these years. It is not right to tell him to stay back. He should come along.'

So the four of them started their journey.

They passed through a dense forest. They saw many wild animals and experienced many exciting moments. Suddenly one day, they came across a heap of animal bones.

One of them said, 'I think this is a wonderful way to put our knowledge to test. Let us bring this animal back to life.'

The two other friends agreed, but the fourth one said, 'I feel these are the bones of a very big animal, so we should not attempt to do such things.'

The other three laughed at him and called him a coward. They said, 'If you had knowledge like we do, you will not feel so afraid of such things. Keep quiet and watch us.'

The three proceeded with the experiment.

One of them arranged the bones in a way that it looked like a proper animal. Then he chanted some verses, sprinkled holy water on it and the bones suddenly took the shape of a skeleton. They were amazed by the power of their knowledge.

The second one came forward, chanted a few more verses and sprinkled more water on it. The skeleton suddenly got covered with muscles, flesh, blood and a coat of fur. It was a lion and lacked only life.

The friends were amazed at themselves.

The third friend came forward and said he would infuse life into it.

The fourth friend gave another warning but they laughed at him. He then slowly climbed up a tree and sat there watching.

The third friend waved life into the lion's body and the lion came to life.

With one roar, the lion advanced towards the three of them. They looked up to see where the fourth friend was. He was perched up on the tree watching the whole scene.

The lion made short work of them.

Knowledge is a tool. It doesn't directly lead to intelligence. It is just a tool. As long as we use it as a powerful tool where needed, it is good. It can do amazing things. The mistake we do is giving our whole lives to the hands of knowledge. On the other hand innocence leads directly to pure intelligence.

Innocence grasps dimensions that cleverness misses. Innocence may miss the facts but it catches the Truths. Cleverness is too busy with facts. When cleverness combines with innocence, it becomes a rare combination of intelligence and innocence. Setting aside knowledge for the sake of innocence is intelligence. I don't mean that you have to stop gathering knowledge. Just understand that knowledge cannot substitute innocence.

If you observe villagers who are not educated you will see that they exhibit pure intelligence! That is why you will find that when you are stuck, a villager effortlessly pitches in and helps you out! Innocent intelligence has that capacity.

Today all universities work on sharpening the intellectual faculty of the individual. They teach us how to make ourselves more useful to society and how to be productive or effective. There is nothing wrong in being productive and effective, but in the process we forget how to be innocent and receptive. We forget how to open up to the cosmos, to Existence. We forget how to move in synchronicity with the cosmos, how to make productivity happen in tune with the cosmic plan, which is the source of all productivity. This happens because we are caught in 'doing' and 'having', we forget the '*being*'.

There are three important states: being, doing and having. Right now, we move from doing to having. We continuously 'do' things. We learn and we put the learning into useful action. We then 'have' what we want, whether it is money, relationships, comfort, and what not. Then we want to have better things or have more things and so we continue doing. We are all the time between doing and having. In the process, the being is forgotten. Our real restfulness lies only in the state of being. Because of this, however much we do and have, we still search for restfulness. This feeling is the 'call of the being'.

If we nurture the being and cause the doing to happen from the quality of the being, then we don't have to work so much for the having. That will simply happen as a byproduct. This is the secret of Existence. But this is not seen as a direct utility to society by the universities. That is the problem. But this is what gives the real utility of every individual, not only to society but to the whole of the cosmos. We should always be concerned about the Whole.

In the ancient Indian universities like Takshila* and Nalanda*, the preparation of the students was always at the being level. Outer world learning happened as a natural consequence. India has always focused on nurturing the innocence of the being because only that will lead to strength of the being. When there is strength of the being, anything can be achieved.

Paramahamsa Yogananda* beautifully describes the intent of spiritual learning. He says, there are trillions of cells in the body. Every cell is like an intelligent being. Every cell has the DNA* substance in it which has the information and intelligence to grow a whole new body and brain. This dormant intelligence needs to be awakened so that the mind doesn't move towards suffering and remains in bliss.

He goes on to say that spiritual education magnetizes the cells by sending life current around the brain and spine, ensuring evolutionary advancement of the individual. With this divine magnetism, every cell becomes a brain alive and ready to grasp every bit of knowledge. With these awakened brains, the mental capacity of the individual multiplies multifold and all sorts of knowledge can be effortlessly comprehended! Such is the impact of spiritual learning.

Alexander, the emperor of Greece, had conquered three fourths of the world and traveled downward to Asia to conquer it. He settled down in the banks of the river Sindhu to conquer India.

On the banks of the same river lived a hermit.

As Alexander and his army passed by, the hermit was meditating and did not stand up to salute him.

Takshila - A center of learning mentioned in the Hindu epics of Ramayana and Mahabharata, now a world UN heritage site in North eastern Pakistan.

Nalanda - A great Buddhist center of learning in modern day Bihar comprising a university and library.

Paramahamsa Yogananda - An enlightened master well known for his book 'Autobiography of a Yogi'. He founded Self Realization Fellowship movement in USA in 1920.

DNA - Deoxyribonucleic acid, the building block of all living beings containing the genetic code.

Alexander felt humiliated and shouted at him, 'How dare you do not salute me!' And he took out his sword to chop his head off.

The hermit looked at him and laughed.

Alexander was shocked. He asked, 'I am going to kill you and you are laughing?'

The hermit said, 'I wonder what you are trying to kill! I can never be killed. I am immortal, eternal and imperishable. Weapons cannot cut, fire cannot burn, water cannot wet, wind cannot dry up this soul.' He quoted from the Bhagavad Gita.

Alexander dropped the sword and saluted the hermit saying, 'India has such great people who are fearless about death. I offer my salutations to this great country.' He retreated from the Indian soil a wiser man.

The teachings of olden day universities created the possibility for supreme knowledge and confidence to flower in individuals, at the same time preserving their innocence. Then every student acquired the quality of a sage. A sage has the vast knowledge of the outer world and the utter innocence of the inner world.

A person may go on and on reading something here and there, and entertain himself. If his intention is just reading books it can be good entertainment, but not enlightenment. Entertainment is different from enlightenment. Just because he has been entertained by some good books, it doesn't mean that he is enlightened. The books which help you sharpen your logic give you the feeling that you know. There starts the problem.

One more thing: one cannot blame modernization for loss of innocence also. Lord Krishna says, 'I am Time.' When Krishna says that, you need to understand that modernization is also the divine play of Existence. Man should understand modernization in the right light and not take it as a replacement to the ancient foundation of growing.

Be vulnerable

When you are innocent, you are vulnerable to everything that Existence wants to teach you! If you are closed, you create a wall around you. The wall neither allows fresh breeze to touch your being nor does it allow you to step out and touch the cool breeze. Vulnerability is breaking the wall and inviting the cool breeze to touch your very being every time it blows.

Vulnerability is allowing *everything* to touch your being. The entire cosmos comes to you when you are vulnerable.

Vulnerability is not weakness. The wall when broken will not cause you danger. The wall itself was built out of a deep fear of exposing your reality. Your reality is your vulnerability and you are so afraid of opening it to the cosmos. You know deep down that if you let go and open up you will simply be swept away in innocence. So you close yourself up. But it is suffocating to be in there because it is the same air that is circulating. You experience the same patterns that the mind knows. Then of what use is the wall? When the wall is broken, you will realize that

When you say 'yes', your energy starts moving in a new direction.

nothing leaves you. Instead, you only gain freshness of life.

Two astrologers met on the road on a beautiful autumn day. One of them commented, 'Beautiful autumn. It is something we have never seen earlier.'

The other replied, 'True. I am reminded of the autumn of 2070.'

When you are vulnerable, you experience everything at the being level. Otherwise, it becomes an experience through the head. The being is poetry, the head is prose. Life is poetry.

One night a wife found her husband standing over their baby's crib.

As he stood looking down upon the baby in the cradle, she saw his face assuming a mixture of emotions of disbelief, awe, skepticism, doubt, amazement and what not.

She slowly went up to him, put her arm around him and said, 'A penny for your thoughts.'

The husband replied, 'It's amazing. I can't imagine how anyone can make a crib like that for just 45 dollars!'

With the head you cannot be vulnerable! And when you are not vulnerable, you are sitting behind the great wall of your house. Life has not yet started. Life happens with vulnerability.

With vulnerability you move towards the truth in a different path, in a joyful path because every moment you are receiving directly from Existence. Existence is able to give you because you are vulnerable and ready to receive it! Existence has its own ethics. Enlightened masters have their own ethics. When there is vulnerability, they can simply shower on you. When there is a wall, it becomes difficult. Their ethics does not permit them to penetrate. So they wait for the wall to break.

When you become vulnerable, you are saying a 'yes' to Existence. Existence is the greatest mystery and the eternal teacher. When you say yes to it, your energy starts moving in a new direction. It moves from the head to the heart and you start receiving the teachings from your very being. Whatever you said 'no' to earlier will start becoming a yes. Then you will see that the world is very different from what you thought.

People ask me how to 'be' in my presence. Just be completely vulnerable and innocent. With openness, you can receive the truth directly in your being. The master is a pure expression of Existence. By allowing him, you are allowing Existence to enter into you. When Existence enters it leaves an impression of the truth in your being. With every *darshan* or touch from the master, the impression becomes deeper. This impression is greater than any teaching he can impart to you.

A master can't teach you spirituality, but you can learn by being open and trusting towards him. Spirituality has nothing to do with words. It is an experience. You need to imbibe it by watching the master's body language, by smelling the enlightenment that radiates from him. You can catch it if you are aware.

When you are vulnerable, you are open in your entire response system. You are not in a hurry to ask your questions. You give space for the intelligence of the cosmos to act through you.

To just express with vulnerability is to be free like a bird, not worried about any past or future, to just *be*. That is what Zen masters taught their disciples.

Surrender with trust

Immense trust leads to surrender. Surrender is simplicity of the heart. It is the knowing that you do not have to decide about the Truth, that you just have to go by it. When you awaken to the powerful presence of the Truth, surrender happens.

If you observe your pet dog, you will find that even if you cheat him once in a while, he will come back to you with utmost trust. His trust is absolute and innocent. The trust comes with no reason. He has no questions, so no answers need to be given. He sees no utility in anything. He just exists like an open book, that's all.

Two gold fish were in a water tank. One asked the other, 'Do you trust in god?'

The other replied, 'But of course. Who do you think changes our water everyday?'

It is only innocence that is capable of taking the leap into trust and surrender. Knowledge somehow sees utility in everything. It looks for reason in everything. Surrender and reason are mutually exclusive.

Only innocence is capable of taking the leap into trust and surrender.

Surrender is to do with trust. Surrender is possible only out of innocence, because out of innocence arises trust.

Out of surrender arises deep relaxation. Out of surrender arises a fresh intelligence that knows on a different plane. On this plane, there is no worry of result, there is only action driven by pure energy. And energy *is* intelligence. Trust does not mean inaction. It means continuing to be in action with intelligence instead of intellect. It is having trust in thought, and intelligence in action.

A disciple came riding on his camel to the tent of a Sufi master. He dismounted from the camel, walked into the master's tent, bowed down low and said, 'Master, so great is my trust in god that I have left my camel outside untied, convinced that god protects the interests of those who love him.'

The master shouted, 'Go tie your camel you fool! God cannot be bothered doing for you what you are perfectly capable of doing yourself!'

Trust is an attitude. It is not a substitute for appropriate action. The spirit of trust is the essence of life. It leads to innocence, surrender, relaxation and bliss. If it is followed out of complete understanding, there is nothing to lose in its path. Until then, you are still on the path to trust.

Enlightened masters are established in the knowing that nothing is impossible in the space of Existence. They are living embodiments of trust. Their bliss is an expression of this. They have access to all the knowledge of the world but are yet utterly innocent. They know that their knowledge is the knowledge of Existence. Their knowledge is not knowledge but a flowing experience of the truth of the moment.

We too have knowledge. But the problem is that we think *our* knowledge is the only right knowledge and all other knowledge is wrong. Understand: the ultimate knowledge is the same for everyone. Anything in between is just a bunch of borrowed ideas. If this is known clearly, surrender will happen and we will drop the burden of knowledge and become innocent.

How to start knowing that we don't know? Mere clarity that we don't know is enough. Just meditate on Existence, the source of all knowledge. Be in a prayerful and surrendering mood to it all the time. Be firm in surrendering to the knowledge of Existence. You will see that miracles start happening around you.

There is a story about Hanuman, the monkey god in Hindu mythology who was a devout disciple of Lord Rama*.*

*Hanuman*was once asked what day of the lunar month it was.*

He replied, 'I don't know anything about the day of the month or the positions of the stars. I think of Rama alone.'*

When you are established in the wonder of the Truth, you become so innocent, that your very life becomes meditative and miraculous. It was Hanuman* who crossed the ocean from India to Sri Lanka with just one leap by chanting the name of Rama*. Rama himself had to build a bridge to cross over with his army! Such is the power of innocent surrender to Existence and all its forms.

One more thing: when you are trusting and surrendering, it becomes difficult to cheat you. Innocent trust always protects from deceit. It radiates that kind of energy.

There was a great Sufi Saint by name Habib Ajami. He went to bathe in the river one day leaving his coat on the bank of the river unattended.

One man passed by at that time and saw the coat. Thinking someone had left it there carelessly and it had to be protected, he decided to stand guard over it till the owner came by.

Habib came back looking for his coat. The man asked him, 'In whose care did you leave the coat when you went to bathe?' It might as well have been stolen!'

Habib replied, 'I left it in the care of Him who gave you the task of guarding over it!'

When trust happens with the utmost understanding, nothing can be lost. In the quality of trust is its true essence. I always tell my disciples about the monks I have seen in the Himalayas during my spiritual wandering days. The monks come to the Himalayas to meditate leaving everything behind. But there they fight for their small

---

Hanuman - The monkey god revered by Hindus and a disciple of Rama.

Rama - Prince of the kingdom of Ayodhya in the Indian epic Ramayana.

water pots! Just the object of possessiveness changes, that's all! Understand this. When you trust, all material possessions will seem like they belong to Existence. The very attitude of possessing then drops. That relaxes the mind. That is the space for relaxing.

In the year 2004, we went as a small group to the Himalayas. In a lifetime at least once you should visit the Himalayas. We went to Gomukh*, which is the source of the sacred river Ganga. The trek is on mule back taking almost five hours up and five hours down. The path is just four feet wide. If you miss your footing you will go into the gushing Ganga river beneath! Once we reached Gomukh* we spent some time there, and the group returned while I stayed back with a few disciples.

The group that returned started at dusk. I told them not to worry and that Existence will take care. Through pitch darkness, not knowing if the mule was taking the bend of the mountain or going straight ahead into the darkness, the entire group made its way back. The next day, I asked them how the experience was. One of them said, '*Swamiji*, we experienced what blind trust means!' If those trusting moments could be extended, they can be the very essence of your life. Then, you can simply *do*, leaving the result to Existence.

Another important thing is unless innocence happens, intimacy cannot happen. Intimacy is the language of Existence. The mind doesn't know intimacy. Only the being knows it. With intimacy there is openness and

Gomukh - Source of river Ganga.

Unless innocence happens intimacy cannot happen.

you can say and do everything that you feel genuinely and earnestly about. There will be authenticity in your words and actions. You will radiate energy that spurs the others around you to be innocent and open. Then the real beauty of Existence can be experienced.

Spirituality – the way to innocent obeisance

There is a famous saying, 'If you worry, then you didn't pray. If you prayed, then don't worry.'

Spirituality is a straight path to surrender worry and be free. It is a tremendous relief for the modern day man. It is a proven science. In today's world of science and knowledge, the call of the being needs to be addressed compassionately and immediately. Spirituality is the way. Spirituality restores the cosmos with its sanctity and mysticism. It reminds man that he is not the greatest creature on the planet. It reminds him of the powerful Existential Energy that pervades the universe. It creates not-knowing and innocent surrender in the mind.

Spirituality is not a ritual. It is the science of merging with Existence. From time immemorial, the first thing that all world religions did was to create a space for the Divine to become a part of life. A temple is a space to reconnect with the cosmic energy and be restful in it. That was the core purpose of all world religions. And when the connection deepened, it became a blissful space within oneself. Religion was a clear stepping stone to spirituality.

When man pursues science alone, he becomes too knowing because his inventions and discoveries seem to be his own findings. Everything seems to fall under the purview of his intellect. Spirituality on the other hand keeps the mystery of the cosmos alive. It creates humble obeisance towards a life force that is mightier than the intellect. That is why spirituality can restore innocence.

There is an immediate need to pay obeisance to the cosmic force and calm the intellect. With obeisance comes fresh intelligence that sees the cosmic consciousness as the central core of activity. Then, man will no more be afraid of the unfathomable cosmos. He will simply fall in tune with it with deep devotion, love and in ecstasy.

The greatest saints of India who had the power of willing the cosmos to lovingly respond achieved this power through spirituality.

There was a man by name Muruganar who was an ardent devotee of Shiva. Everyday before break of dawn he would bathe in the cool waters of the river, gather flowers from trees, fields, the river and creepers and make garlands for the Shiva deity in the temple.

He would walk to the temple every day taking care while walking not to disturb the flowers in their setting in the garland! After offering them to the deity he would chant sacred verses for long hours.

It is said that he attained enlightenment through just this innocent worship.

Today he is worshipped as one of the 63 saints called Nayanmars* who attained enlightenment through innocent devotion to god.

Those who shun spirituality are those who have not tasted its transforming sweetness. They are the ones who think spirituality is seriousness. No! God is always an embodiment of bliss, then how can spirituality be seriousness? Man has made it serious by reducing it to mundane rituals.

Our masters have even specified the times in which to connect to the deeper realms of our being through prayer. They have said it is good to pray in the early morning. What is the reason for this? The intellect has rested well in the night and does not as yet start functioning in the morning. When spirituality is practiced at that time, the impact on the mind is greater. The impact is made while the mind is still fresh and innocent, while the mind has not yet started chewing on the intellect. Not for nothing have the great masters gifted spirituality to us. When the intent is understood, spirituality becomes a straight route to restoring innocence and trust.

Nayanmars - Tamil devotee saints of enlightened master Shiva, 63 in number, whose life stories are told in the book Periya Puranam.

A small story:

One evening, a farmer on his way back from the market found himself without his prayer book. The wheel of his cart came off right in the middle of the woods and he felt sad that the day should pass without having said his prayers.

So he made up a prayer to god. He spoke aloud, 'Oh god, I have done something very foolish. I have left behind my prayer books today. And my memory is so poor that I can't recite a single prayer without the book. So this is what I am going to do. I will recite the letters of the alphabet five times very slowly and you, who knows all the prayers, please put the letters together to form the prayers I can't remember.'

And god said to his angels that day, 'Of all the prayers I have heard today, this one was undoubtedly the best because it came from a heart that was simple and sincere.'

Spirituality is an opening to express innocence in its purest form. Innocence itself is an offering to god. Innocence itself is the greatest prayer to god.

Religion is by itself not any belief as it is made out to be. Every religion is the result of the deep spiritual experience of the great master who founded it. What they experienced, they gave as a religion to humanity, through which humanity can get the same experience. There was no other intent. If this is understood, any person can practice any religion. That is the beauty of all original religions.

The same is true when you are around a master. Be in a mood of innocent surrender. When you are innocent and prayerful, the master's silence penetrates your being. The religion of silence is the greatest religion. It is the religion of the great masters and disciples. That is true spirituality also.

Drop cunningness and become spontaneous

When I told the story of Satyakama to a group of people, one person asked me, 'Swamiji, maybe these techniques are for highly evolved souls. In that story, the disciple gets enlightened when the master just blesses him. He must have been a highly evolved soul for that to happen.'

I told that person, 'No, it is not for highly evolved souls. It is for highly innocent souls!' Understand this. Highly evolved people don't need techniques. Techniques such as those given to Satyakama are given to innocent people who are tired of being cunning. Understand these words, 'tired of being cunning'.

What is cunningness? It is the opposite of intelligence. You can be either cunning or intelligent, never both at the same time. Cunningness is also the opposite of vulnerability. When you are cunning, you cannot be vulnerable. When you are vulnerable, you are pure like a child. A child can be intelligent and innocent at the same time. Over time, his intelligence grows but the innocence invariably takes a turn to become cunningness. Then he is no more pure like a child. Societal conditioning causes the

Calculation is alright for arithmetic, not for the being.

innocence in the intelligence to take the turn into cunningness. Children if left to themselves remain innocent. But we teach them so many things that they become social animals. Understand this. We hold a great responsibility in bringing up children without making them cunning.

The poet Khalil Gibran* says beautifully about children,

You may give them your love but not your thoughts,

For they have their own thoughts.

Cunningness is division. It is a constant calculation. It hinders free and innocent expression. It knows to express only through calculation. Calculation is alright for arithmetic, not for the being. We calculate for the wrong reasons. Do we ever calculate our blessings? No, never! They are just taken for granted.

Cunningness starts with division of the Whole. Innocence is lost when the mind is taught to divide. Once it picks up the thread, the mind continues and moves far away from its original innocence.

Two babies were in a pram next to each other in a mall.

One of them turned to the other and asked, 'Are you a girl or a boy?'

'I don't know,' the baby replied.

The first one said, 'I can tell.' And he dived beneath the clothes and came out and said, 'You are a girl and I am a boy.'

The baby girl was surprised and asked, 'How did you know?'

Pat came the reply, 'That's easy. You are wearing pink booties and I am wearing blue ones!'

From a very early stage, the child is taught division by people who are themselves struggling with cunningness. The child unconsciously trades his innocence for cunningness.

The danger with cunningness is that it grows roots in many directions and solidifies as the very nature of the individual. The person will not even know he is cunning. He won't even know that his struggle with himself is because of his cunningness.

One person came to me and started telling me, 'Swamiji, I have extra marital relationships.' I asked, 'Do you feel it is wrong?' He said, 'Yes, I know it is wrong, and I am very clear that I am doing something wrong.' I told him, 'Then stop it.' He said, 'No, only you can stop it.' I told him, 'Hey, I am not the one having the relationship to stop it! You are the one having it, so it is you who is supposed to decide and stop!' He stood silent. I asked him, 'What do you mean by I should stop? Do you mean that I should take your car keys and not allow you to go there? What do you mean by I should stop?'

Khalil Gibran - 20th Century Lebanese American poet best known for his 'The Prophet'.

This is cunningness. He told me, 'No, I have surrendered myself to you, so you should take care of it.' I told him it was a good story! Then I told him, 'You told just now you have surrendered everything to me. Alright then, just sit here and meditate.' He asked, 'What are you saying *Swamiji*?' I told him, 'You were the one who said just now that you have surrendered everything to me! Then just do whatever I say. Don't move from here, just sit.' That he was not ready to do!

A small story:

The rivers one day gathered together and made a complaint against the sea. They asked the sea, 'Why is that when we enter your waters fresh and fit to drink, you make us salty and undrinkable?'

The sea hearing itself being blamed replied, 'Don't come. Then you won't turn salty.'

If you are not ready for the simple solution, then be assured that you are playing a cunning game! Unless you are tired of being cunning, you can't be helped. No technique can help you because your cunningness knows how to escape from every single technique. People come and tell me, '*Swamiji*, whatever you are saying is correct, but...' Understand this. The moment you say 'but' to me, you have missed! The moment you say 'but', it is over. You are trying to escape with your cunningness.

Some people tell me, 'Whatever you say is right, but please make me do whatever you say.' What do you mean? Should I have two or three people continuously watching you and make you do things? Drop your cunning game, then automatically you will start doing what I say. Cunningness is a pure hide and seek game that you play with yourself. You can't play it with me. I straightaway know where all you are hiding. I don't need to come to you to find you. So understand that you are just playing with yourself. Just take a strong decision to be completely sincere and authentic to yourself. Only then you can drop your cunningness.

When cunningness dissolves, authenticity and sincerity happen and you will enlighten quickly. Also, with authenticity you will not indulge in any kind of gossip. Gossip is a pure expression of cunningness. When you are so cunning that you can't tell a person anything on his face, you talk behind his back.

When you drop cunningness, spontaneity flowers. Spontaneity is the opposite of calculation. Intelligence plus innocence is spontaneity. Intelligence plus cunningness is calculation. Spontaneity is nothing but a flowing expression of your innocence. It is a non-calculating state of mind. It is called *sahaja**, being yourself without any burden. The burden is the burden of constant calculation.

Understand this, with cunningness, you may think you are gaining a lot of things, but the truth is that you are losing your innocence. Losing your innocence is like losing your entire life. You can afford to lose anything but not your innocence.

Sahaja - Spontaneous divine joy.

> **The problem of falsity comes because society teaches you to be someone special all the time.**

Innocence, Totality, Maturity

Dhammapada[*] says:

Light the lamp within, strive hard to attain wisdom. Become pure and innocent, and live in the world of light.

When you came into the world, you came as an innocent infant. You radiated the beauty of your innocence until society gave you the mind. Now, you want to get rid of your mind and become innocent again. The regained innocence is what is called maturity. It is possible to regain it. Just believe that you were innocent once upon a time. Trust that the innocence is still within you. Then it is possible to start radiating it again. This understanding will start the process again.

Maturity causes us to live in totality. Totality is functioning out of immense innocence and giving your whole to the moment. There is no opinion, no judgment, no fragments within you. There is only intense enthusiasm for the moment. The openness to the moment is the innocence.

To become mature you need to go *in* first, because maturity is all about falling at ease with your true nature with no pretensions. Making your natural self to be your very nature is maturity. The best way to become your natural self is to keep your core at ease.

Let the core of you be at ease all the time, irrespective of where you might be or what you may be doing. Then you can retain your purity. Always feel your natural self at your core with no strain, with no effort or pretensions.

The problem of falsity comes because society teaches you to be someone special all the time. There is no need to be someone special all the time. It is an immature idea to be someone special all the time. Once this idea is renounced, the mind relaxes. It feels no pressure to be shrewd. This relaxation gives birth to innocence.

To feel the urge to regain your innocence you may have to go astray, because when you go astray and face the consequences, introspection starts. The introspection triggers the need to regain innocence. Don't condemn yourself for going astray. Just bring in the awareness to integrate yourself into the right path forever. If maturity is going to happen this way it is definitely worth it.

Maturity is taking a strong decision not to delude yourself anymore. It is to awaken to the consciousness within. It is to integrate yourself with honesty. When this happens, you start to become a child again. As a child, you were innocent but not with awareness. Somewhere in the process of growing up you lost the innocence. You are regaining it now. The new innocence will be with full awareness and that is the real innocence.

Dhammapada - Teachings of Buddha in scriptural form.

When you regain the innocence, you flower with the understanding that there is nothing more priceless than becoming childlike again. That is the process of enlightenment.

That is why a child's innocence is to be nurtured with utmost care. For every innocent observation that a child makes, if we can be without imposing our knowledge on it, the child will grow up preserving its innocence. For example, if the child asks, 'Why is it that the sky is blue sometimes and white sometimes?' just tell the child that the sky is blue sometimes and white sometimes. He will anyway learn that in his lessons in school. But if you can tell him they are just the way they are, he will straightaway understand the spontaneity of nature. He will not be looking for further knowledge to feed himself with. The universities take care of that anyway.

At home, when you are still the most influential person in his life, if you make him understand that this is the way things are, that there is no need to know it all with knowledge, the innocence in him survives. He doesn't catch the thread of passing judgment on nature. He learns to see without bringing words in. He learns to just see and be. The moment words are brought in, the innocence is lost. Then it is no more seeing. It becomes looking. The whole beauty of it is then lost.

Growing up is always considered to be a serious thing. If you grow up in seriousness you only grow old. If you grow up in playfulness, you remain young! It is a good thing to see what children, animals and other creatures are doing at times because they all live with innocence and playfulness. It will help understand and reconnect with innocence.

Childlike innocence discovers many things but cannot understand most of it. It enjoys it at the level of its innocence, that's all. Whereas innocence regained not only discovers these new things, but also understands all of them. That is the difference.

Childlike innocence is beautiful but not enough. It has to be lost to life and regained with complete awareness and maturity.

It is said that a mad man and a mystic look alike. Both of them will be eccentric in their ways, laughing abruptly and doing things incomprehensible. But they are actually at the extreme two ends of the same spectrum! Extremes always look alike. Outwardly they appear to be the same, that's all. Similarly, a child and a saint may look alike in their innocence, but they are actually at the two extreme ends of the same spectrum. The child has not even started its achievement of regained innocence, while the saint has finished it.

The innocence of the child is still the god given innocence he came with, not the innocence that he regained through life. The innocence of a child can be easily disturbed, whereas the innocence of a sage can never be disturbed. Getting the innocence disturbed and working to regain it permanently is the process of maturity. That is the travel through to the other end of the spectrum in becoming a saint.

With innocence regained, you will once again be able to look into the eyes of the other.

251

When you regain your innocence, you are called *dvija*, reborn.

Your innocence not only makes you vulnerable, it also makes you integrated. With knowledge, you are fragmented within you. With regained innocence, you are integrated and honest to yourself and to others. That honesty will radiate from your eyes and touch the other. That honesty is maturity.

Just the longing to become innocent again is enough. It will start destroying all that is not *you* inside you. After all, it is just layers of conditioning. But it is important to hold your will strong until the process is complete. The will is a constant reminder to be sincere and honest without cunningness. Decide not to rest until the de-conditioning is total.

The beauty of maturity is that it allows you to function as a mature person when required and as a child at all other times. It easily allows you to flow from one to the other so that you are in perfect harmony with the Whole.

When you regain your innocence, you are called *dvija**, reborn, mature. The key is not to give up in your effort in regaining your innocence. The journey may be frustrating at times, because it is taking time and not happening. It is so because society has conditioned you with many layers. The onion has to be peeled layer after layer to reach the center. Frustration is a precondition to burst open with transformation. So don't relax, that is enough. It will happen. Remember,

innocence is already in you. It is not about any end objective outside. Just this remembrance will give you the relaxation after every frustration.

Everyday just sit for a few moments, sit by yourself and calmly go into your innocence. Feel the innocence in you. Feel the purity in you. Feel the overflowing from within you. Let it spread through your body, mind and being. Feel how beautiful you are in your innocence. Do this everyday. Soon you will see that you will awaken to it as your very nature. All that is not you will be burnt and the real *you* will emerge.

Innocence has a totality about it. This totality is called grace. That is why enlightened masters appear to be so graceful and beautiful all the time. Innocence manifests itself as wondrous beauty to the eyes of the beholder. It is so total that even the most cunning mind cannot deny it. It simply defies all logic and touches you.

We always think children are immature. We think that the grownups who cry are immature. We are conditioned to believe that expression of any emotion is immature. Expressing the emotions in an unfiltered way is a sign of innocence. The cunning ones edit even their emotions. Once in a while it is good to cry in front of people. What is wrong with it? What are you trying to hide? By crying you are only expressing your true feelings. What is there to hide? The problem is that society has always taught us to hide our true

---

Dvija - Twice born. Refers to the state of awakening of Consciousness.

nature and show only our projected personality. That is why with time we forget what our nature is. We forget how to be innocent.

One teacher told the parent during the parent teacher meeting, 'Your daughter is very good in all her activities. She is just a little emotionally immature. But she will be alright.'

The parent looked at her in a puzzled way and asked, 'At three, how else do you expect her to be?'

Just by being with children as their friend, as their playmate, it is possible to get back in touch with the innocence. When you are with them don't pretend to be like a child. Take it really seriously and *become* a child! It is the greatest favor you can do to yourself.

There are umpteen ways to rediscover the child hiding in you. Just play hide and seek with children or learn how to make cookies or watch Tom and Jerry cartoons or eat different color cotton candies or make mud dolls! All these will bring out the child in you. Your solid identity will dissolve. You will become fluid like a river and flow. The weight of your seriousness will drop and you will become light and blissful.

Seriousness is ego. When you are afraid of getting hurt, when you are afraid of losing your control or power, you become serious. When you are too centered on yourself this happens. When you let go and play and touch your innocence again, you will suddenly enjoy a break from yourself. That break is the falling of your seriousness. In that gap you will realize there is nothing to hold on to. There is only free spirit. When you become aware of this you can work on it consciously and move towards becoming completely innocent and sincere.

Innocence is keeping the consciousness at the level of the heart, not allowing it to settle in the head.

You Are Part of the Collective Consciousness

We now move to a slightly more complex subject. It is about the relationship that we have with the world around us. Why do we see what we see? How do we see what we see? How do we fit into the scheme of Existence?

Matter, energy and beyond

What is this world made up of? Our five senses of sight, hearing, smell, taste and touch are our gateways to perceiving this world. They tell us that this world is made up of matter – objects in various forms, shapes, colors and qualities.

We see ourselves living in a three dimensional world fundamentally made up of the five basic elements - earth, water, fire, air and space. We see all the objects in this world undergoing change with time. They all undergo creation, sustenance and dissolution with the passage of time.

Classical physics tells us that matter is governed by the laws of physics like the three laws of motion, the law of gravity, the laws of fluid dynamics and so on. All objects are considered to be made up of molecules, which are made up of atoms, which in turn are made of three types of particles - protons, neutrons and electrons. We learned all these fundamental things in school.

But according to modern science, the world is not fundamentally made up of matter; the fundamental particles are not protons, neutrons and electrons. Modern science says matter itself is actually energy!

Albert Einstein's famous equation, $E=mc^2$ (where E is energy, m is mass of the object and c is the speed of light) proves the equivalence of matter and energy. I was reading a very recent article, also published in the US Journal Science (http://www.physorg.com/news146415074.html), on a research that proved Einstein's equation. The fundamental particles in the nucleus themselves are considered to be made of smaller particles called quarks, which are bound by gluons. The surprising thing is the mass of gluons is zero and the mass of quarks is only five percent. The study says, the missing 95 percent comes from the energy of

> **Matter is actually energy vibrating at various frequencies and manifesting itself in various forms.**

the movements and interactions of quarks and gluons. So, energy and mass are equivalent.

This truth discovered by science a few decades ago, was declared by the Eastern *rishis** in the *Upanishads** - the essence of the *vedic* knowledge. The very first line of the *Isa Vasya Upanishad**, written thousands of years ago, declares, *Isa vasyam idam sarvam* which means all that exists is energy!

Matter is vibrating energy

Matter is actually energy vibrating at various frequencies and manifesting itself in various forms. We are not able to see this vibration with our eyes because the frequencies of vibration are too high. It is just as when movement is too fast, the eye cannot perceive the moving objects as independent frames. The eye sees the objects merging into each other continuously.

In the same way, the vibration of energy cannot be perceived by the eye. It appears to be solid matter! Energy in gross form is matter. Matter in subtle form is energy. The body is the gross manifestation of the subtle mind. The mind is the subtle manifestation of the

gross body. An important thing to be understood here is that the perception of the world varies from person to person because the functioning of the mind varies from person to person!

Even interactions between people are only energy interactions. For example, an atom that consists of a nucleus with a cloud of electrons around it can be compared to a football field. The nucleus is like a peanut in the center of a football field and the cloud of electrons is like the empty space in the field. Another comparison I came across is, if you were to remove all the space between all the atoms on planet earth, the remaining matter would come to just about the size of a sugar cube!

What we see as solid matter, as the football field in this example, is actually the electron clouds - huge empty spaces - interacting with each other. In the same way, our interactions and contact with other people and objects are also only interaction of energies. There is an exchange of energy that happens. You give some of your energy and you get energy from that person or object!

The world of infinite possibilities

Now, what is the origin of matter and energy? What is the origin of the body and mind? From where does the energy in all

---

Rishis – Seers of ancient India.

Upanishads – Texts from the *vedic* tradition of enlightened masters and disciples in ancient India.

Isa Vasya Upanishad - One of the major and oldest *vedic* scriptures.

objects arise? What then is the reality behind this perceived world? If we are not able to see reality as it exists through the senses, what is the nature of reality?

This question is asked in the *Shiva Sutras*, an ancient *vedic* scripture on the science of enlightenment. Shiva's* consort Devi* asks Him, 'What is the nature of this wonder-filled universe?' As a response, Shiva delivers 112 enlightenment techniques which, when practiced, give the answer as a direct experience!

This question about reality leads us to a world beyond matter and energy, beyond the limitations of space and time. This is the world where all the possibilities exist as seed. It is the essence and the origin of thoughts, and it is the essence and origin of events in the material world.

In this world-beyond, ordinary logic does not exist. Cause and effect relationships do not exist. The happening of one event does not *cause* another event to happen, but it is *correlated* with the other event that happens. This correlation has no dependence on space and time. So what we call the seed is the ocean of infinite possibilities from which the waves of events arise.

This whole Existence and all its events happen as causeless auspiciousness, like waves arising in an ocean. Existence is an ocean of bliss and ecstasy. Out of the causeless, overflowing

> **Existence is an ocean of bliss and ecstasy.**

ecstasy, the wave of Creation rises in the ocean of Existence! That is how things happen. The Divine, playing with its infinite manifestations in innumerable universes is called sustenance. Dropping from the play and relaxing into Itself is called dissolution. Dissolution is the settling back into the Absolute or *Parabrahma*✻ state. Then... for no logical reason, the play starts again...! This continues. What we see as results are the infinite happenings in the universe.

The real nature

We see this causeless and ecstatic play of Existence through our own individual perception! Our very perception collapses the beautiful happening into a localized reality. Each individual 'boils down' the beautiful happening into his own individual reality.

Someone asked me, 'I see this table here. All the people in this room see this same table. Then how can you say that this table is not a reality?' Please understand that what you see as this table here is not the same as what the other person sees! Each person in this room sees this table differently! That is the truth. That is what I am trying to explain here.

As long as the mind tries to perceive, what is perceived is not the ultimate reality. Only an infinite being can perceive Reality exactly

---

Shiva — Enlightened master.

Devi - Supreme goddess in Hinduism, Cosmic Mother.

Parabrahma - Supreme Being.

> **When we observe, we observe through our own set of conditioning or engrams.**

as it is happening. He cannot explain it in words because words cannot describe what is beyond space and time. He can only tell you to wait for it to become your own experience! That is why Shiva answers not with philosophy but with techniques. He directly gives techniques for Devi* to experience the Reality – the nature of the universe.

Let me explain this concept based on the energy-matter idea. We saw that matter is actually energy. Classical physics said that the electron is a particle. However, quantum physics says that it is a wave. Actually, the electron exhibits the properties of both a particle and a wave in different situations. Physicists have now concluded that the electron has a dual nature as a 'particle-wave'!

The act of observation collapses possibility into reality

Since the electron is a particle, what is the location of the electron? Since it is a wave, what is the momentum of the wave? The answers to these questions lead to a very surprising discovery that the particle-wave can be either a particle or a wave or *even both* at the same time. But you cannot determine both the location and the momentum of the

electron at the same time, because the very act of observing the location of the electron will change its momentum, and the very act of determining the momentum of the electron will change its location! This is what is known in science as the Heisenberg Uncertainty principle.

The particle-wave is both a particle and wave at the same time until the act of observation comes into play. This act of observation can now be connected with our act of observing the causeless happenings of Existence. When we observe, we observe through our own set of conditioning or what we call engrams which are preconceived and deeply engraved memories and conclusions. Each individual's act of observation is colored by his own conditioning or engrams. Based upon that, he boils down the happening to suit his own experience of reality!

In the case of the particle-wave, the very act of observation 'collapses' the wave-particle to a particle or wave. This leads us to a deep understanding that both possibilities exist simultaneously, and it is the very act of observation that changes the possibility into a particular reality.

Let me give another scientific experiment that highlights how the very act of measuring distorts the beautiful reality. You may have heard of the double-slit experiment with light.

In this experiment, a beam of light is aimed at a barrier with two vertical slits. On the other side of the barrier is a photographic

---

Devi - Supreme goddess in Hinduism, Cosmic Mother.

plate that is used to record the light as it falls on it after passing through the barrier. If only one slit is open, the pattern on the photographic plate is as expected, which is a single line of light aligned with the slit. If both the slits are open, we would expect two lines of light on the plate aligned with the slits, but what is observed are multiple lines of light and darkness in varying degrees. This is the principle of interference where light beams behave as waves that interfere with each other.

Now, if the light beam is slowed down enough so that instead of a stream of light particles or photons hitting the plate, each photon *individually* hits the plate, then there should be no interference and the plate should show a light pattern aligned with the slit. But, the resulting pattern still showed interference!

How is this possible? There is only this one photon, what can it be interfering with... other than itself? It was concluded that each photon not only goes through both the slits, but also simultaneously takes every possible path on the way to the target!

To see how this can occur, experiments were done to track the individual photon paths. But what happened was that the measurement in some way disrupted the paths of the photons. Whenever an attempt was made to observe, there were only two bright lines on the photographic plate aligned with the slits! If they didn't attempt to measure, again the pattern became the multiple lines of light and darkness!

The very act of observation changes the possibility into a particular reality.

Understand, each photon moves simultaneously in a number of paths. But an effort to measure the paths causes it to collapse to a single path! In the same way, our very effort to perceive the infinite risings of the ocean of Existence causes it to appear as what our limited mind perceives!

Once a student asked a Zen master, 'What is the path?' The master replied, 'Everyday life is the path.' The student asked, 'Can it be studied?'

The master said, 'If you try to study, you will be far from it.' The student asked, 'If I do not study, how can I know it is the path?'

The master said, 'The path does not belong to the perception world. Neither does it belong to the non-perception world. Perception is a delusion and non-perception is senseless. If you want to reach the true path beyond doubt, place yourself in the same freedom as the sky. You name it neither good nor not-good.'

Physiology of perception

Let us start with what really happens on a physical level when we perceive things.

When there is a perception of physical reality, the various parts of the brain show a change in neural activity as the neurons, which are the basic building blocks of the nervous system, fire in synchronicity. This results in the random visual patterns of light being perceived as specific shapes and forms. This is how the input from each of our senses is perceived, as an experience of particular sound, touch, smell, taste or sight.

If you now step back and look, you can see that before the observation or the perception, both the world as well as you, that is the seen and the seer, existed in a dynamic and chaotic state of activity. The act of perception changes that chaotic state into some sort of an order that becomes both, the seen in the outside world *and* the process of seeing in the seer (as the activity in the nervous system) at the same time. At the moment of seeing, the probability of what is seen collapses into a specific form.

In the Bhagavad Gita*, Krishna, the lord and master, chooses to give Arjuna* the experience of Krishna's cosmic form. Until then, Arjuna had seen Krishna only as the six foot tall, handsome friend. But upon Arjuna's request, and after Krishna sees that Arjuna is ready to receive the cosmic form experience, He decides to give it to him. Arjuna then sees Krishna as the manifestation of the entire cosmos – in all its seeming chaos.

He cries out, 'O Lord! I can see all the gods and deities in Your body. I can see all the sages and divine serpents. O Lord of the Universe, I see many arms, stomachs, faces, eyes and your limitless form. O Universal Form, I cannot see your beginning, middle or end.'

Arjuna is unable to bear the experience because he loses his intellectual control over things! He begs for equilibrium, meaning he wants his mind to be under his intellectual control again. He wants to know the cause and effect of things and feel that they are in his control, because the experience rips him away from his perception of the cause-and-effect logic itself.

As long as cause and effect logic is under your control, you feel you are perceiving reality! Your ego is strong and steady. But the moment the logic is shaken, you feel tremendous fear. You feel you are just a drop in an ocean. What Arjuna sees is the absolute Reality, but he is afraid of that very Reality because it doesn't conform to his logic. He begs to revert to the earlier state of perception through his five senses alone, through his own solid identity, his own solid ego.

Perception of space-time

Let us analyze what space is.

The 1D, 2D and 3D worlds

Take a basic element, a point, a one-dimensional object. When a point traces across a direction, it generates a line.

Bhagavad Gita – Ancient scripture delivered by enlightened master Krishna, and considered to be the essence of spiritual wisdom.

Arjuna - Warrior prince and the third of the five brothers of the Pandava family in the great Indian epic Mahabharata. He was a disciple of enlightened master Krishna who received the wisdom in the Bhagavad Gita from Krishna.

Point   Point traces a Line   Line

Now, let us trace the motion of a line, a two-dimensional object. If it moves in the same direction as it is in, of course it will just continue to be a line. If it moves in a direction not

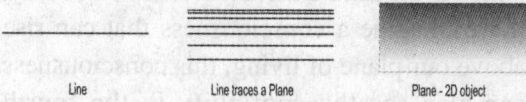

Line   Line traces a Plane   Plane - 2D object

contained in it, it traces a surface or a plane.

Similarly, if a surface or a plane moves in a direction not contained in it, it will trace a

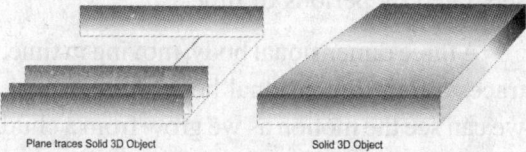

Plane traces Solid 3D Object   Solid 3D Object

solid, a three-dimensional object.

So, a line is an infinite number of points. A surface is an infinite number of lines. A solid is infinite number of surfaces. Similarly, we can imagine a four dimensional space as an infinite number of three dimensional spaces.

Now, just as we built up these higher dimensions from the lower dimensions, we can also see the lower dimensions as parts or sections of a higher dimension space.

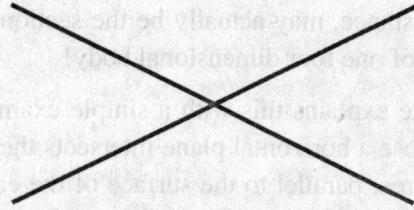

Point - Intersection of two lines

For example, a point is the intersection of two lines. So, a point is a section of a line.

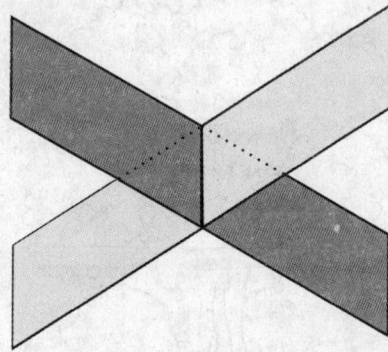

Line - Intersection of two planes

A line is a section of a surface. A surface is a section of a solid.

Extending this, we can say a solid is a section of a four-dimensional body. Our three dimensional space is a section of a four dimensional space. P.D.Ouspensky*, in his book Tertium Organum, explains these very beautifully. He extends this to say that many separate three dimensional bodies, like humans

---

P.D.Ouspensky - Russian philosopher, mathematician and student of enlightened master George Gurdjieff.

for instance, may actually be the sections or parts of one four dimensional body!

He explains this with a simple example. Suppose a horizontal plane intersects the top of a tree, parallel to the surface of the earth. Now, on this plane, the sections of branches seem to be all separate, not connected to each other. But, from the three dimensional space, we can see that these are all sections of branches of one single tree.

A 3D tree when seen in a 2D plane appears like separate circles

The four dimensional world of space-time

In our four-dimensional world, the maximum dimensions in space can be only three. We can call this fourth dimension time. So, the four dimensional world can be looked at as a space-time continuum. It can be said that time is the fourth dimension of space.

We understand time in three forms – past, present and future. We think that the past is

over and does not exist anymore. The future has not yet happened, hence it does not exist. The present thus happens at the transition of the non-existent future to another non-existence, the past.

In the three dimensional world, we see that the seemingly separate sections of the tree in the two dimensional world are actually joined in the third dimension. In the same way, if we imagine a consciousness that can rise above our plane of living, this consciousness can also see the continuity in the fourth dimension of time - past, present and future all existing simultaneously. This consciousness sees the simultaneous happening of events, which the ordinary consciousness sees as distinct events separated by periods of time.

A three dimensional body, moving in time, traces a four dimensional body. Across time, we can see the motion as we grow from a child to youth, to adult, to elderly person. But we are not able to see or feel this 'four-dimensional body' because of our limited perception. Being in the same three-dimensional world, we see only the section of the four dimensional body that is the normal three-dimensional body. It is like one of a series of pictures on a cinema roll.

To understand how a four-dimensional world is perceived in three-dimensional form, let us first see how a three-dimensional happening is seen in a two-dimensional world.

Suppose you are in a two-dimensional world, the world of planes and surfaces. Your life, your perception is restricted to a plane, like a vertical wall. Now, imagine a wheel with each of its spokes painted in a different color is rotating perpendicular to the plane in which you live.

How will you perceive the motion of this wheel? When a spoke of the wheel intersects the plane, you will see a line of a certain color at the intersection of the wheel and the plane. Then, after one spoke passes, there will be a gap when you will not see anything. Then, the next spoke of a different color will pass through the plane. So, you will perceive the motion of the wheel as lines of different colors happening at regular intervals of *time*.

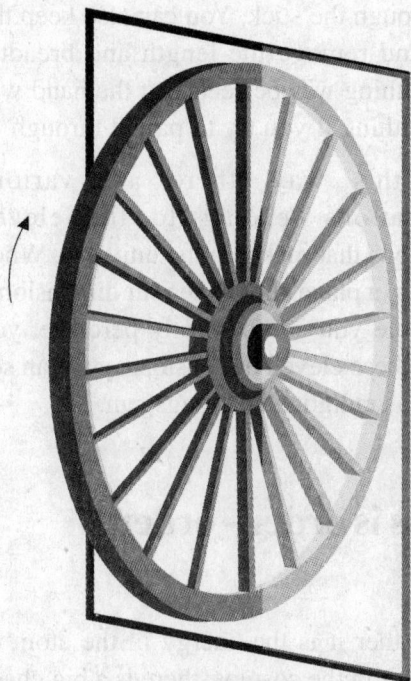

A rotating 3D wheel when seen in a 2D plane appears as lines appearing at regular intervals

What is happening is that the limited perception in a l o w e r dimensional world is changing the perception of space to a phenomenon in *time*! Since you can see only two of the three dimensions of space, you see the third dimension only when it becomes manifest on your plane over time. Hence, you see it as unrelated to your two dimensions of space, and you call it a phenomenon in time.

The limited perception in a lower dimensional world is changing the perception of space to a phenomenon in *time*!

Now, imagine when a green spoke passes through the plane, simultaneously another independent phenomenon occurs, say the barking of a dog. In the two dimensional world, it will be seen as a correlation between the appearance of the green line and the sound of a dog barking, when in reality it is not!

It is not possible for the two-dimensional being to believe that there can be a rise of events outside his plane of perception. That means, to understand the three-dimensional world, he cannot be in the two-dimensional consciousness, he has to rise to the three-dimensional consciousness. Similarly, to understand the four-dimensional world, we have to be in the fourth-dimensional consciousness.

Is this possible? Is it possible for us to go beyond the perception of the senses which give us only a three dimensional view? Can we actually see reality instead of mere

What we feel as reality everyday of our life is also a 'virtual' reality. glimpses of reality as phenomena in time? The answer is YES.

Through indepth research and development, the Eastern mystics and sages have discovered that it is possible to understand Reality as it exists and to experience it also. This can happen as a natural way of life, not just as a chance happening. This experience has happened in them.

Through meditation, it is possible for us to experience this same state of awareness.

A beautiful Zen story:

Once, two soldiers were looking at a flag flying in the wind. One of them said, 'The flag is moving.' The second one said, 'No, it is the wind that is moving.'

A Zen master passing by saw the argument going on. The soldiers requested the master to help them resolve this serious issue.

One of the soldiers asked, 'Master, I say the flag is moving. But he says the wind is moving. Which is correct?'

The master says, 'Neither is correct. Only consciousness is moving.'

As of now, what we feel as reality everyday of our life is also a 'virtual' reality. It is only a perception of things being separate in space and time. If you look deeply, you can see how our very perception of the world itself is questionable. From whatever quality of consciousness we see, THAT appears as our reality, not the absolute Reality.

Reality consists of eleven dimensions

We think we live in a world of the three dimensions of space and the fourth dimension of time. However, there are actually eleven dimensions. The fundamental dimensions are length, breadth, depth, time and consciousness. The higher dimensions are combinations of these fundamental dimensions.

For example, a stick has length, breadth and depth. It is in time and space. Now, if we keep length and breadth and just remove the depth, the stick will be seen, but the hand will pass through the stick. You can also keep the depth and remove the length and breadth. Then nothing will be seen, but the hand will hit something if you try to pass it through.

In this way, there are various combinations leading to the eleven dimensions that make up the universe. When you are in a plane above the four dimensional space-time you can currently perceive, you can see these eleven dimensions, you can see Reality as enlightened beings can.

Chaos is order - order is chaos

Whether it is the energy in the atom or the energy in the cosmos, there is a big chaos in the energy play. Within that chaos, there is an order that you cannot even imagine.

The whole universe is a spiritual being.

Chaos is energy

Anything in chaos is wild and energetic. Anything that has order is dull. Any rule curbs freedom, reduces the energy. Any regulation brings your energy down. Even in your house, if somebody says, 'Do not sit in that place,' you will feel like sitting only in that place. But until that rule is made, you will never even bother to sit there!

Even habits like smoking are maintained for the subtle mental satisfaction that you are wild, that you are not bound. If you scan yourself consciously, you will understand that almost all of your happiness comes only when you break some rules, when you are chaotic!

Chaos is order

The whole of Existence is chaos. In the universe, so many planets are moving. There are no traffic signs or cops or sign-boards! Yet, the planets are moving so beautifully in order. In the same way, in quantum physics, the smallest elements are not even particles; they are both particles and waves, and a multitude of probabilities! But there is an order in that chaos.

If the universe is chaos without any order, it will head toward destruction. 'Chaos in order' is what I call 'cosmic intelligence'.

I had an opportunity to meet Dr. Charles Townes[*], the Nobel laureate and physicist, who is well-known for his work on the laser and maser devices. He told me so beautifully, 'I feel the whole universe is something special, the whole universe is a spiritual being. It has its own intelligence. Even though I am not able to specifically prove it with mere words, I feel it is an intelligent and spiritual being.'

The cosmos is not just a force. It is 'force plus intelligence'. It responds to your thoughts, to your prayers, to your being - because it is intelligence.

Once somebody asked Buddha, 'Who is the creator of this universe?' Buddha replied, 'The universe itself is its creator.'

If the creator and the created are two separate entities, it means only the creator is intelligent and the created is not intelligent. The cosmos itself is the creator because it has its own intelligence. The cosmos is a living energy. You are sitting inside a living energy.

Believing the world is just matter is the basic mistake. This belief is the root of all terrorism and violence on planet earth. As long as we believe the universe is just dead matter, it is going to create only more and more thirst for power.

Only when we realize that the universe has its own intelligence, when we realize the universe is a spiritual being, the seed of peace is sown. Only when we understand that our thoughts are responded to, our way of life is rewarded, our prayers are answered, there is a living intelligent force and there is an order in the chaos, only then we can realize and work

Dr. Charles Townes - Nobel laureate in physics for work related to maser and laser.

The universe itself is its creator.

for peace, bliss and spirituality. Then, instead of trying to own or expand our boundaries and borders, we will try to expand our consciousness. The moment we start believing or trusting that the universe is 'intelligence', we can simply relax, trusting It.

Order is chaos

There is a beautiful Zen story:

A disciple goes to a Zen master and asks, 'Master, please explain to me how you started, how you traveled the path, how you attained the ultimate experience.'

The master says, 'When I started, mountain was a mountain, river was a river and tree was a tree. When I was traveling, mountain was not a mountain, river was not a river and tree was not a tree. Again, when I attained, mountain is a mountain, river is a river and tree is a tree.'

Before achieving, even though you think you are extraordinary, you are ordinary. After achieving, even though you are extraordinary, you understand you are ordinary.

You are not just a simple body. You are not just a microcosm. You are the macrocosm in miniature form. You realize you are the ultimate, endless ocean of potential energy just like the universe. Only when you realize the cosmic consciousness in your body, the macrocosm in your microcosm, you will really become orderly, you will really learn how to be orderly without reducing your energy. As long as you try to become orderly, you will

only suppress your energy, and you will also be suppressing everyone else.

First, when you realize the order in the chaos, you will become a spiritual being, you will experience love and bliss. When you realize the chaos in the order, you will become a compassionate being. When you realize the order in the chaos, you will experience the experience part of love, bliss. When you realize the chaos in the order, you will express the expression part of love which is compassion.

Seer-seen-seeing

We see two things in the process of 'seeing' - the seer and the seen object. Actually, what is happening in the process of seeing? (Though the example of eyes is taken here, it applies for all the senses.)

From the seer, consciousness takes a jump continuously to the seen, because it is not able to relax into the seer itself. Because of its restlessness, it gives life to the seen.

The continuous jump that happens between the seer and seen - from the seer to the seen, from the seen to the seer, again from the seer to the seen and again from the seen to the seer - is what is *SEEING*.

When the seer is not completely in bliss within himself, he starts becoming restless - and jumps. When he jumps, he gives life to the seen. Because he gives life to the seen, the process of jumping becomes *SEEING*.

  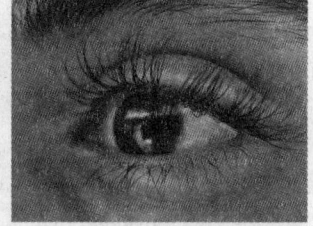

Seen   Seeing   Seer

There are two ways to drop this process of seeing. Either the seer or the seen has to drop for the process of seeing to stop.

When the seen is renounced, it loses its power over the seer. There is no point in jumping because there is nothing to be seen. When there is no place to jump, the seer relaxes in the seer himself, then seeing does not happen. When seeing is not there, the seer is enlightened.

A person who stops this jump by dropping the 'seen' is a renouncer, a *sannyasi*. He takes away all his desire to see things, to believe that any of the sense objects hold value for him. The seen becomes unexciting, and the jumping stops. He becomes enlightened through renouncing. This is true self-knowledge – *gnana*.

In the path of *gnana*, the seer experiences detachment and a complete

 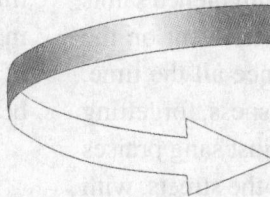 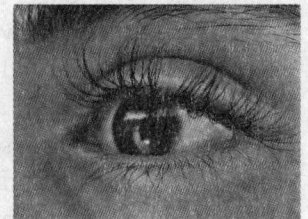

Seen dissolves   Seer relaxes in Seer

Gnana - Knowledge.

267

Seen

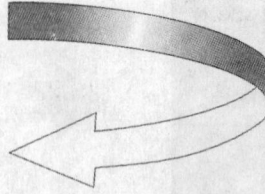

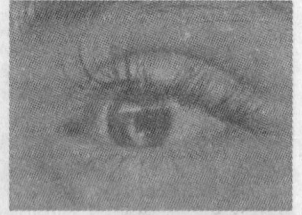

Seer dissolves in seen

witnessing of life. In this way he tries to discover Reality. The main objective is the development of a sharp and pure intelligence through which Reality can be experienced.

On the other hand, when the seer himself drops, what remains is the seen, and again the jumping between the seer and the seen stops. Reality is seen. The seer becomes enlightened through devotion or *bhakti**.

When the identity of the seer drops, dissolves into the seen, deep devotion to Existence happens! Everything becomes an exciting manifestation of Existence for him! His identity is no longer there. He merges into Existence itself. That is why enlightened saints like Meerabai* from India, who went on the path of *bhakti*, were in a trance all the time, merged into the god consciousness, forgetting their own identity. Meerabai just sang praises of god and walked around on the streets, with no self-consciousness whatsoever.

So, in some way, either the seer or the seen has to drop. Only then the jumping between the seer and the seen will stop. When the jumping stops, the process of seeing also stops.

Whether you are stuck with the seer or with the seen, get completely stuck - and you are enlightened! If you are jumping between the seer and the seen, not relaxed in either, you are under the illusion of a separate existence of the seer and seen. This jumping is what manifests as your individual seeing.

When the frequency of the seen is more than the seer, the seer can be changed or manipulated by the seen. When the frequency of the seer is more than the seen, the seen can be changed or manipulated by the seer.

Bhakti - Devotion.

Meerabai - Princess of Chittor, a devotee of Krishna, mystical poetess and singer, who was ill-treated by her husband for her devotion to Krishna.

Collective Consciousness

We are not disconnected and separate islands as we think. Maybe in the physical layer, we all seem like individual islands. But whether we like it or not, whether we accept it or not, whether we want it or not, we are all interlinked by the collective consciousness.

It is like this: if the food is poisoned, only the person who eats it will suffer, not everyone. In this sense, you can think of yourself as an individual. But as you move towards the subtler levels of Existence, you can see our interconnectedness more clearly. For example, if the air is poisoned, whoever is breathing it will suffer, even if they are a long distance from each other. This connection is at the breath level. This means that in the subtler energy layers, the distance between us is reduced.

Even more than the physical and breath levels, we are connected more closely at the mental level. When I say mental level, I mean the level of thoughts. Our thoughts affect not only us but also everyone around us and beyond. Your thoughts are more infectious than your cold. In fact, people may escape from your cold, but they cannot escape from your thoughts.

If an individual mind is polluted, not only the individual, but a much bigger group suffers. For example, if one person who has a disturbed mind sits as a leader of a city, the whole city will be affected by the decisions that he makes! His disturbed thinking will result in wrong decisions and hence will be harmful for the whole city.

Going a step further, if one corrupted visualization leads to a particular action, the action can have tremendous impact on a huge population, not just on that person with the corruption.

For example, take the case of the atom bomb. It is nothing but a 'visualization' of the nuclear theory! The basis of the nuclear bomb can be found in the famous formula $E=mc^2$, that was discovered by the physicist, Albert Einstein. But corrupted visualization of this formula led to disturbance of the whole planet earth. We are all now threatened by this one theory, by this one invention. Today, planet earth has enough atomic weapons to burn itself 700 times, over and over again.

Just see this diagram here. I shall try to explain the truth on the basis of this diagram.

These seven circles represent the seven energy layers in us. The first layer is the physical body, the body that you can feel as

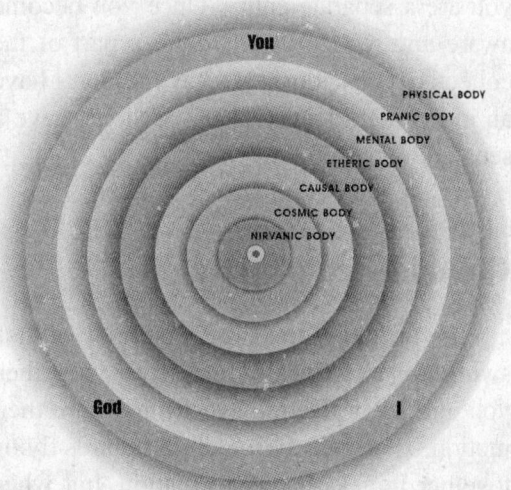

You

PHYSICAL BODY
PRANIC BODY
MENTAL BODY
ETHERIC BODY
CAUSAL BODY
COSMIC BODY
NIRVANIC BODY

God   I

> **Once you become aware and realize that you are a part of the collective consciousness, you don't suffer.**

your hands, legs etc. The second layer is the *pranic* body, the body in which your *prana* or life energy or breath circulates. Like this, there are seven energy layers that make up the total body, with the physical body being just one of those layers.

Now, in the physical layer, you, god and I can be represented as three different points in the circle. In the physical level, the distance between us is great.

If you go inward a little to the *pranic* level, the distance between us is reduced. If you go in deeper to the mental level, the distances are further reduced. When you go deeper and deeper, it finally merges into one. You can see that at the innermost point of all these layers, god, you, and I are one. There is no distance. That is the Truth even at the gross level! It is only your perception that causes you to think you are a separate entity. Once you become aware and realize that you are a part of the collective consciousness, that you don't have an individual identity, that you don't have a separate ego, you don't suffer.

Coincidence of thought

If you have observed a school of fish swimming or a flock of birds flying together, you will see a fleeting synchronicity in their motion. There may be hundreds of birds flying together in a V-shaped formation, but when they have to change direction, they will all do so at the same time, with no confusion or time delay! Scientists have been trying to understand how this is possible. Even studies of insects and animals have shown that when faced with threats, their responses are so fast that they cannot be explained by normal methods of communication.

An interesting experiment was done to study the power of thought on dogs. The dog owners were asked to leave the house with no intention of going to any particular place. After leaving the house, they were given instructions to go to specific places and then at random times, they were asked to come back. It was found that at the time the owner started back home, almost always at the same time, the dog would go to the door and wait for the owner.

In the huge tsunami that rocked the Andaman and Nicobar islands of India, it was found that before the tsunami hit the islands, all the animals, including the huge ones like elephants, had all moved to higher grounds, safely away from the ocean. There have been a number of accounts of animals and insects being aware of upcoming earthquakes minutes before the earthquake actually strikes. What is the difference between these animals and us? It is their connection with nature! Being in tune with nature enables them to sense nature's signals. In the case of humans, because of our false sense of identity and ego, we have lost touch with nature and have become insensitive to the direct signals of nature.

Tuning into the higher intelligence

You can see so many instances in history where the same discovery was made at about the same time by people in different parts of the globe and by people who did not even know each other. The reason is that the ideas are floating in the collective consciousness. It is like this: there are hundreds of electromagnetic waves in the air but your television set picks up only the waves of the frequency to which it is tuned. Similarly, the minds that are ready and waiting for the floating ideas will tune in and convert that potentiality into reality!

Just as the universe gives us so many hints of its existence as one being, we can find hints from nature about the nature of reality. In a series of experiments in the 1920s, it was found that no matter what portion of a rat's brain was removed, the rat still retained its memory of how to perform complex tasks it had learned prior to the surgery. The rat's brain actually showed 'holographic' memory. Scientists proposed that memories are encoded not in neurons, but in the patterns of nerve impulses that crisscross the brain, similar to how a hologram is formed by various patterns of laser light crisscrossing each other. This might explain how the human brain can store up to ten billion bits of information in the brain, which is the small size of two fists!

The universe is a hologram and we are a part of that hologram. In a hologram, every single part of the hologram, even if split, reflects the totality of that hologram. Likewise, we too reflect the totality of the universe. The universe is not an assortment of living and dead matter. It is a huge interconnected Whole. You are very much connected to your fellow beings around you and the trees, animals, birds and rocks on earth, as well as the planets, stars and galaxies in the universe. Whether you perceive it or not depends on the plane of consciousness from which you perceive it all.

Global Peace Begins From You

When we realize our role in the Existential scheme of things, we can no longer feel separate from all those around us. We can only feel separated when we feel unconscious of our role, when we are unaware.

The time has come to create a critical mass of enlightened people on planet earth. Only by creating more and more people who are awakened, who are enlightened, can the collective influence of individual negativity be destroyed. All calamities around the world are created only by unconscious human beings. Global warming, HIV, religious terrorism, fanaticism, and piles of atomic weapons, are all because of this negativity. Today we are facing so many dangers that unless we create a peaceful, blissful, joyful, and enlightened society, we will not be able to preserve this beautiful planet earth.

My mission is to create a peaceful, joyful, blissful, conscious, enlightened society.

Global Peace – a byproduct of individual bliss

Self-contradictory thoughts

Actually, a majority of us are caught up in fighting with our own selves. We are caught in a web of self-contradictory thoughts and desires. Our thoughts and words are so powerful, but we use them so casually.

For example, say you have a headache, what do you do? You tell yourself, 'How I wish this headache would go away!' By uttering these words, you give as much power to the word 'headache' as you give to the words 'go away'. This is what I mean by self-contradictory thoughts. By your very thought, you contradict your original desire. Even your positive intention is caught in the fight, the dilemma of your own thoughts and words. You will then ask, 'How do I get rid of this headache?' Just say, 'Let me be healed!' that's all.

My mission is to create a peaceful, joyful, blissful, conscious, enlightened society.

When we infuse healing thoughts into our system again and again, we give power to positive words and thoughts. They get embedded in our very muscle memory. So at times of low mood and depression, these healing thoughts will automatically come up in our inner space and pull us out of the low mood.

Individual peace by its nature touches the world

A beautiful story from the life of Buddha:

Devadatta, a cousin of Buddha, joined Buddha's order of monks. He was hungry for power and status. He wanted to become the head of the order of monks. But Buddha would not allow such an immature person, who was running after status instead of enlightenment, to lead his mission. So Devadatta harbored jealousy and ill feelings towards Buddha and even made several attempts to kill him.

Once Devadatta persuaded the royal elephant-keepers to release a fierce elephant on to Buddha's path. The elephant was intoxicated and let loose on the streets where Buddha used to walk regularly. The mad elephant ran wildly. People panicked and fled in all directions.

The elephant came upon Buddha. Buddha kept walking, radiating the same peace and calm even in the face of this danger. His bliss and peace was not at all affected by the threat of the wild elephant. The elephant came rushing towards Buddha in a mad fury. Once it reached Buddha, it immediately calmed down completely. Its wild nature simply dissolved in Buddha's enlightened presence. Buddha touched the elephant's forehead and stroked it gently. Calmed by the patting, the elephant bent on its knees and bowed down to Buddha.

The people watching the whole scene were simply shocked!

The waves of bliss radiating from a peaceful person naturally and automatically touch the people, animals, trees, and rocks and affects everything nearby.

To make the whole world blissful and happy, you don't have to do anything. Just change your center. When you are seeing a horror movie, your world will be filled with fear. But if you just change the channel to say a comedy movie, you can see how your whole world changes!

When the inner awakening happens, the higher emotions happen. It all finally boils down to your own experience of what is happening. If you want to save the world, all you need to do is save yourself!

Everything is actually happening in this world – great spiritual sessions where enlightenment is being shared and at the same time terrorist training camps where violence is being shared. According to what you tune with, the world that you attract and see will also appear to be. You will attract the same type of people and situations in your life.

Even one person struggling for enlightenment, seeking, raises the consciousness of at least a million people.

How to handle the suffering in the world

First, we have to understand that every major decision taken at the higher level of power and governance is an expression of collective positivity or collective negativity, because it is the mass consciousness or collective consciousness that creates the leaders. So before blaming others, be they leaders, politicians, or officials, if we can put a little bit of energy towards ourselves and start working to create more positive consciousness in our inner space, we will be doing something really useful.

It is time…

Let us create more positivity from our side.

Let us bring more love to our actions.

Let us increase the frequency of our individual consciousness.

Instead of getting upset or disturbed by negative decisions, just create positive energy so that the people around you and around the world are also affected by this positive consciousness. Then you will see that it radiates through the leaders also. When more and more people begin to transform themselves, the collective positivity has to express itself through the right politicians and the right leaders.

If you get upset and disturbed, what is going to happen? Nothing will happen except that you will have a little more depression, a little more negativity. And because of that, you yourself will add more negativity to the world, you will add more mass to the negative consciousness.

So revolution is not the way. Evolution is the way.

Every revolution promised the truth or the ultimate solution. But what do we see if we look back? In the last 3000 years of the history of planet earth, we have had 5000 recorded wars! Researchers have estimated that in the last 3000 years of the history of planet earth, there have been at least 9000 peace treaties, and the average life span of these treaties was just 8 years!

Just create positive energy so that the people around you and around the world are also affected by this positive consciousness. Then you will see that it radiates through the leaders as well.

Studies of the effects of meditation on peace

Various studies have been done to measure the effects of group meditation on communities. Some studies observed the effect of a critical mass of people who meditated using the technique of Transcendental Meditation™. These studies showed an eight percent decrease in the crime rate in the cities where group meditation was conducted. Other reports showed a significant seventeen percent reduction in acts of violence and a thirteen percent increase in cooperative, helpful acts. In war-stricken areas there was more than fifty percent drop in daily war deaths and more than twenty five percent drop in war injuries. The overall statistics showed reduced crime rates, fewer hospital admissions, and reduced violence, leading to an increase in the overall quality of life.

Global Peace meditation

21 September is observed as the International Peace Day. Millions of people worldwide come together in prayer, meditation, celebration and collaboration for world peace and global harmony.

On this occasion every year, Nithyananda Mission's centers conduct collective group meditations worldwide. The collective consciousness is raised in a much more powerful way when meditation is done as a group.

When matter is shared, it reduces in size. For example, if an apple has to be shared by four people, it has to be cut into four pieces. It reduces in size. When it comes to electrical energy, when the voltage is shared, it does not reduce, it remains the same. For example, if we have ten volts of electricity in a wire, one person touching the wire will feel ten volts, and four people touching the same wire will also feel ten volts.

But it is different in the case of the powerful, subtle energy of meditation. When meditation is done by a group of people, it multiplies! Rather than diminishing or staying the same, the benefit is shared and amplified among the entire group and beyond. If one person meditating generates 10 'volts' of energy, then 100 people sitting together in a collective meditation generates 10 x 100 or 1000 'volts' of energy. Just imagine! The strength of energy that is generated will simply cleanse the entire space where the meditation is done. That is why collective, group meditation is encouraged.

The unavoidable loving touch of enlightened beings

A story from the life of Buddha:

There was a bandit by the name of Angulimala. He used to live in a forest that many people had to cross. He used to ambush the people and rob them of their valuables. Then he would cut off the little finger of the person and make a garland of all such fingers. That is why he was called Angulimala – garland of fingers.

Once when traveling, Buddha was about to cross the forest. People warned him about the terrifying Angulimala. But Buddha was unperturbed and continued walking. Deep inside the forest, Angulimala jumped out of the bushes and shouted threateningly at Buddha, 'Stand still!'

Buddha stopped and replied, 'I am still. May you be still.'

In the presence of an enlightened being even natural enemies lose their enmity.

Angulimala for the first time in his life was shaken to his very being. Something about Buddha touched him deeply. He could not even force himself to attack Buddha. His hands froze. He just fell at the feet of Buddha crying and begging for forgiveness!

This story illustrates one of the truths of the impact of enlightened beings. Without effort or intention, an enlightened being simply radiates tremendous peace and compassion which has the power to simply transform others.

This effect is not limited just to human beings. Even animals are touched by the pure love and compassion radiated by an enlightened being. Everything is changed when it is exposed to that high frequency energy field.

There is a beautiful story from the life of Adi Shankara, an enlightened master from ancient India:

Shankara was wandering in South India in the town of Shringeri. One day, a strange and beautiful scene happened in front of him. Two frogs were sitting on a rock. It became very hot, so the frogs were about to jump into the water. Just then a cobra raised its hood and spread it over the two frogs giving them shade. The frogs enjoyed the cool shade and sat back for sometime. After some time, they plunged into the water. The cobra also folded back its hood and went away.

Shankara was watching this and was amazed. He was a very sharp intellectual person. He did not leave the incident at that. He immediately recognized that unless the place was sanctified in some way by some higher energy, it was not possible for animals to forget their enmity and co-exist in such a beautiful fashion. He went around and asked for details about the place. He learned that some time in the past, a great enlightened sage had established and maintained his ashram* there for many years!

Shankara was so moved by the whole incident that he decided that someday he too would set up his mission in that very place. Years later when he was passing by the same place, he stopped and established his first ashram* there, called the Shringeri Math. To this day it stands as one of the key seats of spiritual wisdom in the world!

An enlightened being effortlessly radiates his all-encompassing inner space, which creates a collective positivism.

As Patanjali says in the Yoga Sutras*, 'In the presence of an enlightened being even natural enemies lose their enmity.'

Ashram - A monastery for Hindu or Buddhist monks.

Yoga Sutras - The book on yoga authored by enlightened master Patanjali.

The Nithyananda Mission

My advent on planet earth is to create a new cycle of individual consciousness causing Collective Consciousness to enter the Superconscious zone.

To achieve this,

One hundred thousand people will be initiated to live as *Jeevan Muktas* – liberated beings experiencing 'living enlightenment'

&

One billion people will be initiated into Nithya Dhyaan – Life Bliss Meditation – designed to cause a positive shift in the individual consciousness on planet earth.

Meditation technique for Global Peace

The way to achieve global peace is to create individual peace. The meditation for global peace is a collective meditation. This is a very simple but very powerful meditation.

Sit in one circle or concentric circles, holding hands so that you hold the hand of the person on your right with your right hand - palm facing down - signifying 'giving' peace and bliss, while you offer your left hand - palm facing up - to 'receive' peace and bliss from the person on your left. This connected circle of people generates a powerful energy cycle. The meditative energy of one person is shared by all others. This meditation can be done for at least 21 minutes.

Sannyas is the Ultimate Gamble

Our ability to be in tune with others and Existence depends entirely upon how we conduct ourselves. It depends on the priorities we choose in life. What if we do not choose? What if we accept things as they happen to us?

It is time to talk about renunciation. Renunciation is not running away from life. Renunciation is flowing with life without resistance. The Sanskrit word *sannyas* refers to this state of trust with Existence that allows us to let go all other things in life.

Sannyas...

There is a beautiful story from the life of Buddha:

After enlightenment, Buddha visited many places preaching his dhamma or teachings, and initiating people into spiritual life.

On his way, he entered Kapilavastu, his birth place. He walked on the streets with his disciples, wearing the saffron robe. Everyone watched him with great wonder.

Buddha's wife, Yashodhara, heard the noise in the street and asked what it was. Her maids told her that it was none other than her own husband who had returned as the Buddha, the enlightened soul. She did not go to meet him. Instead, she called for her son Rahul. Rahul was born the night that Buddha left home in search of enlightenment.

She asked Rahul, 'Do you see that radiant figure there who holds a begging bowl and yet looks like a king? He is your father. Go and ask him for your inheritance.'

The young boy ran downstairs and pushed his way through to where Buddha stood. He fell at Buddha's feet and boldly repeated what his mother had told him.

Buddha lifted him up gently with a smile and looked at him. He simply removed the gold hemmed cloth the boy was wearing and replaced it with a saffron one.

The boy, seven years of age, was given his inheritance. He was the first and only child allowed into the monastic order of the Buddha.

Someone asked me, 'If everything in life is evolving naturally by the process of evolution

The right revolution leads to evolution - or enlightenment. That is _sannyas_ – the greatest revolution of an individual.

like monkey into man, and bad into good, would man not ultimately evolve into god? Where then is the need for meditation, _sannyas_…where then is the need for inspiration?'

I replied, 'It took five thousand years for the monkey to become man, and it would take equally long for man to become god. If you are willing to wait that long, it is alright with me!'

On the other hand, you can decide to live consciously with a clear understanding about life, the laws and structure of the universe, and meditation. You can revolutionize the process of your evolution. The right revolution leads to evolution or enlightenment. That is _sannyas,_ the greatest revolution of an individual. It is to live like a Paramahamsa, like an enlightened being.

Adi Shankara, the enlightened master from India, beautifully says in his work Vivekachoodamani*:

For all living creatures, a human birth is rare,

and even rarer is to have a sattvic (goodness) attitude,

and more so to have steadfastness on the path of spiritual activity

as explained in the Vedas*…

These words had a very powerful effect on the life of Swami Vivekananda, an enlightened master from India who lived thousands of years after Adi Shankara. When Swami Vivekananda was preparing for his law examination, these very words landed on him like a thunderbolt. He could not read further. He left his books and started running along the road. He was running to his master, Ramakrishna Paramahamsa. While he was running, the truth of Adi Shankara's words was ringing in his very being. He thought to himself, 'I have gained all these three: I have been born as a human being. I have gained the desire for liberation. I have got a great master….then why am I still wasting my life? Why am I still wasting my life?' Again and again, these words were haunting him. Swami Vivekananda went on to become enlightened and spread Ramakrishna Paramahamsa's mission worldwide.

Sannyas is the path for those who want to win over themselves, who want to be free of the clutches of jealousy, anger, stress and depression forever. People think _sannyas_ is chosen by losers. No. Of course, sometimes those who don't know what to do with their lives take up _sannyas_. But that is not the spirit of _sannyas_.

Vivekachoodamani - Enlightened master Adi Shankara's philosophical work.

Vedas - Ancient scriptural texts explaining the deep spiritual Truths. There are four main Vedas – Rigveda, Yajurveda, Samaveda and Atharvaveda. These texts explain about the performance of sacrifice and consist of stories and chants. The Vedas are considered to be revelations of the Truths that happened to the mystics and seers.

Sannyas is the effort to become conscious for the first time, conscious of the mechanism that surrounds you as a human being. You are part of Existence. Existence moves with its own mechanism, with its own music. Falling in tune with it is the science of *sannyas*. *Sannyas* is a being level relationship, being in tune with the whole of Existence. That is the shortest path to success in life.

To hear the song of Existence, you need to start moving in the right space. To find that space, you need to first drop any other thing you know, and listen to the song with deep awareness. You will find it. In that space, life will flow like a river moving towards the sea. Any other path will take longer.

When life becomes a flowing river, it has to merge with the sea. There is no other way. *Sannyas* is the science of flowing with the natural course of Existence and finally merging with it.

Flow like a river

The river heads only towards the sea. It does not stagnate anywhere. A *sannyasi* heads only towards his goal of enlightenment. He knows no distractions. The river flows blissfully, whatever be the things thrown into it on its way. So many things are thrown into the river – flowers, twigs, food, animals, birds, dead bodies, etc. But the river flows, not bothering about anything.

Similarly, a *sannyasi* moves blissfully, untouched by anything that comes his way.

> ***Sannyas* is a conscious decision to live the truth immediately in your life.**

The current pulls the river over its obstacles, and it gurgles with a constant music, moving towards the sea. The cosmic intelligence pulls the *sannyasi* over obstacles as he moves towards the ultimate goal. He knows not what obstacles are. For him, they are all stepping stones on the path to bliss.

One Zen master was asked, 'What is Zen?'

He replied, 'Walk on!'

Zen Buddhism beautifully says, life is like the river that flows and fills each form, and bursts its own limitations to expand its capacity. This is the essence of life, and *sannyas*. *Sannyas* is learning in action as life moves, not philosophizing. It is a force, not a dogma. For a real *sannyasi*, life simply moves in the right direction. The learning happens during the movement, not as a separate thing.

Sannyas is nothing but straightaway practicing the truths every passing moment. There is enough philosophy in the world but no one to follow it. *Sannyas* is simply a conscious decision to live the truth immediately in your life.

A Zen master tells his disciple very beautifully, 'Studying the truth as a philosophy is just collecting preaching material. Remember that unless you practice constantly, your light of truth may go out.'

Practice is nothing but continuously flowing in the right direction without stagnating. Even

> **A *sannyasi* continuously moves with the intelligence of Existence with an attitude of surrender.**

in stagnation, there will be movement around the obstacle - trying to find the flow again. There is no stopping.

A *sannyasi* continuously moves with the intelligence of Existence with an attitude of surrender. By surrender, I don't mean inaction. I mean action with an attitude of surrender. There is no stopping. He lives in the moment, spontaneously and according to the need of the moment, which is what is called fluidity.

Sannyas Is not renunciation

Sannyas has always been wrongly associated with renunciation. You don't have to renounce anything. You just need to understand that you are a temporary custodian of some wealth, which is a part of Existence, just as you are as well. Then you won't need to renounce because you never possessed anything in the first place! Even if you have to part with wealth, you will not feel that you are giving away or losing your possessions. The problem starts with the attitude of possessing, with the feeling of 'mine'.

Neither does a *sannyasi* need to renounce the world nor does a *samsari**** need to be afraid of renouncing. Just the plain understanding that Existence gives and takes at the right moment

is enough. Then you know that what is happening is the right thing for the moment and life is flowing as it should. This creates a mental gap between you and your wealth and that gap is called renunciation! It is just a gap, a break in the attitude of possessing, nothing else. It has been wrongly used in the context of *sannyas*.

A small story:

Two monks were traveling together. One of them strongly believed in acquiring wealth. He practiced spirituality through it. The other strongly followed the path of renunciation. They were discussing the two ways of life. As they were discussing, it became nighttime and they reached a river that they had to cross.

The one who believed in renunciation did not have money with him. He said, 'We don't have money to cross the river. Let us spend the night here and some one will take us across the river tomorrow morning.'

The other one replied, 'That is not possible. We will be eaten by wild animals if we spend the night here. I have money with me. Let us pay the boatman and cross the river.'

Once they crossed the river safely, he asked his companion, 'Now do you understand the value of money? If I too had been a man of renunciation, what would have happened to us?'

The first one replied, 'It was your renunciation that brought us across safely. You parted with your money to cross the river!'

Samsari - One who is caught in *samsara* or cycle of birth and death.

Renouncing is 'having' without the idea of having, and 'parting' without the idea of parting. Otherwise, by merely renouncing outer wealth, you will not gain anything. You will only feel the pain of sacrificing the 'mine'. *Sannyas* is not escaping from the 'mine'. It is going beyond the 'mine'. And that is possible only through a proper understanding. If you renounce with understanding, it is okay. Otherwise, the 'mine' will simply persist wherever you go. Not only that, if you renounce with the idea that you are renouncing 'yours', it becomes the right action but for the wrong reason! By merely renouncing outer wealth, you can never be a *sannyasi*. *Sannyas* is a change in the inner mental setup, not a change in the outer material setup. Renouncing outer wealth to be a *sannyasi* is like doing the right action but for the wrong reason.

Wealth and *sannyas* are not mutually exclusive. In fact, *sannyas* is the art and science of creating wealth flawlessly.

If you read the *vedic* scriptures you will see that they always talk only about the abundance of life. They never teach escaping from it. They teach loosening the attachment over possessions, not renouncing or hating it. *Sannyas* is seeing the vast abundance of life as one whole, and therefore not being attached to your own small possessions. It is knowing that wealth is also a manifestation of Existence and not the essence of life itself.

Sannyas is not suicide. It is life. *Sannyas* is living in tremendous beauty, both inside and outside you.

Understand, outer beauty and wealth are not enemies to the path of *sannyas*. They are complementary. *Sannyas* adds inner wealth and beauty to your outer wealth and beauty. It gives us the intelligence to handle the outer wealth and beauty without any suffering related to it.

Samsar and Sannyas

Samsar literally means the 'world' or the 'path'. It refers to the worldly life that causes endless cycles of birth and death.

There are two ways to move in any path: either with baggage and people or by yourself. In the first case, you may have to wait for a long time. In the second case, you can reach even this very minute.

Sannyas is the decision not to carry any baggage while moving. You can have everything, but you don't have to carry it. When you don't carry anything, Existence brings to you what you need for the moment. That is *sannyas*!

There is a beautiful story from the life of Buddha…

Buddha's disciples gathered around him one day and asked him to teach them the essence of sannyas. He told them a small story:

One man was living on an island by himself. Suddenly he got the feeling it was time to move from the island. He did not have a boat. So he made one with some twigs, branches, leaves and whatever he could

A *sannyasi* uses the boat to cross the ocean of life. A *samsari* carries the boat even beyond the time it is needed, not knowing he can drop it.

find. It was a difficult journey but somehow he crossed and reached the other side.

Buddha asked the disciples, 'After reaching the other side, should the man keep the boat or discard it?'

The disciples came out with different answers.

Buddha continued, 'The man of sannyas discards the boat knowing that he will be provided for as needed in the future. The man of samsar keeps it so that his effort doesn't go waste if he wants to journey back!'

A *sannyasi* walks with his thought on Existence. A *samsari* walks with his thoughts on how to exist. A *sannyasi* uses the boat to cross the ocean of life. A *samsari* carries the boat even beyond the time it is needed, not knowing he can drop it. That is the difference. There is nothing right or wrong in this. It is just two different ways to live.

Let me explain *sannyas* in the context of *karma* because *sannyas* is the shortcut to exhausting *karma*.

Karma is nothing but the unfulfilled actions of your past that pull you again and again to take birth to fulfill them. It is the very cause of the cycle of birth and death. It makes you take birth again and again in this world until it is exhausted.

There are three types of *karma* – *sanchita**, *prarabdha* and *agamya**. *Sanchita** *karma* is your entire bank balance of unfulfilled actions (*karma*) accumulated over many lives. *Prarabdha karma* is that portion of *sanchita** that you bring and come to exhaust in this one birth. Every time you take birth, you bring with you a small portion of *sanchita* as your *prarabdha* to exhaust. It includes all your unfulfilled desires, lust, anger, fear, and such things. The third or *agamya** *karma* is the new *karma* that you create in this birth because of new, unfulfilled actions.

Ultimately, these three things need to be done in order to exhaust all *karma* completely. First, the new *agamya** should not get created because it only adds to the bank balance or the *sanchita* at the end of the lifetime. Second, the *prarabdha* with which you came should get exhausted, or fulfilled, in this life completely without a trace. Third, the volume of the *sanchita* itself should somehow be burnt so that the number of times you take birth reduces. This happens by fulfilling the *prarabdha* without accumulating the *agamya* in a lifetime.

If the *prarabdha* is exhausted in the right way, *agamya* will not get created. The same

---

Sanchita - Bank of accumulated *karmas* from which we choose to bring into this birth a few as *prarabdha karma*.

Agamya - The actions one constantly does out of free will after taking birth on planet earth. These are not born out of true desires but from desires borrowed from society, by looking at others.

intelligence that properly exhausts the *prarabdha* will take care of not creating new *agamya*. The *sanchita* itself can be exhausted only by the grace of an enlightened master.

Now understand clearly: if the fantasy of your *prarabdha* is greater than your intelligence, then *samsar* (marriage) is the path for you. If the fantasy of your *prarabdha* is lesser than your intelligence, then *sannyas* is the path for you! In the path of *sannyas*, your intelligence wins over your *prarabdha* and brings it to control and exhaust it. In the path of *samsar*, life teaches you in different ways and you exhaust your *prarabdha* through millions of births.

In Patanjali's Yoga Sutras*, there is an eightfold path to enlightenment. All eight parts have to be followed simultaneously. Three of the parts are *pratyahara*, *dharana* and *dhyana*. *Pratyahara* is drawing the mind inwards, away from the five senses. The next is *dharana*, the merging of the mind with the inner Self. The third is *dhyana*, meditation.

Withdrawing the mind from the five senses itself can happen only when the mind merges with the inner Self! For example, you can release the foot from the lower rung of the ladder only after establishing yourself in the higher rung, is it not? You can let go of the lower branch of the tree only after clinging to the higher branch. We all think that only after renouncing worldly attachments, we can attain god. No! The truth is, only after attaining god can you really shake off the worldly things.

Only after you experience *nithyananda* or eternal bliss, you can shake off *mithyananda* or worldly fantasies.

> **For a *sannyasi*, the mind is happy all the time. What he gets is what he wants.**

If you can become aware of and hold on more firmly to the higher rung you may let go of the lower rung more easily. That awareness is called *sannyas*. It is the process of understanding and moving to the higher rung and leaving the lower rung. As you move, renunciation happens as a byproduct. Because you realize that to climb higher you don't need anything but yourself! Anything you take with you is only going to make it more difficult to climb.

A *samsari* moves to pursue his fantasies. He *goes* to places to see the beauty of Existence. A *sannyasi* sees everything around him as already divine and beautiful! He is fantasized by what he sees! When the *samsari* starts turning inward, he becomes a *sannyasi*. Until he finds the burning need for that, it is better for him to continue with what he is doing. For a *sannyasi*, the mind is happy all the time. What he gets is what he wants. He is always living in the mood of grateful and welcome acceptance. For a *samsari*, the mind is occupied with too many conflicts. He keeps trying to get what he wants. With intelligence, the *samsari* can awaken to the truth, that what he is getting is what he needs for that moment and for his ultimate fulfillment.

Yoga Sutras - The book on yoga authored by enlightened master Patanjali.

The *samsari* is concerned with material things and living life in a limited way. The *sannyasi* is concerned about death – death of all that is not him, which is his ego, possessiveness, lust, anger, fear, jealousy and discontent. He knows he is something beyond all this. His whole quest is to find this, because once he finds it, he has found the higher rung of the ladder and he can leave the lower rung where the constant push and pull of all these emotions and material things reside.

Sannyas is the search to answer the question 'Who am I?' A *sannyasi* puts his whole energy into discovering the answer to this question. If people ask you, 'Who are you?' you will generally reply, 'I am so-and-so's son, I am an engineer, I am a professor.' But those words describe who you are in your relationships with the world. If there were no world, then who are you?

The great enlightened masters who founded the world religions have said repeatedly, *'Aham Brahmasmi'* meaning, 'I am That' in the Hindu tradition, or 'Be still and know that I am god' in the Christian tradition, or *Anal-Haq* meaning 'I am the Truth' in the Islam tradition. Experiencing that you are god is the purpose of human life.

Once this purpose is experienced, the inner bliss that all these great masters talk about starts happening. Then you understand that the outer world is a beautiful stage where the divine play is happening. There is ultimate freedom from all worldly difficulties. You do, and yet you don't do, you speak and yet you don't speak. You cry and yet you don't cry.

Your inner Self remains untouched. You are in 'eternal bliss' – *nithya ananda.*

The problem is that people generally think *sannyas* is a hindrance to worldly life. They think *sannyas* is seriousness. No! *Sannyas* is a certain quality for living life to its optimum. Seriousness will never help one live life to its full potential. Only sincerity and laughter will help. Laughter is the greatest spiritual quality.

A master was seated with his disciples. He was in an expansive mood and his disciples decided to ask him about the various stages he passed through to reach the Divine.

The master beautifully started explaining...

'God held me by the hand and first took me to the Land of Action. I stayed there for several years. Then god returned and took me to the Land of Sorrow. I fell into deep sorrows but eventually went beyond them. I felt happy. Then, suddenly I found that god put me in the Land of Love. I went through burning emotions and found myself cleansed thoroughly. Then, he took me to the Land of Silence. There I learned the mysteries of life and death.'

The disciples asked, 'Was that the final stage of your quest?'

The master said, 'No. One day god said, Today I will take you to my very heart... and he led me to the Land of Laughter.'

Sannyas is your very energy. How can it be a hindrance to anything? Not only that, with the energy of *sannyas*, you are always young. With the energy of *sannyas,* you are ready for the challenges of life.

People ask me, 'Why can't we continue in *samsar* and live with the consciousness of a *sannyasi*?' You see, the nature of man is such that unless a *conscious* decision is taken, it is difficult to bring about a permanent transformation in the consciousness. *Sannyas* is a *conscious* decision to transform the consciousness. *Sannyas* is a conscious decision. That is why *sannyas* needs to be taken. With a conscious decision, there is continued awareness. Continued awareness decreases the chance of slipping back. Without it, there is nothing binding one to keep on the path. It becomes easy to slip.

With *sannyas*, you will continue to do what you are doing but in a much better way. With *sannyas*, you start watching everything. You become a witness. Because of this witnessing, a gap is created between you and the other person. That gap is misunderstood as 'renunciation'. If you notice, the gap was not there earlier. Each one was suffocating the other. Now the gap is there. The gap is not a gap of distance but a gap of awareness.

Sannyas is also living without the burden of the inner woman or inner man. What is meant by inner woman or inner man? It is nothing but the lust hidden in your mind, the fantasies that you have created in your mind. Shiva says beautifully in the Tantra*, 'A man who has abandoned the woman in him, in his inner mind, is a *sannyasi*, even if he is still in the family.' On the contrary, if thoughts of a woman persist in a *sannyasi's* mind, he cannot be called a *sannyasi*. This is the scale to measure if a man is a *sannyasi*.

In Buddha's teaching, The Four Noble Truths, the second truth deals with the cause of suffering. He beautifully says that suffering is because of the demands we make on life every moment. It is like asking a banana tree to bear mangoes! We will understand this habit only when we bring in awareness.

Not only that, when you watch, you start seeing exactly how transactions are happening in relationships. You see how expectations are driving the whole thing. You see the ulterior motives in everything.

A *sannyasi* takes responsibility for the whole of Existence. He doesn't know the difference between his family and the rest of the world.

The responsibility of a *sannyasi*

There is a little known truth about a *sannyasi*, that a *sannyasi* takes responsibility for the whole of Existence. He doesn't know the difference between his family and the rest of the world. All are the same. He wishes for the liberation of anyone who comes his way. On the other hand, a *samsari* takes responsibility for one family or maybe for a few organizations. This taking of responsibility

---

Tantra - Ancient *vedic* tradition of achieving enlightenment through spiritual techniques or practices, meditations and ritual worship.

is always towards a definite cause. It is either to accumulate the credit of serving, to fulfill some obligation, or to co-exist easily with the people around him.

The nature of a *sannyasi's* responsibility is completely different. For him, the whole world is his family. There is no obligation driving him. Responsibility happens completely out of the quality of his inner space. Also, a *samsari* can rest after fulfilling every duty at that stage in life. A *sannyasi* continuously works, because people are constantly in need of truths in their life.

A *sannyasi* is established in rich relationships. People think *sannyasis* run away from relationships. A young girl asked me while I was addressing a college gathering, 'Was it failure in love that caused you to become a *sannyasi*?'

I told her, 'It was success in love that caused me to become a *sannyasi*!' Actually, *sannyas* is what softens you into real love; love towards not just one person but towards the whole of Existence.

Ordinary love comes with a reason, or with lust. Real love knows no reason. It is just a causeless overflowing energy towards everything in Existence.

In reality, *sannyas* is living like a king. *Sannyas* is the beginning of a kingly life because when you have cleaned yourself of all your suffering, then you have gained everything you can ever gain! You gain far more than mere wealth can give you.

A *sannyasi* recognizes the unending abundance of Existence. His vision is oceanic. He is not stuck in narrow perceptions. He perceives the whole of Existence as one. He feels part of the whole. That is why he is rich. A rich man who feels he owns a few acres is not really the rich one. The man who feels the abundance of Existence is really the rich one.

Understand that the very word 'rich' has been misinterpreted. How can a person who is enjoying just a few bungalows be rich? He cannot be! The rich person is the one who is enjoying everything around him continuously. His richness is the richness of the whole Existence. He enjoys everything with no attachment to anything.

Integrity – the trait of a *sannyasi!*

The word 'penance' means nothing but integrating yourself, making yourself a single entity. You may ask, 'Are we not like that now?' If you look closely, you will see that we exist as different entities, never as one. There is everything else in our life except integration.

If you look deeply inside, you will understand that there are hundreds of voices continuously talking inside you. The moment the mind says, 'Let us do this,' the very next moment the thought will arise, 'No. Let us not do it!' After thinking of the side effects and after effects, the mind starts oscillating.

Integrating the fragmented parts of the mind is the very essence of life. Integrating the feelings and the mind, integrating your face and your mind, ensuring that your face shows the same thing as what your mind thinks, is the essence of life.

If you study the lives of great masters and try to search for one basic essence in all of their lives, you will find that it is not knowledge or devotion. It is integrity! What they believed in, they lived. That's all! Their integrity was solid. They were ready to lose even their very lives, but not their integrity.

Chaitanya Mahaprabhu*, the great enlightened master from India, used to move around on the streets just singing devotional songs. He never bothered about what others said about him. What he felt, he expressed. To be like this requires a deep sense of sacrifice. It takes courage to sacrifice anything to live with integrity!

That is why anything that these great masters did in their lives always culminated in eternal auspiciousness! Everything they did was an effort to integrate themselves with deep sincerity and devotion. The intense effort to integrate oneself completely is what is called penance. Penance always ends in auspiciousness. There will be innumerable things happening in your life all the time. Enduring all those things and intensifying your integrity with them is called penance. On the other hand, if you allow life's happenings to shake you, then you land in disgrace. What way you wish to go is up to you.

> # It takes courage to sacrifice anything to live with integrity.

Adi Shankara was a great enlightened master from India. As a young boy, he was caught in a dilemma when he wanted to pursue the path of sannyas. He wanted to leave home with the permission of his mother, but she was unwilling to let go of him.

One day, he went to bathe in the river. Suddenly, his mother heard him crying out loud for help. She ran out and saw that a crocodile had caught his leg. He was struggling to be free.

Suddenly, by a flash of thought, he cried to her, 'Mother, if you give me permission to become a sannyasi, I will be freed from this crocodile now to continue with my life.'

The mother was surprised and asked how. He explained, 'According to the Vedas, if I enter a new ashrama or stage of life, it is equal to being born again. So, if you give me permission to enter into sannyas, then maybe god will give me a fresh lease on life!'*

The mother was totally helpless. She quickly made up her mind. It was better to have

---

Chaitanya Mahaprabhu - A 15th century mystic from Bengal, India steeped in devotion to enlightened master Krishna. His followers are known as Gaudiya Vaishnavas.

Ashrama - The four stages in one's life: *brahmacharya* as a student, *grihastha* as a married householder, *vanaprastha* at the end of a productive married life and *sannyasi* as a person who renounces all material aspects in life.

her son as a sannyasi than see him dead. She agreed.

Immediately the crocodile released the grip! Adi Shankara ran to his mother with great joy. He had lived the truth he sought at that moment... and it worked.

See, there are three things:

Thinking the Truth

Speaking the Truth

Living the Truth

The first two are easy to follow. But the third, living the Truth all the time, is difficult. It is very rare. *Sannyas* is the courage to live what we think is the Truth. We give importance to speaking the Truth. But living the Truth is most important. If you start living your Truth, your respect for yourself will increase. That is the beauty of it.

When you integrate and live the Truth, you drop hypocrisy. Hypocrisy is pretending to be what you are not. Hypocrisy is hiding in many places so people can't see who you really are. The fragments in you dominate over each other and make you hypocritical. When you fight with your own fragments and win, you are a *dheera*, a courageous one! It is easy to fight with others and win. When you fight with others and win, you are a *veera*, a warrior. But fighting with yourself requires more courage. You don't fight unless you are tired of yourself. Only when you are tired, you accept that you need to start the fight.

Once you integrate, for the first time, you know who you really are. All the masks drop. You are ready to expose yourself in relationships. You become more authentic. You suddenly realize that you were missing things because of *you*! *Sannyas* is all about becoming more authentic. When I say authentic, I mean that you will radiate your individuality instead of your personality. With fragments, you are a personality. With integrity, you are individuality. Individuality is seeing your authenticity through your own eyes. Personality is a built up image in the eyes of society. The master's work is to create a space in you where you don't have to guard your personality, where you can be free, where just understanding can cause transformation.

Buddha used to tell his disciples, 'Count your life only after you have taken *sannyas*.'

Someone asked me if taking the vow of *brahmacharya** or *sannyas* will lead to enlightenment. Whether taking the vow leads to enlightenment or not is secondary. But if you observe the vows strictly for one month, successfully, the respect you have for yourself will tremendously increase. That is enough! It is called *asatya sadhana* or doing the seemingly impossible task successfully. It is making you do whatever your mind says you cannot do! Techniques like fire-walking are in this category. Ordinarily, the mind will say that you cannot walk on a fire bed. Once you do it, the respect you have for yourself will increase! Then you will come into integrity.

Brahmacharya - Literally means walking in reality. The first stage of life in the *vedic* tradition as a celibate.

Integrity needs to be understood in two ways.

The first part is integrating the fighting parts of the mind into one. See, the very life gets wasted in the oscillation of the mind. If you can follow any one path, you will attain it. For example, let us suppose there are two paths to reach Bangalore. One path is 30 kilometers while the other is 30,000 kilometers. You are oscillating between these two paths not knowing which to choose. If you choose any one path and proceed, you will reach Bangalore.

But if you keep oscillating, if you go on one path for half hour, and then change your mind and go on the other path for the next half hour, what will happen? You will never reach Bangalore! At least if you decide and take the 30,000 kilometer path, you will reach Bangalore, even if it takes you one year! But if you keep oscillating between these two paths, even if it takes thirty years, you will not reach Bangalore.

Even if the chosen path is wrong, the one who moves with integrity automatically comes to the correct path. He achieves what needs to be achieved. There are only two types of people on planet earth – those who live with integrity and those who live without integrity, that's all! The scale to measure a person is not the path on which he went but whether he lived with integrity or not.

Integrity is the strength to live your belief, come what may.

Second, not getting diluted by external influences is also integrity. It is the ability to not alter our integrity or dilute ourselves due to inner confusions or outer influences. The person who lives with integrity, even if he dies on the train platform, will die with the satisfaction that he lived completely. The person who lives without integrity, even if he dies in the best hospital, will die with dissatisfaction. The scale to measure the quality of a person's life is to see how much he lived in tune with what *he* felt was life. For example, if he is an aethist, if he lived as a strong atheist and died as a strong atheist, there is nothing wrong. He will attain! That very strength, when it goes deeper and deeper in him and searches, will show him the truth!

Integrating the mind is the essence of life. Decide you will always say and do only what you feel is right. Then, you will come to tremendous clarity and conviction in the inner and outer worlds.

Swami Vivekananda recounts in his life that his master, Ramakrishna Paramahamsa[*], died leaving him the responsibility of the mission. At the same time, Swami Vivekananda's father died leaving behind a family of utter poverty. Swami Vivekananda was the only hope for his family. He stood between saving his family and saving the world. No one recognized the mission he spoke of. He says beautifully, 'Who will sympathize with the imaginations of a boy?' He was, after all, a young boy!

Ramakrishna Paramahamsa - Enlightened master from West Bengal in India. His chief disciple was Swami Vivekananda.

With the strength of integrity comes utter freedom and bliss. He describes those few days as 'unimaginable hell'. He was with a small group of boys, with no money, with only one thing: the integrity to live the life they believed in, the life taught by their master. Ten years later, he says, 'Ten years ago, I could not get one hundred people to celebrate master's birth anniversary. Today there are fifty thousand!' *Sannyas* is taking a strong decision not to allow the unconscious to hinder the consciousness and to establish consciousness firmly on the master and his words.

Swami Vivekananda was questioned as to how he could desert his family at that time. He beautifully replied, 'I believed that Ramakrishna Paramahamsa's teachings could rationalize India and many foreign races. With that belief came the realization that it is better that a few persons suffer than for such ideas to die out of the world. What if a mother or two brothers die? It is a sacrifice. Let it be done. No great thing can be done without sacrifice. The heart must be plucked and the bleeding heart placed upon the altar. Then, great things are done!'

Such was his integrity.

Not only that, those who said that Swami Vivekananda deserted his family do not know the correct facts. He continued to fulfill his duty by giving them the bare minimum requirements. He also went to the court of law to attend to some legal issues they faced.

A small story:

During the civil wars in Japan, an invading army entered a town and took control of the whole town. Before the army arrived in one particular village, everyone fled except a Zen master.

Curious about this master, the general went to the temple to see what kind of a man the master was. The master did not even acknowledge the general. The general became very angry when he was not treated in the usual respectful way to which he was accustomed.

He took out his sword and shouted, 'You fool! Don't you realize you are standing before a man who could run you through without blinking an eye?'

The master remained calm and asked, 'And do you realize that you are standing before a man who can be run through without blinking an eye?'

With the strength of integrity comes utter freedom and bliss. With freedom and bliss there is no fear in the inner or outer world!

Life is for enlightenment!

The very goal of life is enlightenment. You may have other goals, but knowingly or unknowingly, they are just different names that we give to the goal of enlightenment. In the same way, whatever else you may seek, what you actually seek is *sannyas* itself. But you don't know it. That is the problem!

You may think your goals are to have more money and more relationships. The truth is that even the one who searches for money actually searches only for enlightenment! See, there are only two things. One is money, and the other is name and fame. Name and fame mean nothing but to have more relationships. Whatever experience you feel you are going to get through money or relationships, you will only get through enlightenment!

That is why the soul never rests until enlightenment happens. No amount of money satisfies the soul. No relationship satisfies the soul. When money and relationships don't give satisfaction, it is called the 'depression of success'. This is what happens after reaching the peak of our career. People come to me and say, 'I have achieved all that I wanted to achieve, but *what for* I wanted to achieve, I have not achieved. I feel incomplete.' Understand that this is the call of your being that seeks no other goal except enlightenment. The response to it is *sannyas*.

Not properly understanding the goal of life is the root cause of all problems. *Sannyas* is recognizing the goal properly and integrating to achieve it. Whatever goal you may be running behind in your life, be it money or relationship or whatever, your end goal is only bliss. There is no other separate goal in life!

There are only two types of people. One group knows the word 'bliss' or 'enlightenment', and the path to it. They live their life according to that. The other group does not know the word or the path, so it comes around in circles. That's all! The former is *sannyasi*, the latter is *samsari*.

> **You have achieved the human body which gives you the highest possibility to take the jump in consciousness.**

You have achieved the human body which gives you the highest possibility to take the jump in consciousness. The glass is already reflecting the sunlight. Now all that the glass needs to do is to see the *source* of the reflection. That's all! Merging with the Source is what I call enlightenment. It is merging of the individual consciousness with the cosmic consciousness.

If this happens, then the goal of life, the purpose for which the glass was created, is achieved. Then, even if the glass breaks, there is no problem. But without achieving that, if the glass is broken, it is the greatest loss ever. If the human body perishes before enlightenment, there cannot be a greater loss than that.

Sannyas is the means to this achievement. *Sannyas* is not the end of life. It is the beginning of life. *Sannyas* is moving towards enlightenment, the only and permanent purpose of life.

Conditioning is the culprit

If the purpose of life itself is enlightenment, where are we stuck right now? In what areas of our lives are we moving in the wrong direction? Understand that the problem is in recognizing the correct goal. If the goal is right, you have achieved it. If your goal is right, it means you are already living it.

293

By taking *sannyas*, you are taking the first conscious step to drop the past and enter a new world.

'Conditioning' is the reason that you miss the goal. When you were born, you came as a free bird, a Paramahamsa or the supreme swan, to flit and fly blissfully around and enjoy the whole of Existence. But after coming, not only did you fly around, but unknowingly you also landed on planet earth. That was the problem. There are many people waiting to catch such birds that land! Society waits to fit you into the frame of country, religion, caste, community and creed.

You were a sweet soul when you landed on planet earth. You were not a Hindu, or an engineer or a worker. But understand that society wants engineers and workers. It is not bothered about your consciousness. Actually, neither your parents nor society are aware that there is something called consciousness. They themselves don't have that intelligence. They teach you what they were taught. That's all. Their conditioning is not a deliberate attempt to restrict or condition you.

Conditioning is the unwanted dowry that has been handed over for generations and lives, from person to person. First, there is parental conditioning. Then there is societal conditioning. Based on these two, you create certain ethics for yourself. This is the self imposed conditioning, your own *dharma**, your own path of righteousness.

Because we create so many layers of conditioning, we are unable to see the Truth directly. We are not able to perceive the goal directly. We are not able to live the goal directly. We are caught in the conditioning and forget who we truly are. The conditioning creates certain limitations in us, and we start thinking that the limitations are the real us. Even the clothes that we wear condition us to believe we are the clothes!

Many of the conditionings are created in society in order to peacefully co-exist. For example, for easy communication, many languages are taught. There is nothing wrong in learning a language, but taking it up as a conditioning and making the language your very life, and creating sorrow for yourself and others is wrong. That mental attitude is wrong. So many people have sacrificed their lives for the sake of language. If the conditioning were not there, so many deaths would not have happened! The very history of mankind would have been written differently. Conditioning is the reason for terrorism among human beings. Today, conditioning-based-divisions go right down to the level of belonging to specific political parties!

By taking *sannyas*, you are taking the first conscious step to drop the past and enter a new world. The past is familiar, so you like to carry it. The mind always likes familiar patterns. Also, society teaches you to carry the past so that it can put guilt and fear in you that are based upon the past incidents. The past is unwanted baggage. *Sannyas* is

---

Dharma - Sanskrit equivalent of the Pali word *dhamma* used by Buddha. Also translated as 'righteous behavior'.

disconnecting from the past. When you disconnect from the past and move to a new future, initially, there is utter insecurity. *Sannyas* is utter insecurity. In utter insecurity, there is nothing else to hold on to, so you will find god!

Why do you think I give you a spiritual name? I give you a spiritual name to help you more easily disconnect from the past. The new name that I give you will constantly remind you of the psychological revolution that has happened in you, the new understanding that has happened in you. The name also indicates your individual spiritual path, according to your own innate nature, which will lead to the ultimate flowering of your consciousness.

A *sannyasi* works for the present moment. He works to give his whole life to Existence and doesn't care about the results. The results take care of themselves. That is his way. He knows only the moment, nothing else. Therefore, he learns directly from Existence every moment. That is why he has no doctrine, no religion. He moves in synchronicity with the whole of Existence and learns through it.

There is a Sufi saying, 'The Sufi is the child of the moment.' In Sufi texts, every moment is called a breath. And the Sufis are called 'the folks of the breaths,' because they live in full awareness of every breath, of every instant. According to them, every moment, a new Self arrives. That is the spirit of *sannyas*, it is being fresh every moment. A person of the moment learns from the moment. For him, Existence is his teacher.

When the great Sufi mystic Hasan, was dying, somebody asked, 'Hasan, who was your master?'

He said, 'I had many masters. If I relate their names it will take months or even years, and it is too late now. I am going to die any time. I will tell you about three masters.

The first one was a thief. Once I got lost in a desert, and when I reached a nearby village, it was late and everything was closed. At last I found a man who was trying to make a hole in the wall of a house. I asked him where I could stay and spend the night. He said, 'At this time of night it will be difficult. If you don't mind staying with a thief, you are welcome to stay with me.'

I stayed with this man for one month. Each night he would tell me, 'Now I am going for my work. You take rest and pray for me.' When he came back, I would ask him, 'Did you get anything?' He would say, 'Not tonight. But tomorrow, god willing, I will try again.' He was always happy and hopeful, never in a state of hopelessness!

When I was meditating for many years, and nothing was happening, many times the moment came when I was so desperate, so hopeless, that I thought I should stop all this nonsense. And suddenly I would remember the thief who would say every night, 'God willing, tomorrow it is going to happen'

My second master was a dog. One day, I was going to the river to quench my thirst. A dog came and he was also thirsty. He looked into the river, and saw another dog there, which was his own image. He became afraid. He would bark and run away, but his thirst was so much that he would come back. Finally, despite his fear, he jumped into the water and his own image disappeared. I realized that the message had come from god to me: one has to jump in spite of the fear.

The third master was a small child. I went to a town where a child was carrying a lit candle. He was going to the mosque to put the candle there.

I asked the boy, 'Have you lit the candle by yourself?' He said, 'Yes.' Then I asked him, 'There was a moment when the candle was unlit, and then there was a moment when the candle was lit. Can you show me the source from which the light came?'

The boy laughed, blew out the candle, and said, 'Now you have seen the light going. Where has it gone? You tell me!'

My ego was shattered and my whole knowledge was also shattered.

It is true that I had no master. That does not mean that I was not a disciple. I accepted the whole of Existence as my master. I trusted the clouds, the trees. I learned from every possible source.

Sannyas is the joyful awareness that the 'moment' is guiding you closer to your enlightenment. All you have to do is be vulnerable, that's all.

Tomorrow also comes in the form of today. So why not focus on just today? When you are in the moment, there is no space for pain or suffering. Only when you live in the past or future, you create the space for suffering. When you live in the moment, you automatically create a space where everything is beautiful. Life itself becomes a romance with Existence! You resonate with the whole thing. You are in love with everything and everyone for no reason at all. That is *sannyas*. Then you don't amass. You don't fear. You don't worry. Things happen around you like a beautiful dream.

A *sannyasi* is an eternal wanderer in spirit. Even if he is in one place, his spirit wanders without any pattern, touching so many things far away. He doesn't care to accumulate anything. He gives away whatever comes his way. He receives much more than he needs. He lives like a king.

Enjoy the transience!

Sannyas is the understanding of the transient nature of everything. All desires, possessions, and emotions are moving and changing. Everything is changing and moving. Nothing is permanent. If you analyze your own desires, before a desire is fulfilled, it looks like a mountain, a huge goal. After being fulfilled, the same desire looks like a molehill. Before being fulfilled, it will seem like your very life. After fulfilling one desire, you simply move to the next desire! Understand that the process itself shows that desires are neither solid nor permanent. They are just changing fantasies of the mind.

Sannyas helps you see the temporary nature of desires. Slowly, desires stop getting

Although you live in it, nothing in the material world really pulls you.

created. Then all the energy that was locked up in desires is freely available to you. Automatically, your potential will take a jump. You are ready to do anything. Although you live in it, nothing in the material world really pulls you. Even if you see something beautiful, you don't wish to possess it. You just enjoy it and move on. That's all. That is *sannyas*.

Sannyas works like the log of wood that is used to burn the dead body and finally gets thrown into the same pyre. It burns out all the fantasies in you and finally gives itself to the same fire. It is a tool.

Adi Shankara beautifully says in his famous song, Bhaja Govindam*:

Even when days and nights,

winters and springs have gone,

and life almost comes to an end,

the grip of desire is still there!

Desire has such a pull at the unconscious level that liberating oneself from it is the greatest liberation.

A small story:

Once there lived a stone cutter. He was not satisfied with his position in life. One day he was passing through a wealthy merchant's house. Through the gate which was open, he noticed many possessions and important visitors in the merchant's house. He thought that the merchant must be very powerful. He became jealous and wished that he could be like the merchant.

To his great surprise, the stone cutter suddenly became the merchant, enjoying more luxuries and power than he had ever imagined.

One day, he was standing on the road when he saw a high official pass by. He was carried in a beautiful chair, accompanied by attendants and escorted by soldiers beating gongs. Everyone, no matter how wealthy, had to bow down before the procession.

He thought, 'How powerful that official is! I wish I could be a high official!'

Immediately, he became the high official, and he was carried everywhere in his beautiful chair.

One day it was extremely hot, and he felt very uncomfortable in the sticky chair. He looked up at the sun. It was so bright and beautiful in the sky. He thought, 'How powerful the sun is! I wish that I could be the sun!'

He became the sun! And he enjoyed his powerful position over everything.

One day, a huge black cloud moved between him and the earth, so that his light could no longer shine on everything below. He was surprised. He thought, 'How powerful

---

Bhaja Govindam - Collection of 32 (sometimes 34) devotional verses composed by enlightened master Adi Shankara. This is considered to be the essence of Vedanta and Advaita, non-duality.

Even in the most difficult times, a *sannyasi* remains with the awareness that life is a fleeting dream.

that huge black storm cloud is! How I wish I could be a cloud!

He became the storm cloud, flooding the fields and villages.

Soon he found that he was being pushed away by some great force, and realized that it was the wind. He thought, 'How powerful the wind is! I wish to become the wind!'

He became the wind and powerfully blew over the roofs of houses and through forests.

One day, he came across something that would not move, no matter how forcefully he blew against it. It was a huge and towering rock. He thought, 'How powerful that rock is! I wish to become the rock!'

Then he became the rock, more powerful than anything else on earth. But as he stood there, he heard the sound of a hammer pounding a chisel into the hard surface, and felt himself being changed. He thought, 'What could be more powerful than a rock?'

He looked down and saw a stone cutter far below him!

This story clearly illustrates how the mind always thinks that which has not yet been achieved is greater than that which has been achieved. The grass on the other side is always greener. But when we go to the other side, what happens? We feel the grass on the opposite side is greener! We jump from one thing to the other, from one desire to the next,

from one point of view to the next, but we are seldom happy.

A *sannyasi* is one who clearly sees that everything is changing all the time, and everything is beautiful just the way it is. He also knows that beauty is in the eyes of the beholder. That is why he sets out first to clean his eyes. Eyes are the windows of the soul, so his work is at the core level. If you see the world through a red colored lens, everything appears red. If you see with a green colored lens, everything is green. If you see with clear eyes, everything looks clear and beautiful. Existence has always been beautiful, but we missed seeing it. *Sannyas* is the decision to see with clear eyes.

If life itself is changing all the time, then why are we trying to frame it? Buddha says in his Dhammapada[*], 'Life is like a flash of lightning in the sky.' Life is transient. Then what are we trying to do? We are trying to do an impossible job. Our job is to see, enjoy, and move on. If everything is a passing manifestation of Existence, then where is the scope for ego or fear or greed? *Sannyas*, as such, doesn't change anything. Everything remains the same. But it changes the way *you* see things. *Sannyas* happens in you. *Sannyas* has nothing to do with the outer world.

Sannyas is awakening the charioteer. Man's body is like a chariot and his consciousness is the charioteer. The charioteer is fast asleep, and the chariot is moving according to the horses. The five horses are

---

Dhammapada - Teachings of Buddha in scriptural form.

the five senses, each with its own different idea. Not one of them is the truth. They are just transient ideas!

Even in the most difficult times, a *sannyasi* remains with the awareness that life is a fleeting dream! He carries a completely different definition for success and failure. He doesn't carry success or failure itself. A *samsari* on the other hand carries success and failure with him wherever he goes. There starts the problem.

Surrender, love, compassion, *sannyas*

Sannyas is saying 'yes' to Existence. Saying 'yes' is surrender. Saying 'yes' is love and compassion.

The human mind is trained to always say 'no'. Saying 'no' boosts the ego. 'Yes' makes the ego vulnerable, so the mind continues to say 'no.' *Sannyas* is saying 'yes' to Existence. Existence created you. It is waiting to express its divine play through you. By saying 'yes,' you allow the divine play to happen through you. When the divine play happens, things happen exactly according to the flow of Existence. Then, everything becomes auspiciousness!

In the effort to say 'yes,' you start softening. *Sannyas* is about becoming soft. As long as you say 'no,' you remain hard. When you make an effort to say 'yes,' you start softening. When you make a conscious decision to say 'yes,' it starts. That is where

the master plays a role. *Sannyas* is saying 'yes' to the master without asking for an explanation. When you start trusting the master completely, *sannyas* starts happening in you. Somewhere you get the click that the master knows better than you. Then you start letting go of your hold over your mind and start holding the hands of the master. The master's hands are always stretched out, but you were not ready to hold them. Once the 'yes' starts happening, you hold his hands.

Then a space is created where love starts happening. Love happens only when you start saying 'yes.' By saying 'yes,' not only do you start loving, you allow the other person to love you as well. Then your inner space that was like a rock earlier, starts becoming like cotton! It becomes soaked with love. The love is not just towards one person or for any reason. It is an overflowing energy. It is towards the whole of Existence for no reason. You start communing with the trees, with everything around you. You feel that life is a song, the song of Existence of which you are a part. You are in a deeply resonant mood with everything and everyone around you, including yourself. Your actions simply become an outpouring of the joy and ecstasy that is enveloping you all the time.

A small story:

A Zen master arrived at the meeting place of the Cambridge Buddhist Society. He found everyone dusting and cleaning the whole place in anticipation of his visit.

They were surprised to see him because he was not supposed to arrive until the following day.

> **An enlightened being's love and compassion is boundless. *Sannyas* is living like an enlightened being. It is living enlightenment.**

He simply tied back the sleeves of his robe and joined the preparations. They could not believe that he wanted to help. He asked, 'Why can't I also prepare for the grand day of my arrival!'

When you are resonating with Existence, you enjoy everything, including yourself. You don't see yourself as separate from anything else. You see no separate reason for anything. There are people who commune with nature but fail miserably when it comes to people. Then, even their communion with nature is not real communion. Feeling only for nature is not a scale by which to measure love.

People tell me that they are already communing with Existence. Trees and animals don't create trouble for you. That is why you claim to commune with them! They keep quiet. You can simply express anything to them. You can thrust your feeling on them, pull it out, and feel good, that's all. It is just an ego trip. The essence is in the ability to commune with the whole of Existence, even when faced with trouble! If you can create that space of love under those conditions, then you are communing.

A poet once wrote a love song and sent it to his friends. A few days later, he received a letter from a lady to whom he had sent the poem.

She wrote to him saying, 'I am so touched by your poem. Please come home, meet my parents, and ask them if you can marry me.'

The poet was surprised. He wrote back to her, 'That was a poem of love from my heart that I wanted to sing to a few souls. It was nothing more than that!'

She replied, 'You are a hypocrite. Because of you, I will never again entertain a poet in my life.'

The problem is, everything happens with the reason of the intellect. Love has been reduced to mere lust for the other person's body. That is the problem. Real love is an expression of the overflowing energy that starts happening in you when you start saying 'yes' to Existence.

The famous poet Kabir[*] says that when love possesses you, don't even think twice. Just dive into it. If you start thinking, it is like arranging your pillows when deep sleep of rest has come to your eyes. He says, 'Even though the head itself must be given, why should you weep over it!'

The master waits many lives for you. But *you* have to say 'yes'. Remember, the master is a gentleman. He gives you the freedom to remain in bondage. He waits. Once you say 'yes,' he takes you in his arms. The master is the only one who can show you the power of love.

An enlightened being's love and compassion is boundless. *Sannyas* is living like an enlightened being. It is living enlightenment.

Kabir - Mystic devotional poet of India.

A *sannyasi* is one who is established in love and compassion in the inner world, while being established in concentration and precision in the outer world. A real *sannyasi* has the precision of a sword. When he closes his eyes, the outer world is no more. When he opens his eyes, his work is perfection, perfection not only in work, but in relationships also! He is a father, a mother, a brother and a friend, all at the same time.

He moves, guided by inner intelligence. That is why he is in the present moment all the time. He responds to the moment. That is the ultimate sense of responsibility – responding to the moment spontaneously. True love and compassion are spontaneous responses to the moment. That is why they surface irrespective of people or situations.

A small story:

One man went to a Zen monastery and told the master, 'Master, I wish to practice Zen for the rest of my life but I have never stuck with anything for very long. I always look for shortcuts to everything. Is there a shortcut to enlightenment?'

The master told him, 'You are accepted into this monastery for two days. In these two days, you will be taught the shortcut to enlightenment. Is there anything that you like to do in particular?'

The man said, 'Since I don't stick to anything for a long time, I am unable to tell what I like to do most. But I like to play chess.'

The master called for a young disciple who was supposed to be a good chess player. He asked the two of them to sit down and placed a chess board between them. He then took out his sword and placed it in front of the two of them and said,

True love and compassion are spontaneous responses to the moment. They surface irrespective of people or situations.

'Both of you have to play. The moment one of you loses, the loser will have his head cut off.'

They were shocked at the master's words! They started the game and played.

They concentrated on the game like they had never done before.

Initially, the young monk made good moves, and it looked like he was going to win. Then suddenly he made a mistake. The man took the opportunity and took over the game. Soon, he was clearly on the way to winning.

Suddenly, he looked at the young monk and thought with what dedication and devotion the monk lived his life with the master at that young age. Then he thought about his own life and how he had wasted it. Suddenly he decided, if at all anyone should die, it should be himself. He deliberately made a wrong move. The young monk saw that and took over the game again.

The master was watching the whole thing. At that point, he took the board away, and the coins fell in the air. He said, 'Nobody wins. Nobody loses. The game is over. There are only two things needed for enlightenment, they are concentration and compassion. Today, you learned both. Stay with me and study the way you have played chess today. Enlightenment will be yours!'

Sannyas is bringing together concentration and compassion. With concentration, you never forget the goal of life, which is enlightenment. With compassion, you are ready to sacrifice your very life so that the other may reach the goal! When both are there, both you and the other will reach! That is the greatness of *sannyas*. That is the space of *sannyas*.

The greatest quality of a *sannyasi* is his immense trust in Existence. Society trains you to always protect yourself from everything. That is the problem. You are made to believe Existence is the enemy from which you have to protect yourself. You apply the same rule and protect yourself from the master also. The master happens in your life with just one intention - to destroy your ego and allow the attitude of *sannyas* to flower in you.

Sannyas is nothing but finding out exactly where you are going wrong. That exact place is known as nothing but the ego. If you understand this, you will simply open up to the master and allow him to strike the ego. You will simply drop all your defenses and open up. Being closed to the master's presence is like closing your nose with your fingers when there is a fragrant breeze blowing. When you open up to him with trust, you will see miracles happen all around you.

Trust has amazing power. It works beyond logic. Anything that works beyond logic is the direct truth. It never fails. When you trust the master, when you surrender to the master, you

are giving him the responsibility of you. He never fails! It does not mean you can surrender to him and then do foolish things. No! The first thing to realize is that when real surrender happens, it will never prompt you to do foolish things. Only surrender in the name of surrender will attempt to do foolish things. Real surrender is a consciousness, not a concept for trial.

Sannyas is a consciousness that flowers in groups of people in the presence of the master. Over the years, *sannyas* has always happened in groups. All the great masters have ordained groups of *sannyasins*. When a group of people start dissolving in love, when a group of people start melting, *sannyas* starts happening. Suddenly, so much beauty radiates. Suddenly, Existence appears to be profoundly mystical and beautiful. The power of coincidence becomes a way of life. Tremendous energy starts flowing. For no reason, life looks tremendously beautiful. Everything seems to be perfect. There is an inexplicable feeling of blossoming all round.

It is not that Existence has become more beautiful. Existence is always the same. You have started responding to it, that's all. Your own human qualities have enriched tremendously. That is *sannyas*! When you start responding to Existence with enriched qualities, when you start melting into Existence, when you start yearning for it, *sannyas* starts happening to you.

When *sannyas* happens, you automatically add more beauty to Existence. You become a creator. People think *sannyas* is renouncing creativity. No! *Sannyas* is moving one step closer to god, and god is the ultimate creator. The very energy of *sannyas* is creation. This is a little known fact about *sannyas*.

When *sannyas* happens, the moment is right ...

A small story:

One day a young man approached Socrates*, the Greek philosopher, and said, 'O great Socrates*, I come to you for knowledge.' Socrates* took the man to the sea and pressed his head down into the water for a few seconds.

When he released him, the man came up gasping for breath. Socrates asked him to repeat what he wanted. The man said, 'I want knowledge.'

Socrates put him under the water again, this time for a longer period. Then he released him and asked, 'What do you want?' The man replied, 'Knowledge'.

Socrates repeated this a few times.

After a few times, Socrates asked again, 'What do you want?' The man gasped, 'Air. I want air!'

Socrates said, 'Good. When you want knowledge as much as you wanted air, you shall have it.'

Sannyas is a deep urge that rises from within you. It is a deep yearning. Even if the longing is not completely consistent over time

and space, it is alright. You can take the jump. It may not become consistent. But becoming consistent is not the criterion needed. When it takes root, that alone is enough. You are ready. Once you jump in, everything takes care of itself.

One man was walking towards the Himalayan mountains in the winter months. An old man saw him and asked, 'It is so cold in the mountains. Are you sure you can make it?' The man replied, 'My heart is already there. So it is easy for the rest of me to reach there.'

The initiation itself will trigger the process. The outer adornments of *sannyas* will take care of the inner adornment. That is why, with the initiation, a new name and saffron clothing are given. They will do most of the job for you. They will keep the awareness alive every moment.

But if you start analyzing the decision to take the jump, you will miss it. *Sannyas* is linked to your energy. Just by seeing your energy, I can tell you are ready for *sannyas*! You cannot analyze energy with logic. Energy is beyond logic. When you take *sannyas*, the moment is right, that's all. Even if you drop it later, have no regrets. The seed has been sown. Once a *sannyasi*, always a *sannyasi*. It will happen again at the right time. That time may be the final time.

Sannyas is a decision taken by intelligent people. When life comes to the boiling point, to a peak of depression, to a point where you

---

Socrates - Greek Philosopher. Contemporary of Plato.

303

feel the outer world is of no use, when there is nothing further that can be done to help your situation, there are three choices you can make.

The first choice you could make is suicide. Suicide appears to be immediate freedom but actually it creates terrible suffering. People think that suicide takes courage. Courage is a beautiful word wrongly used here. Do you need courage to rub chili powder in your own eyes? No! It is simple foolishness. In the same way, it does not require courage to commit suicide. It is simply foolishness. There is nothing courageous about it.

Understand the science behind suicide. Suppose your normal life span this birth is ninety years of age and you commit suicide when you are forty-five. For the remaining forty-five years, you have to wait as a spirit. Only at the end of ninety years can you choose the next body to take birth. These forty-five years will be the worst hell you can ever experience. It will be worse than the struggle that happened when you were in the body. Suicide is not the relief you think it is.

The second choice is to resort to some sort of addiction, like drugs or alcohol, and slowly poison the system until it dies. This is equally as foolish because you are knowingly abusing the body.

The third and most intelligent path is to look into yourself. When the outer world seems to be over in your mind, the time has come to look inwards. *Sannyas* happens when you decide to look in and introspect. *Sannyas* is the alchemy of transforming your entire lifestyle, directing your whole energy towards enlightenment. When the first thought to look in comes, when the first thought to embrace spirituality happens, the intelligent one takes the jump into *sannyas*. *Sannyas* is the shortcut.

A small story:

A fifty year old student of enlightenment approached a Zen master and said, 'I have been studying spiritual studies since I was a small boy. I have learnt that even the grass and trees will become enlightened. This seems very strange to me.'

The master asked, 'Of what use is it to discuss how grass and trees become enlightened? The question is how you can become enlightened. Have you ever considered that?'

The old man answered, 'I never thought of it in that way.'

The master said, 'Then go home and think it over.'

Sannyas is a focused appointment with yourself. It is a conscious commitment to yourself that you are going to destroy 'all that you are not', and cleanse yourself completely.

Once you make the commitment, your seeing, hearing, talking and feeling will start being different. The same things will cause a new understanding in you. That is what commitment to *sannyas* does to you. *Sannyas* is going to be the only solution for the future, because it is the only thing that teaches you to be established in yourself and yet learn to act in the outer world in a playful, joyful, ecstatic way. *Sannyas* allows you to play any number of roles without identifying with any of them. It keeps you in continuous excitement and ecstasy all the time. It makes you experience the very essence of taking birth on planet earth.

Real love doesn't stand in the way

A true mother is one who lets go of her child when the time is right. A mother who is too possessive of her child should probably hesitate to give birth in the first place! Even giving birth is a form of letting go because she is allowing the child to leave her body! Only a mother who is ready to allow the next level of explosion to happen, a mother who is ready to let go, can only be a real mother.

If you are possessive, if you feel sad just thinking about separating from the child, then you should not even give birth to the child! You should continuously feed him through the umbilical cord. The umbilical cord connection should be continuously kept alive! Just as the child grows physically only after you deliver him into the outside world after nine months, likewise, he can grow psychologically only if you allow him to break from you.

Physical disconnection is birth. Psychological disconnection is *sannyas*.

In that way I am very fortunate. When I went and told my mother that I wanted to leave home for *sannyas*, it was late at night, around eleven o'clock. I went to the temple, spent some time as usual, and came home at my regular time. I opened the door with my key and walked in. I wore wooden sandals, normally worn by wandering ascetics. They made a loud noise on that granite floor! My mother's usual custom was to wake up, prepare the food of my choice, and serve me the moment I entered. If I had finished my dinner at the temple, I would tell her and both of us would go to sleep.

That particular night, she got up and was about to prepare food. I called her and told her, 'I have decided that I am leaving home for *sannyas*. You can give me food tonight, even though I have already eaten. I will eat now because tomorrow I will be leaving.'

It was a very casual announcement from my side. Of course, she was shocked, but she did not say anything. One thing is that all of my family knew from the beginning that talking and trying to convince me to do otherwise would never work. They knew that before saying anything, I would be very clear about it inside. Only after knowing what to do would I say it out loud. When I say something, it means it is going to be done - that's all!

Tears started pouring from her eyes. I looked at her and asked, 'What do you mean by crying? Do you mean that I should not go?'

She shook her head and said, 'No, I am not saying you should not go. I am crying because I am not able to control myself. I am not able to accept it. I can't say that you cannot go.'

> **Physical disconnection is birth. Psychological disconnection is *sannyas*.**

She knew all along that one day this would happen. One day or the other I would leave. It was predicted in my horoscope. The beauty of it was, she never said 'No!' Not only did she not tell me I couldn't go, she broke the news to my father as well. My father thought she had shouted at me and created some problem and that was the reason I had decided to go. He asked her, 'Did you shout at him? Did you create any problem?'

My mother said, 'No, I did not shout or say anything. He came of his own accord and told me this.' Then my father calmed down.

It was a straight and simple declaration. My father came to me, sat down and asked, '*Swami*, your mother is saying a few things as your words. Are these things true?'

Funnily, they used to call me '*Swami*' even in those days!

I told him, 'Yes. I have decided to leave home to pursue *sannyas* and become enlightened.'

It was a shock to him. But he saw that I was very clear, balanced, cool and relaxed. He made only one statement. He said, 'If you fall sick, please inform us. We want to take care of you.' That's all. He simply said, 'If you ever fall sick anywhere during your travels, please inform us. We want to take care of you. That is the only thing we want, nothing else. Otherwise, do what you want.'

My parents never stood in my way. Understand: any relationship, including the parental relationship, is a healthy relationship, only when the person is ready to allow the next phase to happen. I have seen thousands of youngsters who are so inspired, who are bold enough, who are courageous enough to take up this path of seeking. However, they don't even give themselves a chance to explore because of their parents.

Parents simply fall into the regular way of life, living to satisfy other people's ego, and bringing up children. Very rarely, a few souls get the inspiration and courage to explore. Try to understand that I am not asking you to train your kids or force your kids to become *swamis*. No! I am saying that if at all they feel that click towards *sannyas*, do not stand in their way. You will be blessed if you do not stand in their way.

Have the intelligence to see the path the child has chosen. He has chosen the ultimate path. Even if he cries and struggles and becomes a failure, there is nothing wrong – if that is your fear. I might have been a failure in my previous ten births. That is why this time I am successful! Understand, when the struggle is for *sannyas*, even if enlightenment does not happen, it is not a failure. It is a great success because you lived with integrity and that too in the conscious field. In the conscious field, Existence watches over you completely. You are taken care of at every step. So understand that any exploration, any research, any adventure in the conscious field should be encouraged, allowed, and supported.

I feel eternally grateful to my parents for not standing in the way.

Enlightenment is the Key to Your Kingdom

We now reach the ultimate, or what I call the peak experience. Realization of who we are and our role in this universe is the ultimate knowledge and experience that we can have. From the darkness of ignorance we move into the light of truth. We become enlightened.

Why enlightened beings happen on planet earth

When you see somebody swimming, you understand three things. The first thing is that swimming is possible, that a man can float on water. Secondly, you have a tremendous urge: 'If he can do it, why not me? Why can't I? I can too.' The third thing is, 'Let me jump in!' You get inspiration and courage!

In the same way, when you see an enlightened being walking on planet earth, when you live around him, you also understand three things. The first thing is that enlightenment is possible. You can live like a god on this planet earth. The next thing is, 'If he can attain enlightenment, why not me?' because he radiates such simplicity and ordinariness, which is close to your own human nature. You naturally get confidence that it is possible for you too. The third thing is courage, 'Let me jump in!' All these three will happen only if you live around an enlightened master and continuously watch his body language. Nothing else can trigger this in you.

Enlightenment is...

1. Experiencing the limitless continuum

Living with the limitless continuum is enlightenment. The limitless continuum will happen when you relax from the identities you hold of yourself in the outer and inner worlds.

If you are settled in that limitless continuum and are able to be active, you are living enlightenment. If you are not able to settle down in it, but you had at least one experience of it, then you have experienced *satori*.

2. Realizing the self, world, and god

The basic thing needed for enlightenment is a 'psychological revolution', a new clarity about the self (*jeeva**), world (*jagat**), and god (*Ishwara**).

How you think, why you think, how you are driven, what is your inspiration, what motivates you in life - this understanding is the clarity about the self or *jeeva**.

How to achieve your desires in the world, how you avoid fears and other things forced upon you by the world - this understanding is the clarity about the world or *jagat**.

Clarity about *Ishwara* or god means understanding the source of both the individual self and the world. Achieving the source, knowing all these three, is enlightenment.

When you have a clear understanding about why you think and how you think, this very understanding gives you the clear experience of the self. When you understand how to connect with the world, achieving what you want, and avoiding what is not needed, you gain a clear experience of the world. The third is experiencing god, *Ishwara**, the source of the self and the world.

Gaining a true understanding of the self, world and god is enlightenment.

Jeeva - Usually the imperishable spirit that dwells in all living beings.

Jagat - Universe.

Ishwara - Supreme.

3. Intense excitement for no reason

People ask me, 'After enlightenment, can enlightened beings enjoy?' I tell you, only after enlightenment can you enjoy! Before that, you can only think or imagine you are enjoying.

After enlightenment, you don't even need sense objects to enjoy. You will simply be enjoying all the time. There will be such an intense excitement for no reason.

If I have to define enlightenment in two words, I will say it is 'intense excitement' for no reason, intense passion directed towards no object. There is no object, but there is intense passion. There is no reason, but there is intense excitement. That is what I call enlightenment. Enlightenment does not mean escaping somewhere. Tasting life here and now is what I call enlightenment.

4. Seeing others as you see yourself

What I call enlightenment is experiencing the same intensity of life that you feel inside yourself, outside your skin also. You are not alive just inside your body, but you are also alive inside every other individual, tree, and rock. Your hold over your physical body is transformed into a hold over the cosmic body!

You are alive in every cell in the cosmos. Every cell is a complete, fulfilled part of the cosmos.

Understand, I am alive as much outside as I am inside my skin. So, I am alive in all the millions of heads, eyes, and feet and all the millions of beings in the cosmos.

To achieve this, start seeing everything as if you are seeing for the first time, without bringing in your engrams, your past engraved memories. Then you will start experiencing the same life and intensity that you experience inside your skin, outside also. Try this for ten days. Once you get a glimpse, you will never miss it! You will see you are in ecstasy for no reason. You are in excitement for no reason. You will never take things for granted again. You will always be in joy.

5. Being unclutched

As of now you connect all the past experiences of your life and create a shaft. All your future experiences depend on how you have created this shaft. They depend on which words from the past you have picked, and how you have formed the shaft. Your future emotions, reactions, thoughts, and words depend entirely on this shaft. But after enlightenment, life is very different from this. Thoughts arise, and if they want to work, the body pursues the thoughts. Once the work is done, the thoughts disappear. Then the next time something needs to be done, thoughts arise again, and the process continues. The whole thing happens beautifully by itself.

There is no shaft at all.

Currently we all carry constant irritation from the moment we get out of the bed until the minute we go back to bed. Constantly we carry some irritation or other. We are waiting to jump on people. We only need some excuse. After enlightenment, the constant fear or guilt or desire, something that constantly irritates is not there. When you unclutch from the shaft for even one moment, you get a glimpse of enlightenment.

Enlightenment is intense passion directed towards no object.

The shift from the shaft happens in a fraction of a second. If you are deeply aware, you can catch that precious moment when the unclutching happens. All our *tapas*, spiritual training, is only preparing us to catch that shift. The shift happens many times. You just need to be really aware and you can catch it. When you permanently unclutch from the shaft, you are enlightened.

6. The four permanent changes

I can say that a few changes happened permanently in me when I became enlightened.

The first thing was that all inner chatter disappeared. By inner chatter, I mean the constant chatter of words that goes on inside us normally. In the gap between my words as I talk now, even in those few seconds, there is no chatter inside. It is simply pure space, silence.

Even a simple thing creates intense excitement.

The second thing is that the idea that my boundary ends here at this body, and there starts the rest of the world disappeared. Border consciousness dissolved. I don't feel I am just this six foot form. I see and feel myself in everything. If you watch me, I will be the first one to enjoy all my photographs after a photo shoot or on the book covers! I will just play with them for four or five days.

The third thing is that even though the body is a male body, the inner identity of male or female disappeared. The psychological idea that 'I am male' or 'I am female' doesn't exist in me anymore.

And the fourth thing is that there is a constant excitement within, everything excites. Even small things give big excitement. Even a simple thing creates intense excitement and joy.

I can say that these four changes are permanent things that happened in me after enlightenment.

7. Ultimate but not final

Be very clear, enlightenment is not the end. It is the ultimate experience, but not the final experience.

You need to understand these two words 'final' and 'ultimate'. They are very different. For example, after the first day of discourse in a series, one person came to me and said, 'You have said everything. Why do we need one more class?' The next day, another person said, '*Swamiji*, on the first day, I thought you could not take us any deeper; it is over. And today, suddenly I felt that you have taken us deeper than yesterday, and you cannot take us any deeper than this. Every day I feel that you cannot take us much deeper than this, but we do keep going deeper.' Every day the person felt that the experience was the ultimate.

Ultimate means living every moment totally, completely. Ultimate is not final. It can be updated.

There is a big difference between these two words, ultimate and final. If it is ultimate, it is happening every moment. It is not final.

When a being becomes enlightened, not only does he experience his potentiality, but he also starts creating more enlightened beings. He starts creating the possibility of more enlightened beings.

8. No verbalization, visualization

When you are enlightened, there will not be any movement of letter or word or thought between your navel and throat. Words will come only from the throat. I can say this is one of the precise descriptions of enlightenment. There will not be any word, thought, syllable, or sound movement between the navel and the throat.

Words will be there only when you are talking. When you are not talking, there will not be any words inside. Only the energy movement will be there. There will be no thought, no verbalization, no continuous inner chattering.

Understand, when you don't have inner chatter, it is not dead silence. It is intense energy! From that energy, whatever needs to be done will come out as a complete visualization. If you have inner chattering, it will come line by line like, 'In the morning, I have to wake up. Then, I have to go to office. There I will work on the new project. In the evening I will come back. Then I may go out for dinner…' In a linear manner, one by one, thoughts and words come out.

When you don't have inner chatter, when you are just with yourself, the whole visualization comes out as one package, one piece of information. That is what we call intuition. When you go through the logical process, it is called inner chatter, it is intellect. But when you don't have that inner chatter, things start expressing in you intuitively. Straightaway, you know.

9. Integrated inner chatter and outer words

The person who has removed hypocrisy from his inner space will experience enlightenment. Ramakrishna Paramahamsa, the enlightened master from India, says beautifully, 'Integrating your inner chatter and your spoken words is enlightenment.' He says, just integrate your inner chatter and the words that you utter. Let both of them be integrated

and you are enlightened.

10. Research & Development from superconscious awareness

After someone achieves enlightenment they have a very sharp superconscious awareness. With that superconscious awareness, it is easy to do research, experiments and analysis. Even after enlightenment, I have been doing so many experiments, so many practices along with scientists and researchers of the outer world and inner world, and by myself.

Understand, when an enlightened being does spiritual practices it is not just for him. It is to create the right formulas for the disciples, so that he can reproduce the same experience in them.

11. Transcendence of the human state

Someone asked me, 'Is enlightenment the natural human state or is it a transcendence of the human state?'

Surely, enlightenment is the transcendence of the human state. Whatever you think of as the human state is not complete. You are only a seed, a potential, a possibility. You are not a

> When you don't have inner chatter, when you are just with yourself, the whole visualization comes out as intuition.

You are a spiritual being with a human experience. tree. You are not actuality. Your actuality is enlightenment.

You are called a human being in your potential state. In your actual state, realized state, you are called an enlightened being. Be very clear, you are not a human being with a spiritual experience. You are a spiritual being with a human experience!

12. Beyond yogic powers

When you meditate, you can get various yogic powers or siddhis*. But enlightenment happens when you go beyond these powers also. Enlightenment is having the capacity to handle the powers, as well as the intelligence to drop them when necessary.

The other day I read an interesting article about a book 'Occult Chemistry' based on research done by the theosophists Annie Besant and Charles Leadbeater on the molecular structure of various elements. It said that even long before physics discovered that an atom has a nucleus, the theosophists had determined the atomic structure of many elements, and that too down to the 'quark', the most fundamental particle known today in quantum physics!

How did they find this out with no modern scientific equipment, before even quantum physics was born? The report says it was through the siddhi, or mystical power, known as anima that has been described in the Yoga Sutras by the sage Patanjali, an enlightened master from India and father of the science of Yoga*. Patanjali described anima as 'the ability to acquire knowledge of the small, the hidden, or the distant, by directing the light of superphysical faculty'.

With yogic training, they could experience visual images of minute objects too small to be seen by the normal eye. They found five new elements through these yogic powers. They even went beyond the quark as well as its detailed structure, into the sub-quark, which science is yet to find. These very same findings have also been made by at least three other people from different places in the world at different times, through such occult capacities.

They concluded that all matter is like bubbles in space, just like pearls on an invisible string. The report says that the researchers not only 'saw' the subatomic particles, but they could also see inside the atom down to the sub-quark, for which science needs a very powerful particle accelerator that costs billions of dollars!

There are many yogis who have these kinds of siddhis or powers that come about as a result of meditation. They are good as long as you don't get caught in them. Otherwise, you will lose sight of the ultimate goal of enlightenment.

Siddhis - Yogic powers that arise during spiritual journey.
Yoga - Literally means 'uniting' of body-mind-spirit.

13. Clear, undisturbed peace

Enlightenment is having such a strong and clear sense of peace inside you that even your thoughts cannot disturb you.

Do not think enlightened masters don't have thoughts. It is just that their inner space is so big that the mind is a negligible part. For you, if you have a ten-acre mind, all ten acres are like a zoo. With an enlightened being there are a million acres, but still only a ten acre zoo. In a million acres, if there is some movement in ten acres, can you consider it as something disturbing? No! It is negligible. It is practically not there. That is why an average person feels 'I am the body' but an enlightened being feels, 'I am the body also.'

It is not that the idea 'I am body' disappears. It just expands to 'I am also the body.'

14. Beyond bliss

'Always being intense' is the main mark of an enlightened master. When you see that, you understand it as 'bliss' or 'happiness'. To tell you honestly, I myself do not feel that I am a separate blissful being. All I know is that something extraordinary is constantly happening in me, very intensely. Only an outsider feels it is 'bliss'. Actually it is not even 'bliss'. It is the quality that cannot be described, that cannot be conceived by the mind.

15. Merging of the experience, experiencer, and experienced

As of now, you see three separate things: the experiencer, the experience, and the experienced. For example, you are reading this book now. You are the experiencer that is the reader, the experience is of reading, and the thing being experienced is the book. When you get enlightened, all these three – experiencer, experience, and the experienced, become one. You are only the experiencer having the experience of you, who is also the experienced!

Living enlightenment

1. Enjoying the chaos of the cosmos within the frame of the body

As of now, you are not mature enough to hold the chaos, the cosmos, inside the frame of your body. You need to put the chaos in order because you are not able to handle the cosmos as is. The six feet frame of your body is not mature enough to hold the chaos as is, to experience and enjoy the cosmos as is.

The body, mind and brain being awakened, tuned to experience the cosmos as is, is what is living enlightenment.

For this, the body, mind and brain need to be prepared. The body can be prepared with techniques like Nithya Yoga.

The mind is like the software. It consists of the conscious mind and unconscious mind. The conscious mind can be cleared by teachings, removing the wrong ideas and taking in the clear, correct ideas. The unconscious mind can be cleared by meditation techniques.

But ultimately, for the software change to be permanent, the hardware also has to change. Your very brain grooves have to change to hold the experience of and radiate living enlightenment. This can happen through initiation, through the touch of the master. Initiation is directly transmitting the energy after which different dimensions of you will start getting awakened.

2. Living a conflict-free life

Living enlightenment has nothing to do with married life or celibacy. It is just living a conflict-free life where your actions and knowledge are in tune with the desire.

3. Reduced number of thoughts

Not being in the extremes of anything, not being caught in the extremes of emotions is what is called the Middle Path. Being in the middle path, the *madhyapantha**, suddenly you see a reduction in the number of thoughts that arise before any action starts. That is the period called 'living enlightenment'. When thoughts completely drop and you are able to do all your activity without thoughts, you are enlightened.

4. Awakening of the non-mechanical parts of the brain

When you are centered in *sattva**, positive energy, you have a clear understanding of the *jeeva**, the self. You have the clear understanding of how to relate with the *jagat**, the world. Because of the clarity of the self and the world, naturally you will fall into the source, *Ishwara**, god.

The very understanding will give you clarity. That clarity will automatically awaken the non-mechanical parts of your brain. When that awakening happens, a chaos will start happening in your routine. Your routine will start getting re-arranged by itself. Just cooperate with it. That is what I call 'living enlightenment'. Cooperating with the awakening that happens in you is what I call being a disciple or living enlightenment.

Madhyapantha - 'Middle Path' prescribed by enlightened master Buddha. It represents the power of witnessing that causes one to be in moderation without being pushed and pulled into extremes of emotions.

Sattva - One of the three *gunas* or attributes of nature. Attribute of passive action.

Jeeva - Usually the imperishable spirit that dwells in all living beings.

Jagat - Universe.

Ishwara - Supreme.

5. Living the great Truths

'Living enlightenment' is the right word. When you are living these great truths you are enlightened, that's all.

You are supposed to live the truths. Living the great truths in your life is enlightenment. Enlightenment does not mean you will leave your body and die. No! You will live in a center that is beyond the five senses, but with the five senses. Only your center will be shifted. The cognitive shift will happen within you. This is what I call *jeevan mukti*, living enlightenment.

Ego Vs Enlightenment

Your ego is not powerful enough to take away your enlightenment! Understand, your ego is not so powerful that it can take away your enlightenment.

You need to stop thinking that you have an ego. Even your ego is not as big as you think. You are not as big as you always think! So even your ego cannot take away your enlightenment.

Whether you believe it or not, experience it or not, you *are* eternal Consciousness.

Your logic is also not as strong as you think. I always tell people, your ignorance is not so strong as to take enlightenment away from you. Even in your ignorance or ego you are not that big a person, and that is the truth!

For the sheer grace and blessing - deep want, no qualifications

Cooperating with the awakening that happens in you is what I call living enlightenment.

People ask me, 'If a master wants, whether a disciple is qualified or not, can he give him enlightenment?'

An enlightened master can enlighten anybody just by one touch – not even touch, just a thought is enough. Nothing else is necessary. He can liberate anybody.

The greatest happening on planet earth is an un-enlightened being sitting with an enlightened being and becoming enlightened.

The master can simply download the software of an enlightened physiology into anyone. When you are completely open, the software of an enlightened physiology can be downloaded into your system. Your body learns that it can be better than what it is now. Your bio-memory learns the lesson of the possibility for a better existence.

A small story from the life of the enlightened master Buddha:

Buddha was once asked, 'Why don't you give enligh-tenment to everybody?' He said, 'Please ask in the village who wants enlightenment. Bring them to me and I shall give.'

The man went through the whole village that day asking who wanted enlightenment.

Enlightenment can be had by giving yourself to Existence.

He came back to Buddha in the evening with a low face. Buddha asked him, 'What happened? Nobody wants enlightenment, is it?'

The man replied a little cheerfully, 'No, no, two people want enlightenment.' Buddha replied, 'Ok, get them right now. I will give them enlightenment.'

The man replied in a low voice, 'No, they don't want to come here. If you send it to where they are, they will take it!'

Nobody really wants enlightenment in the real sense! They just want it as a utility or to keep in their showcase! Understand, god gives you the freedom to be in bondage also. Enlightenment can never be forced on you. If it is forced, even freedom will become bondage.

There are two things: qualification and wanting.

There is no qualification needed for enlightenment, but the deep feeling, the deep wanting that 'I want it', should be there.

Please be very clear, I also had ALL the problems that you are having like not being able to trust Existence or not being able to trust myself. All I can say is, there is no qualification for enlightenment. For somebody to become enlightened, they do not need any qualification.

Enlightenment can be had by giving yourself to Existence. Giving yourself is not an equal thing for what you receive. Even if you give your life, it is nothing more in effort or value than buying a lottery ticket.

After it happens, you will understand that the whole thing is nothing but the pure grace and blessing of Existence. The result or the transformation will be so big, so great that you can't think of a reason why you were chosen for it, why it was showered on you! No qualification is necessary, but the deep need, the seeking is necessary. Fulfillment is always a gift. To receive a gift, there is no such thing as being worthy.

Ramakrishna used to say, 'Suppose you are living in poverty, dying with no food and no clothes. But somehow you know that there is a lot of wealth kept locked in the next room. Even if you take it nobody will know. Will you be able to sleep restfully now? Either you will try to open the door or you will break down the door. Unless you have that wealth under your control, you will not be able to sleep.'

In the same way, you should know you are in spiritual poverty right now. You should know that inside you there is a room in which there is immense wealth that is kept under lock and key. That knowledge, that attitude, that intensity, that mood is a basic necessity. With that, the seeking can simply transform your whole life.

Your dedication is powerful enough to lead you to enlightenment.

Actually, enlightenment is practically like cooking. Something has to be added, something has to be removed. You have to add the intense seeking. Whatever is unnecessary, like restlessness, etc, will come out automatically, and enlightenment will happen!

Enlightened society

During the *vedic* times in India, the whole life, the whole society was based on enlightenment where seventy percent of the people were enlightened and the remaining thirty percent were seeking, working towards enlightenment.

Arts, sciences, education, lifestyle and every sphere of life, every action was directed towards the ultimate experience of enlightenment. Classical dances like Bharatanatyam, traditional vocal and instrumental music, traditional architecture of temples and sculptures, classical paintings and art forms, the science of languages like Sanskrit, the sciences of astrology and *vaastu**, the unique *gurukul** system of education, traditional ceremonies right from birth through marriage to death – every single activity in every dimension of life was an expression of the enlightenment of the great seers, as well as a means to get enlightened.

The ultimate energy that can stand the test of time

Your dedication is powerful enough to lead you to enlightenment.

There can be nothing more than the enlightenment experience on planet earth. No philosophy, no system, no theory, no ideology, stands, survives, or thrives for more than one generation if it does not have an enlightened base or the base or inspiration from an enlightened being.

In ancient India, there were at least 3000 kings ruling at different times. Not a single king or kingdom that was not guided by an enlightened master was able to flourish. Even today if you go to South Indian villages, you will see huge temples built of stone, installed by enlightened masters. But the palaces that were constructed by the same kings for themselves no longer exist.

Understand, the same king and the same architect who built the temples to hold the enlightened energy, also built the palaces for the king to stay. One might think the king would have used better material for his own palace! But today, if you see, the temples are still standing while the palaces have disappeared with time.

Vaastu – *Vedic* science of construction and interiors of a house based on the energies of the physical and metaphysical elements

Gurukul – *Vedic* educational institution.

> **As long as there are enlightened masters on planet earth, planet earth can never be destroyed!**

In my own village Tiruvannamalai* in South India, the village in which I was born and brought up, we have a temple that has twenty-five acres of built up area. The palace built by the same king is not there. It is just ruins. But the temple built by him is still alive because the enlightened master's energy is there.

The greatest service to mankind - keeping the science of enlightenment alive

The biggest service you can do in your life, the best use you can make of your life is to keep this science of enlightenment alive on planet earth. Planet earth is alive today in spite of all the atomic weapons we have piled up, all the depletion of forests, minerals, and natural resources. It is so because of the presence of enlightened masters. As long as there are enlightened masters on planet earth, planet earth can never be destroyed!

Tiruvannamalai - Temple town where Nithyananda was born and raised.

Top 10 reasons to get enlightened

1. **No Worries, Be Happy!**

   Express spontaneous creativity for assured success!

2. **Intensely Enjoy Life!**

   Enjoy every moment of life with pure excitement!

3. **Always Auspiciousness!**

   Whatever happens in life will be auspicious!

4. **'Always-Right' Strategic Planning!**

   Relationships, business, or life – always make right decisions!

5. **Ultimate Experience Every Moment!**

   Expand and explode in all dimensions of life!

6. **No Study, Just Download!**

   Science, arts, religion, business, cooking… Just download from the cosmic archives!

7. **No Greed, No Fear!**

   Nothing to gain or lose – get all you want right here, right now!

8. **Un-clutch - the Fastest Gear!**

   Master-mind – Forever free from the clutches of the mind!

9. **Being God!**

   Master of your destiny – create your reality!

10. **Beyond Space, Time, and Mind!**

    Enjoy being in the lap of eternal bliss!

You are eternal bliss - *nithya ananda*!

Powerful free discourse clips online for free, watched by 8000 people per day from 120 countries. Over 500,000 views on www.youtube.com/LifeBlissFoundation have resulted in Nithyananda becoming #1 watched spiritual leader.

The Mission activities can be seen across over 18 websites featuring meditation programs, yoga, education, sacred arts, online shopping and humanitarian services. Main website: www.dhyanapeetam.org

Encouraging a green Mother Earth

The sacred ancient healing banyan tree in Bidadi, the spiritual headquarters of the Mission, represents the enlightened energy and is a mystical energy hub in the Bidadi ashram.

Accommodation for participants of meditation programs, Bidadi ashram, India

Participants of various residential meditation programs are provided comfortable accommodation in the energy field of the ashram. Dormitory accommodation is also available for program participants and for those who wish to stay in the healing energy field

Vedic temple, Ohio
Over 1200 full-time volunteers run the various ashrams, Vedic temples and mission activities worldwide.

Vedic Temple, Montclair, USA

Hyderabad ashram, India
Nithyananda mission includes numerous ashrams and hundreds of centers worldwide which are 100 percent volunteer based and stand to serve society by providing meditation programs and social services in fields like health and education.

Nithyananda Mission in St. Louis, USA

Nithya Yoga classes are conducted in over 10 countries to date in various places like yoga studios, colleges, bookstores, prisons etc

Free food serving
Nithyananda Food Temples worldwide serve an estimated average of 20,000 meals are served daily.

Common utility items for orphanages

Over 100 service activities have been conducted by the Nithyananda Youth Foundation. These include bread distribution in hospitals, donation of bicycles, school books, bags and footwear as well as scholarships for students, meditation classes, food, rice and clothing distribution, donation of road safety barricades, blood donation camps, donation of artificial limbs, prayer and worship for prosperity, donating household items to orphanages, free counseling, free saplings to encourage the green drive and support to old age homes.

Free bicycles for rural students

Blissful gathering (satsang) of the Nithyananda family in Brazil

An estimated 5000 satsangs have been conducted across 50 countries. The satsangs include free Nithya Spiritual Healing services, discourses, group meditations and counseling.

Blissful meditation group, London

Life Bliss Program Level 3, Guadeloupe led by a senior swami of Nithyananda order

Over 300 ordained meditation and yoga teachers worldwide conduct basic to advanced levels of courses in meditation and yoga.

Life Bliss Program Level 1, New Zealand

Life Bliss Program Level 1, Dubai

Nithyananda addresses various forums to create awareness of and spread the message of global peace and religious harmony.

Second Kumbh Mela, held in Los Angeles on 9 September, 2007

Nithyananda Mission centers participate in the unique spiritual gathering of Kumbh Mela conducted currently in various locations in India and USA to raise the collective positivity of planet earth.

Yearly Himalayas Yatra

Nithyananda leads people on yatras or spiritual journeys to energy fields like Himalayas, Varanasi, Angkor Wat and so on.

Varanasi yatra, June 2008

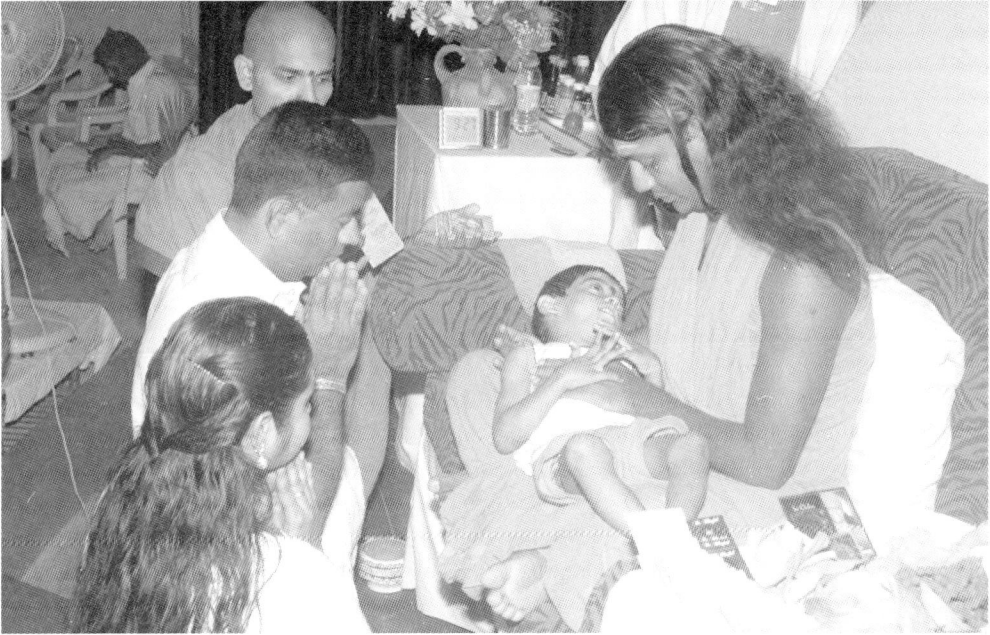

Free healing darshan, Bidadi, India, March 1-31, 2008

Nithya Spiritual Healing is a unique science of healing through the cosmic energy. Nithyananda personally heals people and has initiated over 5000 Nithya Spiritual Healers providing free healing service to an estimated 20,000 people worldwide per day.

Addressing a healers' meet at the Bidadi ashram, India
Nithyananda regularly meets various groups of people - volunteers, ordained healers, teachers and devotees at large.

Thousands at the Life Bliss Program Level 2 at an engineering college in India

Mass meditation program, Pondicherry, India

Meditation programs have been conducted in about 30 countries by 300 ordained teachers

Sitting with a group of ashramites in front of the 'Laughing Temple' in Bidadi ashram, India, 2006.
This is the rare gift of upanishad – sitting with the master which can directly lead one to live enlightenment.

Taking classes for the gurukul students
Nithyananda Gurukul revives the unique vedic tradition of gurukul education. It is a modern scientific approach to education combined with the vedic system of learning – protecting and developing the innate intelligence of the child who flowers without repression, fear or peer pressure, into a confident, responsible and fulfilled individual.

Meditation programs in schools and for youth
Thousands of students have benefitted from the specially designed meditation, yoga and memory programs.

Paths to blissful living

Paths to blissful living

- Why meditate?

- Nithya Dhyaan – Life Bliss Meditation

- Nithya Yoga – for the body, mind and beyond

- Eight steps for a blissful life everyday

Why Meditate?

In the following four chapters as well as those on meditation techniques that follow in a later section, I give you the pathways to experience the truths we talked about. By now, you have the intellectual understanding about what needs to be done and why.

We now come to the part of how. All the understanding will remain only theoretical if it is not converted into experience.

What is the real aim of life?

What is your ultimate aim in life?

To earn more… ? To stay forever young, healthy, beautiful…? To have better, longer-lasting relationships…? To improve your personality…?

Each of us is actually searching for bliss, but we search in many different ways. But ninety-nine percent of us are not even aware that bliss is our true goal! We search everywhere in the outside world for something which is there within us, just waiting to be discovered.

A small story:

One evening, a man was searching hard for something in the courtyard in his house. His wife asked him what it was. He replied that he had dropped a gold coin. His wife also joined in the search. Soon, others gathered and practically the whole neighborhood was searching for the lost coin.

Suddenly one neighbor asked the man, 'Where exactly did you drop the coin? How come we still haven't found it?' The man replied, 'Oh, I lost the coin inside the house.' Everybody searching became angry and asked him, 'Then why are we searching here?'

The man replied, 'The problem is I have no lights inside my house. So I started searching by the light of this streetlamp here!'

This is exactly what we do in our own lives. We are all experts in searching for answers in the wrong places. We search for bliss everywhere, be it in money, power, relationships or ideologies. But we don't move in the one obvious direction which is inwards.

321

What is bliss?

In life everyone has experienced some moments of great happiness. But it has always been for a reason. The state of that happiness does not seem to remain forever. It is there temporarily, and when it changes or goes away, once again you feel pain. Only the happiness you experience for no reason at all, which does not die for any reason, is real and permanent happiness. This is what is called bliss. Such happiness doesn't depend on anything outside of you.

The word *'ananda'* itself means, 'that which cannot be reduced, which cannot be lost'. *Ananda* does not translate into 'happiness'. You will be surprised to know, it simply means 'that which cannot be reduced or lost'. And bliss is that thing which does not reduce for any reason.

What is meditation?

Technique to raise consciousness

Any technique, any method which raises your consciousness is meditation.

Meditation can even be a simple breathing technique. It can be a simple repetition of a word or simply sitting. In the Zen tradition, just sitting is meditation. You may think this is the easiest thing to do but in fact, just sitting is the most difficult meditation. Anything can become meditation if it raises your consciousness.

Intensely blissful in the present

Meditation is just being blissful in the moment. When you are at complete peace in the present moment, you are already in a state of meditation.

Recall any moment in your life when you have experienced extreme beauty. Maybe it was the sun rising suddenly from behind a mountain, or the first time you heard a lovely piece of music. Suddenly you became totally still, wordless. In the presence of that beauty you couldn't think any more. You were just silent, relaxed, in thoughtless awareness. You were completely dissolved in that beauty. That moment was meditation!

After a few moments your inner chatter started again. Your mind said, 'What a beautiful sunrise!' The moment the words appeared, you were out of meditation! You can either think or meditate. You can never do both. Meditation is just being. It is experiencing the present moment without resistance.

What is the right way to approach meditation?

The first thing is, be sincere. Keep an open mind. Have the openness to experiment. Be enthusiastic.

There is a beautiful term in the Zen tradition to describe the attitude – the beginner's mind. It means looking at every single thing in life as new, so everything in life excites you.

The second thing is, be optimistic. Bliss is a perfectly realizable goal for you, even if you are completely unfamiliar with meditation.

Once a man approached the great enlightened master Ramana Maharishi and asked him, 'Bhagavan, am I qualified for spiritual life?' Bhagavan answered him with a question, 'Are you alive?' The man was startled. He said, 'Yes, of course!'

Bhagavan replied, 'That is enough. You already have the necessary qualification for spirituality!'

The very aim of human life is enlightenment. The possibility of becoming enlightened lies in the *Kundalini shakti*, an extraordinary potential energy which is hidden inside every human body. If it can be awakened, it will take you to a different plane of consciousness, a different plane of Existence. The possibility to become a different conscious being is present only in human beings. Animals don't have this potentiality to become enlightened, to become different conscious beings.

The third thing is, be playful! Meditation is a big adventure. To become serious about meditation is to miss the whole point. Celebrate meditation. Simply enjoy it!

The fourth thing is, have patience. Don't start worrying about results the moment you start meditating.

The possibility to become a different conscious being is present only in human beings.

A small story:

Three monkeys once found a ripe, juicy mango. Like all monkeys, they fought over the mango for a while. Then somehow, they had a moment of clarity, a moment of intelligence.

Instead of eating the mango right away, they decided to sow the mango. They knew that once the mango seed sprouted and grew into a tree, there would be more than enough mangoes for all three of them.

Each of them decided to take up one part of the task of caring for the mango plant. The first monkey said, 'I will water the plant every day!' The second monkey said, 'I will keep the soil healthy and rich, add fertilizers and ensure that the plant grows well.' The third monkey said, 'I will guard the plant carefully and protect it from harsh weather and other animals.'

One month passed, then two, then three. There was no sign of any plant growing out of the soil. The three monkeys called for an urgent meeting to discuss the issue. The first monkey declared, 'As promised, I have been watering the seed every single day.' The second monkey cried, 'As promised, I have been adding fertilizer and making the soil rich.'

The third monkey said, 'As promised, I have been guarding the seed very carefully. Not only that, I have been taking the seed out every single day to check whether it has sprouted or not!'

If you are greedy for instant results, you actually prevent the process from settling down

323

All our physical and mental illnesses take root in the dream state. in your system. You yourself block the whole process.

The fifth thing is, enjoy solitude. Give yourself a chance to experience your inner environment. When meditation becomes a part of you, bliss will flower naturally.

Why Meditation?

Various States of Consciousness		
	With Thoughts	**Without Thoughts**
With "I" Consciousness	**Jagrat** Wakeful State Thinking	**Turiya** Blissful State State of Full Awareness
Without "I" Consciousness	**Swapna** Dream State Dreaming	**Sushupti** Unconscious State Deep Sleep

There are three states that we constantly experience in our lives – the waking state, dream state and deep sleep state. But there is a fourth state that we have not experienced. It is called *turiya**. In this state the 'I' consciousness exists but without thoughts. It is called thoughtless awareness. Very few people experience this in their lives. Some people experience this for a few seconds and then go back to their regular waking state.

If you get a sudden shock or if you are sitting with nature in a completely relaxed state and in deep silence, it is possible that for a few moments you experience this thoughtless awareness. The identity is alive, the 'I' consciousness is alive, but there are no thoughts. This is the fourth state of *turiya**.

All our physical and mental illnesses take root in the dream state. The dream state starts penetrating and overlapping the deep sleep and waking states. If our waking state is penetrated by the dream state, it is called daydreaming, we fantasize or imagine endless things that we wish to do. If our deep sleep is penetrated by dreaming, it is called disturbed sleep.

Continuously during the day or night, our dream state disturbs us. When our deep sleep state is disturbed by dreams, it results in problems like chronic fatigue and insomnia. When our waking state is disturbed by dreams, we will be daydreaming with much less awareness of the world around us.

The more the dream state penetrates the waking state, the more the frequency of our consciousness decreases. We may be living in the human body, but we will not be living a truly human life. When the frequency of consciousness comes down, we will not be fully aware about the decisions we make. We will not be aware of the kind of words we are thinking. We will not be aware of what is going on inside of us. It will be as if we are living in a house, but we do not know everything that is happening inside that house.

Turiya - Fourth state of consciousness in which there are no thoughts and only awareness.

You ask, 'Why should I meditate?' Meditation is needed to infuse deep awareness into both your waking state and the deep sleep state. Instead of the dream state penetrating the waking and deep sleep states, with meditation the *turiya** or blissful state will start penetrating the waking and deep sleep states!

The purpose of meditation is to experience this fourth state at least once. Once we experience this fourth state, we can bring the influence of it more and more into our waking and deep sleep states. If our waking and deep sleep states are completely influenced by the fourth state, *turiya*, that is what we call *jeevan mukti* or living enlightenment.

Benefits of meditation

Physical health

Meditation has the power to transform you physically, mentally, emotionally, and spiritually.

See, physical health means digesting whatever you eat and having that food become part of your body. Mental health means digesting all the ideas and problems that you encounter and forming a clear solution. In other words, it is living without conflict. Spiritual health means receiving all the great teachings and energy, digesting them and living a liberated life. Having all three is total health.

Meditation is also a complement to medication. Through meditation, you can regulate your blood pressure and blood sugar and you can increase your body's resistance to disease. Through meditation, it is possible to heal even chronic problems like skin allergies, asthma and arthritis. No disease can escape the power of meditation.

Mental health - awakening of intelligence and flowering of intuition

On the mental level, meditation enhances clarity of thought. Meditation is also a proven way to improve concentration and memory power. Above all, meditation leads you from intellect to intelligence to intuition.

With meditation, you go beyond the mind, into the being. In the being no rules exist. You become free to explore your full potential. That's why with meditation you will suddenly find yourself at ease with your surroundings, easily able to cope with new situations. You rediscover your spontaneity.

Self-healing thoughts

You may have a medically fit body. That does not mean you are completely healthy. Of course, I can say from my experience of having seen millions of people, ninety nine per

---

Turiya - Fourth state of consciousness in which there are no thoughts and only awareness.

325

> **Knowledge-weapons are the weapons of Truth that can destroy the depression of your being.**

cent of those who do not have the 'self-healing clarity' in their system are never able to maintain even physical health. When I say 'self-healing clarity', I mean the clarity and understanding to bring yourself out of depression whenever it tries to grip your consciousness.

Just a year ago, I did a small research study. I selected one group of people who had been through some meditation programs and had done some spiritual study. I asked them to write whatever came into their mind without editing for just twenty minutes. Then I also asked another group of people who had never been exposed to spirituality to also write down whatever came into their minds without editing for the same twenty minutes. The results of my study were shocking.

In the case of those people who were not exposed to spirituality, if they had written one hundred thoughts, more than eighty of them were directing them more and more towards depression. Only twenty thoughts were self-healing or bringing them out of depression. But in the case of those who were exposed to spirituality and meditation, I saw that more than sixty percent of their thoughts were self-healing! Only forty percent were taking them towards depression. This is the impact of meditation! It keeps you healthy holistically.

Knowledge-weapons to combat depression

The knowledge of the Truth is what I call 'knowledge-weapons' or *shaastra-shastra*. *Shaastra* means Truth, knowledge. *Shastra* means weapons. Knowledge-weapons are the weapons of Truth that can destroy the depression of your being. The more knowledge-weapons you have, the more depression will be afraid of you! If you have a huge army, naturally the enemy country will be afraid of attacking you. Just by seeing your pile of weapons, the other country will think twice before attacking you. In the same way, the more you accumulate the self-healing thoughts, the knowledge-weapons, inside your being, the more depression will fear to come near you.

Freedom

With meditation, you can live your life in a much better way with greater clarity and greater intensity. You will be more aware, more creative. Yet internally, you will experience a deep and undisturbed silence.

You will no longer be doing, you will only be watching the doer. This is the whole secret of meditation – to become the watcher, to become the witness of your own actions and emotions.

Once you become aware that the real *you* is not the one who acts, that the real *you* is not the one who feels angry or hurt or depressed, then you experience a tremendous sense of freedom. This will happen through meditation. And this is real freedom.

All our life we are searching for freedom. Whether we realize it or not, every single one of us is searching for freedom. We think our freedom is dependent on others. Now you know that the other person is in no way connected to your freedom.

Love and joy for no reason

With meditation, for the first time, you will understand what it means to love for no reason. For the first time you will not be giving something in order to receive. You will give love simply because you have so much to give! You will shower love upon the world in the same way that a rain cloud showers upon the earth or a flower spontaneously spreads its fragrance all around. You will love because you are so full and overflowing!

Work as play

Just try this: whatever you do, act with awareness. If you are eating, eat with awareness. No extra time is needed to do this. In fact, it will take less time to eat because when you eat with awareness, you will eat just the amount your body needs rather than stuffing food down your throat thoughtlessly.

Awareness has tremendous knowledge. Awareness can do better miracles than all your planning. Awareness doesn't contradict, it complements the plans. It will add to the potentiality.

When you are aware, *you* are absent. When awareness is present, your ego can't exist. When your ego exists, awareness can't be present. 'Your absence' will make you live enlightenment.

When you are aware, you will work optimally and use your energy efficiently. So at the end of the day you are just as fresh as in the morning. You see, it is not the work that exhausts you; it is your mind, your attitude. The whole game of meditation is to get out of the work-oriented mind and look at every moment of life as a beautiful Divine play.

With meditation, for the first time, you will understand what it means to love for no reason.

When to do meditation?

The next question is when to meditate. This is always a controversial question! All the youngsters think, 'I can do this in my old age after I have lived my life fully and I don't have anything else to do.' All the elderly people think, 'I should have done this in my young age when I was fresh and energetic.'

So the question is not just how long to meditate everyday, but also when to make the decision to enter into meditation. Please understand, meditation is the basic need for every person. It is not an option. It is a very basic need.

Benefits of Meditation

Health

Meditation results in holistic health. It gives good health on the physical, mental and emotional levels. Specific health benefits reported by some who meditate are:

1. The stabilization of high or low blood pressure, blood sugar, body heat and heartbeat.

2. The balancing of mind/body rhythms.

3. Reduction of muscle tension, stronger bones, immunity from disease.

4. Cleansing - quicker elimination of toxins and body waste.

5. Overcoming insomnia and improved quality of sleep.

6. Enhanced energy, increased work capacity.

7. Longer life span - improved body metabolism and body cells with a longer life span.

8. Secretion of healthy body chemicals - increased secretion of natural anti-depressants, enhanced secretion of endorphins, the body's 'happy chemicals'.

9. Relationships - Meditation inherently puts you in tune with yourself and others. The direct result of this is deeper, more meaningful interpersonal relationships with family, friends and with everyone you encounter in your daily life.

10. Intelligence - To work efficiently, one needs intelligence. Meditation ignites your innate intelligence making you more aware and sharp. The natural result of this is improved, efficient and effortless performance in whatever you do.

11. Creativity - Each of us holds within us an undiscovered treasure of talent and potential. Meditation reveals and helps you realize your inner talents and latent creativity.

12. Authenticity - Meditation allows you to touch base with the real you, and makes you realize your uniqueness. Self-confidence then becomes a natural by-product.

13. **Balance** - Most of us live life as a roller-coaster ride, held in the sway of emotions like worry, jealousy, discontentment, fear, anger, guilt, etc. over which we have no control. Meditation enables you to be centered in yourself, have a solid inner balance and thus, be the master of your own self.

14. **Relaxation, peace, bliss** - A natural byproduct of meditation is something we spend almost a lifetime trying to attain: inner relaxation and peace. With meditation, you automatically drop out of the vicious cycle of fear, greed and stress, and enter the virtuous cycle of bliss.

15. **Holistic spiritual growth** - To measure intellect, we have IQ or Intelligence Quotient, which is measured by many standardized tests. Of late, another measure is gaining importance, especially in the corporate world, namely EQ or Emotional Quotient. However, the most important factor of our lives which is inner satisfaction and fulfillment, is what matters at the end of the day. Meditation enhances this very important factor of life, SQ or Spiritual Quotient, besides also increasing IQ and EQ.

16. **Life** - As of now, our mental setup is rigid and reflects our personality. Because of this self-image we carry in our minds, we face a lot of troubles in life and are not able to enjoy life completely. Meditation simply reprograms the software of the mind so that we can live life completely.

17. **Ultimate potential** - You are like an airplane with the potential to fly, but you think you are an ox-cart because you have not actualized your potential. Meditation simply makes you realize and experience who you really are and the enormous capabilities you have been born with.

Kinds of meditation

There are three kinds of meditation.

The first is bringing the truth or awareness into your life.

This meditation is supposed to be done all twenty-four hours a day. Breath-related techniques like *vipassana** or techniques where you bring your awareness to the present moment all the time belong to this category of meditation. It is not a part of your routine. It should become the very quality of your routine. You may be doing anything like writing, reading, cooking, discussing, but this thread of meditation should be happening simultaneously like an undercurrent.

With the second kind of meditation techniques, you need to spend a particular time, like one hour in the morning or one hour in the evening, or any other convenient time.

The *Mahamantra** meditation technique, where you hum for a few minutes and then remain a witness for a few minutes, can be given as an example for this category of meditation. *Nithya Dhyaan* is another example of this type of meditation, since it is practiced for a specified time each day.

Then there is the third kind of meditation techniques, where just the very remembrance of the technique is enough.

Examples of this are the statements of the great timeless truths. When you are in a highly mature state, you don't need any separate technique. You don't need to practice the whole day or at any particular time. Just the very remembrance of these truths will put you in the elevated state. This is the third type of meditation. Examples of this are the beautiful Zen *koans**. They are profound truths written in a concise way. Just the very remembrance of them will transport you to the zone of truth!

There is a very beautiful story in the *Upanishad** where a disciple comes to the master and asks for a technique or a method for enlightenment. The master just says, *'Tat tvam asi, Tat tvam asi, Tat tvam asi'* - 'Thou art that, Thou art that, Thou art that', and the story says, the disciple became enlightened!

It seems like a very strange story. The master just repeats a few words and the disciple is suddenly enlightened. How is it possible? It seems unbelievable! Actually it is not so. If we have done the first two types of techniques, the technique that needs to be done the whole day and the technique that needs to be done at a particular time, then the very maturity that happens out of that practice will cause you to experience the Truth the moment you hear it from the master!

Vipassana - Teaching of enlightened master Buddha to look inwards by observing breath.

Mahamantra - Humming meditation that energizes the *anahata chakra* and taught as part of Nithyananda's Life Bliss Programs.

Koans - Riddles given as techniques in Zen to aid Self Realization.

Upanishad – Literally means, 'sitting at the feet of the master'.

Reality as dream

You may wonder, 'How is it that every day when I come back to the waking state, I see the same world but every night when I go back to the dream state, I don't see the same world? So, can this be used as a scale? With this can we say that this waking-state world is real?'

Let us analyze one night's dream. For example, let us say that you go to sleep on the night of the fourteenth, and on the morning of the fifteenth, you wake up. You sleep for around ten hours. I am sure many of you have had experiences of having lived around ten to twenty years of your life in one night's dream, in just ten hours' time.

Perhaps the dream starts in your college days and moves slowly, step by step, up to your marriage, your having a son, your son's marriage, etc. In this way, you live even twenty years of your life in just one night's dream, am I right? If you have experienced this at least once, you can follow very closely what I am going to present now.

You see, while sleeping, we go through the dream state and the deep sleep state. Maybe for half an hour, you fall into the deep sleep state. Then you go to the dream state and have some dreams. Again you fall back into the deep sleep state for perhaps twenty minutes, and then once again, you come back to the dream state. In this way you keep moving from the dream state to the deep sleep state and back.

Understand: in one night, you dream that you have lived twenty years of your life. In the first episode of your dream, you are in college. In the second episode, when you come back to the dream state after a gap of deep sleep, you are getting married. In the third dream episode, you have a son. Maybe in the fourth episode, you see your son getting married.

An important thing you need to understand: when you fall into the deep sleep state and then come back to the dream state, and then repeat this process, in these different episodes, you do see the same world even in your dream state. Am I right? Sometimes you do see the same world even in the dream state.

Understand, it is a very subtle point, a very subtle understanding. If you can catch this, it will lead to very great clarity, which can really revolutionize the way in which you think about your life, the way in which you try to solve the problems of your life.

Imagine a man is dreaming. In the dream he sees a tiger chasing him and he starts shouting, 'Oh, a tiger is chasing me! Save me, save me!' His wife is sleeping next to him. She wakes up and sees the husband shouting! The wife is confused, 'What am I supposed to do?' She just needs to tell him, 'Hey, wake up!' Instead of that, if she tries to supply some weapon to kill the tiger in the dream, what will happen? He may kill himself or he may kill her! Any other solution she may try to find will only lead to more problems, more difficulties. All the husband needs to do is wake up.

331

If you understand these basic things, suddenly you will see that your very decision-making is revolutionized. The cognitive shift happens in you. The way in which you think and the way in which you make decisions, the way in which you find solutions for your problems, will be entirely different. You will start working towards the right solutions.

When you are dreaming, in a span of ten hours, you can easily live twenty years. You fall into deep sleep and come back to the dream state many times. Whenever you come back to the dream state from deep sleep, even though there was a break from the last dream, you see the same world. So, you have to understand clearly that just seeing the same world after the break in the dream state cannot be the quality to define it as reality. Only when you wake up from sleep, do you realize you have 'lived' twenty years of your life in a mere ten hours.

In the same way, only when you wake up from this 'waking dream' in which you are living now, suddenly you will realize you have dreamt maybe ninety years of your life in a few hours! This life in the waking state may be another long dream!

When you are in a dream, you think the dream is reality. Where you are, that is reality for that moment. There is no other scale. In the dream you can never imagine, 'It is a dream.' In the reality, you can never think, 'It is one more dream.' When you come out of the dream, the dream looks like a dream. But when you are in the dream itself, it will not look like a dream.

In the dream, even if you remember about your real life, you think it is a dream. In the reality, even if you remember about the dream, you think it is a dream. So it just depends on the frequency in which you are. There is no other scale to explain which is reality or dream.

Realizing and understanding there is a possibility that this very waking state could be one more long dream will turn much of your attention and awareness to the center, to the consciousness, to the ultimate reality. When you go beyond the frequency of this waking state, it will also look like one more dream.

This is the first step in spirituality. This is the first step in psychological revolution.

Again and again, your suffering gives you a clear statement that you are not living in reality.

Many times I am asked another question along the same lines, 'Not only am I seeing this world, even the people who are living around me are seeing the same world. How can you say it is a dream?'

Understand, in a dream if you are seeing a particular city, and if in that dream you are going to that city with your whole family, then not only you, but the family with you inside your dream, will also see the same city, because they are also projections of your mind! So, just because the people around you see the same scene as you do, it does not mean that the scene is reality. Those people around you might be a projection of the same scene!

The ultimate truth is that the stuff out of which your dream world is made is the same as the stuff out of which this waking world is also made.

If your attention is centered on the stuff, naturally the inner healing cannot happen. If your attention is equally distributed on the consciousness and the stuff, that is what I call healthy life or balanced life. You will have physical health, mental health and a vibrant life.

If your attention is totally centered on the consciousness, not on the stuff with which these worlds are made, that is what I call 'living enlightenment' or *jeevan mukti*.

Whether you want *jeevan mukti* or not, whether you want enlightenment or not, is secondary. But if you can turn a little bit of your attention towards the 'I' consciousness, towards the Truth, towards the center, suddenly you will see that a tremendous inner healing happens.

For example, if you are facing some big difficulty or depression, if you realize very clearly and consciously that this whole thing is a dream, you will experience such a relaxed feeling or the inner healing happening in you. That inner healing is what I call meditation. That restful awareness that happens in you is what I call *satori*, the first glimpse of *samadhi*.

A basic cognitive shift or a basic psychological revolution, with the simple understanding that what you are seeing may not be reality as you think, can bring

tremendous inner healing inside you, can bring a great restful awareness inside you.

Glimpse of scientific research on meditation

Science is just now getting glimpses of the tremendous power of meditation to completely change the entire body-mind structure itself. The benefits of meditation are countless and across all planes, be it physical, mental, emotional or spiritual. Meditation can simply change the very quality of life.

Increased brain power

Until recently, it was believed that in the brain, the connections among the brain nerve cells were fixed in childhood and did not change, so the brain growth stopped early in life. Now scientists are finding that the brain actually grows and forms new connections all throughout life, they call this neuroplasticity.

The other day I was reading in the papers (*Washington Post*, January 3, 2005), about research done by the University of Wisconsin to study the effects of meditation on the brain. The study was done on a group of Tibetan monks who had been meditating for years, and also on a group of students who were new to meditation but had been taught how to meditate.

They found that the awareness was more and the brain activity was faster and much better organized and coordinated in the meditating monks than in the students who were new to meditation. Not only that, the brain region associated with happiness, positive thoughts and emotions, was also much more active in the monks than in the students.

One more important thing, the researchers found that the brain activity of the meditator monks was more intense and organized (than that of the students), even before the monks started meditating. So the benefits of meditation are actually permanent. Meditation can simply change the very circuitry and the inner workings of the brain.

Many top universities in the USA like Yale, Harvard and MIT (Massachusetts Institute of Technology), have also studied[*] the effects of meditation.

Studies using MRI (Magnetic Resonance Imaging) showed that meditation actually increased the very thickness of the brain in areas related to awareness and attention, as well as cognitive processing and emotional wellbeing.

The researchers found that the blood vessels become wider, the support structures also increase in number and they have more branches and connections.

Meditation Vs Sleep

There was another research[**] done at the University of Kentucky where they studied the effects of sleepiness on a person's awareness. A group of people was made to look at a screen and they were supposed to press a button as soon as an image came on the screen. Normally a person who has had less sleep takes much longer to respond to the image than a person who has had normal sleep. Sometimes they even completely miss seeing the image coming up.

The researchers tested the participants before and after forty minutes of sleep, meditation, reading or some light activity.

They found that with meditation, the response was the fastest for every single participant, even though the participants were not experienced in meditation. In fact, their response was even better after keeping awake the whole night!

Improved concentration and speed of response

There have been many studies to learn the effect of meditation on the speed and correctness of perception and response.

A couple of studies were done at Liverpool John Moores University in Liverpool, England.

---

[*]http://www.news.harvard.edu/gazette/daily/2006/01/23-meditation.html

[**]http://www.asianresearch.org/articles/2848.html

In one study, the participants were given lines of letters with different numbers of dashes marked above the letters. They had to cross out the letters with multiple dashes, as quickly as possible.

In another study, the participants were shown the words like 'RED', 'BLUE' or 'GREEN' printed in different colored inks. They had to quickly name the color of the ink the word was written in. Normally, this is difficult because your brain tends to read the word rather than look and identify the color of the ink that the word is written in!

They found that the meditators were much faster and made about half the number of errors as the non-meditators.

Meditation directly and significantly improves awareness, attention, memory, concentration, response time, visualization, emotional wellbeing, and general health.

Science has just started exploring the vast dimensions of the effects and benefits of meditation. But for thousands of years, right from the *vedic* times, man has been enjoying the benefits of meditation which is the ultimate way to the Ultimate! It is a foolproof, time-proven technique to realize oneself.

Nithya Dhyaan - Life Bliss Meditation

The master technique

There are some meditation techniques that are specific for specific times and people, and there are a few that are universal. Nithya Dhyaan is the meditation for the seeker of today. It is the cyber age meditation.

The birth of Nithya Dhyaan

First I would like to tell about how this meditation technique Nithya Dhyaan happened. Up to the age of 11, I experimented with numerous meditation techniques. At the age of 12, I had my deep spiritual experience. From 12 to 21 years, I consciously scanned and analyzed the benefits of several techniques. For three years after my enlightenment, I worked on creating a sound technology to reproduce this experience of enlightenment in others. The essence of this entire inner world research I have done to date is formulated in the Nithya Dhyaan meditation technique.

Nithya Dhyaan is a formula and a technique that works on the entire being to transform it and make it ready for the ultimate experience of enlightenment. Each segment of this unique technique complements the other steps to help raise the individual consciousness. It is an everyday meditation for eternal bliss - *Nithya Ananda*.

Chakra awareness

To understand the technique, we need to understand a little about the *chakras* or subtle energy centers. Working on the seven *chakras* is like awakening new channels of energy. It is like tuning to a new channel on television.

There are seven energy centers in us, each center associated with a particular emotion. The seven emotions are lust, fear, worry, attention-need, jealousy, ego and discontent. Currently, man can think only based on these seven emotions. His body itself moves only due to the utility of any one of these emotions. Some people will move because of desire, lust or touch. For some, only fear will move them. There is nothing wrong in being driven by emotions such as desire. But you should experience the other higher dimensions like love as well. You should understand that it is possible to function out of sheer energy, not just out of these emotions.

By awakening the *chakras*, you will be released from the mental setup of these emotions. You will start working as a free being. If you are liberated from such mental setups, only then you will understand the value of the freedom.

For example, if you are liberated from a particular *chakra*, say the *chakra* associated with jealousy, you will experience a new world in that dimension, a jealousy-free world! On whatever identity your personality is now standing, on whatever idea your life is now standing, that identity or idea will just melt down. You will experience a new energy altogether.

For example, if you suddenly get interested in the share market business, you start collecting updates from television, magazines, people etc. about the share market. After a month or so, you start feeling that the whole world is becoming more aware of the share market. You feel more surrounded by people related to the share market. It is not that the world has changed, it is your perspective that has changed. When you shift your energy center, you will start gathering such kind of people around you.

If you shift your energy center, you can change the world that you see. In Hindu mythology, they say there are seven worlds. This is what they actually refer to - the seven emotions that decide how you see the world.

Nithya Dhyaan meditation technique

This is a five-step technique, each step being of seven minutes.

1. Chaotic breathing

Duration: 7 minutes

Sit in *vajrasana** (sitting with the knees folded and your feet tucked under, with the bottom resting on the heels). Normally in our body, the energy flows from the *sahasrara chakra**(crown center) to the *muladhara chakra** (root center). *Vajrasana** posture

---

Vajrasana - A Yoga *asana* posture of sitting with the knees folded and your feet tucked under, with the bottom resting on the heels.

Sahasrara chakra - The seventh and final energy center at the crown of the head. Considered to be a gateway rather than an energy center.

Muladhara chakra - Subtle energy center at the root of the spine, related to the emotions of greed and lust.

The quality of breathing changes depending on your state of mind.

helps reverse this flow and supports the upward movement of energy.

Sit with eyes closed, hands on your hips and breathe chaotically. Inhale and exhale deeply and chaotically, without a particular rhythm. Just focus on the breathing. Your entire being should become the breathing.

This first part is very physical - sitting in *vajrasana** and inhaling and exhaling intensely, chaotically. You will see if you have any digestion problem, it will be completely healed. Your body will be ready.

When the body intensity is heightened, you will have a beautiful digestion system. This first part of the *Nithya Dhyaan* is for creating a healthy body.

An important thing you need to understand is that the quality of breathing changes depending on your state of mind. Your emotions have an impact on the breathing process. When you are in anxiety, your breathing changes. When you are angry, your breathing changes. When you are in tension, if you take a deep breath, suddenly you feel light, more relaxed and the tension is released.

The breath and mind are inter-related, changing one automatically changes the other. Emotions may not be in our hands, but our breathing is. If we control our breathing or bring about some change in our breathing pattern, we will directly impact our emotions and state of mind.

We tend to breathe in a fixed pattern. Our past *samskaras*, past memories locked in our unconscious zone, create a particular type of breathing pattern in our system. As a result, we attract similar emotions and *samskaras*. We get into a vicious cycle where our past *samskaras* create our breathing pattern and the breathing pattern in turn, attracts similar *samskaras* and incidents in the future. This vicious cycle has to be broken.

Nithya Dhyaan begins with chaotic breathing. Since the breathing is chaotic, it has no fixed pattern or rhythm. The pattern of the mind that forms its existence and expression is broken. Thoughts cannot follow the pattern they have been following so long for so many years.

Our muscles store all our past memories in the form of energy bio-memories. The deep chaotic breathing will start releasing the tension in the muscles, and these engraved memory patterns in the muscles and body parts will be expelled. Our muscles are normally under stress. Chaotic breathing will loosen the muscles and start clearing the engraved memories.

Each emotion within us gives rise to a particular breathing pattern. You might have seen that children breathe deeply and blissfully. But as they grow, they are conditioned by

---

Vajrasana - A Yoga *asana* posture of sitting with the knees folded and your feet tucked under, with the bottom resting on the heels.

Humming is an excellent technique to reduce the inner chatter. society, picking up from society the perceptions of pain, pleasure, guilt, beliefs, etc. Then the quality of the breathing changes totally. In order to shake this pattern which has been created due to the habitually suppressed emotions, we have to insert chaos. Inserting another pattern is not the solution.

You have to create utter chaos in your system to dig out all the past impressions. So I don't recommend any rhythmic breathing pattern like *pranayama** in this meditation. Just breathe chaotically. This chaotic breathing will destroy the emotional attachment to all your past memories. It is like shaking a tree that is full of dead leaves. All the dead leaves will fall down. Similarly chaotic breathing is like shaking your suppressed system. All the past engraved memories will be released.

Deep chaotic breathing also infuses tremendous oxygen and releases carbon dioxide from the body. It creates hyperventilation and as a result you feel more vibrant and fresh. Through increased intake of oxygen in the blood, automatically more bio-energy is generated in the cells and all aspects of the body come alive. The bio-energy that is generated will start clearing the *samskaras*, leaving you feeling light, energetic and blissful.

2. Intense humming

Duration: 7 minutes

Continue to sit in *vajrasana*, form *chin mudra** with your fingers, and place your hands on your knees, palms facing upwards.

In this posture, with your mouth closed and lips together, produce a humming sound as intensely as possible, as loudly as possible and as lengthily as possible.

Produce the sound 'Mmmm...' from within your body. If you were to put your face inside an empty aluminum vessel and make a humming sound, the sound generated will be similar to this. Note that this is not 'Humm...' or 'Omm...', it is simply keeping your lips together and producing 'mmm...' sound. The humming should be as lengthy as possible between breaths. It should be as deep as possible (from the navel center) and as loud as possible. There is no need to make an effort to take in deep breaths. The body itself will take the correct amount of breath when needed.

Pranayama - Breath control, one of the eight limbs of the *Ashtanga yoga* of Patanjali.

Chin mudra - Palms upraised with thumb and forefinger forming a circle and other three fingers outstretched.

The humming will create a healthy inner chattering and a heightened emotional awareness.

Put your complete awareness on the humming. Become the humming. Continuously there is talking going on within the mind. Humming is an excellent technique to reduce this inner chatter. Inner chatter is nothing but the flow of independent thoughts continually happening in us. Humming lets you feel your body as energy. The moment you start humming, you start feeling light, as if you are floating. You don't feel the heaviness in the body because humming matches the vibrations of the mind with the vibrations of the body. You start experiencing yourself as energy.

Don't become tense. Just do it in a relaxed manner. Immerse your whole being and energy into creating this vibration. Try to minimize the gap between the humming sounds. After some time, you will feel that the humming continues without your effort and that you have simply become a listener. The body and the mind start resonating with the humming vibrations.

The humming will create a healthy inner chattering and a healthy heightened emotional awareness.

3. *Chakra* awareness

Duration: 7 minutes

Continue to sit in *vajrasana* or sit cross-legged if you wish. Keep your fingers in *chin*

mudra. Now take your awareness to each *chakra* (energy center) starting from the *muladhara chakra* (root center) to the *sahasrara chakra* (crown center). You should become that energy center when you are asked to put your awareness on each energy center. Feel the energy center completely as if your whole being has become that energy center.

Each of these seven energy centers is associated with a specific emotion in our being. Kirlian photography* has captured these *chakras* and proven their existence at the energy level. These emotions themselves are a result of the engraved memories accumulated in the past. The memories pull us to react in the same old ways to situations and people, and that reaction is

Chin mudra - Palms upraised with thumb and forefinger forming a circle and other three fingers outstretched.

Sahasrara chakra - The seventh and final energy center at the crown of the head. Considered to be a gateway rather than an energy center.

Kirlian photography - High voltage photograms used to record auras of living beings.

what is called emotion. The rising emotions block the particular energy center, causing physical and mental disturbances. So in this step we focus our complete awareness on each energy center, starting from the base of the spine and moving to the crown. When we flood anything with awareness, the negativity in it dissolves. This is true for physical pain as well. If there is pain in one part of our body, if we flood that part with awareness, we will see that the pain shrinks to a point and disappears!

Flood each of the seven energy centers with full awareness for a minute each. Feel that only that particular center exists in the whole world. There is nothing else. Just become that energy center. Feel the energy center completely as if your whole being has become that energy center. Then move to the next center. At the end of this step you will feel completely energized with positivity and lightness.

By the time you come up to the higher and higher centers, your livingness, intensity also will come up. You will become very intense. This visualization helps to create a healthy mind and emotion, healthy inner chattering and heightened emotional awareness. At the end of this step you will feel energized and light.

If you concentrate on the energy centers, your mind will not wander as easily, it will just settle down because these are living energy centers. If you try to concentrate on some other part of the body, your mind can wander easily.

4. Be unclutched

Duration: 7 minutes

In this step, carry the understanding with you that your thoughts are unconnected, irrational and unclutched. Even if you have thoughts, neither try to suppress them nor try to react to them. Just watch them with the understanding that they are un-clutched. Automatically, the witnessing consciousness will start happening in you.

Understand that whether you realize it or not, accept it or not, you are already enlightened. By your very nature you are unclutched. Sit silently and experience the un-clutched state, the state of pure being and bliss. This is the ultimate technique to experience the state of enlightenment.

Please refer to the chapter 'You can unclutch from the mind maze' for further details.

5. Guru Puja*

Duration: 7 minutes

We end Nithya Dhyaan with the connecting, relaxing and resting into the whole Cosmic energy.

Guru puja - Ritual worship of the master.

Just sit in a relaxed way, connected to the whole Cosmos. If you have love for the master, or love for some god, just sit in a very deep and passive way, feeling connected to the Cosmos, or god, or your master, that's all. Just relax and settle down.

Just sit silently in a blissful mood and listen to the *Guru Puja** *mantras* being chanted. Feel connected to Existence and feel the vibrations of the powerful *mantras* within your being. The *mantras* are a way to express gratitude to Existence and to the master for bestowing upon us this great wisdom which liberates us from ignorance and helps us attain the state of eternal bliss, *Nithyananda*.

The chanting is in Sanskrit which has both linguistic and phonetic importance. By centering ourselves on the vibrations created when chanting these Sanskrit sounds, we can go beyond the words of the mind to the peace of our very being. Even if we don't understand the meaning of the sounds, the phonetic value of Sanskrit will transform our mood and purify our whole body and mind, creating positive vibrations inside our being.

You can also choose to perform the *Guru puja** (offering gratitude to the master) in this step by reciting the *mantras* and performing the rituals (For details please refer to the 'Do Guru Puja Yourself' book).

Practice this meditation technique once a day and you will start experiencing a new dimension of your being. Nithya Dhyaan will prepare your body and mind to experience the state of pure consciousness and bliss.

Benefits of Nithya Dhyaan

The half hour of Nithya Dhyaan meditation can give you:

- Relief from stress
- Improved relationships
- Inner peace and fulfillment
- Awakened intuition
- Regulated blood pressure
- Enhanced sleep patterns
- Increased clarity
- Increased energy levels for the whole day
- Connection to the Divine energy

You can get your family and friends initiated into Nithya Dhyaan. This will directly contribute to the collective positivity of planet

---

Guru puja - Ritual worship of the master.

earth, as more and more people will live in an 'unclutched', liberated way as *jeevanmuktas* (liberated beings). This shift in the individual consciousness will result in a positive shift in the collective consciousness which will in turn impact all of life on earth.

Nithya Yoga - For the Body, Mind and Beyond

Yoga* is not about physical fitness alone. It is also to help prepare the body for realizing the aim of uniting body, mind and spirit. Nithya Yoga is the technique designed in the body language of Patanjali for this uniting. In the same manner as we spoke about Nithya Dhyaan amongst meditations, Nithya Yoga is the yoga for the jet age.

What is yoga?

Patanjali, the father of the ancient science of yoga, says at the very start of Patanjali's Yoga Sutras, the foundational scripture of yoga:

Yogaha chitta vritti nirodhaha

He says, 'Yoga is the cessation of the mind.' Understand, it doesn't mean that yoga ends with the cessation of mind, rather that yoga begins where the mind *ends*. Actually, yoga never ends, it can only start. It is a continuous happening.

To understand how yoga is a continuous happening, we need to understand this important truth: whatever is happening is auspicious. Be very clear, every experience raises your consciousness and makes you more mature. Even losing your wealth gives you some maturity. Losing your health gives you some understanding. When you are able to internalize this truth, you suddenly see life as a wonderful happening every moment.

A small story:

There was once a ship sailing in the ocean. Suddenly, the captain of the ship saw bright lights ahead and rushed back to warn that ship to move out of the way. He quickly announced, 'Please divert your course fifteen degrees north to avoid a collision.' A voice spoke back, 'We recommend that you divert your course fifteen degrees south to avoid a collision.'

Now the captain of the ship got angry and replied in a proud and threatening way, 'This is the largest ship in the country. We are accompanied by three destroyers, defense equipment and many support ships.

Yoga - Literally means 'uniting' of body-mind-spirit.

Yoga begins where the mind ends.

I demand that you change your course fifteen degrees north or counter-measures will be undertaken to ensure the safety of this ship.'

The voice replied in a straight tone, 'We are a lighthouse!'

Understand, Existence is happening continuously and guiding you also so that whatever happens to you does so in the best possible way. Just fall in tune with it, that is the best course! Yoga is a path to fall in tune, just like tuning a radio to a higher frequency! The word 'yoga' literally means 'uniting'.

Patanjali – founder of Yoga

Patanjali is the founder of the yoga system. He was the first master who created a clear, scientific, logical system to reproduce the experience of enlightenment.

Patanjali was the first master, or I can say the 'spiritual navigator', who created the map and gave complete directions to enlightenment. He created clear-cut directions, step by step formulas to reproduce the experience of enlightenment. Just as scientists create a formula to reproduce the understanding of the outer world phenomena, Patanjali created a beautiful formula, a technology, to reproduce the understanding of the inner world, of enlightenment.

Raghupati Yogi – master of Yoga

I had the great fortune to be around a living master of yoga, Yogiraj Yogananda Puri, also called Raghupati Yogi. He had mastered the whole science of yoga as discovered by Patanjali.

He had mastered all aspects of yoga including the physical aspect of bending the body into various postures called *asana** or Hatha Yoga, working with *prana* or the life energy, working with the mind, working with visualization power, working with emotions and all the dimensions of yoga. He had a deep insight into the core truths of yoga.

Only the person who has experienced the consciousness of Patanjali can bring Patanjali back to life. I had the great fortune to be with such a master who had experienced that consciousness or the inner space of Patanjali.

He had amazing strength and unimaginable physical power that he expressed so casually. He would tie an iron rope around his chest and exhale completely, then he would inhale and the iron rope would break into pieces!

Usually a logical mind cannot accept or understand that all this is possible, but this great yogi made everything possible. I had the good fortune to be around him and see him levitating, not once but at least twenty times.

Asana - Physical posture and one of the eight paths of yoga in Patanjali's Ashtanga Yoga. *Asana* must be stable and comfortable.

He would inhale deeply and hold the breath. The moment he did that, the body would lift from the ground like an inflated balloon!

From the age of three to thirteen, I had the fortune to be at his feet, under his guidance and care. Every day from morning until noon for at least four to five hours a day, he would make me do all the traditional yogic techniques like various *asanas**, *neti** and *dhauti** where I would have to swallow a long cloth to clean the intestines and the internal system!

Just move the body with the intention and get the result!

On some days, Raghupati Yogi would ask me to sit still and be very peaceful, to meditate on stillness, peace and tranquility. Then after ten minutes, he would suddenly tell me to stand up and run around the entire temple as fast as I could!

He would make me bend this way and that way. In the temple where he would teach me yoga, there were twenty to thirty pillars. He would make me climb every stone pillar and come down. And I had to use only one hand to climb the pillars and come down!

I would ask him why he was making me climb all the pillars, because I couldn't find any books or any *sutras** saying climbing pillars was a part of yoga!

He said a beautiful thing, 'For whatever purpose you bend your body or move your body, that memory and idea will become completely inserted or completely recorded in your body and mind.'

For whatever purpose you move your body, that memory gets completely recorded in your body and mind.

It was a very shocking revelation! He said, with any intention that you move your body, bend your body, or make your body active, and that intention, that purpose, will be recorded into your body, that *samskara* will start expressing in your body.

Today, especially in the West, there has been too much connection of disease and *asanas** as in for this disease, you have to do that *asana*, for this problem you have to do that technique. Understand, doing *asanas* for solving a disease is not the purpose of yoga! When you think of a disease and do yoga with that thought in your mind, you are actually pushing the imprint of the thought of that disease into your system!

Asana - Physical posture and one of the eight paths of yoga in Patanjali's Ashtanga Yoga. *Asana* must be stable and comfortable.

Neti - Nasal cleansing technique of yoga.

Dhauti - A yogic practice of cleansing intestines.

Sutras - Spiritual techniques offered in epigram form.

Your body itself is made out of your memory. Raghupati Yogi says, any *asana* practiced, or any physical movement practiced for some purpose or with some intention, will create that effect in your body. He says that this is possible even with ordinary sitting. If you strongly believe that by sitting you will have health and you just sit for health, you will see health simply happening in you.

Understand, your body itself is made out of your memory. Your mind, what you think of as you, makes up the building blocks of your body.

Every memory is recorded in your muscles. So when you change the memories, you can simply change your system also. Your system can and will respond to the memory you create. This is how the transformation in the body-mind happens through Nithya Yoga. The inner space is cleaned first so the mind falls in tune. Then the body follows as the physical movement is done with the intention. The intention gets inserted into the very muscle memory and cellular intelligence.

Scientific evidence

'We are what our perceptions are. As are our perceptions, so become our actions. As are our actions, so becomes our destiny.' This is not a quote from the *Upanishad*, but from 'The Biology of Belief', a recent book by Dr Bruce Lipton[*], a cellular biologist who has presented a new theory on how cells behave. We have all been taught that we behave the way our genes are designed. Dr Lipton[*], after his research, says the opposite - our genes are designed the way we behave!

There have been many recorded incidents of the ability of intention and visualization actually resulting in the intention becoming physical reality itself! For example, people have cured their own fatal diseases like cancer or overcome tremendous physical handicaps by pushing their limits and going beyond what they thought was their capacity. These things have happened through the power of intention which transforms basic cellular memory.

This ancient truth is now being proven with the support of modern scientific findings. It has been found that whatever we think deeply and continuously has a profound effect on us physically, mentally and spiritually.

Purpose of Nithya Yoga

Nithya Yoga is my offering to the world. It is the science, the formula, that will give others the same experience of enlightenment which happened in me.

The purpose of Nithya Yoga is simple - to experience and express bliss. With Nithya Yoga, the capacity to experience bliss will just explode in your inner space. The capacity to radiate bliss will start happening in your body.

Dr. Bruce Lipton - Molecular cellular biologist and author of 'The Biology of Belief', renowned for his seminal work in relating genetics to conditioning.

As of now, your system may not be prepared to stay in that enlightened space, to radiate that same experience continuously. Nithya Yoga prepares your body to experience and stay in and radiate the inner bliss, the eternal bliss.

Through Nithya Yoga, I am training seekers not only to experience the bliss, but also to stabilize the experience in them, and to radiate that experience continuously in their life. The purpose of Nithya Yoga is to help people unclutch and experience eternal bliss. People may also find that physical healing results as a byproduct or side-effect. But, be clear that yoga is for much more than physical health, which is just one benefit of yoga. The emotional benefits are also tremendous but these are also more like byproducts!

In the same way, meditation is not just for mental well being. Mental well-being is just one side-effect happening through meditation. The goal of Nithya Yoga is making your whole life, every activity and every movement transformed into yoga, into bliss.

Nithya Yoga is not about adding more movements to your life. It is about adding more *life* to your movements.

Nithya Yoga is conducted today worldwide. Every session of Nithya Yoga deepens the uniting of the body-mind-spirit by bringing together all the eight limbs of Patanjali's Ashtanga yoga*, by including all the elements like asana, *pranayama*, *mudra* etc.

Nithya Yoga is not about adding more movements to your life. It is about adding more *life* to your movements.

If you are present, if you are aware, and if you are totally in the moment while doing anything, it *is* yoga – Nithya Yoga.

Ashtanga yoga - Eight limbs or paths of Patanjali's Yoga: *yama* (discipline), *niyama* (rules), *asana* (body postures), *pranayama* (breath control), *pratyahara* (withdrawal of senses), *dharana* (concentration), *dhyana* (meditation) and *samadhi* (bliss).

Pranayama - Breath control, one of the eight limbs of the Ashtanga yoga of Patanjali.

Mudra - Signs formed with hands during *yoga* practices, especially meditation, to distribute and seal energy within the body.

Eight Steps for a Blissful Life Everyday

Living in bliss

- The eight-fold path of blissful living or *Ananda Ashtanga*

Ananda Ashtanga or Blissful Living is a simple eight-fold pathway to living enlightenment. These are simple techniques that take you into the experience directly without the need to understand and absorb.

These are:

1. Blissful Laughter
2. Blissful Affirmation
3. Blissful Cleansing
4. Blissful Yoga
5. Blissful Meditation
6. Blissful Tools
7. Blissful Energy
8. Blissful Chant

Blissful Laughter

- Laughing meditation or *Hasya Dhyana*

Meditation

As soon as you wake up in the morning, even before you get up from your bed, laugh for five minutes! Just laugh at yourself. Laugh without a reason!

Laughter is a wonderful meditation technique. The technique of the ancient Zen tradition of masters and disciples is to touch no-mind through laughter. Laughter works whether we believe it or not. It has an immediate effect. With other techniques, we need to practice to see the result, but with laughter we don't need to practice. It happens the first time and every time. It goes in deep and heals us physically and mentally.

Laughter itself is born out of health and creates health. It is an overflowing energy. It releases emotional suppressions.

Laughter is the greatest spiritual quality. In laughter we become Buddha, the enlightened one. Buddha is 'no-mind'. When we laugh, we are in a no-mind state for those few moments. Either laughter or our mind can exist, never both at once. When we laugh, for that moment, our mind disappears and we become one with the energy of Existence. We don't feel our identity. Can we experience ourselves as separate in the peak of our laughter? No! That ceasing to exist is the momentary no-mind and merging with Existence. That is why we need to laugh more. The moments of the self's disappearance can be extended so that we finally lose our identity and live as one with the energy.

Laughter is known to heal a number of diseases, especially diseases related to the nervous system and throat. A hearty laugh is said to squeeze out harmful byproducts of cellular functioning.

Blissful affirmation

- A vow of bliss or *Ananda Sankalpa*

Ananda means bliss. *Sankalpa* means vow. *Ananda sankalpa* is a vow of bliss.

You can decide to be blissful. It is a choice you make. In fact it is not even a choice that you make. If you allow yourself to flow in a

---

Abdullah - Abdullah Ansari of Herat, a Sufi master.

choiceless manner along with whatever Existence intends for you, you will be in bliss eternally. This attitude of being choiceless can be cultivated.

Part of this meditation has its origin with the Sufi mystic Abdullah*. Sufis are the most ecstatic sect ever. Their prayer is gratitude, nothing else. Abdullah* was famous for his ever-smiling face. It is said that even on his deathbed, he was laughing. Finally some of his disciples couldn't help but ask Abdullah* how he was always blissful. They asked him, 'Master, what is so funny about dying?'

Then Abdullah gave them the secret that his own master had taught him. He said, *'Remember that your happiness is always in your hands. Your happiness is 100 percent your own choice. Every day, life gives you a chance to be happy or miserable. What you choose is up to you!'*

Meditation

There can't be a simpler meditation technique than this. Yet it is the most effective one.

Every morning, as soon as you get up, even before you open your eyes, sit up in bed.

Call out your name loud. If you don't wish to disturb people around you by calling out loud, then just speak silently to yourself.

Ask yourself (using your name…in the first person), *What do I choose to experience today? Do I choose happiness or sadness?*

Naturally, first thing in the morning, you are not going to choose misery! So your mind will say, *I choose happiness.*

Then reply, *Ok* (your name), *be happy, that's all!*

Then, with your eyes closed, for a few minutes, strongly and consciously, come to the understanding that nothing can make you suffer without your silent permission. You suffer because you agree to be affected by external circumstances. You have the power within you to be happy all the time. Now open your eyes and live your affirmation!

You will see during the day that just by the strength of your affirmation, you have changed the whole course of your mind. You will see how until then you were blaming others for your misery, while actually you were choosing to become disturbed at every turn of events. You will develop an attitude of being happy, not *because* of external circumstances, not *despite* them – but *irrespective* of them. You are happy because you are happy, that's all.

Blissful cleansing

- Oil pulling

The tongue is said to be an indicator of what is going on in the body. By examining the tongue and its color, it is possible to guess the medical condition of a person. According to *ayurveda**, the tongue is mapped to different organ locations. Specific sections of the tongue are connected to specific parts of the body, like the kidneys, lungs, etc. When we do oil pulling, the oil pulls mucus, bacteria and toxins from your body through your saliva and tongue. According to *ayurveda** medicine, mucus is a poison that must be removed.

Meditation

Early morning, before brushing your teeth, eating or drinking anything, take one full tablespoon of either sesame or refined sunflower oil. Put it in your mouth, sit in one place, tilt your chin up so that the oil gets to the back molar teeth, and slowly pull through your softly gritted teeth for fifteen to twenty minutes.

Ayurveda - Traditional Indian system of medicine, *Ayurveda* literally means knowledge of life.

Don't multitask while doing this. When the time is up, spit out the oil in a washbasin and brush your teeth well. If you have pulled properly, the oil that you spit out will be thin and whitish in color. Drink two glasses of water after rinsing and cleaning the mouth.

Note: do not swallow the oil that you pull. It will contain parasites and bacteria.

If you have to pull oil after meals, wait at least four hours before you do it.

Oil pulling is said to address many conditions, including anything from cracked heels to cancer. Exhaustive research reports on the benefits of oil pulling are available on the web.

Blissful yoga

-Sun Salutation or *Surya Namaskar*

Surya Namaskar is part of Nithya Yoga. The uniqueness of Nithya Yoga is that it directly brings to life the original teachings of Patanjali by adapting it to suit the modern mind. Sage Patanjali, from southern India, is considered to be the Father of Yoga.

Surya Namaskar is a daily salutation to the sun. Not only does it help keep the body at peak functioning, it also brings a complete awareness of the body-mind connection.

Benefits of Surya Namaskar

The practice of Surya Namaskar awakens the body intelligence to directly draw energy from the sun. Surya Namaskar is designed to access the etheric energy around us. It has tremendous effects on the mind, body and spirit, when practiced facing east in the first rays of the morning sunlight, along with the appropriate breathing technique and the corresponding *mantras**. Nothing more needs to be done.

Surya Namaskar works on all body parts, every organ, system and *chakra* (vital energy centers in the body). It is a sequence of postures done dynamically and fluidly with appropriate breathing.

Every morning, you may do six to twelve repetitions of Surya Namaskar. Of all the yogic postures, Surya Namaskar is considered the most effective way to tone up the limbs, stretch and strengthen the entire body and spine. Surya Namaskar is regarded as the king of all postures.

Significance of Surya Namaskar *mantras* (chants)

A *mantra* (chant) is a composition of syllables, words, phrases or sentences that, when repeated with awareness, has a very powerful and penetrating influence on the mind and body. The Surya Namaskar *mantra* comprises a *bija** (seed) *mantra* and a

---

Mantras - Literally means 'that which shows the way'. Sacred syllables that have a powerful positive vibrational effect.

glorification *mantra*. The glorification is to the Sun god.

The *bija* (seed) *mantra* has no meaning by itself but the vibration created by chanting it is very powerful in the human system. The 'Theory of Vibration' expounded by modern scientists was put to direct application thousands of years ago by the ancient inner world scientists, our *vedic* seers!

Scientific studies conducted by Dr. Masaru Emoto* of Japan have clearly proven that sound vibration has a profound effect on water. Since water makes up over sixty percent of the human body, it is evident that sound vibrations can and do influence our entire mind-body system also.

Unconscious thoughts and emotions create strong vibrations within us in the form of stored memories or *samskaras*. We need to dissolve them with awareness. Then we will experience the completely positive consciousness that already exists deep within us.

There are six *bija mantras*. They are:

Om hraam

Om hreem

Om hroom

Om hraim

Om hraum

Om hraha

The glorification *mantras* highlight the glorious qualities of the sun. Beginning with the first, each *mantra* is chanted with complete awareness before every cycle of Surya Namaskar. The *mantra* is empowered to imbibe the same qualities of the glorification in the sincere practitioner.

Through this simple set of steps, we can realize that the outer sun symbolizes the shining intelligence of our inner Self. We come to understand our connection to the cosmic energy that is all pervasive.

Surya Namaskar *mantras* (formed by combining the *bija mantras* with the glorification *mantras*)

1. ~ *OM hraam mitraaya namaha*

Salutations to the Eternal Friend of all

2. ~ *OM hreem ravaye namaha*

Salutations to the Eternal Shining One

3. ~ *OM hroom suryaaya namaha*

Salutations to the Eternal One who Induces Activity

4. ~ *OM hraim bhaanave namaha*

Salutations to the Eternal One who Illumines

5. ~ *OM hraum khagaaya namaha*

Salutations to the Eternal One who Moves swiftly

Bija - Seed.

Dr. Masaru Emoto - Japanese scientist and author of 'The Hidden Messages in Water' showing the effects of one's thoughts and words on water and therefore on living beings.

6. ~ *OM hraha pushne namaha*

Salutations to the Eternal Giver of Strength

7. ~ *OM hraam hiranya garbhaya namaha*

Salutations to the Eternal Golden Cosmic Womb

8. ~ *OM hreem mareechaye namaha*

Salutations to the Eternal Lord of Dawn

9. ~ *OM hroom adityaaya namaha*

Salutations to the Eternal Son of Aditi, the Infinite Cosmic Mother

10.~ *OM hraim saavitre namaha*

Salutations to the Eternal Benevolent Mother

11. ~ *OM hraum arkaaya namaha*

Salutations to the Eternal One who is Praiseworthy

12. ~ *OM hraha bhaaskaraaya namaha*

Salutations to the Eternal One who Leads to Enlightenment

Breath control

In Surya Namaskar, every movement of the body is synchronized with the breath. With every inhalation and exhalation, visualize clearly you are taking in and sending out bliss energy. Feel the bliss energy moving in every cell of your body and revitalizing your body-mind.

Meditation

This should be done on an empty stomach preferably in the morning.

Asana (Posture) Sequence of Surya Namaskar:

1.   Stand with the feet slightly apart for balance. Bring the hands together into *namaskar* (prayer position) in front of the chest. Keep the eyes open throughout the practice of Surya Namaskar. Chant the corresponding *mantra*.

2.   Inhaling, gracefully sweep the arms up over your head and gently arch the spine backwards.

3.   Exhaling, sweep the arms forward and down so the hands touch the floor on either side of the feet and close to them, and the forehead comes in close to the knees. You may bend the knees to allow for greater ease in doing this.

4.   Inhaling, step the right foot backward as far as you can and lift your heart center, looking up at the same time.

5.   Holding the breath, step the left foot back and come into a plank position with the spine, neck and head in one straight line, your hands placed directly beneath your shoulders and eyes looking down at the floor.

6.   Exhaling, lower the knees, chest, and chin to the floor and assume *ashtanga namaskar* (salute with eight parts or points of your body touching the floor). Let your stomach be off the floor with your hips lifted up gently, the elbows tucked in.

Surya Namaskar

11

1

10

2

3

9

4

8

5

7

6

7. Inhaling, point the toes out, relax your stomach to touch the floor, keeping the elbows bent at a ninety-degree angle. Then, gently pushing with your hands, lift the chest off the floor. Come into *bhujangasana* (cobra pose).

8. Exhaling, push with your hands, raise your hips upwards and backwards into the air, and assume *adhomukha svanasana* (downward-dog pose). Spread the fingers wide and gently push your heels toward the floor. If you are unable to touch the floor with your heels, don't bother about it. But don't shift your position in order for them to touch.

9. With a soft gaze look forward between your hands and step the right foot forward as far as you can, between the hands and in line with them if possible. Inhale, lifting your chin and chest.

10. Step the left foot forward to meet the right foot, bending your knees slightly if you need to. Exhale and bring the head in close to the legs.

11. Inhaling, sweep your arms up over your head and gently arch the spine, saluting the sun.

12. Exhaling, bring your arms down, and your hands back into prayer position in front of your heart.

Each cycle consists of two such movements of twelve positions each. In the first half of the cycle, lead with your right leg in steps 4 and 9. In the second half of the cycle, lead with your left leg.

Complete at least 6 such cycles and if possible 12. Before starting on each cycle chant the *mantra* in sequence.

Blissful meditation

- Life Bliss Meditation or *Nithya Dhyaan*

Up to the age of eleven, I explored and experimented with numerous traditional meditation techniques. At the age of twelve, I had my deep spiritual experience. From twelve to twenty-one years of age, I consciously scanned and analyzed the benefits of several techniques. For three years after my enlightenment, I created and perfected a technology to reproduce the experience of enlightenment in others. The essence of this entire inner-world research to date is formulated in the Nithya Dhyaan meditation technique.

Nithya Dhyaan is a formula and a technique that works on the entire being to transform it and make it ready for the ultimate experience of enlightenment. Each segment of this unique technique complements the other steps to help raise the individual's consciousness. It is an everyday meditation for eternal bliss - *nithya ananda*.

Meditation

This is a five-step technique, each step being of seven minutes duration. Please refer to the Nithya Dhyaan chapter for meditation instructions.

Blissful tools

- Knowledge-weapons or *shaastra-shastras*

Meditation

Everyday for half an hour, read the books of an enlightened master or listen to his discourses.

A master's words are straightaway *shaastra* – ultimate knowledge, Truth.

Weapons used to slay your ignorance are called *shastra*.

When words become the very weapons to slay the ignorance it is called *shaastra-shastras or* knowledge-weapons!

The master's words are the knowledge-weapons that can directly slay the ignorance. A master continuously expresses many ideas. Suddenly, some idea will click for you. It will bring you out of depression. It will give the solution to some problem. That is a click. And that click is what is called *initiation*.

The person who gives these knowledge-weapons through his words, techniques and body language is a master.

The person who receives these knowledge-weapons through the master is the initiate.

A master is a person who has created a technology to reproduce in others, the same ultimate experience that happened in him. Initiation is the technique. The knowledge–weapons are the techniques to raise ourselves again and again to Higher Consciousness. The totality of these knowledge-weapons sitting inside us is our inner master. Till the inner master is awakened, the outer master works on us. He works through words, techniques, his body language, and gives us the confidence to use the knowledge, and above all to live the life of an enlightened being.

Blessed are those who have had the click with enlightened beings. This click is not through logic. Suddenly, some words from the master will get connected to our heart. The first time it happens, we will suddenly know that he is our master, that this is our path. That click is the first initiation. Whoever has felt this click through the master's words, his teachings, books, blessings, techniques, energy, or body language, is blessed.

Understand: the seed is always afraid of breaking open, of rupturing. But only the seed that ruptures and opens becomes a tree. Then the tree needs to give courage to the other seeds by saying, 'Don't be afraid, you will never die by breaking, you will only live. You will only expand like me.' But the seed is waiting for the tree to happen and the tree is waiting for the seed to open! That is the problem.

I know the Truth that I am speaking. Oh! Sons of Immortality, have the courage to sprout and become the tree!

This energy, this inspiration is the master. The advent of the master is the greatest adventure in one's life. Once the master has entered our inner space, all we need to do is stand up with trust, courage and confidence.

Again and again, use the clicks that have happened in your life. Any weapon not used will not only lose its power on us, but we will also forget how to use it. Again and again, the weapons that are actually used will bring us clarity and courage and we will also have the intelligence to use them.

Add more and more clicks to your life by listening to the master's words. Add them to your inner space. Creating a family, friends, a spiritual circle, will constantly give us the courage and inspiration to use the knowledge-weapons.

One more thing, when we watch the master talk, we are watching the body language of an enlightened being. A person's body language radiates his own truth and totality. A master is an embodiment of the ultimate Truth of Existence. His body language is therefore the very body language of Existence. By watching him, the Truth will work on us beyond our logic.

Blissful energy

- Harnessing the energy of Existence or Shakti Dharana

This technique is taken from Tantra Shastra (Kularnava Tantra). It is a beautiful technique to relate with the Existential energy.

It is ideal to practice this meditation at night just before going to sleep. This can also be done in the morning but it must be followed by at least fifteen minutes of rest, or else you would be in a state of blissful intoxication because of the effect of the meditation. This meditation leads to your merging with the energy of Existence. The importance of *Shakti Dharana* meditation is that it leads you to the threshold of the state of *turiya*, where you are in a state of total awareness but without thoughts.

Meditation

Stand on your knees and balance yourself well. Do not sit on your haunches. Close your eyes and raise both hands upwards with palms facing skywards. Tilt your head slightly upwards.

In this position, feel the Existential energy flow through you. Visualize that a light-beam of Existence is flowing through you. To start with, you can visualize the blissful face of any enlightened master. Just as a miser is at the peak of his energy when counting money or a lover is at the peak of his energy when he is with his beloved, so also a master is at the peak of his energy when laughing or smiling.

That is why I tell you to remember his blissful face and allow the energy to flow through you. Also, it is better that you think of a master than allow your mind to wander and think of something else!

As the energy of Existence flows down your arms, you will feel a tingling sensation, a gentle vibration, or a slight tremor in you. It would be as if a tender leaf is dancing in the breeze. Just allow the tremor to happen. Help the tremor, let your whole body vibrate with the energy. Just allow and help whatever happens to happen. You might feel as if the earth below and heaven above are merging, as if the male and female energies are merging. You might feel as if you are floating or merging. Allow any feeling, just drop yourself completely. There is no 'you'. You have simply dissolved into Existence.

After two or three minutes when you feel that your being is completely filled with the energy of Existence, bend down, rest on your elbows and forearms, and kiss the earth, or at

least let your forehead touch the ground. You become a medium or a passage for the divine energy that you attracted to unite with the energy of the earth. Allow all your energy to flow into mother Earth. You may visualize the feet of the master when in this posture. It will help to be in a mood of surrender to mother Earth while offering the energy.

Now, regain your original posture and repeat this cycle at least six times. You will do seven cycles totally.

This meditation tremendously improves energy circulation in the body. All troubles related to the backbone will simply vanish by doing this meditation, as the energy goes straight to the *muladhara chakra*, an energy center which is at the base of the spine.

After completing the meditation, you may go to sleep in the same meditative mood. The sleep that follows this meditation will be intense and dreamless. When you wake up the next morning you will experience great freshness and energy.

This is a very powerful technique. When done consistently, a new life, a new meaning, a new Truth will start flowing into you. A beautiful and alive connection between Existence and you will be created. You will experience much joy and each day will become a celebration!

Blissful chant

- Chanting the Bliss *mantra* or *Purashcharanam*

Mantras are chanted in the *vedic* language, Sanskrit. The beauty of Sanskrit is that all the possible sounds are described in its fifty-one syllables. The Sanskrit language not only conveys meaning; its phonetic sounds also transmit special vibrations along with them. Even if you don't understand the meaning of the *mantras*, the vibrations will work on you.

In the East, Sanskrit *mantras* are used for initiations. The master will utter a *mantra* and the *mantra* itself will give the awakening initiation to the disciple. The vibrations will straightaway enter his being and start working.

The Guru *mantra* is:

Om hreem Nithyanandaya namaha

In Hindu thought, every simple act is imbued with multiple layers of understanding. This understanding happens depending on the level of awareness of the individual's consciousness. The word or sound '*Om*' means many things at many levels.

Om is the elemental sound. The whole of Creation is believed to have stemmed from it. It comprises three utterances - A, U and M. The syllable A (*aah*) stands for Brahma, the Hindu god who creates the universe; U (*ooo*) stands for Vishnu, the Hindu god who sustains the universe, and M (*mmm*) for Shiva, the Hindu god who destroys to create the space for further creation to happen. The combined sound *Om* is therefore the manifestation of the entire universe.

At a deeper level, the gods are representations of the energies of creation, sustenance and rejuvenation that happen at a cellular level in our personal universe, our body-mind entity.

The vibration of *Om* when chanted gives one the staying resolve of mother Earth. It dissolves anger, desire and psychosomatic illnesses in us. It fills us with the expansiveness and boundlessness of mother Earth. It frees the mind from negative thinking. It releases tremendous energy and rejuvenates the brain. It brings peace of mind and great power of concentration. It is a jumping board to quiet the mind and enter into the Self.

Hreem is the *bija mantra* of Devi, the sacred feminine principle.

The sages of ancient India practiced chanting these primordial sounds and experienced deeply at the levels of mind, body and being. They presented the science and method of practicing them to humanity so that they might experience what the great sages experienced. Chants from the *vedic* times are all research reports of such sages whose love

for the ultimate experience caused them to share it with humanity.

Chanting of *Om* and *Hreem* together awakens the masculine and feminine energies residing in us.

Nithyananda is chanted to invoke the name of the master as the expression of the ultimate Truth. It is the *poorna moola mantra* (the complete and 'Source of all' chant) because it is the straight path to both *Shakti* or success in the material world, and to *Shiva* or success in the cosmic world or enlightenment.

The word *Nithyananda* also means 'eternal bliss'. By chanting this, we give a clear intention to our being and the universe about our ultimate desire for eternal bliss or enlightenment.

Namaha means *I am not.* By saying *I am not*, we surrender our ego to Existence or to the master who is the pure form of Existence. The word *namaha* when repeated strengthens the experience of surrender. It brings humility and obeisance into us.

Meditation

Chant the Guru *mantra* fifty-four times every day for eleven days or continuously whenever it is remembered. The chanting can be done either out loud or silently in the mind. The speed of chanting varies from person to person.

The *mantra* has the property of energizing your inner space and preventing unwanted thoughts from rising. Thoughts arise as silent words from the navel region, the *manipuraka chakra*, which is the vital energy center at the navel region. When you chant the Guru *mantra*, the *manipuraka chakra* gets

completely cleansed. This automatically leads to the removal of all worries, negative thoughts and emotions.

The Guru *mantra* purifies the energy behind speech, which is called *vak* energy. It causes continuous bubbling of energy and intense enthusiasm and excitement for life.

The vibration of this *mantra* can change the vibration and frequency of the being. The important thing is to keep the awareness on the *mantra*. When you persistently bring your awareness back to the *mantra*, you move closer to your inner consciousness.

Like in a water tank, if we keep blue powder at the base, the rising bubbles will also be blue, in the same way, when you keep this *mantra* at the center of your consciousness, your entire thinking system will be purified.

Slowly you will see, the *mantra* will begin happening effortlessly, on its own. And you will fall into a naturally meditative state.

The *mantra,* when done with a particular affirmation, becomes an intense prayer. Medical research has proven that prayer has remarkable effects on the body, mind and spirit.

Leading universities in the United States of America have found that prayer causes a forty percent lower death rate from heart disease and cancer, up to fourteen times higher survival rate after surgery for heart patients, decreases the stroke rate by half in the elderly, and reduces hospitalization time up to three weeks. There is a large database establishing the positive effects of prayer on the web.

364

Master - The Living

Enlightenment

Master – The Living Enlightenment

Master - The Living Enlightenment

Chitram vadataror mooley vriddhah shishyaa gurur yuvah

Gurostu maunam vyaakhyaanam shishyaastu chinnah samshayah

Beneath the banyan tree they sit

the disciples, old men, the guru a mere youth!

The guru speaks through Silence alone

But lo! The disciples' questions dissolve on their own!

Understanding of concepts will remain academic, and techniques will remain as tools without the power to transform, unless the master's presence catalyzes the process. One needs the master to realize god.

In the *vedic* tradition, the spiritual teacher, the guru, is more important than god. Scriptures say that the guru is mother, father and god, all in one and beyond all.

God is a concept to most of us. There are few who can speak with authority based on one's own experience about the divinity one has experienced. It is said that one who

experiences does not express, and one who expresses has not experienced. The master, is one who has experienced and who communicates that experience to others not merely as expressions but through his very body language and life style.

The master is the doorway to one's own divine experience. He leads the disciple by the hand through it to experience the fundamental truth of one's own inner divinity. In the process the disciple becomes a master and the cycle continues.

This virtuous cycle of enlightenment resulting in the experience of one's true nature, breaks down the vicious cycle of desires and suffering that all of us are caught in. It is with deep understanding that Buddha said that all desires are suffering. Buddha's reference was to human nature that seeks to fulfill these desires externally through the senses. This can never happen. Desires grow again and again. It is only the experience of the inner bliss arising out of the understanding of one's own infinite potential, that can eliminate the suffering which has become human nature.

The master is a mirror. He is an intelligent mirror of energy that leads us to the discovery of who we are. Let us now begin this journey.

Lion and cub story

A small story:

Once upon a time, a pregnant lioness attacked a herd of goats while hunting for food. As she jumped at one of the goats the strain became too much for her and she died giving birth to a cub.

The newborn cub could barely open his eyes. He made some sounds and moved around on the ground helpless. The goats saw the orphaned cub and felt compassionate towards him.

You may wonder how goats can feel compassion towards a lion cub. Understand, when the enemy does not disturb or hurt you and you don't feel threatened in any way by his presence, you will feel compassionate towards him even if he is your enemy by nature. In the same way, since the goats did not feel threatened by the lion cub they started showing love towards him.

The goats sensed the cub was not going to attack them and because of this they were able to express compassion towards him. They looked after him, bringing him up in the manner they knew best. They showed him how to eat grass, drink goat milk, live like them and even how to bleat like them!

The lion cub also picked up the body language of the goats. Right from his birth

no one had ever told him he was a lion, so he never knew what it was to be a lion. So, the cub grew up continuing to live like the goats. The goats also were quite comfortable with the cub being one amongst them.

As the lion cub grew, he began to express his strength in a manner that was natural to him. When the other younger goats fought with him, he used to hit them with a strong blow. The young goats would complain to the mother goat, 'He is hitting us!' The mother goat would try her best to patch things up between the cub and the goats by consoling the young goats and advising them to forget about the fight.

One day a lion attacked the herd of goats. The frightened goats scattered in different directions. The lion then saw a lion cub running away with the goats bleating like them. The lion could not believe his eyes! He could not understand why the cub was running away upon seeing him and why he was bleating like the goats.

The next day the lion returned not to hunt but to look out for the young cub. When he saw the cub he slowly went up behind him and caught hold of him. The moment the lion caught hold of the cub, the cub started shouting, 'Let me go! Let me go! Baa, baa...'

The lion said, 'Fool! Don't be afraid. I am not going to kill you. Don't you know who you are?' The cub cried, 'I am a goat. Let me go! Let me go!'

The lion said, 'Fool! You are not a goat. Don't be afraid of me!' But the young cub was terrified and not ready to listen to anything. Somehow he managed to break free and he ran away.

The next day the lion came back to where the goats were. He managed to catch the lion cub again. This time he held him firmly.

The cub was struggling under the grip, but while one part of his mind told him strongly to escape, another part of him felt good at being touched by the lion. The assuring, comfortable feeling of the lion's touch awakened something deep within the cub. Seeing the struggle of the cub, the lion let him go saying, 'I will come again tomorrow. But at that time I will not be chasing you.' And the lion went back into the forest.

The lion cub stayed awake the whole night unable to sleep. His mind was filled with so many thoughts… 'I cannot accept what the lion said to me,' 'But I think there may be some truth in what he said,' 'No! No! No! I don't think whatever he said is correct. I know I am a goat. I have known it from birth. And what he says does not make any sense to me. He is just lying to get something from me.'

Understand, the lion has penetrated the cub in a way beyond the cub's logic. Let me be very clear, if the presence of the master affects you beyond your logic, the master in you has already been awakened!

You cannot feel connected to the lion unless the lion in you awakens. If you feel some ecstasy, some comfort, through the touch of the master, the lion, and if you find yourself trying to recreate again and again the same feelings that came up in your memory when you were with the lion, even if it is through visualization, be very clear,

the lion has touched you deeply! A part of you has already started feeling soothed. A part of you has already started feeling there is something in what the master says.

The next day when the lion arrived, the cub was standing there waiting for him. The cub was standing patiently at the edge of the forest looking out for the lion. But when the lion appeared, the cub started moving away from him towards the herd of goats. But he did not turn his face away from the lion as he did not want to lose sight of the lion!

He just took a few steps back cautiously telling the lion, 'You stay where you are and I will stand where I am now. We can still talk. It is true that I am not able to forget you. But let us keep this distance between us.' The lion replied, 'That is alright with me. You stay where you are. Now let us talk.'

The lion continued, 'Understand, you are a lion! You are ignoring your true nature by trying to be something else! Look carefully and you will see the difference between you and those goats.' The cub cried, 'No! No! How can that be? I eat the same grass as them. I live exactly as the other goats do.'

The lion said, 'Fool! Understand this very basic thing. See for yourself. No other goat feels attached to me. No other goat is waiting for me. They are all terrified of me. Only you are waiting for me. Understand from this alone that there is something happening within you. What is the need for you to wait for me here? Come with me to the river nearby and look at your reflection in the water. You will be able to see your face and mine.'

The cub felt scared to go with the lion and told him, 'No. Let us just stand here and talk. You stand where you are, I will stand where I am. You say whatever you want to say. I will stay right here and listen.'

Then the lion said, 'Alright, let me tell you this. If you allow me, I can show you your true self in the river and prove to you that you are like me. But I will not force you. I will return after one week. If you are ready, come back to this place and wait for me. I will then take you with me to the river. If not, just forget me. Don't even try to remember me, just get lost!' The lion then left.

After a week as promised, the lion arrived. The cub's mind was still confused, 'Should I go or not go to meet the lion?' Deep within, the cub really wanted to meet the lion but at the same time he was very afraid of the lion.

Finally, the cub reached the place where he had met the lion the last time and found the lion there. The lion looked up at him and stood up. He led the way and slowly they started walking towards the river. As they were walking, the lion moved a little closer to the cub. The cub got scared and started shouting, 'No! No! You stay where you are. You just show me the path to the river. Please do not walk so close to me. I can walk to the river on my own!'

The lion moved away a little and started telling the cub stories about when he was a cub himself and how he grew up to become a fully grown lion. Listening to these stories, the cub got so engrossed he forgot to keep the distance between the two of them. As they walked, the lion started getting closer

to the cub. The cub was completely involved in the stories of the lion and was asking him, 'Is that so?' 'Is that how it happened?' 'Did you also have all these problems?'

Without the cub realizing it, the lion had slowly come so near that he was now touching the cub as they continued their walk! Suddenly the young cub noticed this but he found that it did not bother him at all. He felt the gentle touch of the lion on him so relaxing! He did not protest.

The lion continued talking and the cub was saying, 'Oh! That was nice... that was interesting...' The lion was now almost holding the cub, but the cub was fully engrossed in the 'small stories' about the lion's early days.

As soon as they reached the river the lion caught the cub and took him to the water. The cub knew now there was no escaping. But he was surprised that he no longer had any desire to escape!

Understand: the cub knew that not only could he not escape, but he also did not want to escape! But then, a little ego hiding in a corner of his mind troubled him and he said, 'No! No! Let me go! What are you doing to me? Why are you holding on to me?' The cub still had some fear in him; so he asked, 'What are you doing to me? Tell me please, what are you doing to me?'

The lion replied, 'I am not doing anything to you. Just look into the water.' The cub looked into the water and said, 'Okay, I am looking into the water.' The lion then asked, 'What can you see in the water? Can you see two forms?' The cub replied, 'Yes.'

The lion said, 'Well, one lion is me and the other lion is you.'

The cub repeated, 'Two reflections: one mine and the other yours.' Then suddenly he realized what he was saying, he could not believe it and started shouting, 'May be not! No! No! No! Both the reflections in the water must be of you!'

The lion shouted, 'Fool! Look! I am raising my hand. See which reflection is raising a hand.' The cub pointed to the reflection in the water and said, 'Only that reflection is raising its hand.' The lion then said, 'Okay, now you raise your hand.'

The cub raised his own hand, looked at the reflections in the river and cried out, 'Yes! Yes! Yes! I see! I see!' Then in a small, confused voice he asked, 'But… How can I be a lion? Am I not a goat?'

The lion simply looked at him and said, 'I am not here to play with you.' That is when a feeling of ecstasy began to rise up in the cub. He could sense something incredible was about to happen.

But then again his mind stepped in and his mood went into a low and he started doubting in his mind, 'I think I have been hypnotized. This is not my true nature!

But then again his mind stepped in and his mood went into a low and he started doubting in his mind.

Something has happened to me. This is not me. I have never felt so blissful, so joyful! This is not me! He is doing something to me. He has already done something to me!'

The cub still resisted. He struggled to escape, but it was only a half-hearted attempt, an act actually, because he actually had no real desire to escape.

The cub started protesting, 'No! No! No! Let me go! Let me go! I know that you are a lion. As an offering for you, I will bring the grass which I eat everyday. I will bring the milk which I drink every day. I will devote my time to serve you.'

Finally the lion thought, 'I should leave him now. He can only understand this much for now.' So, he told him, 'Alright, be very clear, we shall meet again tomorrow. I will not come to the boundary of the forest to bring you here. I will be in my own home. If you want to see me, find out where I live and come on your own to meet me there. I have no time to waste by coming all the way to your place to bring you here! If you don't want to come to me through your own effort, let it be!' The lion told him this and left.

This time the cub did not run away as he usually would. He walked back very slowly. He did not want to go, but on the other side his mind was pushing him to go back to the goats. Three legs of the lion cub were not moving. Only one leg was able to move. Big drops of tears began to fall from his little eyes at the thought of this farewell.

The next day the lion was seated in a majestic pose in his home. Slowly, very slowly, the cub approached him with freshly-cut green grass thinking, 'This is the best grass available anywhere' and set it down in front of the lion saying, 'Please accept this offering I bring you.'

The lion watched and thought to himself, 'Alright, if I take this grass this fellow will feel connected to me. He might even allow this relationship to become more intense. Through this he might feel more connected to me.' Thinking this, even though a lion never eats grass, he picked up the grass, put it in his mouth and started eating! He praised the cub saying, 'This grass you brought for me tastes really good!' The cub was very happy with himself. The relationship started deepening between them when the lion began to eat the grass.

Understand, the lion comes down and eats grass only to be able to bridge the gap between the cub and himself. Even though he never really eats grass, he acts as if he is eating it and loving it.

Slowly the relationship grew between the lion and the cub. Sometimes when the lion tasted the grass brought by the cub he shouted at him, 'Fool! Don't you know which type of grass you should bring to me? What kind of grass is this? By now you should know what I eat. Next time bring me the right grass!'

The lion cub began to think, 'He is getting angry. I also get angry sometimes. So he speaks my language and I can speak his language. He is just like me!'

When the lion eats the grass, he comes down from his level, from his plane, from his consciousness, to connect with the cub.

The cub immediately felt very comfortable. It could now connect with the lion. Now the cub decided, 'I must bring the right grass and fresh milk next time. I must do things the right way. Maybe I should have the grass packed properly.' The cub made plans, thinking he had been scolded by the lion because he did not do his work properly! This is how the relationship started happening between the cub and the lion. Now the cub started feeling free and he started coming to the forest to see the lion whenever he felt like it. The cub started feeling very comfortable around the lion, very relaxed. It did not know the 'master' plan of the 'master' lion.

One day when the cub came as usual with grass and milk, he saw the lion sitting with a large chunk of meat in front of him. The moment the cub saw the meat he got afraid and started shouting, 'Why do you have meat on your plate? What is this? Are you a non-vegetarian? I did not know you are a non-vegetarian! You are such a loving and charismatic person. You cannot be a non-vegetarian! You eat all these terrible things! I am a vegetarian! I can't digest this!'

This time the lion did not take the time or energy to explain anything. He simply caught hold of the neck of the cub, picked up some meat and forced it into the cub's mouth. The moment the meat entered his mouth, the cub tasted the blood from the meat and something suddenly happened within him.

The cub could not understand what was going on. The cub had tasted meat for the very first time! He was overwhelmed with the feeling that rose in him. This is what happens in your first experience of satori, bliss! When you experience it, you will understand!

On tasting the meat, the cub let out a roar like a lion! He started roaring announcing his true nature. He expressed his true nature. Now the lion looked straight into the eyes of the cub and said, 'Tat tvam asi' - That

You are neither man nor the identity you think you are.

art Thou – you are That.' The initiation happened. *The lion became a lion. That was all. The lion who thought he was a goat became a lion!*

You are a lion, not a goat!

Understand, you are neither man nor the identity you think you are.

You are very much like the goat. In fact, you *are* the goat. Look at me and understand. I too thought I was a goat, but just look at the way I became a lion. Just take a close look at my own life. Then you will understand how foolish you are to think of yourself as a goat, and you will automatically become a lion!

This is what Krishna means when He says, 'When you understand *My* life, you will be liberated.' A liberated man's life liberates you because it shows exactly where you stand now. The liberated man too was ignorant once and stood in the same place you are standing now. This will give you the tremendous courage that you need to swallow raw meat to taste your inherent nature that is bliss and to start roaring instead of bleating. When this experience happens you roar instead of bleating.

How long did it take for the cub to realize he was a lion? Hardly a second! The moment the meat and the blood went into his mouth he started roaring. But remember how long it took just to get the meat into the mouth of the cub!

371

**The master is the
only scripture that
is alive.** It takes time
to enter the
master's cave. The relationship, the bridging
needs to happen before that. That is why it
takes some time.

Enlightenment itself does not take time.
The bridge, the trust to transmit that
experience takes time.

Significance of a master

It is very difficult especially for the modern
mind to understand the need for a master.

The master is the one who gives you a
glimpse of the Real, the truth of who you are.
He is not here just to teach. He is here to
awaken.

The master is the only scripture that is
alive.

Surrender towards god is difficult because
you don't know where god is or who god is.
God is a mere concept to you. But the master
is one with the Whole. He has reached the
Ultimate. To him god is reality. He lives with
god or Existence or whatever you wish to call
it. And the master is real to you. He is tangible.
So he can become your door to reach god.

Through him you can take the quantum
jump into the arms of god.

The only thing standing between you and
your true nature of bliss or god is your ego.
The process of becoming a disciple is the
process of renouncing your ego. The ego is
very difficult to drop. Dropping the ego means

losing the solid identity that you have been
carrying all these years, thinking you need it
for survival. Dropping the ego looks like death
when actually it is the ego that stands between
you and life!

Dropping the ego is possible only in a
relationship of deep trust, love and reverence
with the master. You gradually gather courage
and then risk dropping the only thing you have
clung onto throughout your life, your ego. You
drop the ego only when you fully know that
even if you fall, you only fall into the net of
infinite love and compassion of Existence
embodied by the master.

As of now, most of the experiences that
you add to your being bring in more and more
fear or greed. Instead, any experience can add
more strength and awareness to your being
also. This is the cognitive shift, the
psychological revolution the master does on
you that results in your complete
transformation.

Learning from master

You may ask, 'Why do I need a master? I
can learn from life.'

Learning from the master is a very sweet
experience, a very joyful experience. The
master first puts you in his lap and gives you
the anesthesia of love before he starts his
operation on the tumor of your ego. Because
he showers his love, you will not even
experience the pain of going through the
transformation. Even if it is mildly painful, you

MASTER - THE LIVING ENLIGHTENMENT

will endure it only with the joy and awareness of being with the master.

Master is intense life. Not only does he teach you, he also sees to that you go through the whole transformation blissfully.

A small story:

The father of a young boy was telling his little son to move a big stone. The boy tried his best, but he was not able to move it. He stood completely tired. The father said, 'You have not used all your potentiality. Use all your potential power.'

The son was completely tired. He shouted at his father, 'What are you talking about? You are saying I have not used all my potential power. I am tired. Are you not able to see?'

The father said, 'Why, you could have asked me. I am also your power!'

In the same way, you can also use the master's presence. Please understand, you can ask me. You can take the master's help. You have never done that. You have never considered the master also as your potential. So much of help is available, you can have so much, but you never ask or you never take it!

Life itself can be your master. But then it will become difficult to know from where to learn, what we should learn and from whom to learn. Dattatreya*, a great master says, 'I never had a master because life has always been my master. I learnt how to concentrate from the hunter who tries to concentrate on the bird. I learnt how to save money for the future by watching ants!' Life can become a master if you have the intelligence to pick up right things from it. But many times, you pick up the wrong things.

> **Not only does master teach you, he also sees to that you go through the whole transformation blissfully.**

A small story:

King Harishchandra lived his whole life based on truthfulness. The story of Harishchandra* says that he lived for the truth and at one point he even sold his wife and children to maintain his truthfulness.*

Once in a village, a preacher was narrating the story of Harishchandra. After the narration he asked a man, 'What did you learn from this story?' The man replied, 'I learnt that I should always speak the truth, no matter what happens in life.' The preacher was happy. Then he asked another man, 'What did you learn?'*

The second man said, 'I learnt another important lesson. In an emergency, you can even sell your wife, nothing wrong!'

Understand: you can learn two different things from the same story!

You may not have the intelligence to always learn correctly from life, which is why the master happens in your life. He shows you the path because he has already tried it and succeeded.

Dattatreya - Representation of the Hindu Trinity of Brahma, Vishnu and Shiva in one incarnation.

Harishchandra - Legendary Indian ruler who was renowned for keeping his word at whatever cost.

The master opens out the gates to the sweetest experience of life, of your own

See, by giving some medicines also, tumors can be removed. But it may take years and years. The master simply removes the tumor in no time. One more thing, the pain you will have living life with the tumors will be much worse than the pain you experience when master removes it. The pain with the master when he removes it, is hardly anything. But living with the tumor is dangerous and difficult. That is why it is better to go to the master.

Life is too deep a mystery which cannot be captured by our desires. Our desires may appear big and worth a whole lifetime for us. Because of our narrow view of life, we attach so much more importance to insignificant things while there are so many significant and more meaningful experiences just waiting at our doorstep. But the problem is that we can't even imagine them because we have never seen the likes of these.

That is where the master comes in. He has seen the wholeness of life. He can see things which you cannot even imagine, leave alone desire. He is there just to help you move towards realizing that fulfillment in your life too.

All you need is the trust to move with him. Then as things start happening you will be convinced about this truth. Then you enter the virtuous circle. More trust leads to more experiences which lead further to more trust.

The master does not impose anything on you. He simply removes what is not necessary and what has been imposed on you and leaves you fresh and new. You become a beautiful empty canvas upon which you can create your own unique painting. You can compose your own song and you can dance your own dance. The master opens out the gates to the sweetest experience of life, the experience of your own uniqueness.

Understand the difference between technique and process. Technique can be done again and the effect will be the same. But with process, you can't get the same effect every time and you won't even be able to do it on your own.

Technique done with master is a process. Process done without master is technique.

The eternal relationship

What is a relationship?

Relationship is that which can reveal to you dimensions in you that you don't even know exist inside you. It gives you the experience and proves to you that you are also capable of loving someone or something. It shows that you can also love and you can also sacrifice to an amazing extent for the sake of someone.

When we are born, we are born with completeness. But we are not aware of many of our dimensions and when we are not aware, the outer world too does not know of it. Relationships have the power to awaken our unknown dimensions and make us experience them and show the same to the outer world.

Relationship awakens the unknown dimensions in you.

A relationship with anyone or anything, no matter who or what, will lead you to the ultimate relationship with the master.

When you fall in love, whether it is with a man, woman or child, deity or master, you will see dimensions of you that you never knew existed inside you. With the flowering of such love, you become more responsible. You experience the very juice of life.

The relationship with the master, who is one with Existence, is deeper than any other relationship. It is a being level connection.

Generally all other relationships will create bondage but the relationship with the master has the power to lead you to freedom and finally to eternal bliss. Even if you try to create bondage in this relationship, it will only lead to eternal bliss! Bondage can never happen in this relationship.

The form of the master is the bridge between the Ultimate and you. Because the form is an embodiment of the Ultimate, it has both the dimensions, of man and god. When you relate with not only the form but the truth that the form stands for, you reach the knowledge of the Ultimate.

The master is all forms and no form. He refuses to be captured in a frame, to be turned into a stone or worshipped as an image. The master is beyond forms, beyond dimensions. He has infinite dimensions - infini-D!

Relationship awakens the unknown dimensions in you.

Frozen into one frame, whether as mother or lover, he is easy for you to capture and retain. He becomes easier to market. But the master is not interested in business for him. He wants you to be confused so that you look in and become enlightened. He wants you to die so that you become awake.

Come to the master with your ignorance. He will show you the path. Don't hesitate to fall into his arms with love. You will soar with him into bliss.

The master relates to us on multiple frames and planes, each one of which unveils the beauty and intensity of the unique relation he has with every single being that has the fortune of entering his space.

Each one in the quest for the Truth traverses a uniquely beautiful path with the master as he leads from the darkness of ignorance to the light of knowledge. It is a delicate love affair. It is the merger of two beings in such deep trust and communion that the flame from the master just jumps from his being to the disciple's being. The spark of awareness is thus lit.

Different relationships unleash various dimensions in you. A lover unleashes the love feeling in you. Friends around you unleash the feeling of friendship in you. Your kids unleash the motherliness dimension in you. Your parents, grandparents unleash the childhood dimension in you. But only the master can unleash all the dimensions in you. Master is the person who awakens the unknown

> **Master is the person who awakens the enlightenment dimension in you.**

enlightenment dimension in you. You cannot calculate the transformation the master-disciple relationship creates in you. The master reveals himself in various dimensions and makes you transcend those and lets you experience the Ultimate through communion.

God and master

The poet-mystic, Kabir* sings beautifully,

'Master and god both appear before me. To whom should I prostrate?

I bow before the master. He introduced god to me.'

Vivekananda*, in one of his discussions with fellow disciples of Ramakrishna Paramahamsa*, referred to Ramakrishna as god. Another disciple objected saying, 'Surely this is taking it to the extreme. I agree that the master is enlightened, but how can he be god?'

Vivekananda asked him, 'What do you know about god?' The disciple said, 'Oh, god is omnipotent, omniscient and omnipresent.'

Vivekananda asked, 'What do you mean by saying that god is omnipresent?' The disciple said, 'God is everywhere.' Vivekananda said, 'Surely, then you must be able to see him now.' The disciple was confused and did not know what to say further.

Vivekananda told him, 'To you god is a concept that you cannot see, a notion that you don't even know or understand. But here is the master in front of you who is god in reality.'

Someone asked me, 'What is the difference between god and master?'

I asked him, 'What do you know about god? All you know is a bunch of words, concepts. You have no clue as to what you are talking about when you refer to god. To you he is just an idea, an imagination of what you believe to be the ultimate energy and universal consciousness, or whatever name you wish to give something you know nothing about!'

The Brahmanda Purana* says,

Master is *Shiva** sans his three eyes,

Vishnu* sans his four arms

Brahma* sans his four heads.

Kabir - Mystic devotional poet of India.

Vivekananda – Disciple of enlightened master Ramakrishna Paramahamsa.

Ramakrishna Paramahamsa – Enlightened master.

Brahmanda Purana - A collection of 12,000 verses in what is usually considered the last and eighteenth Hindu *purana* or epic. This *purana* is the story of the creation of the universe by Brahma.

Shiva - Rejuvenator in the Hindu Trinity of gods.

Vishnu - Sustainer in the Hindu Trinity of gods.

Brahma - Creator in the Hindu Trinity of gods.

He is *Parama Shiva** himself in human form.

The master is real. He is the reality of the ultimate cosmic energy. He is here and now. He is in the present; He *is* the present. He is the bridge between you and the concept of god. In that sense he is greater than god.

People ask me, 'Are you god?' I tell them, if you do not know what or who god is, how can you ask me whether I am god? God cannot be defined. He can only be experienced.

Let me tell you one thing clearly, I am not here to prove that I am god. I am here to prove that you are god. I am not here to prove my divinity. I am here to prove your divinity.

The master is like a forest fire that is happening on one side of the river. The disciple is on the other side of the river. The river is the *'samsara'*, the river of births and rebirths. Between the master and disciple, if there can be a bridge made of any material, the fire can move, cross over the bridge and reach the disciple. The material of which the bridge is made is immaterial. It can be made of wood or with cement but the forest fire has the capacity to move over the bridge and reach the disciple. In the same way, irrespective of whatever relation you may have with the master, just get totally dissolved into that.

If you dissolve into that, it will simply fulfill your feelings and lead you to the ultimate state of eternal bliss. If you under-stand this truth deeply and try to practice this with the determination, 'I will focus on my feeling and get dissolved into the master-disciple relation', it will lead you to that state. Don't think that you don't know how to dissolve in that. The sheer determination is enough; it will happen automatically in you. Any hurdle between the master and disciple will dissolve just by focusing on the dissolution that happens between the master and disciple.

> **I am not here to prove my divinity. I am here to prove your divinity.**

Five Ways to Relate with the Master

There are five attitudes with which to relate with the master. Through each attitude, a different path unfolds, taking you closer to yourself.

One path is the attitude of the mother towards her child, looking at the master as your child. This is called *vatsalya bhava* – which is how Yashoda, Krishna's foster mother, related with Him.

Another is the attitude of the child towards the mother. This is called *matru bhava*. This is how Ramakrishna Paramahamsa related with goddess Kali, looking at the master as mother.

The third is the attitude of a friend, looking at the master as your friend. This is called

---

Parama Shiva – Supreme.

sakha bhava. This is how Kuchela[*] and Arjuna related with Krishna.

The next is the attitude of a servant. It is called *dasa bhava*. It refers to the master-disciple relationship wherein the disciple feels like a faithful servant of the master. This was how *Hanuman*, the monkey god, related with Rama in the famous Indian epic Ramayana[*].

The ultimate is the attitude of the beloved. It is called *madhura bhava*. This is how Radha[*], the milkmaid lover of Krishna, saw Krishna. This is how Radha[*] felt about Krishna, it was the attitude of the beloved. The attitude of a beloved is in no way connected to whether you are a male or female. It is in no way connected to the body. It is completely beyond the body. It is from the being.

If the master is male and you are also male, then too *madhura bhava* can happen. Or if the master is female and you are female, then also *madhura bhava* can happen. *Madhura bhava* is in no way related to gender. It is beyond gender consciousness. It is a feeling of intense connection.

The last is the *maha bhava*. It is all the other five *bhavas* put together and something more! That is what the master–disciple relationship is all about. Sometimes with the master you will feel he is your son. At some other time you will feel he is like your mother.

Sometimes you will feel he is your lord. Other times you will feel he is like your friend. Sometimes you will feel he is like a comforting beloved. The relationship with the master is all these five put together plus something more.

You can relate with the master in any one of these five attitudes or *bhavas*, or all the five put together.

Stages of master-disciple relationship

There are many levels in the master-disciple relationship. The first is purely at the intellectual level, based on doubt more than anything else. Numerous doubts keep coming up all the time. You think, 'Eh! He seems to be hardly thirty years of age. How can he be a master? He doesn't seem to be highly educated or qualified. How does he get thousands of people to listen to him?' You have your doubts. You are cynical. In the zone of pure intellect the relationship never happens.

The next step is from intellect to intelligence. From the negativity of doubt you move to, 'Why not attend this program and see what this person is really doing?' Instead of remaining with 'What can he do?' you move to 'I think he means something. But I

Kuchela - Childhood friend of enlightened master Krishna who exemplifies the relationship of friendship between master and disciple.

Ramayana - Hindu *itihasa* or epic about prince Rama. The original version was written by poet sage Valmiki.

Radha - Chief among the *gopis* or cowherd women devotees of enlightened master Krishna.

neither believe nor disbelieve. Ok, let me see.' The intellect starts to become intelligence.

Then next, if you continue to look in, you move from intelligence to intelligence with emotion like 60% intelligence, 40% emotion. You feel that the master is a good friend. You think, 'He can guide me a little bit here and there, wherever I need guidance. I have an idea of how my life should be, so he doesn't have to teach me everything, but wherever I need help to make some decisions, I can take his help.' This is looking at the master as a friend. That is what we call *sakha bhava*, the friendly attitude.

This is like using a stick to walk with. You use the stick when there are ups and downs. After that, by and by, slowly, when you go through some serious problems like depression and low mood, when you are not able to help yourself with his words, you ask him, 'Your teachings are great but at this moment I am not able to follow them. What do I do?' Then he supports you mentally, psychologically also. You realize that the stick alone may not be enough, that you need more support. Then you reach out for his hand and with his help you start walking again. The gratitude towards him increases while holding his hand.

If you have only the stick, then it is a friendly attitude, the intelligent emotion. If you start holding his hand, he will start lifting you, then slowly it becomes emotion-intelligence. This attitude is what I call feeling the master like a father or mother.

From being a friend he becomes a father or mother. Slowly, very slowly, the relationship deepens. You settle down and think, 'He is not just a friend. He is not just a person who gives me suggestions and ideas. He takes me out of my problems also.'

Then slowly, again and again when you are helped every moment beyond your expectation, the feeling within you toward him becomes more emotion. He fills you, he fills your heart. You have a problem forgetting him. That is the moment you feel like bowing down to him like a servant, not with shame but with revered humility that you have found someone to surrender all your problems to. This was how Hanuman felt towards his master Rama in the Indian epic Ramayana[*]. He was completely devoted to Rama. A deep connection of high emotion happens with this kind of relationship. This attitude is much more emotional than the earlier one. It is a mix of 60% emotion and 40% intelligence.

Then, by and by, you move in deeper emotionally and you become protective of the master. Instead of asking attention from him and taking help from him, you want to support him, love him and attend to him. Your attitude becomes that of a nurturing mother. This is a state of pure emotion. It is the primal need of a mother to ensure the wellbeing of her child.

In these four states of intelligence, intelligence-emotion, emotion-intelligence and pure emotion, your life is separate and independent from the master's life. You just

---

Ramayana - Hindu *itihasa* or epic about prince Rama. The original version was written by poet sage Valmiki.

The master is such a live energy that you *will* be a new consciousness. take help from him to help your life, to enrich your life, that's all.

When the emotional attitude ripens, you start feeling that your life is no longer separate from his. You then move from the emotional level to the being level. You feel like sacrificing yourself to take care of him and dedicating your life to him. There is a merger at the being level, even stronger than the emotional connection of a mother and child. It is a connection of deep love, without any gender consciousness. This is what is called *madhura bhava,* an intense mix of emotional and being level attitude.

When the *madhura bhava* becomes intense, suddenly you experience that there is no 'he' and 'you'. There are no two different beings. You and he are one and the same. You start experiencing the *maha bhava* - experiencing *you* as the master. You experience the ultimate - *tat tvam asi* - That art Thou.

First intellect, then intelligence, then 60% intelligence and 40% emotion, then 60% emotion and 40% intelligence, then 100% emotion, then 60% emotion and 40% being, then pure 100% being.

This is how step by step you start experiencing and growing in the master-disciple relationship. But at any time, any one attitude may be more prominent than the others.

Everyone grows collectively in energy, yet each one's relationship with the master is unique. That is the beauty of it! Be it *dasa bhava*, the master-servant relationship as existed between Rama and Hanuman, or *vatsalya bhava,* mother's love, as between Yashoda and Krishna, or *sakha bhava,* friendship, as between Krishna and Arjuna, or *matru bhava,* child's love for mother as between Ramakrishna and Mother Kali, or *madhura bhava*, love of the beloved, as was between Radha* and Krishna - each *bhava,* the attitude, is unique to that relationship, between that disciple and the master. Each disciple progresses with the master in search of his reality in the path that is best for him to progress.

How to be with the master – be open

When you are with the master, be completely open. Don't be frozen. Understand that life is a lot more than logic. Let go of your logic and be completely open and aware.

When you let go and are open, the master is such a live energy that you *will* be transformed. You *will* be a new being, you *will* be a new energy and you *will* be a new consciousness.

Radha - Chief among the *gopis* or cowherd women devotees of enlightened master Krishna.

I can say it in just one statement: you *will* be new! You will be 'new' and 'clear', you will be 'nuclear'!

You will feel lighter. You would have lost the weight of the 'tumors' you were carrying but were not part of you, that were a disturbance in you. Something that is supposed to be an inherent part of you can never be a disturbance to you. If it is a disturbance, it was never meant to be a part of you. So just be open so that the 'master surgeon' can remove these tumors you have been carrying for life over life.

When you are with the master, be total. It is not a question of whether you agree or disagree with what the master tells you. You have to go beyond agreement and disagreement. When you see the sun rise, can you say you agree or disagree with it? No! It is, that's all. In the same way, the master is, that's all. Once that feeling becomes a part of you, nothing more needs to be done from your side. Then you have given the master the permission to reveal yourself to you.

To be a disciple means to be completely open to the master, not afraid in any way, not hiding yourself in any way, but being totally authentic to the core.

Then the master can do his work on you. He will push you in directions you would never have thought you are capable of handling. He will inspire you into moments and situations you would have been otherwise afraid of. He will expand your boundaries continuously till you ultimately realize there are no boun-daries, there are no limits. Then you also become like

him. You too become a completely free, limitless *Paramahamsa!*

To be a disciple means to be completely open to the master, being totally authentic to the core.

All you need to do is be open to the master, to Existence. When you are open, you are expressing your trust in the master. This trust is all that is needed to form the beautiful bridge between you and Existence.

A small story:

A disciple fell into the river Ganga. His master was sitting on the banks of the Ganga. On seeing him the disciple shouted, 'Save me! Save me! God, save me! Master, save me!'

The master replied, 'Fool! Stand up. Save yourself.' The disciple shouted back, 'Teach me your philosophy later. First save me. My life is in danger. Just save me!'

The master did not even move. He repeated, 'Fool! Save yourself! Stand up.' The disciple cried out, 'I thought you were my master. Save me, save me!' Now the master shouted in a loud voice, 'Idiot! Stand up!'

The disciple got frightened and stood up... and saw that the water was only up to his waist!

You also struggle because you have 'fallen into water' but do not realize it is only up to your waist! It is only when you listen to the master and stand up do you realize the water just reaches your waist and you can simply relax. All the worries that you thought were destroying your life don't really exist in reality. They are mostly only in your imagination. They

> **When you are caught in an engram, just be in the master's presence. You will be completely healed.**

never come out true.

So understand, when I say 'I will take care', I am actually giving you the stick with which to stand up. When the master says, 'I will take care', if you doubt it, you simply miss an opportunity to stand up.

Burn your *samskaras* in the master's presence

A beautiful incident from the enlightened master, Ramana Maharishi's life:

There was a disciple who was writing the Ramana Purana*, verses in praise of Ramana Maharishi. But he had what you call the 'writer's block' and he was stuck at one point. Somehow, whenever you write with ego, the 'writer's block' will happen. Anyhow, that disciple came to Ramana Maharishi and said, 'Bhagavan*, I am not able to write further, please help me.' Bhagavan* said, 'Put that paper down and leave. I will talk to you later.'

The disciple put the paper down and went out. The next day when he came back, he saw that the whole poem had been completed! Ramana Maharishi had written 300 lines

himself. When the book was printed, the writer enclosed those 300 lines within quotes and below he put a footnote, 'These 300 lines were written by Bhagavan* Himself.'

Bhagavan saw the book and asked, 'Oh! So then, the other lines are written by you? Alright!'

The disciple later says, 'Something simply broke in me when he said that. Tears rolled down, and I just dropped at the feet of Bhagavan and never got up again.'

Just that one comment was enough for this disciple Muruganar* to become enlightened!

Understand, just like Muruganar's* one engram or engraved memory of writer's ego, you also carry many engrams. When you are caught in an engram, just be in the master's presence. You will be completely healed of it.

The big problem is that the engram will not allow you to acknowledge that you even have an engram. It will justify itself because it is a question of survival for itself.

That is why I always tell people, when you are caught in engrams, when you are overwhelmed by these powerful unconscious drivers of anger, lust, greed, fear, depression or jealousy, never make a major decision. Just be in the master's presence. Never miss that

---

Ramana Purana - Stories about enlightened master Ramana Maharishi.

Bhagavan - Used as a title of veneration with great masters, literally meaning 'prosperous'.

Muruganar - A disciple of enlightened master Ramana Maharishi and Tamil poet who composed many verses about Ramana.

wonderful opportunity. You will be completely healed and you will be able to come out of it. Never escape from the master when you are caught by engrams.

Whenever somebody is depressed and he leaves me, I feel so much for him. It is not because I have one person less in the mission. No! It is because he left me at the time of depression. If this same person leaves me when he is happy, it is alright. It is a normal relationship. He will carry me in him wherever he goes. But if he is in a depressed state, not only will he not grow, but he will never come out of that engram also. It will become a serious wound in him like a cat that is burnt by hot milk. It will never again go near milk.

Never decide on anything when you are in the low mood. The low mood will naturally itself distort the facts for you. It is not the right condition to take any big decision. You have to wait to swing to a good mood when things will be clearer. Always take a big decision only when you are in a cheerful mood, when you are in a positive state of mind. Just like how you decide anything in the light of day when you are awake and not in the dead of the night when you are asleep, in the same way decide this too when you are in awareness and not when in turmoil.

Be very clear, the low also will pass just like the high mood passed. That is the very nature of the mind, it is like a wheel. What is down has to come up. Neither the 'up' nor the 'down' can be said to be more real than the other. They are both there, that's all.

Trusting the positive more is a choice that you have.

The very nature of the mind is like a wheel. What is down has to come up.

If someone decides to leave when they are in depression or low mood, the problem is his mind will come back to a high and when that happens he will repent his decision. Then it will be difficult to come back because he will be caught in guilt and will not feel qualified to come back.

I always tell people, never leave when you are depressed. If you are depressed, that is the right time to be around me. Trying to move away from me when you are caught in engrams is just as if you are sick and you do not want to be with a doctor! This is actually the right time to be with a doctor!

Awakening to the purpose of your life and the master

Understand, the disciple will not know about his ignorance because he is in darkness. The responsibility is of the person who is in the light, not of the person who is in darkness.

A small story:

There was a born blind man wandering in the Himalayas. He was searching for a stick to guide him. He stumbled upon a frozen snake. He thought that it was a stick and started using it.

An enlightened master saw this and started shouting, 'Fool! It is a snake, drop it.' The blind man started shouting, 'No! I think you

> Awakening to the master in your life is awakening to this deep yearning and purpose of your life.

don't have a stick. So you are asking me to drop it so that you can pick it up!'

The master said, 'Fool! I don't need it. What you are carrying is not a stick, it is a snake. The sun will rise soon, the snake will come back to life and it will kill you.' The blind man was not ready to drop it. Then the master said, 'Even if you don't believe me, now it is my responsibility to save you.' So he snatched the snake and tried to throw it away. The blind man started beating the master with the same stick.

But the master said, 'Even if you beat me, it is ok. It is my responsibility to save you because you don't know.' He took the snake and threw it away.

You don't know how many births you have struggled or prayed to have a master. You are not even aware of your own true yearning. A master happening in your life is not a joke. You yourself don't know how many births you have struggled and prayed intensely to have a glimpse of a living master. Awakening to the master in your life is nothing but awakening to this deep yearning and purpose of your life.

End of the psychodrama of life

All your relationships are mere characters and life is just a drama. Please understand clearly, everything that happens as a relationship is just a psychodrama.

You should understand the truth. You take birth in a family with somebody as your mother, father, brother and sister and play with them as family members. You might have seen kids playing with dolls. The child will have a few dolls; he will dress one as father, another as mother and similarly dress two other dolls as brother and sister. Then he will enact a day of their life. He will make sounds as if the father is going to work, pretend that the mother is cooking something in the kitchen, show the brother going to school and the sister refusing to go to school and crying instead. The child will play all these roles himself and enjoy the whole game.

Now just look into your life. You are also trying to possess more and more, whether in terms of relationships or material things. You try to expand the movable and immovable possessions and suddenly the drama ends with your death.

Again you take birth in some other family with a different father, mother, brother and sister and play the same game once more. Our entire life is nothing different from the game which the kids play with the dolls. This is the psychodrama of life. For one who experienced the complete master-disciple relationship, the psychodrama will not happen again in his life.

Surrender – the ultimate technique

In the Bhagavad Gita, Arjuna is confused completely about what is the path he should follow. The ultimate teaching imparted by Krishna to Arjuna in the last chapter is the best technique to realize the Ultimate. After giving various techniques like meditation, devotion and knowledge, finally Krishna reveals the straight, sure and ultimate technique, which is that of surrender.

Be very clear, when you surrender to an enlightened master, you are actually surrendering to one who has no ego, no identity and hence no vested interest of his own. He is one with and overflowing with Existence. By holding his hand, you ask him to take you also to the ocean of bliss he is in.

Worry and tension come when you think you are the doer. And you get tired soon. But if you shift the sense of ownership to a higher energy and continue to do your work blissfully, you will feel tremendously relaxed!

A small story:

There was once a bank manager who used to take all the cash to his home everyday and bring it back with him the next morning. He did this for a month and could not do it anymore.

He found himself trembling all the way while driving back home and was not able to sleep at home with all the money in his custody. He finally asked his boss to be relieved of the job since he could not bear the stress any longer.

His boss told him that even if the money was lost, he would not be blamed and that he could continue with his job. The manager slept peacefully from that day onwards.

> **The best technique to realize the Ultimate is surrender.**

What was the difference in him? He was doing the same job, but why was there no more fear and tension? Because the responsibility had been shifted to a higher authority, that's all. He continued to do what he was doing.

When you surrender to the higher energy, you can never feel drained and exhausted because you are directly connected to the one who is an embodiment of the infinite energy. This is the gift of surrender.

Three levels of surrender

I will now explain to you the three categories of surrender: surrender of the intellect, surrender of emotions and surrender of your very senses.

The first is surrender of intellect which means trusting the master's intellect more than your own intellect. This is just intellectual surrender. At this stage, you follow the lifestyle that the master shows you.

The second is trusting the master's emotions much more than your own emotions. This means trusting that the relationship with the master is the ultimate relationship, more than any other relationship. If god appears before you and asks you to choose one person on planet earth as the only other person who can be alive except you, who will you choose? If you choose the master, then emotional surrender has happened to you.

Of course, the master can never be destroyed, but that is different! Never think that just because you choose him he is alive! He will be alive whether you choose him or not.

If you feel that your emotion towards the master is stronger than any other emotion, then emotional surrender has happened in you. Be very clear, 99% of the people remain in the first level. Only a few people move deeper to the second level. The rest remain standing where they are.

There is the third kind of surrender, surrender of the senses.

In Krishna's life there is a beautiful incident.

After the Mahabharata *war, when Krishna and Arjuna are relaxing, Krishna says, 'Hey! Arjuna, look there, there is a green crow!'*

Arjuna says, 'Beautiful! A green crow!' Krishna says, 'Fool! It is black, not green.' Arjuna says, 'Yes Krishna! It is black, not green.'

Krishna asks, 'What has happened to you? When I say green, you say green. When I say black, you say black. What is going on with you?'

Arjuna says, 'Krishna, let me be honest. I don't know what color that crow is. But when you said green I saw it as green. When you said black I saw it as black. I know nothing else!'

Arjuna's very senses trusted Krishna. He trusted the master's senses much more than his own!

Placebo effect or more?

In medical terms, we have a term called 'placebo effect'. A patient takes a dummy medicine but he is told it is actually the real medicine, and he is cured of the ailment! But recent research indicates that the placebo effect is actually far more revealing.

I read about an interesting research at the University of Turin in Italy. They tried an experiment where they connected electrodes to the person and gave him controlled electric shocks. First they established a pain scale for the person by finding the minimum current he could feel and the maximum current he could bear.

Now, before they gave the shock, a red or a green light would appear on the screen in front of the person. Green light meant the shock would be a mild one. Red light meant the shock would be stronger. The person was supposed to then rate the pain from the shock on a scale of 1 to 10, from mild to strong.

The participant tried this for fifteen minutes. At the end he felt that in the beginning the shocks were strong while in the end the shocks were mild.

But the shocking thing was actually it was exactly the opposite. The last series of shocks were all strong. Then how did the shocks get perceived as mild? Just before the mild shock was administered, the light shown to the person was green indicating that the shock about to come was a mild one.

So the person's mind was prepared, conditioned to believe the shock coming up was going to be a mild one. When the shock was actually administered, even though physically it was a strong one, because his mind was anticipating a mild shock his body actually felt a mild shock!

So researchers are now saying that the placebo effect is much deeper and has lot more significance than what was thought before.

They have found that even drugs do not always have the direct effects. Their results can be influenced by expectations. Doctors have found that if the person is not told that he is being given an injection of a painkiller, he has to be given a larger dose to get the painkilling effect. Whereas if he knows that he is getting a painkiller, much lower doses give the same effect!

The mind is so powerful, it can directly create a physical change in you. Just like the senses can surrender to the mind, in the same way the senses can surrender to the divine consciousness too. This is exactly what happened in the case of Krishna and Arjuna when Arjuna saw a green crow when Krishna told him to see the 'green' crow.

Your senses say you are a human being. But I say you are a spiritual being. As long as you trust your senses, you will be a hu-man being. When you trust the master you will experience that you are a spiritual being. That shift is what I call the 'cognitive shift'.

Master – the ultimate luxury

When the master happens in our lives, nothing else is needed.

Master is the ultimate luxury in your life. When the master happens in our lives, nothing else is needed. If he does not happen, nothing else is of use. He is a channel to bring wisdom to our life and to update it, according to our need.

Life energy and the master are not two different things. Masters again and again emphasize the beautiful concept called experiencing the master inside. Only until you experience the master inside, you think you need the master from the outer world. Once you experience the master inside, you don't need the master from the outer world.

The presence of the master

See, when a meditation technique is done with a master, it becomes an alchemy process. If you do it alone in your home it is called meditation. When you do it along with the master, in the presence of the master, guided by the master, it becomes alchemy. It is like boiling you. The process becomes so alive and intense.

A small story:
There was a young lady who did not know cooking. But she wanted to make something for a potluck dinner that she was going to.

She got hold of a cookery book and tried making a dessert.

She was holding the book in one hand. The instructions said, 'Put the vessel on the stove.' She did. Then it said, 'Put half a cup of flour.' She did so. Then, 'Add water half a liter, add a little sugar and stir it for twenty minutes.' She followed every instruction exactly but nothing happened even after twenty minutes.

Why? Because the book did not tell her to light the fire!

In the same way when you are doing meditation on your own, sometimes you may forget to light the fire. The master's presence itself is fire. It will ensure the product happens, the alchemy happens.

People ask me, '*Swamiji*, why should you insist on the presence of the master?' Of course, you can listen to my words on an audio CD or a DVD. But when you sit here, the honesty that radiates in my eyes, the truth that expresses in my body language will catch you. You will catch it. You will feel the click, the connection, 'Yes, he is talking the truth.'

Even if you want to suspect, suddenly you will see your logic has no power over you anymore. These words are simply entering you beyond your logic. This will happen only when you sit in the presence of the master. We call that as *Upanishad* - just being around, sitting, and opening up to the master.

Open yourself with trust and just drop yourself into trust. You will see the master standing there to hold you. Just drop yourself from your head and fall into the abyss of the heart. The master will be there to hold you and make you enlightened, that's all.

Upanishad

Upanishad means 'sitting'. When a disciple sits in the presence of the master the same experience that happened in the master is reproduced in the disciple.

The disciple who experiences the master and within whom the master has been reproduced, writes down his recollections on how this process happened. The disciple or the master or someone else writes an account of how the experience was reproduced in the disciple - what happened when the process began, how it ended and what happened when it ended. This report is referred to as an *Upanishad*.

How *upanishad* happens – beyond the law of cause and effect

We have heard of the law of cause and effect. If you drop a ball, it falls down. If you heat water, it becomes steam at 100 degrees C. If you put salt in water, it will dissolve. This is the law of causality. Any action will result in a particular effect. Science has its foundation on this law of causality.

But this is not the only law in Existence. An important law in operation every moment is the law of intuition or as the philosopher Carl Jung* calls it, the law of synchronicity.

Here, it is not that something happens and another happens as a result of it. Something happens and a *corresponding* thing happens.

We are so used to seeing things as cause and effect. We can see the relation between the cause and the immediately following effect. But life is filled with instances where the effect happens so much later that you are not able to relate to the original cause. It is just like when you throw a stone in the water, you can see the immediate ripples are because of the stone. But if you came a few minutes later, you see the secondary ripples, but you cannot be sure what caused them.

You may have experienced instances like this in your life. You think of asking your friend to make your favorite dessert and you land up at her place and she has made exactly that! She just felt she should make it on that day. This is the power of synchronicity.

This happens between the master and disciple even more than in close relationships of friends, lovers or spouses. Because the master-disciple relationship is the deepest relation possible in Existence, it is the ultimate love affair.

It is the most mysterious because it is beyond the narrow range of logic. In fact, life begins only when you have touched something that is beyond logic, which cannot be framed by the mind but which pulls the strings of your heart. It brushes aside the arguments of the mind, always looking to criticize.

The true disciple is not a disciple because of something the master said, rather it is because of what the master is. That is why just sitting with the master, the disciple starts falling in tune with the beautiful rhythm of the master. This is *upanishad*. This is true disciplehood. It is being open to the master so that he can shower his love on you and you can receive it in all its glory and divinity and grow.

Hardware and software change

The unconscious zone in the mind is like the software that can be cleansed by meditation. The hardware, the brain itself, will be tuned to hold this new software by the *darshan* or grace of the master.

When you clean the conscious and unconscious with meditation and create a change in yourself, the hardware may not be able to hold and sustain that effect from day one. If the master's *darshan* or blessing happens, the hardware also changes to hold that effect. If you don't get that blessing, constant meditation and teaching will eventually help change the hardware.

If the hardware is old, once the new software is installed, the hardware will also get updated gradually. However, if you want a change immediately in the hardware,

Carl Jung - Renowned 20th Century Swiss psychiatrist and contemporary of Sigmund Freud. He was renowned for his work on the 'collective unconscious'.

darshan is the right thing. Straightaway it will change the hardware.

Sometimes, without even installing the new software the hardware can be changed and the person will straightaway start radiating the new software's quality. That can happen when a disciple is completely open to the master. Sometimes a disciple falls in love with the master for no reason. He may not be attracted to the teachings or be familiar with them, he may not be attracted to the meditation techniques or be familiar with them, but he just falls in love. If he is in love with the master for no reason at all, the master can straightaway change the hardware along with the software. These disciples will be simply radiating the quality of the teachings and meditation without even learning any of them.

As of now, both the hardware and software are directed to the outer world, the material world. The conscious portion of the software starts turning to the inner world through listening to teachings, and the unconscious portion of the software starts turning through meditation. But even if the software turns inwards, the hardware will not be able to handle it. Then naturally the hardware will try its best to maintain its original nature. If the software is too strong and stays in the same tune, then the hardware will change. But immediately after the teaching and meditation is given, if the *darshan* and blessing is also given, the hardware will also change and it will start holding the change. It

will be prepared to hold on to the same experience.

DNA phantom effect

There is an interesting research done by the Institute of HeartMath, USA:

In this experiment, the characteristics of light-photons were studied in a light scattering chamber. The graph looked like a typical plot representing random motion of the photons.

Next, a DNA* sample was placed in the scattering chamber. The graph now changed showing an interaction between the DNA* and the photons of light.

Then the DNA was removed from the chamber. When the DNA was removed, you would anticipate that the graph would be the same as before the DNA was placed in the chamber. Surprisingly, the graph after the removal of the DNA looked clearly different from the one obtained before the DNA was placed in the chamber.

In spite of the removal of the DNA, it influenced the behavior of the light-photons. Not only immediately after removal but for several more days, the lingering effect of the DNA on the light-photons persisted.

One interesting observation is that this effect is not seen with the DNA of lower forms of consciousness. So, one can conclude that the consciousness of a particular object or a

---

DNA - Deoxyribonucleic acid, the building block of all living beings containing the genetic code.

particular person is always radiating and it contributes its own effect. We can also note that in nature, the higher forms of consciousness, by their very presence, will influence the other forms of lower consciousness. *(The complete paper is available at http://twm.co.nz/ DNAPhantom.htm).*

You can then imagine how a superconscious energy, that of an enlightened being can influence the consciousness of everything and everyone around them.

Energy to hold the transformation

Staying in the presence of an enlightened being will straightaway change the hardware for it to hold on to the transformation and the software and the entire process.

Understand, even your physiology changes with enlightenment. When a master touches, that software of enlightened physiology is also downloaded into you changing your physiology.

When you are completely open during the touch, the software of enlightened physiology is downloaded into you. Your body learns that it can be better than what it is now! Your bio-memory learns the lesson that the possibility for better existence is there.

Vasudeva Kutumbaha

With the master's love comes love for the fellow disciples. It is no longer 'I', but 'we'. A bond develops with fellow disciples, that is stronger than even biological family bonds. There are no conditions here except for the need of radial love for the master. The peripheral love automatically flourishes. '*Vasudeva Kutumbaha*', Krishna's vision that the whole world is our family, becomes true.

You grow collectively in energy, yet the relationship with the master is unique to each individual. The affair may start with the intellect or the heart. Very soon it ascends to an affair of the being. When a being merges with another, the disciple's with the master's, it is liberation, everlasting bliss.

Living enlightenment is living with the master…it is that easy!

Q&A

Does the master choose the disciple or does the disciple choose the master?

First thing, it is actually the disciple who chooses the master. Because master never chooses. The master just showers. He is like the sacred river Ganga. He just flows. If you want, you will enter the river, immerse yourself, drink or play. You can do whatever you want. But Ganga itself just flows. It does

Feel my responsibility, the responsibility of Existence.

not choose. So it is with the master. The master is a choiceless energy, choiceless bliss.

So I can say that the relationship is established by the disciple. The disciple has got the ultimate freedom, the last freedom in establishing the master-disciple relationship. After establishing, whatever freedom he has will be lost because he will become enlightened! The last activity that you can do, the last choice which you can make in your life is choosing your master, that's all. The moment you choose the master, you disappear as you. Then you are no more an individual. You become master.

How do I become your disciple?

Actually, if you are unclutched, you can get into my circle. Being unclutched directly connects you to me. A tremendous energy starts flowing through you. What do I mean by unclutched? Being relaxed without clinging on to any person or thought or thing.

I always tell people that the person who feels only his pain and comes to me for healing is a devotee. The person who has complaints only about his own problems is a devotee.

The person who feels *my* pain and takes the responsibility which I have taken as this whole mission is a disciple!

The person who after taking my responsibility realizes, 'How can an enlightened being have pain? Whatever I

thought as a pain before taking this responsibility is not a pain, it is *nithyananda* or eternal bliss,' then you become an insider!

So now you know how to become a disciple. Feel my responsibility, which is the responsibility of Existence. Then you will become a disciple.

How does a seeker know he has reached his master, or can he have many masters?

When you reach the master, this question, 'Is he my master or not?' will disappear. People ask me, 'Should we accept you as our master?' I tell them, 'Never do that mistake. No. I never promote myself. I can never tell you to accept me as your master.'

If I am your master, there will be something beyond your intellect and you will not be able to forget me. Now I challenge, if you can forget me, forget. Then I am not your master. Relax and continue your seeking. You will get the right master. Don't worry.

If you can't forget me, only then I am your master.

I always tell people, never accept me as a master. If I am your master, I will be there in your mind the whole day and whole night. I will be there even in your dreams. If thoughts of me fill you day and night, then I am your master.

People ask me, '*Swamiji*, should I remember you? Should I meditate on you?' I

MASTER - THE LIVING ENLIGHTENMENT

tell them, 'No. Forgetting me will be the problem. Remembering me will not be the problem. Only then I am your master. If you can forget me, forget and continue your journey. That is good for you.'

If you are not able to forget me then I am your master. Even if you have one doubt in one corner, that is a solid proof I am not your master. Relax. Don't struggle. Don't suffer. Don't torture yourself. Just say a beautiful goodbye and continue. My love, respects and best wishes for you to reach the right master, the master who is for you. Start searching, you will see the right master. I myself have sent many disciples to many masters. I have guided many people that way. This is not like a shop. It is not as though if you come to my shop, you can't go to another shop. It is not a business.

If you can't forget me, only then I am your master.

I always tell people that even if you are my disciple, do not stop learning from all other masters. Pluck flowers from all gardens and make a beautiful bouquet for yourself. After all, life is to be enriched.

First thing: this very question of whether you are my disciple or not will not arise in you if I am your master. If you have this doubt, be very clear I am not your master. Continue your seeking.

Second thing: even if the doubt has completely disappeared and you think I am your master and you feel completely connected, even then do not stop learning from all the other sources, all the other masters. Learn from all possible sources.

Meditations for

Living Enlightenment

Meditations for Living Enlightenment

Living Enlightenment is the Ultimate Meditation Technique

Static meditations

1. Third eye meditation

See the whole world as a dream and awaken to the higher intelligence within you.

Duration: not applicable

This meditation is to be done before going to sleep.

Sit straight on your bed. Close your eyes. Be aware of the third eye, the *ajna chakra*, which is the subtle energy center between your eyebrows. Do not concentrate, do not strain. Just be fully aware, in a very relaxed way.

Be aware of the *ajna chakra* and of the movement of *prana*, the life energy. Watch how the *prana* flows into your body, how the incoming breath brings more energy and the outgoing breath relaxes your body. Just feel it.

Again, do not concentrate. Just be aware, in a very relaxed way of the *ajna chakra* and the flow of the incoming and outgoing breath.

Now, get into a sleeping position. Be aware of the third eye when you are falling asleep. When you lie down on the bed, decide, 'Yes, now I am going to fall asleep.' Be aware when your consciousness gets diffused, when you are just disappearing into the darkness, into deep sleep.

Before going to sleep, if you are aware of the third eye it is enough, because your *prana* is hovering there during the waking state. As you fall asleep, the *prana* will start moving downwards from the third eye.

Next, throughout the day, whenever you remember, think that this whole world is not real, that you are just dreaming, that whatever you are seeing is just a dream. Consciously remember that whatever you are doing, be it eating, sleeping, walking, drinking, driving or sitting in your office, it is all just a dream.

Immediately you will tell yourself, 'How can I think that this world is a dream? This world is in fact a reality.' Please be very clear, there is a distinction between fact and truth. 'The whole world is a dream' may not be a fact according to you, because the scale by which you measure whether something is a fact or not, is itself not accurate!

Once you try to practice this technique, in a few days, you will understand the truth behind these words. It will lead you to the truth. It may not be a fact for your logical mind, but it is a fact *and* truth at a deeper level.

So throughout the whole day, whenever you remember, tell yourself, 'This world is a dream. Whatever I am perceiving is a dream.' And slowly, you will see that the whole projection just gets diffused. You will then see the *screen* on which this whole dream is taking place!

Just try this for the next eleven days. Whatever is happening in front of you, whatever you are experiencing, is a changing dream. Just remember this, that's all.

One important thing to know, any idea that you continuously remember the whole day for eleven days will penetrate your dream state. When you are dreaming, you will know you are dreaming. If you remember you are dreaming in the dream, you will be awakened.

Continuously for eleven days, if you tell yourself that you are a doctor but actually you are a lawyer by profession, in your dreams, you will see yourself as a doctor. If you want to change your identity, eleven days is enough. You will start expressing that new identity.

If this idea penetrates your inner being, the dream state, you will experience a tremendous healing effect over your entire being. This one experience is enough, you will be tremendously balanced in your day-to-day life. Not only that, suddenly you will see that you have the energy to change what you think of as reality. Situations which you thought you would never be able to change will start changing. The screen on which you project this whole dream and see is what I call consciousness or *prana*. When you start seeing the screen on which you are projecting this whole dream, you will also see the same screen with awareness when you are dreaming.

The next question that the mind will ask is, 'If I am dreaming, why should I continue doing anything at all?' Even if it is all a dream, you can still be doing. There is nothing wrong with that. You don't want to continue doing because you take yourself seriously. If you remember you are dreaming, then your dreaming or non-dreaming is in no way going to change anything. You will then relax and let life happen. You will be in the flow of life.

Suddenly your intelligence will be awakened. You will be awakened to the truth that the whole thing is your projection. Then you will not be the same person anymore because you will see the truth.

2. Include everything in you

Expand your consciousness

Duration: 21 minutes

Step 1: *Duration: 2 minutes*

Sit straight. Now feel clearly the boundary of your body. Look at the room in which you are sitting.

Step 2: *Duration: 5 minutes*

Now close your eyes and feel the room inside you, as a part of you. Your space has expanded from beyond the boundary of your body to include the entire room.

Step 3: *Duration: 2 minutes*

Open your eyes, go outdoors and look at the trees and buildings around you.

Step 4: *Duration: 5 minutes*

Now close your eyes and feel yourself expanded to include all the trees and buildings around you.

Step 5: *Duration: 2 minutes*

Open your eyes and look at the open sky.

397

Step 6: *Duration: 5 minutes*

Now close your eyes and feel the entire sky inside you.

This is a very powerful meditation to include everyone, everything around you as a part of your self. It can become a part of your daily life.

For example, at work, include your work equipment as a part of you and expand your sphere of awareness. Say you are working on your computer, sitting on a chair with your computer on the table. Include the computer, the chair, the table, and your office space, all as part of you. Close your eyes and feel them as part of you.

Include people working around you as a part of you including your colleagues, your co-workers and the people in your group. Enjoy your individual consciousness expanding to become a group consciousness. If your entire group practices this meditation, then individual personalities beautifully melt and ego clashes get resolved automatically.

3. Find the source

Find the source of your thoughts and awaken to the ultimate source that is Existence

Duration: not applicable

When you just sit, naturally, some thought will arise in you. See from where the thought is rising or which part of the body experiences movement or feeling through that thought.

You will see, one by one, each thought creates some sensation in some internal organ in your body. Try to see which thought is connected to which sensation happening inside your body. Try to locate the internal organ feeling the sensation, the organ that produced the thought coming into your mind. Do this with each thought.

When you experiment with this technique, if it clicks for you within twenty-four hours, this is the technique for you. If not, continue to try other techniques. This is a technique that can directly give you the enlightenment experience.

4. Touch the eyelids as a feather

This is one of the powerful techniques to awaken the *kundalini shakti*, the potential energy which you carry within you. This is a beautiful technique to develop sensitivity in the body.

Duration: 30 minutes

Close your eyes and just touch the eyelids with your forefingers as lightly as a feather would. You can use a real feather also if you like. The feather should not bend when touching the eye. If it bends, it means you are applying too much pressure on the eyelids. Too much pressure will not work with this technique. You need to give just a feather touch.

It is as if you are touching, but not touching. It is as if your fingers are on the eyelids but not pressing them. Balance your hands well and touch your eyelids with your forefingers. Your hands may tremble at first and you may touch either too heavily or too lightly, or you may not be touching your eyelids at all.

When you are able to touch your eyelids like a feather, you will be able to see a strong energy connection getting established between the fingers and the eyes. Slowly, you will feel that your fingers and hands have become a part of your eyes.

As of now when you close your eyes, you feel your boundary ends inside the eyelids. But with your feather touch, your eyes will feel like they have expanded! If the pressure you apply is just right, you will have this experience. Your eyes should feel the same sensitivity outside that you feel inside.

Once you start practicing this technique intensely, you will be able to see that the energy circles inside you instead of the energy leaving you through your eyes, as you normally feel it does. If you close your eyes, the outer scenes may cease and the outgoing energy may stop. But even then, inside you, some scenes will be moving and so the energy will continue to be wasted. Only if you stop the inner and outer scenes does enlightenment happen.

This technique takes at least half an hour to balance even once. It might take at least one month of daily practice to balance oneself completely using this feather-touch technique.

Dynamic meditations

1. Blissful dancing

Rejuvenate with the tremendous energy within you. Relax with the deep peace within you.

Duration: 31 minutes

Free dance means dance with no defined steps or rules. It is just allowing your body to move as it pleases, being playful, enjoying yourself and becoming part of the tremendous energy of dancing.

There are two stages to free dance: dancing and resting.

Step 1: *Duration: 21 minutes*

Close your eyes and begin to dance. Don't bother about the steps. Let your body be free to move as it wishes. Don't be concerned about how you look, how your clothes look. No one is watching you, this is not a performance.

As you continue to dance in this fashion, more and more energy will surge inside you, and you will keep going. The more you dance, the more energetic you will be! You will not feel tired at all.

Enter deeply into the dance. Dance as fast as possible, as freely as possible. Forget yourself totally. Just become the dance.

Step 2: *Duration: 10 minutes*

At the end of 21 minutes, wherever you are, in whatever position you are, just drop down on the floor. Lie down. Be silent and still.

In the sudden change from frantic motion to sudden stillness, you will experience a moment of blankness. There will be no thoughts but you will experience a deep silence.

In a few moments, the thoughts will start coming back. Watch the thoughts calmly. Don't fight with them, don't get lost in them. Just remain aware. You will become aware of a lasting peace inside you, a great silence that remains even after the thoughts return. Carry this peace, this silence with you throughout the day. Carry the silence into your sleep. You will wake up feeling new and refreshed.

2. Whirling

Find the unmoving center in your being. Merge with the whole of Existence.

Duration: 31 minutes

This is a beautiful, natural meditation to center yourself.

Do not have any food or drink at least three hours before this meditation.

The meditation has two phases: whirling and resting.

Whirling

Whirling is usually done in a counter-clockwise direction, with the right arm held higher, palm facing upwards, and the left arm lower, palm facing downwards.

If you are uncomfortable whirling counter-clockwise, switch to clockwise.

Start whirling slowly, letting your whole body be soft and unresisting. As you whirl, the passing images will become blurred. Let them flow past. Don't try to focus on anything as focusing will make you dizzy or nauseous.

Slowly pick up speed and become the whirling. There will be action and movement on the periphery of the circle, but at the center you will feel stillness. You will feel as if you are a witness to the whirling.

Resting

When you are whirling so fast that you can't stay upright, your body will fall by itself. Don't plan the fall.

As soon as you fall, turn over onto your stomach so that your navel is in contact with the earth. Feel your body become one with the earth.

Keep your eyes closed. Remain in the same position, passive and silent, for at least fifteen minutes.

After this meditation, remain silent and meditative for a few hours.

Breath-related techniques

Watching the breath continuously is a powerful and effective meditation. It has led more people to enlightenment than any other meditation. Watching the breath tremendously increases awareness. As awareness increases, inner awakening happens, and bliss follows.

1. Awareness of the incoming and outgoing breaths and the gap

Total Duration: 35 minutes

Sit in a completely relaxed position. Let your body be completely relaxed.

Step 1: *Duration: 5 minutes*

Start observing your breath. Start witnessing your breath. Do not increase the length of your breathing. Just witness your normal inhaling and exhaling.

Step 2: *Duration: 5 minutes*

Next, observe only the breath that goes in. Do not bother about the outgoing breath. Witness only the breath going in.

Step 3: *Duration: 5 minutes*

Now witness only the outgoing breath, not bothering about the incoming breath. Witness with your full awareness only the outgoing breath.

Step 4: *Duration: 5 minutes*

Now leave everything else and start witnessing only the gap between the incoming and outgoing breath. Be aware of your breath taking the turn. Be aware only of the gap between the incoming breath and outgoing breath.

Step 5: *Duration: 5 minutes*

Now, be aware of the incoming breath, the gap and the outgoing breath. Be aware of all three. Feel that your whole body is rejuvenated and alive. You are in a silence that is alive and energizing. You are vibrating with high energy.

Step 6: *Duration: 5 minutes*

Now, witness the gap between the incoming breath and outgoing breath. Be aware only of the gap. You may feel you are not breathing at all. Witness that feeling also.

Step 7: *Duration: 5 minutes*

Close your eyes and relax. Do not meditate. Just relax. Do not think actively of anything. Just let your mind settle down.

Relax and come out of the high-energy zone slowly. At the end of the five minutes, open your eyes very slowly.

2. Vipassana

Vipassana means realizing the Truth step by step. There are three ways in which you can do *vipassana*:

Duration: anytime, anywhere

When you walk, when you move your hand, when you smile, do it all with awareness. Know perfectly well that it is you who is doing that action. Be alert. Not a single moment or movement should pass in an unconscious state. Not a single action should happen in your body without your awareness.

Just like your body, watch your heart and mind. Be aware of every emotion that rises in your heart. Be aware of every thought that passes in and out of your mind. Don't have opinions, don't evaluate anything. Just be a witness.

Watch your breathing

Duration: anytime, anywhere

Feel your belly rise and fall with every inhalation and exhalation. The navel, the source of your life energy, is in the region of the belly. So when you pay attention to the navel, you become aware of the flow of life energy in your body. As you become more aware of the belly, you will see that your heart and mind fall silent!

Watch the breath as it enters your body at the nostrils

Duration: anytime, anywhere

Be aware of the cool air in the nostrils. Feel the ease with which the breath enters and leaves the nostrils.

Vipassana can be practiced both sitting and walking.

Sitting

Total Duration: 60 minutes

Sit in a comfortable position, spine erect, facing straight ahead. Keep your eyes closed and breathe normally. Stay still without shifting positions.

Watch the rise and fall of the belly when breathing in and out. Don't concentrate on the breath, but calmly observe it. If you find other thoughts, feelings or physical sensations coming up, allow them. Witness them also momentarily and then return to watching the breath. It is the process of watching that is important, not what you are watching. Witness everything.

Do this for 45 minutes and rest for 15 minutes.

Walking

Total Duration: 30 minutes

Here your awareness is totally on your feet as they touch the ground.

You can walk in a circle or in a straight line of about fifteen steps, going back or forth. You can practice this meditation simply going from room to room in your house, or out in your garden.

The eyes should be lowered and focused on the ground, on the feet. Just as you watch the belly in sitting meditation, watch and be aware here of the contact of each foot with

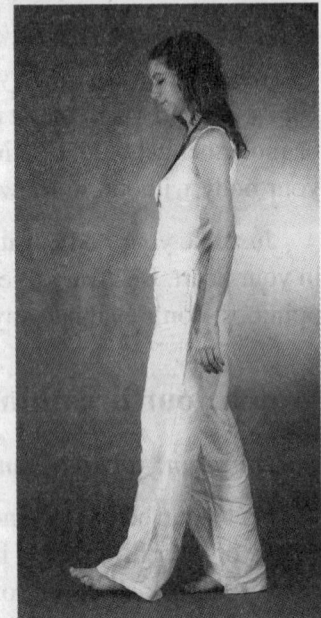

404

the ground. If other thoughts and sensations come up, allow them. Nothing is to be seen as a distraction. When you have finished witnessing the sensation or the thought, go back to watching your feet.

Do this for 20 minutes and rest for 10 minutes.

Powerful instant meditations

1. Just Stop!

This is a very powerful technique to strongly bring your awareness to the present moment.

Duration: anytime, anywhere

Just Stop! was used widely by enlightened master George Gurdjieff.

Just as you have the impulse to do something, stop. Your cunningness is also one more impulse. It is one more impulse for your survival. You always think you will survive only if you are cunning and constantly on guard. Now suspend that cunningness. Just be innocent and trusting.

Second step is whenever you have an impulse like hunger, anger, thirst or sneezing or any other urge to act, when it is about to happen or when you are about to act, just stop. Move to the space of 'being' from the space of 'doing'.

2. Looking through the mirror at yourself

Continuously energize and revitalize yourself

Duration: 10 minutes

Stand before a full-length mirror and look at yourself. Take a good look at yourself from the outside. You are the subject, and the reflection in the mirror is the object of your attention. You will feel your energy flowing towards the object. You are looking, and your reflection is being looked at.

Now imagine a reversal of roles. Imagine that your reflection is looking at you. This can be frightening at first. You are not used to thinking of your reflection in that way, as someone who can observe you.

Even if the feeling is strange and frightening, keep at it. In just a few moments, you will feel a great change. You will feel the energy flowing from your reflection towards you. You have now closed the circuit. By closing the energy circuit, you have ensured that the energy is not wasted, it is flowing back towards you. You are conserving your own energy for yourself.

Practice this technique for a few days, and you will feel a definite change. You will be more energetic, more centered, more at peace with yourself and with others.

You can practice this throughout the day, not just with the mirror and your reflection. Try it with anything or anyone you focus attention on. When you have passed your energy to something or someone, imagine it is returning the energy to you. You will feel the energy flowing back towards you, rejuvenating you, revitalizing you! You can even try this with the computer you work with all day!

3. Limb relaxation

This is one of the fastest techniques for instant relaxation.

Duration: as little as two minutes or longer if time allows

If a private space is available, practice this technique lying down. Otherwise, just make yourself as comfortable as possible.

Close your eyes. Take a big, deep breath. You are going to be holding your breath, so breathe in as deeply as possible.

Holding the breath inside you, start clenching or tensing your limbs one at a time. Start with your feet and ankles, then move upwards to your calves, your knees, then tense your bottom. As you move upwards, do not loosen the previously clenched part of the body.

Now move up to your waist, then to your stomach. Tense your stomach muscles as tightly as possible. Automatically, your groin muscles will also get tensed.

Next, move upwards to your chest and back. Tense all the vertebrae along your back. Tense your arms and hands, starting from your fingers and moving up to your biceps. Tense your shoulder blades, your neck and throat muscles. Especially hold the tension in your neck muscles.

Move to your face. Your face has more muscles than you are aware of. Tense the muscles in your mouth, nostrils, eyes, eyebrows, forehead and cheeks. Squeeze your eyelids shut. Clench your teeth. Screw your whole face into a tight ball. Remember not to relax the rest of your body during this time.

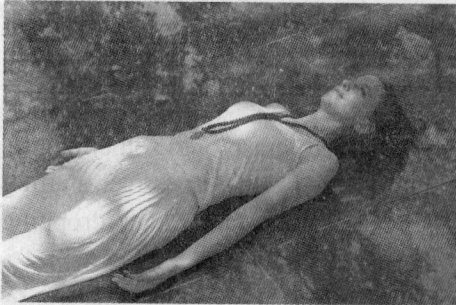

Stay in this state of tension for as long as you can. When you can't hold your breath any more, expel it in one big gush, simultaneously relaxing your body utterly.

Stay in this state of physical and mental relaxation for a minute. This technique relaxes both the body and mind and refreshes you in just two minutes. If time allows, repeat the process three times.

4. Contemplate beyond perception

Experience the bliss of no-mind

Duration: 10 minutes

The moment you perceive anything, the moment you are able to think about it, it becomes past.

For example, in the beginning, when you are told to think of something that is beyond your thoughts, you may think of the entire solar system. But the moment you think about the entire solar system, you have already made that into one more thought! So now, drop that. Next, try to think beyond. You might think about the galaxy, beyond the solar system. When you are able to think of the galaxy, drop that thought. Go beyond the galaxy. When you continuously expand your mind to go beyond, you will be in the present moment.

Understand, the moment you are able to grasp something and think about it, you have already made it into the past, into your property. Your mind can flourish there. So think further and further beyond what you can think. Even if you are thinking about what you can't think about, drop that. The mind will always try to grasp everything and keep it in storage, so it can eat slowly and ruminate, just like a bull! So do not bring the things that you have already grasped back into the mind. Continuously drop them.

Whatever you think is the ultimate in your life, drop it, and expand your thinking to something bigger. Then again your mind will automatically grasp something else. But don't allow your mind to hold that idea, drop it also. Continuously your mind will say, 'If I am dropping every moment, then what will happen to me? Where will it end?'

Don't bother about this ending. Your mind is just trying to grasp onto something by asking you this question. Your mind is asking you to prove the result before even starting the practice. Do not allow it. That is where you get cheated. Constantly keep dropping each boundary, each thought, and keep expanding, going beyond.

Meditate on the real master, or the real cosmos or the real god. You may think you have grasped the essence of god, but it can never be, because your mind can never grasp the real god! If your mind can grasp god, it means your mind is greater than god. So what you grasped is not god, it is just your *idea* of god. Drop the idea and try again. Grasp something bigger than that.

Continuously try to grasp the ultimate truth. Understand, when you throw a particular idea from your mind, not only do you throw that idea, but you also pick up one part of the bone structure from your mind and throw it out. Every time you pick up some thoughts from your mind and throw them out, not only the thoughts are discarded, but one part of the bone structure of your mind is also thrown away. So after discarding and discarding, finally there will not be any bone structure left! Suddenly you will see your whole mind has been thrown out! And you will experience the bliss of no-mind.

Sound

1. Center of the sound storm

Find the center of all sound within you, and transcend all sound.

Duration: 21 minutes

We always live in a storm of sound. Sounds are constantly moving towards us, crashing in upon us, engulfing us. But at the center of this sound storm, there is a silence we haven't heard. This meditation makes us aware of the silence in the center of this storm of sound.

Sit down in some place. The noisier the place, the better! Look for a place with continuous sound. It could be a natural sound, like the gushing of a river or a waterfall or the crashing of the waves on a beach. Or it could be a railway station, or a marketplace.

Sit silently. Feel the sounds coming at you from every direction as sound waves. With sounds flowing at you from all directions, feel yourself to be at the center of this storm of sound. You are at the center, and sounds are flowing towards you.

Feel clearly, at the center, where you are, there is no sound! At the center is total silence. If there were sound at the center, you would not be able to hear the sounds outside. The sounds are entering you, penetrating you, but they stop at the center.

Inside you, there is a point where all sounds stop. It is from that point that every sound is being heard. Try to locate that center.

When you locate it, suddenly, your awareness will turn inward from the outer world of sound. You will be at the center where there is silence, the point where no sound can enter. That point is your center.

Once you have heard that silence, you will never again be disturbed by any sound. You will never be touched by sound.

We always think that we are hearing sounds with our ears. With this technique, you discover that sounds are not heard in the ears or even in the head. The sound is always heard at the navel point, that is the center of sound.

You cannot try this technique with songs because the lyrics will have meaning for you, and you will focus on the meaning. So it needs to be just some noise.

Visualization

1. The lotus thread of light

Allow the intelligence, energy and enlightenment to awaken in you.

Duration: 21 minutes

Mentally scan your spine so that you will be able to visualize it easily in this meditation.

In the center, alongside the spine is a flow of energy like a slender thread, and that is what we call *sushumna nadi**. Observe it so that it will be easy for you to visualize the *sushumna nadi**. It runs from the base of the spine to the crown, passing through each of the seven vital energy centers in our body called the *chakras*. The *ida nadi**another slender thread, begins and ends on the left of the *sushumna nadi**, and the *pingala nadi**, a third slender thread, begins and ends on the right of the *sushumna nadi*. The *ida** and *pingala** spiral around the *sushumna,* crossing each other at every energy center, and all three meet midway between the eyebrows.

Whenever your energy is being sucked by the intellect, the *ida nadi** will be active, and the subtle energy of your system will be flowing upwards. Whenever your energy is being sucked by the sexual center, the *pingala nadi** will be active, and the energy will be flowing downwards. When enlightenment is activated in you, the central *sushumna nadi* will be activated, and your intelligence will be awakened!

All your intellectual thoughts suck the energy upward. All your thoughts of comfort or pleasure suck your energy downward. Now you are going to put your energy in the *sushumna,* the center, so that your enlightenment or intelligence is awakened.

Sit straight and close your eyes.

Let your spine be erect. Visualize your spine to be just like a lotus thread, a small thread from the root of your spinal cord to the top of the head, the crown area. Visualize

---

Sushumna nadi - One of the three major *nadis,* energy pathways in the body arising from the root energy center and ending in the crown center. The central pathway of the *kundalini* energy.

Ida nadi - Energy pathway arising from the root energy center and ending at the left nostril. Feminine, cool, represents the moon.

Pingala nadi - Energy pathway arising from the root energy center and ending in the right nostril. Hot, masculine, represents the sun.

a thin thread of light in the center of the spine, running continuously from the base of your spine to the crown of your head.

Put your attention on this thread of light. Just see the energy flowing from your root to the crown through this *sushumna nadi*. Let your whole awareness be centered on your *sushumna nadi*.

Try this technique for at least twenty one minutes for ten days. In just ten or eleven days, you will experience the intelligence, the energy, the enlightenment, awakening in you!

2. Etheric connection

Expand your consciousness and conquer your emotions

Duration: 21 minutes

Visualize you are a huge body of light. Visualize all your emotional relationships, both loving as well as not-so-loving, being a part of your light body (also called etheric body). If you have somebody who is emotionally connected to you, say in another country, visualize that you have a huge body that extends out to that country, and that person (or persons) is also inside your light body!

Let all the emotional connections, hateful or loving, be inside your etheric body. Secondly, add along with the visualization of the etheric body, the awareness of your center.

Carry this visualization for ten days.

The Touch of the

Divine Energy

- Nithya Spiritual Healing – you can also heal

- Experience the touch of living enlightenment

Nithya Spiritual Healing - You Can Also Heal

Nithya Spiritual Healing

Nithya Spiritual Healing is a gift that I received along with my enlightenment, that I pass on to you. It is not any meditation program. It is an initiation that a master gives you. The initiation puts you in tune with the Existential Energy and provides you the energy to heal.

What is healing?

The enlightened master Buddha gives a beautiful explanation or definition for the word 'healing'. He says healing is our way of expressing our compassion, our care towards somebody to help restore his health to him.

Healing is nothing but helping a person restore his physical, mental and emotional wellbeing.

Health

Good health is not just absence of disease. It is a presence of ease, a sense of wellbeing.

We are not mere humans who are meant to fall sick and then get cured. We are embodiments of bliss. We were created to live with a blissful feeling at the being level all the time. This is what good health is meant to be.

Chakras and the science of healing

According to Patanjali, an enlightened master and the father of yoga, there are seven major *chakras* or subtle energy centers in our body.

These seven energy centers influence our physical, mental and being level activities. They lie in the metaphysical plane within us and are associated with seven major glands in our physical bodies. They strongly influence the working of the corresponding physical gland.

It is only when our *chakras* are affected that disease happens in us. If our body and mind are at ease with each other, we feel this ease as a sense of wellbeing. If our body and mind are not at ease with each other, we feel

When you serve as a healer, you actually get in touch with the deepest level of your being. the *dis-ease,* otherwise called *disease* and the state of the *chakras* reveal this level of ease or dis-ease in us.

Mind over body

The body is like the hardware and the mind is like the software. We try to fix the hardware when the software is what is causing the problem! The software is corrupted, so it continuously gives the wrong instructions to the hardware, the body. Please understand that it is our mental setup that is the root cause of disease and imbalance in our body-mind system.

What is Nithya Spiritual Healing?

Nithya Spiritual Healing is healing through cosmic energy. The cosmic energy is different from the energy that we know in various forms such as electrical energy. Electrical energy does not have its own intelligence. If you put a light bulb into an electric socket, the current will flow and the bulb will glow. If you put your finger in that electric socket, the same current will flow but you will receive an electric shock! The electricity does not have the intelligence to determine what to do while flowing. But cosmic energy is pure intelligence.

Although the cosmic energy is often compared to the electric current, it is very different from it. It can never do anything wrong because it has its own independent intelligence.

Who can receive energy? The person with open heart and mind

Who can receive the energy? Anybody who is in need can receive the energy. It is not restricted in any way. There are a few tips that help a person receive the energy in a beautiful way. People with an open heart and open mind receive the energy more easily and quickly than those who question the energy with their logic.

Try to understand the concept and enter into it with full sincerity, that is enough. Just have the courage and openness to experiment without demanding proof of experience before even experimenting. Integrate your thoughts, intelligence, emotions and spirit and align them towards the concept.

Nithya Spiritual Healers' Initiation

Nithya Spiritual Healers' Initiation is directly related to enlightenment. Healing others is only a side-effect or a byproduct of the process. The main effect is that when you serve as a healer, you actually get in touch with the deepest level of your being.

In Nithya Spiritual Healers' Initiation, the master opens the door to the energy of the *Ananda Gandha chakra*.

Ananda Gandha Chakra

Ananda Gandha chakra is an energy center in us wherein our seven *chakras*, our seven energy bodies, and our five *koshas** all collapse. It is the source of all our energy, and the direct connection to the universal cosmic energy. The *Ananda Gandha* does not exist in the physical body; it has a metaphysical significance.

When a person with enlightened consciousness initiates a healer, he opens the door to the *Ananda Gandha chakra*, so there is access to the divine energy every single moment. When you are in *Ananda Gandha*, you are enlightened because you are one with the cosmic energy.

The master lives in *Ananda Gandha*. A connection to the same energy source is established when we are in *Ananda Gandha*. That is why the healing energy is able to give new life, new energy and heal disease.

Some benefits of *Ananda Gandha* meditation

When you do the *Ananda Gandha* meditation every day, continuously, nothing

from the world outside can shake you inside. Even if everything around you is failing, you will be stable and strong. You will soon reach a state where this meditation becomes your natural state of being. You will eternally be in *Ananda Gandha*!

This meditation gives you:

Sat: **Clarity in everything**

You will have clarity because you will be able to see things objectively without being driven by greed and fear.

Chit: **Consciousness**

You will have enthusiasm for everything you do. Every pore, every cell will radiate energy and enthusiasm. You will simply execute decisions one after another without feeling tired, and more importantly, with the same enthusiasm and intelligence.

Ananda: **Bliss for no reason**

You will remain happy irrespective of whatever happens in the outer world.

Being in *Ananda Gandha* continuously, you will not only have good physical and mental health but also the clarity to handle anything that happens in the outer world.

Nithya Spiritual Healing is a two-in-one technique. As the healer, you will feel bliss and the person receiving the healing will get

In Nithya Spiritual Healers' Initiation, the master opens the door to the energy of the *Ananda Gandha.*

Koshas – Five energy sheaths around the physical body. Described in detail in the *vedic* text, Taittreya Upanishad.

415

> As the healer, you will feel bliss and the person receiving the healing will get healed.

healed. That is why this is the ultimate technique.

Health benefits of Nithya Spiritual Healing

1. Relief from various physical ailments like cancer, chronic asthma, sinusitis, hernia, renal failure, diabetes, high blood pressure, back problems, allergies, seizures, migraine, wheezing, skin problems, insomnia, etc.

2. Relief from psychological problems like anxiety, depression, phobias etc.

3. Quick healing of physical injuries like burns, pains, aches etc.

4. Solutions to gynecological issues, infertility issues etc.

Services

Nithya Spiritual Healing is a service provided free of cost at thousands of healing centers worldwide, as well as at free healing camps conducted regularly. This unique system of cosmic healing is a meditation for the healer and healing for the person receiving the energy, with the safety of no adverse side-effects.

Appendix

Scientific research on Nithyananda and meditation and healing

Paramahamsa Nithyananda was the subject of cutting-edge research experiments that attempted to observe what happened in his brain while he meditated. The goal was to understand, measure and demystify what happens during the mystic phenomena in enlightened beings. Experienced physicians, neuropsychologists, and researchers of the Jim Thorpe Rehabilitation Center Neuropsychology Department, and also the PET Center of Oklahoma, USA, conducted this research.

PET scan studies

Positron Emission Tomography (PET) scans image the metabolically active brain areas at any given time. Nithyananda's PET scans showed that the activity in the frontal lobes of his brain was significantly heightened, even in early meditation stages. The level of activity was several times higher than would be seen in the average human brain under any conditions. The frontal lobes are associated with the functions of intelligence, attention, wisdom and judgment.

They studied Nithyananda's brain when he was in the deepest meditative state. There were two more remarkable findings. First, the dominant hemisphere of his brain was more than ninety percent shut down. Second, the lower portion of his mesial frontal areas lit up in a very significant way. This area roughly corresponds to the reputed location of the mystical 'Third Eye'.

QEEG Studies

Quantitative Electro Encephalography or QEEG measures electrical patterns in the brain, patterns commonly referred to as brainwaves. There are different bandwidths of brainwaves, each different in frequency, and each associated with a different state of mind. For instance, beta brainwaves are small and fast and linked with an awake, alert state of mind. Alpha brainwaves are slower and larger, and are connected to feelings of wellbeing. Theta waves represent a state of consciousness that is close to sleep, a stage in

which there is a sense of calmness and serenity, without active thought.

From Nithyananda's QEEG we can see that he has complete control over his brainwaves. When in deep meditation, his brain smoothly shifted from one state to another, like a talented pianist playing the scales.

Nithya Spiritual Healing

Research was conducted on Nithyananda's brainwave patterns, heart rate variability (HRV) and skin conductance level (SCL) when he was offering healing to another person[*]. The studies showed shifts in the power spectra indicating sympathetic arousal to match the energy of Nithyananda's heart thus indicating that the subject's heart rhythms entrained to Nithyananda's during the healing session.

(JACM, 2004, vol. 10(4); 15th ISSSEEM Conference 2005)

Experience the touch of Living Enlightenment

Ananda Darshan

(Ananda darshan is the time when you are in the presence of the master's surging energy. You go near him and he touches you on your *ajna chakra*, thus transmitting the energy and experience of enlightenment to you.)

Darshan means, 'to see something divine'. *Ananda darshan* means, 'blissfully seeing'. When the Existential energy flowers into a form that your eyes can see and consciousness can perceive, and when it causes a transformation in you, it is called *ananda darshan*! The form that you see is the form of the enlightened master who happens from time to time on planet earth.

Some people ask, 'Is there something called Existential energy?' Yes there is, but it is beyond our intellect. When we reach the peak of our intellect, we will understand there is something beyond which cannot be perceived with our intellect. Many scientists who reached the peak of their intellect saw the next step as infinite Existential energy that lay beyond them. With sensitivity, one can feel the presence of this energy.

There is always a group of people who say that the entire universe is nothing but a divine play of Existential energy. But there is another group who say that the entire universe is an accident and there is no energy or intelligence behind it. The second group can very conveniently exploit their philosophy to manufacture any number of weapons and cause destruction in the world. They don't develop any sensitivity towards anything in the universe because of this very idea that the universe and its happenings are an accident. They continue to exist and perceive at the gross level.

If you belong to the first group, you automatically enter into a subtle level and develop a deep respect for everything in this universe, for every stone, tree, and plant. A deep devotion surges within you. Automatically your very life moves with a beautiful flow like a surfer riding the rising wave of Existence.

It is only because man reached the clarity that a profound and deep intelligence is running the whole show that he is able to create a way of life that allows him to merge

A master's *darshan* is like a huge wave rising in the ocean of Existence.

beautifully and sweetly with the play of Existence.

The whole of Existence is a living being that responds to your every word, feeling, and prayer. Every moment it responds with responsibility to your very consciousness. In order to respond to you in a way that *you* can hear, see, and understand, it takes the form of enlightened masters from time to time. The seeking and praying of millions of people around the world creates a tremendous pull that causes enlightened masters to appear on planet earth, like how a low-pressure area or a depression naturally creates a storm.

A master's *darshan* is like a huge wave rising in the ocean of Existence. The wave never gets disconnected from the ocean, but at the same time expresses itself as tremendous dynamic energy! A river is also connected to the ocean, but it doesn't have the dynamic energy of the wave. It just flows passively, that's all. But *ananda darshan* is the dynamic wave that rises in the blissful ocean of Existence. It creates a churning that can completely transform you.

Now imagine a sand particle inside the wave. Can it have any impurity in it? No! It will be completely pure because it is inside the energy of the dynamic wave. In the same way, when you come for *darshan*, you will be completely cleansed inside and out by the dynamic energy that is expressed. During *darshan*, you are within the very source of the Existential energy. In the presence of the sun, the lotus blooms. In the same way, in the

presence of the master, your consciousness flowers.

All you need to do is co-operate. Actually, even if you don't co-operate, the energy will penetrate you. It is like this: whether the shell in the wave cooperates or not, the wave takes it along. In the same way, whether you cooperate or not, the energy will envelop you and do what is needed. But the shell that cooperates with the wave playfully dances along with the blissful movements of the wave. It gets purified and finally merges with it! Whereas the shell that tells the wave, 'I can't trust you so easily', and collects a few pebbles and builds a wall around itself for protection, suffers resistance. But the sheer compassion of the energy wave ultimately pulls it along into the bliss.

For the person who surrenders joyfully to the wave, his very life becomes *ananda darshan*, not just a moment of *darshan*. During any moment that your consciousness is turned towards the blissful expression of Existence that is the master, *ananda darshan* happens for you! You don't even need to be physically near the master. If you continuously rest your consciousness on that energy expression, your very life becomes *ananda darshan*. On the other hand the person who resists, misses the celebration of merging with the energy, but also merges ultimately.

During *darshan*, tremendous energy radiates from the master. How do you receive this overflowing energy? Just come like a small child, with intense enthusiasm, with a deep prayerful mood, with a melting heart, that is enough. Society has destroyed the power of prayer. Prayer has the power to completely transform you into what you want to become.

What is prayer? When you want to achieve something, you focus your intention and intensity on it with your will. This is called 'your vow'. Soon you realize, however, that to fulfill it, you need the help of some higher energy as well. When this understanding happens, your vow becomes a prayer! You start praying to the energy. 'I can do it' is a vow, 'I need the grace of the energy that is beyond me' is prayer. So come with a deep prayerful mood.

When you open up your feelings in the presence of an enlightened master, it is like putting a slide in front of a projector. What is on the slide gets projected on the screen as reality. In the same way, your desires that need to be fulfilled for your own good and the good of others will materialize. The desires that don't need to be fulfilled will get burnt away along with the unfulfilled feeling that created them. Either the desire is fulfilled or your mind forgets about the desire. Either the seed of the desire sprouts or it is burnt away. Both ways you experience fulfillment.

You carry many desires that need not be fulfilled. The energy of the master works as sheer intelligence to handle this.

A small story:

Once, a tired traveler decided to rest under a tree. The tree happened to be a wish

fulfilling tree. While he was resting, he had a passing thought, 'How nice it would be if I got some good food now!' The moment the thought came, a plate of delicious food appeared in front of him. He was delighted and ate to his heart's content.

After the satisfying meal, he thought, 'It would be good if I could get a comfortable bed to lie on.' No sooner did the thought come than a luxurious king-size bed appeared in front of him. He was amazed! He lay down on the bed.

As his head touched the pillow, he thought it would be really good if somebody fanned him while he slept. In an instant, a young girl appeared with a fan in her hand and started fanning him.

Suddenly, a thought came to the man, 'I am in the middle of a forest! What if a tiger suddenly appears?' The moment the thought came, a tiger appeared in front of him, pounced on him and ate him up!

Before fulfilling your desires, you need to bring clarity to them. When you verbalize your desires in front of the master, they will automatically acquire clarity. That is why, during the program Kalpataru*, I ask you to verbalize your desires to me. As you verbalize, you yourself will know which desires really need to be fulfilled and which need not be fulfilled. Such is the intelligence of the expressed energy.

The kalpataru darshan* sows within you the seeds of:

Kalpataru - Boon-giving tree.

Kalpataru Darshan - A meditation *darshan* program of Nithyananda.

The whole scene of the *darshan* becomes a deep imprint in your consciousness.

Shakti - Energy to change the things that need to change,

Buddhi - Intelligence to accept the things that cannot change,

Yukti - Understanding that whatever may change, Existence itself is an eternally changing dream!

Bhakti - Surging devotion to the unchanging and supportive energy of the master.

Living these four in your life is what is *mukti* or liberation!

Put your energy into changing whatever you can, including simple things that you can change. Don't think, 'Oh, I can change two habits, what about the other ten?' Just change what you can change. Then accept what you can't change. When you have expressed your energy, intelligence will start flowering.

Intelligence is accepting what you cannot change. But until you express the energy to change whatever you can, you won't be able to have the intelligence to accept what you can't change. First try changing what you can. Then you will see a tremendous ability to accept whatever you can't change.

The third seed is clarity. However much you change things, whatever you may change, still the whole world itself is a changing reality, a changing dream. It is a dream that is continuously changing for no reason. It is causeless for no reason. Understand that it is causeless. Because it is causeless, you can call it either a causeless auspicious energy or a causeless chaos. Anybody who thinks this is a causeless auspicious energy is a theist, a seeker. Anybody who thinks it is a causeless chaos is a materialist.

The whole of Existence can appear as either a miracle or a curse. If you think it is causeless auspiciousness, it is a miracle, a continuous miracle. Otherwise, it is a curse.

During *darshan*, many people have visions, healing experiences, intense spiritual experiences, and the direct experience of causeless bliss. Not only that, the energy wave that rises also causes many unconscious fears, guilt, and desires to surface. Some people just go into intense silence. Others feel overwhelmed with tears. You may not even know the reasons for all these because they come from deep unconscious layers that erupt by the energy of the wave. *Darshan* time is a rare opportunity to liberate yourself from these deeply engraved memories. These emotions can be simply wiped out at the root level by the overflowing energy.

During *darshan* time, your being comes alive and celebrates with the energy wave of Existence. The mind disappears for some time. The whole scene of the *darshan* becomes a deep imprint in your consciousness.

I would like to say just one thing. The energy of Existence is like your father's wealth. Don't miss enjoying it! Just say 'YES' to Existence and enter into it like a child.

To draw money, even from your own bank account, you need to sign a check. In the same way, to receive the energy of Existence, you need to be open. That's all.

Remember, only the oyster that opens and catches a drop of rainwater makes the pearl! When you are open to the master, just one word from him is enough. It is like rainwater that enters an oyster to become a pearl.

For the master's presence to work on you, allow whatever happens to happen. Don't be tense, irritated, or resisting. Don't expect anything. Whatever happens, allow it to happen. Just be like the surfer who dances on the energy wave, enjoying its bliss!

Blissful Sharing

Healing experiences

Healing

1. I was struck with Hepatitis B and suffering from cirrhosis, a chronic liver disease generally considered irreversible. All the hospitals had given up hope and I had been living on liquid diet for six years and knew death was around the corner.

On my friend's suggestion, I went to Nithyananda who was then at Erode in Tamilnadu, South India, healing the people who sought him out. He gave me a little holy ash and said to mix it into everything that I ate and drank for the next three days. I followed his instruction and on the third day itself I felt my stomach beginning to feel fine - after six long years! Immediately, as instructed by him, I even ate a full spicy meal for the first time in six years. Since then I have been leading a healthy and blissful life, ever ready to serve my divine master!

- Sri Nithya Sadananda, Senior Swami of the Nithyananda Order
   (nithyaayya@yahoo.co.in)

2. I had been diagnosed with Polycystic Ovarian Syndrome (PCOS), which caused severe hormonal issues. It was detected through an ultrasound which showed that my ovaries were covered by the growth of large cysts. I attended one of Nithyananda's meditation programs during which he said I would be healed, without even my telling him about my problem!

About a month later, I realized I had lost thirty pounds, which I had battled with for a long time having been close to two hundred pounds and not being able to lose weight even through diet and exercise. That is when I realized how emotionally related my weight had been! I understood how any addiction is a call for fulfillment that we try to fill externally but can never fulfill. About a year later, when I went in for an ultrasound checkup, the doctors were shocked to discover that the cysts were completely gone!

- Roshini Nambiar, Meditation Teacher, Oklahama, USA
   (roshininambiar@gmail.com)

3. When my uncle and aunt were visiting us in Singapore, they made a short trip to Tioman islands in Malaysia. When they returned home, both of them were in really bad shape. Apparently, they had a bad experience with the sea, which almost drowned them while snorkeling. They had swallowed huge amounts of sea water as well. They were in a state of complete shock even after returning. My uncle was in shivering fits and was running high temperature.

I just asked him to lie down and relax and started giving him Nithya Spiritual Healing. After about ten minutes he drifted off into deep sleep. The next morning when he woke up, he was perfectly normal as though nothing at all had happened!

- Sri Nithyananda Arpana, Nithya Spiritual Healer, Malaysia
(nithya.arpanananda@gmail.com)

4. One of my American friends was telling me that she was going through chronic anxiety and suffering frequently from 'anxiety attacks'. She wondered if Nithya Spiritual Healing would work on mental problems as well. I explained to her how the healing energy is pure intelligence and it works at all levels. I then gave her healing for about fifteen minutes. She called me the next day saying she felt such a deep sense of peace and relaxation during and after the healing and that she slept exceptionally well that night after four long years, when a major incident in her life had become the source of all her anxiety.

- Premeshwari, Nithya Spiritual Healer, Michigan, USA
(premeshwari.mayi@gmail.com)

5. I am a practicing gynecologist. Many of my patients have had miraculous experiences with the touch of Paramahamsa Nithyananda. Recently I had a case of a woman who had been suffering from tuberculosis. Her uterus lining had become very thin and the endometrium was badly affected. We tried various methods of treatment but none worked. We were thinking of the option of surrogate mother when I suggested to her to take healing from Paramahamsa. She went for healing to Paramahamsa who blessed her with a divine child. It is a real medical miracle that she was able to conceive in the first place and also have a normal delivery!

- Dr. Nirmala, gynecologist, Advanced Fertility Center, Bangalore
(nimmar@rediffmail.com)

Meditation programs

1. I was rated a star in my MNC (multinational company) corporate career. I ran companies and conglomerates, built billion dollar entities and helped start up many dreams. But I was never fulfilled. After Paramahamsa happened in my life, I have learnt how to be successful in the outer world while being equally successful in the inner world!

- Ram S Ram, Business Mentor, Singapore
(ramsram@gmail.com)

BLISSFUL SHARING

2. Five years ago I was the Vice President of Global Supply Chain at a Fortune 500 company. I was diagnosed with diabetes at the age of 32. There is a very long history of diabetes in the maternal and paternal sides of my family. When I met Paramahamsa, on one occasion, I told him about the problem. Almost four and half years have passed since I told him and till date, my blood sugar levels have been well within normal range with no diet restrictions or symptoms of the disease.

I attended an advanced meditation program with Paramahamsa. One of the techniques in that was to verbalize what stopped us from living in bliss all the time. Each of us verbalized where we felt we were stuck. The moment we verbalized this, whatever that was holding us back vanished. All I can say is, there was some intense alchemy that went on in the non-physical plane. It was as if Paramahamsa set up a flame and whatever we verbalized was burnt away from our system once and for all. Now I feel there are no emotional ups or downs in me and I am able to work with utmost intensity and bliss in all fields of endeavor. All I can say is he showered his love and compassion on us and we came out as new beings.

-Sri Nithya Sachitananda, International Coordinator and Senior Swami of Nithyananda Order, Los Angeles, USA
(nithya.sachitananda@gmail.com)

3. Effortless work is something I never thought possible. I learnt through Paramahamsa's meditation programs how to enjoy work and automatically, I started giving results effortlessly, with great creativity and work satisfaction as well.

- Apurvi Sheth, Marketing Director, Singapore (apurvi.sheth@diageo.com)

4. Besides an amazing rise in my energy levels, my business took a quantum jump ever since Nithyananda touched me the first time. My intelligence in taking business decisions entered a different dimension. Also, my relationships have greatly matured at home and outside. My child is in the Nithyananda Gurukul in the Bangalore ashram and I can really see her blossoming into a confident, intelligent and fulfilled person.

- Charanapriya, Businessman, Pondicherry
(sri_charanapriya@yahoo.com)

APPENDIX

About Paramahamsa Nithyananda

Paramahamsa Nithyananda is a living enlightened Master of the 21st century.

He took birth in Tiruvannamalai, a spiritual nerve center in South India. Since a very young age, Nithyananda spent days and nights in meditation in the divine aura of Arunachala. His intense quest for deeper Truths of life led him on his spiritual journey which covered the length and breadth of India, several thousand miles of which he covered on foot. Visiting venerated shrines, meeting highly evolved *yogis* and *rishis*, and practicing intense meditations, he studied Yoga, Tantra, and other Eastern metaphysical sciences. He went through several profoundly impacting spiritual experiences, culminating in his realization of the Ultimate at a young age.

Since then, Nithyananda has been sharing his experience with millions of people worldwide through the activities of Nithyananda Mission which conducts insightful and inspiring meditation programs and a wide spectrum of social services, thus providing life solutions at the physical, mental and spiritual levels. The meditation programs are offered worldwide through the International Vedic Hindu University (IVHU) Florida, USA. Further, free education to youth, encouragement to art and culture, corporate meditation programs, meditation for prisoners, free medical camps, free meals, a one-year residential training program in India called the Life Bliss Technology program, an in-house *gurukul* system of learning for children, and many more such services are offered around the world.

Employing time-tested *vedic* knowledge and modern technology, the Mission ashrams and centers the world over serve as spiritual laboratories where inner growth is a profound achievement. Today, they are much sought after as ideal destinations to explore, experiment and experience through a host of programs, courses and research facilities in diverse subjects from meditation to the sciences.

Established in 2003, Nithyananda Mission has grown today into a worldwide movement for bliss, standing for the ideal of realizing an enlightened humanity and thereby raising the collective consciousness of planet earth.

Programs and Workshops

Nithyananda Mission offers specialized meditation programs worldwide, to benefit millions of people at the levels of body, mind and spirit. A few of them are listed below:

Life Bliss Program Level 1 (LBP Level 1)

- Energize yourself

A *chakra* based meditation program that relaxes and energizes the seven major *chakras* or subtle energy centers in your system. It gives clear intellectual and experiential understanding of your various emotions such as greed, fear, worry, attention-need, stress, jealousy, ego, and discontentment. It is designed to create a spiritual effect at the physical level. It is a guaranteed life solution to experience the reality of your own bliss. When you are liberated from a particular emotion, you experience a new world, a new energy. It is a highly effective workshop, experienced by millions of people around the globe.

Life Bliss Program Level 2 (LBP Level 2)

- Death demystified!

A meditation program that unleashes the art of living by demystifying the process of dying. This program creates the space to detach from ingrained and unconscious emotions like guilt, pleasure and pain, all of which stem from the ultimate fear of death. It is a gateway to a new life that is driven by natural intelligence and spontaneous enthusiasm.

Life Bliss Program Level 3 - Atma Spurana Program (LBP Level 3 - ATSP)

- Connect with your Self!

An indepth program that analyzes clearly the workings of the mind and shows you experientially how to be the master of the mind rather than be dictated by it. It imparts tremendous intellectual understanding coupled with powerful meditations to produce instant clarity and integration.

Life Bliss Program Level 3 - Bhakti Spurana Program (LBP Level 3 - BSP)

- Integrate your Devotion

A program that reveals the different dimensions of relating with others and with your deeper self. It clearly defines relationship as that which kindles and reveals your own unknown dimensions to you. It allows you to experience the real depth and joy of any relationship in your life.

Life Bliss Technology (LBT)

- A free residential life sciences program

Life Bliss Technology (LBT) is a residential program for youth between 18 and 30 years of age. With its roots in the Eastern system of *vedic* education, this program is designed to empower modern youth with good physical, mental and emotional health and practical life skills. By nurturing creative intelligence and spontaneity, and imparting life skills, it creates economically self-sufficient and spiritually fulfilled youth. Above all, it offers a lifetime opportunity to live and learn under the tutelage of an enlightened master.

Inner Awakening

An enlightenment intensive program for sincere seekers offering yoga, powerful teachings, meditation, initiation and more. This program is an intense experience to prepare the body-mind system to hold and radiate the experience of 'living enlightenment'.

Nithyanandam

An advanced meditation program for seekers where the presence of the Master and the intense energy field lead one to the state of *nithya ananda* – eternal bliss. It offers a range of techniques from meditation to service to sitting in the powerful presence of the master.

Kalpataru

An experiential meditation program sowing in one the seed of:

Shakti, the Energy to understand and change whatever you need to change in life,

Buddhi, the Intelligence to understand and accept whatever you don't need to change in life,

Yukti, the Clarity to understand and realize that however much you change, whatever you see as reality is itself a continuously changing dream,

Bhakti, the Devotion, the feeling of deep connection to That which is unchanging, eternal and Ultimate, and

Mukti, the Ultimate Liberation into Living Enlightenment when all these four are integrated.

Nithyananda Mission Highlights

- **Meditation and de-addiction camps worldwide:** Over 2 million people impacted to date

- **Nithya Spiritual Healing:** A system of cosmic energy healing administered free through 5000 ordained healers, through our worldwide ashrams and centers, touching 20,000 people globally every day – healing both mind and body

- *Anna Daan*: **free food program**: 10,000 nutritious meals distributed every week through all the ashram *anna mandirs* for visitors, devotees and disciples thus improving health standards

- **The Nithyananda Order and its training:** Spiritual aspirants ordained as *Sannyasis, Brahmacharis and Brahmacharinis*: who undergo years of intensive training in yoga, meditation, deep spiritual practice, Sanskrit, *vedic* chanting, life skills, and who run the 100% volunteer based ashrams of Nithyananda Mission worldwide, working in all Mission activities

- **International Vedic Hindu University (IVHU)** (the former Hindu University, Florida, USA): Paramahamsa Nithyananda was unanimously elected as chairman (chancellor) of International Vedic Hindu University which provides education in Eastern philosophies, therapeutics, *vedic* studies, meditation science and more through Bachelor of Science, Post Graduate and Diploma degrees

- **Nithya Yoga:** A revolutionary system of yoga in the lines of sage Patanjali's original teachings, taught worldwide.

- **Temples and Ashrams:** Over 30 Vedic temples and ashrams worldwide.

- **Meditation Programs in prisons:** Conducted in prisons and juvenile camps to reform extremist attitudes, resulting in amazing transformation among the inmates.

- **Medical Camps:** Free treatment and therapies in allopathy, homeopathy, ayurveda, acupuncture, eye check-ups, eye surgeries, artificial limb donation camps, gynecology and more

- **Support to children in rural areas**: School buildings, school uniforms and educational materials provided free to rural schools.

- **Life Bliss Technology**: A free two year / three month program for youth teaching Life Engineering and the science of enlightenment

- **Nithyananda Gurukul:** A modern scientific approach to education combined with the *vedic* system of learning – protecting and developing the innate intelligence of the child who flowers without repression, fear or peer pressure

- **Corporate Meditation Programs**: Specially designed and conducted in corporate firms worldwide including Microsoft, AT&T, Qualcomm, JP Morgan, Petrobras, Pepsi, Oracle, American Association of Physicians of Indian Origin (AAPI), with focus on intuitive management, leadership skills and team work.

- **Nithyananda Institute of Teachers' Training:** Over 300 teachers trained to teach transformational meditation programs, Quantum Memory Program, Nithya Yoga, Health and Healing Programs, Spiritual Practice Programs and more

- **Media**: Articles in national and international newspapers and magazines, carrying transforming messages from Nithyananda

- **Nithyananda Publishers:** Over 4700 hours of Paramahamsa Nithyananda's discourses transcribed, edited and published in-house and made available in stores through books, DVDs and CDs

- **Life Bliss Gallerias:** Worldwide stores and mobile shops retailing recordings and books of Nithyananda's discourses and Nithya Kirtan recordings in 23 languages

- **Nithyananda Meditation & Healing Centers:** Worldwide, offering meditation and healing services

- **Nithyananda Sangeeth Academy:** Music, dance and other forms of art taught and encouraged in youth and elderly alike, live and through internet

- **Free Discourses on YouTube:** Over 500 free discourses on www.youtube.com – wisdom from the Master, easily accessible. Ranked top in viewership

- **Support to scientists and researchers:** Continually bridging gaps between science and spirituality through researches on spiritual energy and healing.

- **Nithyananda Youth Foundation**: A collection of inspired youth, building a divine and dynamic society with a common ideology of peace and enlightenment

- **Nithya Dheera Seva Sena:** Through transformation of self, this volunteer force of *Ananda Sevaks* trains and functions in the service of humanity, also serving as relief wing working towards disaster recovery management.

Contact Us

Listed below are some of the main centers of Nithyananda Mission.

USA:

Los Angeles
Los Angeles Vedic Temple
9720 Central Avenue, Montclair, CA 91763
USA
Ph.: +1 909 625 1400
Email: programs@lifebliss.org
URL: www.lifebliss.org

MALAYSIA:

Kuala Lumpur
14, Jalan Desa Gombak 5, Taman Desa Gombak
53000 KL, MALAYSIA
Ph.: +601 78861644 / +601 22350567
Email: murthi.kasavan@gmail.com, nirantaraananda@gmail.com
URL: www.mynithyananda.com

INDIA:

Bengaluru, Karnataka
(Spiritual headquarters and Vedic Temple)
Nithyananda Dhyanapeetam, Nithyanandapuri, Off Mysore Road,
Bidadi, Bengaluru - 562 109
Karnataka, INDIA
Ph.: +91 +80 27202801 / +91 92430 48957
Email: mail@nithyananda.org
URL: www.nithyananda.org

Varanasi, Uttar Pradesh
Nithyananda Dhyanapeetam
Leelaghar Bldg, Manikarnika ghat
Varanasi, INDIA
Ph.: +91 +99184 01718

Hyderabad, Andhra Pradesh
Sri Anandeshwari Temple, Nithyananda Giri,
Pashambanda Sathamrai Village, Shamshabad Mandal
Rangareddy District - 501 218
Andhra Pradesh, INDIA
Ph.: +91 +84132 60044 / +91 98665 00350

Salem, Tamil Nadu
Nithyanandapuri, 102, Azhagapurampudur
(Behind Sharada College), Salem – 636 016
Tamilnadu, INDIA
Ph.: +91 +427 2449711

Tiruvannamalai, Tamil Nadu
Nithyanandapuri, Girivala path
Tiruvannamalai – 606 604
Tamilnadu, INDIA
Ph.: +91 +4175 237666

Rajapalayam, Tamilnadu
Nithyanandapuri, Kothainachiarpuram,
Sankaran Coil Road,
Rajapalayam, Virudhunagar District
Tamilnadu, INDIA
Ph.: +91 +4563 230001 / +91 +98421 30008

Pondicherry
Nithyanandapuri,
Embalam to Villianoor Main Road,
Embalam Post, Pondicherry - 605 106
INDIA
Ph.: +91 94420 36037 / + 91 97876 67604

For further information visit www.nithyananda.org

Nithyananda Galleria

A wide range of products for blissful living:

- Nithyananda's insightful messages on video, audio tapes, CDs and books in over 20 languages.
- Enlivening music and chants for meditation and deep inner healing.
- Meditation and yoga books, kits and CDs for rejuvenating body, mind and spirit.
- Energized rosaries, bracelets, photographs, clothing and gift items for a stimulating life style.
- Ethnic energy bead jewelry for men and women for tranquility and continued high energy.

Visit www.lifeblissgalleria.com for more information.

Suggested for Further Reading

- Guaranteed Solutions
- Don't Worry Be Happy
- Nithyananda Vol. 1
- Instant Tools for Blissful Living
- You Can Heal
- Follow Me In!
- The Door to Enlightenment
- Songs of Eternity
- You are No Sinner
- So You Want to Know The Truth?
- Uncommon answers to Common Questions

Over 500 FREE discourses of Nithyananda available at http://www.youtube.com/lifeblissfoundation

GLOSSARY

Abdulla   Abdullah Ansari of Herat, a Sufi master.

Abhisheka   A ceremonial bath performed in the worship of a deity.

Adhomukha shvanasana
                          The downward-dog posture in yoga.

Adi Shankara   Enlightened master from India who lived only 32 years in the eighth century CE. Greatest exponent of the doctrine of *Advaita Vedanta* or non-dualism, whose movement restored glory to the declining *vedic* tradition and Hinduism during that period. Shankara established the Hindu order of monks which continues unbroken till today.

Agamya   The actions one constantly does out of free will after taking birth on planet Earth. These are not born out of true desires but from desires borrowed from society, by looking at others.

Aham Brahmasmi
                          Literally means 'I am god.' *Aham* means 'I am'; *Brahman* means 'god' or 'supreme being'. The statement refers to the essence of the soul which is ever identical to god.

Ahankar   The false identification of the pure inner self with the outer world; a form of ego that makes you project a false identity of you to the outer world.

Ajapa japa   Chanting a sacred chant involuntarily.

Ajna chakra   The sixth energy center located between the eyebrows. Means 'command' or 'will' in Sanskrit. This *chakra* is blocked by one's own ego.

Akbar   Moghul emperor..

Albert Einstein   Scientist and Nobel laureate.

Allopathy   Generally refers to western medicine.

Amrutasya putraha
                          Sons of Immortality.

Anahata chakra Subtle energy center in the heart region related to love.

Anahata Dhvani The primordial sound of creation *Om*.

ix

Anal-Haq   I am the Truth. Said to have been constantly uttered by the Sufi master Mansur, who was hanged to death for this sacrilege.

Ananda   Literally means 'that which cannot be reduced'.

Ananda Ashtanga

Eight fold path of bliss, referring to eight practices each of which leads to awareness

Ananda darshan Ananda Darshan or Energy Darshan refers to the blessing given by a master imparting his energy to the recipient.

Ananda Gandha chakra

Situated in between the navel or *manipuraka chakra* and heart or *anahata chakra*, Ananda Gandha is the point where all *chakras* collapse into one. Nithyananda's healing initiation to a disciple energizes the *Ananda Gandha* and initiates the disciple into Nithya Spiritual Healing.

Ananda Sankalpa

Blissful Affirmation is the second step in the *Ananda Ashtanga* process.

Anandamaya kosha

Bliss Sheath is the fifth and final energy layer in the five layers known as *koshas*. A meditative journey through the five *koshas* is the essence of Nithyananda's Atma Spurana Program.

Anima   *Anima siddhi* is one of the eight *yogic* powers, referring to the power of decreasing one's body size to that of a minute particle.

Annamacharya   Mystic saint composer of South India.

Annamalai Swamigal

Disciple of Ramana Maharishi in the temple town of Tiruvannamalai, whose teachings led to Nithyananda's deep spiritual experience at the age of 12.

Annamaya kosha Food or Physical sheath, the first of the five *koshas* or energy sheaths.

Annie Besant   Theosophist and Indian freedom fighter, writer and orator.

Anubhava   Experience, especially knowledge born out of repetitive experiences.

Appar   Tamil poet saint and author of Thevaram, devotional songs in praise of enlightened master Shiva. One of the most prominent of the 63 Nayanmars, Tamil saints who were devotees of Shiva.

Arati	Fire ritual performed at the end of most *vedic* worship done with lighted lamps or camphor, accompanied often by devotional songs.
Arihanta	Term used for *Tirthankars*, spiritual leaders of the Jain religion.
Arjuna	Warrior prince and the third of the five brothers of the Pandava family in the great Indian epic Mahabharata. He was a disciple of enlightened master Krishna who received the wisdom in the Bhagavad Gita from Krishna.
Arunachala	Literally the unmoving red mountain in Tiruvannamalai in Tamilnadu in South India, this mystical hill is considered a representation of lord Shiva.

Arunagiri Yogeeshwara

The temple of Arunachaleswara in Tiruvannamalai is built on the living energy tomb of Arunagiri Yogeeshwara, who is considered an incarnation of enlightened master Shiva.

Asana	Physical posture and one of the eight paths of yoga in Patanjali's Ashtanga Yoga. *Asana* must be stable and comfortable.
Ashram	A monastery for Hindu or Buddhist monks.
Ashrama	The four stages in one's life: *brahmacharya* as a student, *grihastha* as a married householder, *vanaprastha* at the end of a productive married life and *sannyasi* as a person who renounces all material aspects in life.
Ashramite	Resident of ashram.

Ashtanga namaskar

Prostrating to a deity or master by lying on the floor with all eight limbs of the body touching the earth.

Ashtanga yoga	Eight limbs or paths of Patanjali's Yoga: *yama* (discipline), *niyama* (rules), *asana* (body postures), *pranayama* (breath control), *pratyahara* (withdrawal of senses), *dharana* (concentration), *dhyana* (meditation) and *samadhi* (bliss).
Ashtavakra	An enlightened *vedic* sage who was born with eight crooked limbs. He is the author of the Ashtavakra Gita.

Atma deepo bhava

Buddha's message to his disciples exhorting them: 'Be a lamp unto your Self'.

Atma gnana	Self Realization.
Atma sharanagati	Surrender of the Self.

Atman	Soul, spirit, consciousness etc as referring to the individual imperishable energy that is a holographic image of the Cosmic Consciousness or *Brahman*.
Atmano mokshartham jagat hitaya cha	
	'For one's own salvation and for the welfare of the world', this is the motto of the Ramakrishna Order coined by Swami Vivekananda.
Ayurvaidyans	Practitioners of the traditional Indian medicinal system of *ayurveda*.
Ayurveda	Traditional Indian system of medicine, *Ayurveda* literally means knowledge of life.
Ayurvedic	Related to *ayurveda*, the traditional Indian system of medicine.
Bardos	Literally 'interval between two things' as in the Tibetan Book of the Dead, referring to different phases of the passage of the spirit.
Bayazid	A 9th century Persian Sufi saint.
Bhagavad Gita	Ancient Indian scripture, delivered by enlightened master Krishna, and considered the essence of the Upanishads or scriptures.
Bhagavan	Used as a title of veneration with great masters, literally meaning 'prosperous'.
Bhagavan Mahavir	
	Vardhamana Mahavira was the 24th and last Jain *tirthankara* or enlightened one, and established the tenets of the religion of Jainism, founded in India and now practiced by millions worldwide.
Bhagavatam	The foremost epic of Hindu religion describing the incarnations of Vishnu, especially his incarnation as Krishna. It was written by Vyasa, who was also the author of the *itihasa* or epic Mahabharata.
Bhaja Govindam	Collection of 32 (sometimes 34) devotional verses composed by enlightened master Adi Shankara. This is considered to be the essence of *Vedanta* and *Advaita,* non duality.
Bhakti	Devotion.
Bhakti yogi	A person who follows the path of devotion, *bhakti yoga*, as a means to enlightenment.
Bharatanatyam	Classical South Indian dance form.
Bhava	Emotional mood, referring here to the five emotional ways in which a disciple can interact with the master.

Bhujangasana	Cobra posture in Yoga, in which the head is raised while lying down.
Bidadi ashram	Nithyananda's spiritual headquarters in Bidadi township, about 30 km from Bangalore city.
Big Bang	Cosmological model of the universe where the universe is considered to have originated from a highly dense initial state at some time in the past, and continues to expand to this day.
Bija	Seed.
Bija mantra	Seed *mantra* or an energized chant that is specific to a deity or master.
Birbal	Advisor to Moghul emperor Akbar.
Black hole	A theoretical region of space in which the gravitational field is so powerful that nothing, not even light can escape from it.
Bodhidharma	A disciple of Buddha and mainly responsible for spreading Buddhism as Zen Buddhism.
Brahma	The Creator amongst the Hindu Trinity of Gods.
Brahmaanda	Cosmos or macrocosm as opposed to *pindanda,* the individual microcosm.
Brahmachari	A *vedic* student, usually referring to a young celibate monk.
Brahmacharinis	A female *vedic student,* usually referring to a young celibate monk
Brahmagnana	Knowledge of the Absolute.
Brahman	Absolute, Cosmic Consciousness, Formless god etc all referring to the Universal Energy source of which the individual energy of the soul is a holographic part.
Brahmanda Purana	
	A collection of 12,000 verses in what is usually considered the last and eighteenth Hindu *purana* or epic. This *purana* is the story of the creation of the universe by Brahma.
Buddha	Enlightened master and founder of the religion of Buddhism.
Buddhi	Intelligence.
Buddhism	Religion founded by enlightened master Buddha.
Carl Jung	Renowned 20th Century Swiss psychiatrist and contemporary of Sigmund Freud. He was renowned for his work on the 'collective unconscious'.

Chaitanya Mahaprabhu

A 15th century mystic from Bengal, India steeped in devotion to enlightened master Krishna. His followers are known as Gaudiya Vaishnavas.

Chakras

Energy centers in the body. Literally means 'wheel' based on the experience of mystics who perceived these energy centers as whirlpools of energy. There are seven major *chakras* along the spine: *muladhara*, *swadhishthana*, *manipuraka*, *anahata*, *vishuddhi*, *ajna* and *sahasrara*.

Chakshu

Energy behind the power of sight.

Chandogya Upanishad

One of the oldest and primary *Upanishads* or scriptures.

Charles Leadbeater Theosophist..

Chidambaram

A place in South India famous for its ancient temple dedicated to enlightened master Shiva in his dancing form as Nataraja and where he is represented as the space energy.

Chin mudra

Palms upraised with thumb and forefinger forming a circle and other three fingers outstretched.

Chitta

Memory.

Chittakasha

The middle part of the three space or *akasha* definitions. First is *ghatakasha* or the physical space. *Mahakasha* is the third infinite space of Consciousness.

Christianity

Religion based on teachings of Jesus Christ.

Cleve Backster

A polygraph expert who studied behavior of plants subjected to threats and affection using the lie detector equipment.

Dakshinamurthy Swamigal

Enlightened master from South India.

Darshan

Literally 'sight', referring to the vision of the divine, a deity or master.

dasa bhava

One of the five forms of relationships between master and disciple. *Dasa bhava* refers to the emotional mood of the disciple as a servant in surrender to the master, exemplified by Hanuman's relationship with Rama.

Dasoham'

Means 'I am the servant' signifying surrender to master.

Dattatreya

Representation of the Hindu Trinity of Brahma, Vishnu and Shiva in one incarnation.

Deepak Chopra	A medical doctor who writes and teaches spirituality in USA. His works on wellness related to mind-body integration have been bestsellers.
Devi	Supreme goddess in Hinduism, Cosmic Mother.
Dhamma	Representing the teachings of the enlightened master. Buddha spoke of the three elements of his mission, Buddha the master, *dhamma* his teachings and *sangha* his community.
Dhammapada	Teachings of Buddha in scriptural form.
Dharana	Concentration. The sixth limb of Patanjali's Ashtanga Yoga.
Dharma	Sanskrit equivalent of the Pali word *dhamma* used by Buddha. Also translated as 'righteous behavior'.
Dharmo rakshati rakshitaha	A *vedic* scriptural statement that means: *Dharma* protects those who protect it.
Dhauti	A *yogic* practice of cleansing intestines.
Dheera	Courageous person. Term used by Swami Vivekananda in exhorting his followers.
Dhyana	Meditation. Seventh of the eight limbs of Patanjali's Ashtanga Yoga.
DNA	Deoxyribonucleic acid, the building block of all living beings containing the genetic code.
Dr Charles Townes	Nobel laureate in physics for work related to maser and laser.
Dr. Bruce Lipton	Molecular cellular biologist and author of 'The Biology of Belief', renowned for his seminal work in relating genetics to conditioning.
Dr. Masaru Emoto	Japanese scientist and author of 'The Hidden Messages in Water' showing the effects of one's thoughts and words on water and therefore on living beings.
Draupadi	Princess in the Hindu epic Mahabharata who was married to all five warrior brothers of the Pandava family.
Dukkha ateeta	Beyond sorrow and pain.
Dukkha Harana	'Removal of sorrows' meditation that is part of Nithyananda's Life Bliss Programs. Addresses the root energy center *muladhara*.
Dvija	Twice born. Refers to the state of awakening of Consciousness.

Electroencephalograph
Machine which uses electrodes attached to the scalp to measure brain wave activity.

Engram
Shortened form for engraved memories, referring to value systems, beliefs and conditioning memories that are stored in our unconscious mind, which drive us in our thoughts and actions.

Freudian
Referring to teachings of Austrian psychologist and father of modern psychiatry Sigmund Freud.

Gananaatha
Refers to Hindu god Ganesha.

Ganas
Devotees of enlightened master Shiva.

Ganga
The most celebrated river in India, considered holy by all Hindus.

Gayatri mantra
Considered to be one of the most powerful *mantras* in the *vedic* tradition, Gayatri was the initiation *mantra* for all young students.

Generalized Anxiety Disorder
Psychological condition of constant worry leading to stress and fatigue.

George Gurdjieff
Greek Armenian mystic and spiritual teacher famous for his principle of Fourth Way, corresponding to the *turiya* state in *vedic* tradition.

Gnana
Knowledge.

Gnana shakti
Energy of knowledge.

Gnana yogi
One who follows the path of knowledge for Self Realization.

Goddess Saraswati
Hindu goddess of learning

Gomukh
Source of river Ganga.

Gopis
Women who tended cows who were devotees of enlightened master Krishna.

Guru
Spiritual master.

Guru Granth Sahib
Scripture of the Sikh religion.

Guru Krupa
Compassion of the master.

Guru Nanak
Founder of Sikh religion.

Guru puja
Ritual worship of the master.

Gurukul
Vedic educational institution.

Gurus	Spiritual masters.
Haasya Dhyana	Laughter meditation.
Hamsa Mantra	Also called *soham mantra*, it is practised by intoning 'hmmm' while inhaling and 'sssooo' while exhaling.
Hanuman	The monkey god revered by Hindus and a disciple of Rama.
Hara	Seat of the soul in Japanese tradition, corresponds to *swadhishthana chakra* or subtle energy center related to fear.
Hatha Yoga	A form of Yoga developed by Yogi Swatmarama focusing on the physical aspects of Patanjali's *ashtanga yoga*.
Himalayas	The mountain range that separates Indian sub continent from Tibetan plateau and home of the tallest peak Mount Everest. In Sanskrit means the temple of snow.
Hinduism	Religion of most Indians. Developed from the *vedic* principles of *sanatana dharma*, the eternal law, that gave rise to other religions such as Buddhism, Jainism, Sikhism etc.
Hindus	Followers of Hindu religion, estimated at over a billion people.
Homas	*Vedic* rituals to connect to the elemental energy of fire.
Hoo kara	*Hoo* sound produced from the mouth during exhalation in meditation.
Hreem	*Bija* or seed *mantra* relating to feminine energy.
Iccha shakti	Energy of desire. The other two are *kriya shakti*, energy of action and *gnana shakti*, energy of knowledge.
Ida nadi	*Ida* is one of the three major *nadis,* energy pathways in the body. Arises from the *muladhara,* root energy center. *Ida* is the left nadi, ends at the left nostril, is feminine, cool, represents the moon.
Idli	South Indian delicacy, a rice lentil steamed dish.
Issac Newton	Physicist and mathematician, pioneer of classical physics.
Institute of HeartMath	
	A not for profit organization promoting heart based living.
Isa vasya Upanishad	
	One of the major and oldest *vedic* scriptures.

Ishwara	Supreme.
J. Krishnamurthi	Renowned Indian philosopher.
Jagat	Universe.
Jain	Follower of the religion of Jainism.
Jain sutras	Scriptures of Jainism, mainly teachings of Mahavira.
Jalaluddin Rumi	13th century Persian Sufi poet..
Janma marana chakra	
	Cycle of birth and death.
Japa	Repetition of a *mantra* or sacred syllable either silently or loudly.
Jataraagni	Inner fire that sustains life.
Jeeva	Usually the imperishable spirit that dwells in all living beings.
Jeevan mukta	A person who achieves liberation from the cycle of birth and death during one's lifetime.
Jeevan mukti	The state of *jeevan mukta* or who achieves liberation from the cycle of birth and death during one's lifetime.
Jesus Christ	Founder of Christianity.
John C Maxwell	Leadership expert and writer.
John Gardner	Author of many leadership books.
Juliet	Female lead character in English poet Shakespeare's play 'Romeo and Juliet'.
Junaid	9th century Sufi master.
Karana sharira	Causal layer, the fifth energy layer in us, corresponding to deep sleep. The source of conditioned memories or engrams.
Kabir	Mystic devotional poet of India.
Kalpataru	Boon-giving tree.
Kalpataru darshan	A meditation darshan program of Nithyananda.
Kamandalu	Water pot carried by Hindu monks.
Kapha	One of the three *doshas* or attributes of the body in *Ayurveda*. Energy related to the elements of water and earth. *Kapha* is structure and lubrication.

Kapilavastu	Kingdom where enlightened master Buddha was born.
Karma	The *vedic* concept of one's freewill actions deciding one's destiny.
Karma bandha	Bound by one's actions, since they are performed with vested interests.
Karma mukta	Free of one's actions, because they are performed without attachment.
Karma yoga	The path of Self Realization by fulfilling one's responsibilities without attachment.
Karmic	Referring to *karma*.
Karurar	South Indian mystic saint upon whose immortal remains, the temple at Tanjore is believed to have been built.
Kathopanishad	One of the major *Upanishad* or scriptures that features the interaction between Yama, Hindu god of death and a young boy Nachiketa.
Kayakalpa	Body rejuvenation and anti ageing technique of *ayurveda*, traditional Indian system of medicine.
Keertans	Devotional songs.
Khalil Gibran	20th Century Lebanese American poet best known for his 'The Prophet'.
King Harishchandra	
	Legendary Indian ruler who was renowned for keeping his word at whatever cost.
King Janaka	Indian king of the kingdom of Videha with the capital of Mithila, well-known for his righteousness.
Kirlian photography	
	High voltage photograms used to record auras of living beings.
Konganavar	Hindu saint and disciple of Bogar, upon whose immortal remains, Tirupati temple is said to have been built.
Koshas	Five energy sheaths of the body-mind system, including the physical body. Described in detail in the *vedic* text, Taittreya Upanishad.
Krishna	Enlightened master from India who delivered the Truths of the Bhagavad Gita.
Kriya	Action.
Kriya shakti	Energy of action. Other two energies are energy of desire and energy of knowledge.

Kshana	Interval between two thoughts.
Kuchela	Childhood friend of enlightened master Krishna who exemplifies the relationship of friendship between master and disciple.
Kulaarnava Tantra	
	Ancient literature said to be authored by enlightened master Shiva.
Kumbh Mela	Spiritual gathering which happens once in three years in India at one of the four places of Prayag, Hardwar, Ujjain and Nasik on the banks of sacred rivers.
Kundalini shakti	Extraordinary potential energy which is hidden inside every human body. If it is awakened, it will take you to a different plane of consciousness or existence.
Kunti	In the Hindu epic Mahabharata, the mother of the five Pandava brothers who stood for righteousness.
Lamas	Buddhist monks.
Leela	Divine play, especially that of Krishna.
Rama	Prince of the kingdom of Ayodhya in the Indian epic Ramayana.
Madhura bhava	The relationship of beloved between master and disciple.
Madhyapantha	'Middle Path' prescribed by enlightened master Buddha. It represents the power of witnessing that causes one to be in moderation without being pushed and pulled into extremes of emotions.
Madurai	Temple town in south India. A major pilgrim center with the temple to Meenakshi and her consort Sundareshwara, an aspect of enlightened master Shiva.
Magnetic Resonance Imaging	
	Equipment and technique for body imaging providing greater contrast to soft tissues than X rays.
Maha bhava	The ultimate expression in master disciple relationship transcending all ordinary relationships.
Mahabharata	The Hindu *itihasa* or epic whose central characters are the five Pandava princes, their hundred Kaurava cousins and enlightened master Krishna.
Mahakaasha	The third space of the infinite beyond.

Mahamantra	Humming meditation that energizes the *anahata chakra* and taught as part of Nithyananda's Life Bliss Programs.
Maharishi Mahesh Yogi	
	20th Century Indian spiritual teacher and promoter of transcendental meditation TM.
Mahavakya	Great sayings from the Upanishads. There are four: *Aham Brahmasmi, Tat Tvam Asi, Ayam Atma Brahma* and *Prajnanam Brahma*. All four mean that You are the Divine.
Mahavira	Vardhamana Mahavira was the 24th and last *tirthankara* or enlightened one, and established the tenets of the religion of Jainism, founded in India and now practiced by millions worldwide.
Mamakar	Inner ego that constantly says that you are smaller than what you think you are.
Manas	Mind.
Manasa sharira	Mental layer of energy.
Manickavasagar	One of the 63 Nayanmars, devotees of enlightened master Shiva from Tamilnadu.
Manipuraka chakra	
	Subtle energy center located near the navel region, related to the emotion of worry.
Manomaya kosha	The third mental energy sheath in the five *koshas* or energy sheaths.
Mantra	Literally means 'that which shows the way'. Sacred syllables that have a powerful positive vibrational effect.
Mara	The demon of evil in Buddhist tradition.
Maslow	American psychologist famous for his concept of the five layered hierarchy of needs.
Matru bhava	The relationship of a child to a mother in the context of master disciple relationship.
Maya	Literally 'That which is not'. The concept that life is but a dream, however real it may seem while being experienced.
Meenakshi	The goddess at Madurai in south India. She is said to be a saint upon whose immortal remains, the temple has been built.

Meerabai	Princess of Chittor, a devotee of Krishna, mystical poetess and singer, who was ill-treated by her husband for her devotion to Krishna.
Milarepa	Tibetan Yogi and disciple of Tibetan Buddhist teacher Marpa.
Mithyam	Impermanent, opposite of *nithyam* which is eternal.
Mithyananda	Someone who represents and teaches impermanent happiness.
Moksha	Liberation through Self Realization.
Mrutyunjaya	Chant for victory over death.
Mudra	Signs formed with hands during yoga practices, especially meditation, to distribute and seal energy within the body.
Mukti	Liberation through Self Realization
Muladhara chakra	Subtle energy center at the root of the spine, related to the emotions of greed and lust.
Muruganar	A disciple of enlightened master Ramana Maharishi and Tamil poet who composed many verses about Ramana.
Na maha	'I am not' or 'I surrender'. Most Hindu ritual *mantras* end with this statement.
Nalanda	A great Buddhist center of learning in modern day Bihar in India comprising a university and library.
Namaskar	Hindu custom of greeting. Means 'I bow to you'.
Namo	Homage, refers to masters and deities as in *Om namo narayanaya*, with reference to Vishnu.
Namo Arihanta	I bow down to Arihanta, the Jain master and deity.
Narmada	Fifth largest Indian river starting from Vindhya Hills in central India flowing east to west joining the Arabian Sea.
Nataraja	Enlightened master Shiva in the dancing form in the temple of Chidambaram in south India.
Nawab	A noble of the Mogul empire.
Nayanmars	Tamil devotee saints of enlightened master Shiva, 63 in number, whose life stories are told in the book Periya Puranam.
Neti	Nasal cleansing technique of yoga.

Neuroplasticity	Changes in brain structure based on experiences.
Nidra devi	Goddess of sleep.
Nile	The longest river in the world flowing through Sudan, Egypt etc in Africa.
Nirvana	Liberation through Self Realization.
Nirvana Shatakam	A collection of six verses sung by enlightened master Adi Shankara at the age of eight to introduce himself to his master, Govindapada.
Nirvanic	Connected to *nirvana*. The *nirvanic* layer is the seventh and final energy layer in our body mind.
Nithya ananda	Eternal Bliss.
Nithya Dhyaan	Meditation developed by Nithyananda as the daily meditation for his followers.
Nithya mukta	Eternally liberated person.
Surya Namaskar	One of the techniques taught in Nithya Yoga, taught by teachers ordained by Nithyananda
Nithya Yoga	Nithyananda's teachings of yoga based on the body language of Patanjali, taught by his teachers.
Nithyam	Eternal.
Nithyananda Spurana	Eternal flowering of bliss.
Niyama	The second limb of Patanjali Ashtanga Yoga, concerning codes of behavior.
Oedipus and Electra complexes	Sexual desire of father to daughter and mother to son as defined by Freud.
Om	The sacred syllable and symbol that represents creation in Hinduism.
Omkaara	The sound of Om.
P.D.Ouspensky	Russian philosopher, mathematician and student of enlightened master George Gurdjieff.
Pancha kriyas	The five activities of a divine being: creation, sustenance, rejuvenation, creating illusion, removing illusion.
Pandavas	The five princes in the Hindu epic Mahabharata. Their father was Pandu.

Parabrahma	Supreme Being.
Parama Shiva	Supreme.
Paramahamsa	Literally means Supreme Swan. Title bestowed on enlightened beings.
Paramahamsa Yogananda	An enlightened master well known for his book 'Autobiography of a Yogi'. He founded Self Realization Fellowship movement in USA in 1920.
Paramasthiti	Supreme state.
Patanjali	A sage of ancient India and author of Yoga Sutras, which is considered the foundation of the system of yoga.
Periya Puranam	A Tamil classic by Sekkizhar on the lives of the 63 Nayanmars, the devotee saints of enlightened master Shiva.
Peter Drucker	Management guru considered to be the father of modern management
Pindanda	Individual microcosm as against *brahmanda* or universe.
Pingala nadi	*Pingala* is one of the three *nadis,* energy pathways in the body. *Pingala* ends in the right nostril, is hot and masculine, represents the sun.
Pitta	One of the three *doshas* or attributes of the body in *Ayurveda*. Energy created by the dynamic interplay of water and fire. They cannot change into each other, but they modulate or control each other and are vitally required for the life processes to occur.
Placebo	A substance given as medicine but without any verified therapeutic effect.
Placebo effect	Effect of placebos in curing people of illnesses.
Polygraph	Lie detector machine.
Pondicherry	A state in South India neighboring Tamilnadu.
Poornima	Fullmoon day.
Prana	Life energy or life force.
prana sharira	The second layer of energy body in the seven layer system.
Pranamaya kosha	The second sheath of energy in the 5 layer *kosha* system.
Pranayama	Breath control, one of the eight limbs of the Ashtanga yoga of Patanjali.
Pranic	Related to *prana* or life energy.

Prarabdha	Mindset and desires that we bring into this world when we are born.
Pratyahara	Fifth limb of Patanjali's Ashtanga Yoga referring to turning away from sensory inputs.
Puja	Hindu ritual worship.
Purashcharanam	Repetition of *mantra*.
Purusha	In Sankhya philosophy it is the male principle pure passive consciousness, as different from the active female principle *Prakriti*.
Purusha Suktam	A *vedic* chant dedicated to *Purusha* or the Supreme.
Quantitative Electro Encephalography	
	Study of brain waves.
Radha	Chief among the *gopis* or cowherd women devotees of enlightened master Krishna.
Raja sannyasi	King amongst monks.
Rajas	One of the three *gunas* or attributes of nature. Attribute of aggression.
Rama	Prince of the kingdom of Ayodhya in the Indian epic Ramayana.
Ramakrishna Paramahamsa	
	Enlightened master from West Bengal in India. His chief disciple was Swami Vivekananda.
Ramana Maharishi	
	Enlightened master, based in Tiruvannamalai in South India. He taught the method of Self-inquiry, asking oneself, 'Who am I?', as the path to Self-realization.
Ramana Purana	Stories about enlightened master Ramana Maharishi.
Ramanuja	Founder of the *Vishishtadvaita* or modified duality principle. Along with Adi Shankara and Madhva, considered to be one of the three great teachers of Hindu philosophy.
Ramayana	Hindu *itihasa* or epic about prince Rama. The original version was written by poet sage Valmiki.
Ras Leela	The spiritual interaction of enlightened master Krishna with the *gopis* or cowherd women devotees.
Rene Descartes	French philosopher scientist famous for his saying 'I think, therefore I am'.

Rishis	*Vedic* sages
Romeo	Male lead character in English poet Shakespeare's play 'Romeo and Juliet'.
Rudraksh	Seed of a tree used for Hindu rituals and for wearing. Retains energy of meditation.
Sadashiva Brahmendra	
	18th century Tamil saint and music composer.
Sadasoham	I am always Brahman. I am always conscious.
Sadhana	Spiritual practice.
Sahaja	Spontaneous divine joy.
Sahasrara chakra	The seventh and final energy center at the crown of the head. Considered to be a gateway rather than an energy center.
Sakha bhava	Mode of friendship between master and disciple as with that of Arjuna and Kuchela with Krishna.
Sakshi	Witness.
Salem	A city in Tamilnadu.
Samadhi	The eighth and final limb of *Ashtanga Yoga*, refers to the uniting of the individual consciousness with the universal consciousness. Same as *moksha, mukti, nirvana* etc.
Samhara	Dissolution.
Samsara	Cycle of birth and death.
Samsara sagara	Ocean of birth and death.
Samsari	One who is caught in *samsara* or cycle of birth and death.
Samskara	Engrams or deeply engraved memories.
Sanchita	Bank of accumulated *karmas* from which we choose to bring into this birth a few as *prarabdha karma*.
Sangha	Community.
Sankalpa	Vow or promise.
Sannyas	Renunciation.
Sannyasi	One who has renounced, a monk.

Saris	One piece garment worn by Indian women.
Satan	Representation of evil.
Satori	High state of consciousness.
Satsangs	Gatherings for prayer, meditation and spiritual purpose.
Sattva	One of the three *gunas* or attributes of nature. Attribute of passive action.
Self	Individual spirit, that which is imperishable when body and mind perish.
Self-Realization	Awareness that one is the Cosmic energy.
Shaastra	Scriptures.
Shaastra-shastras	Scriptures as tools.
shakti	Energy.
Shakti	The supreme female principle, Cosmic Mother.
Shakti Dharana	A meditation taught by Nithyananda to all Nithya Spiritual Healers.
Shanmukhi Mudra	A *mudra* in which eyes, ears, nose and mouth are covered while meditating.
Shastra	Weapon
Shirdi Sai Baba	An enlightened master worshipped by Hindus and Muslims alike. Lived in Shirdi near Nasik in India.
Shiva	Enlightened master from India. The word *shiva* literally means 'causeless auspiciousness'.
Shiva lingas	Representation of enlightened master Shiva as a symbol of rejuvenation combining male and female principles.
Shiva Sutras	A collection of teachings of Shiva in epigram form as techniques. Includes Vignana Bhairava Tantra, Guru Gita, Tiru Mandiram etc.
Shiva Tandava	Cosmic dance of Shiva as Nataraja, seen in Chidambaram.
Shraddha Saburi	Sincere commitment and perseverance. The essence of Shirdi Sai Baba's teachings.
Siddha	One who is a practitioner of the spiritual techniques.
Siddhis	Yogic powers that arise during spiritual journey.
Sister Nivedita	Anglo Irish disciple of Swami Vivekananda.
Socrates	Greek Philosopher. Contemporary of Plato..

Soham'	Same as *Hamsa*.
Sufi	Mystical dimension of Islam.
Sufis	Followers of Sufism, a mystical dimension of Islam.
Sufism	Mystical dimension of Islam.
Sushumna naadi	*Sushumna* is one of the three major *nadis,* energy pathways in the body. Arises from the *muladhara,* root energy center. *Sushumna* is the central pathway of the *kundalini* energy and ends in the *sahasrara* at the crown of the head.
Sushupti	Deep sleep.
Sutra	Spiritual techniques offered in epigram form.
Svadharma	One's right path.
Swadhishthana chakra	
	Spleen energy center between base of spine and navel. Blocked by fear.
Swami	A honorific term used for a sannyasi, a monk.
Swami Sri Yukteshwar Giri	
	Master of enlightened master Paramahamsa Yogananda.
Swapna	Dream.
Taittreya Upanishad	
	One of the major *Upanishads* or scriptures that explains the concepts of the five elements and five *koshas* or energy sheaths.
Takshila	A center of learning mentioned in the Hindu epics of Ramayana and Mahabharata, now a world UN heritage site in North eastern Pakistan.
Tamas	One of the three *gunas* or attributes of nature. Attribute of inaction.
Tanjore art paintings	
	Devotional paintings from South India that use semi- precious stones and gold as adornment.
Tantra	Ancient tradition of achieving enlightenment through spiritual techniques or practices, meditations and ritual worship.
Tapas	Spiritual penance.
Tat tvam asi	One of the great Truths meaning 'That Art Thou'.

Tathata	Suchness.
Thanjavur	Town in South India famous for its massive temple and learning and cultural heritage.
Pratyakatma chaitanya jagrat	
	Awakening of the Consciousness and inner Self.
Tirupati	Famous temple to Vishnu as Venkateshwara or Balaji in Andhra Pradesh, South India.
Tiruvannamalai	Temple town where Nithyananda was born and raised.
Transcendental Meditation-Sidhi	
	Yogic powers said to occur upon practice of advanced TM techniques.
Transcendental Meditation™	
	Meditation technique popularized by Mahesh Yogi.
Turiya	Fourth state of consciousness in which there are no thoughts and only awareness.
Tyagaraja	18th century south Indian Carnatic music composer.
Upanishad	Scriptures that form the essence of the ancient texts of the Vedas. Literally means 'sitting with the master'. There are eleven main *Upanishads* that have been commented on by enlightened master Adi Shankara.
Vaastu Shastra	*Vedic* science of space, how we interact with the space around us.
Vajrasana	A Yoga *asana* posture of sitting with the knees folded and your feet tucked under, with the bottom resting on the heels.
Vak	Energy behind speech.
Vakya	Statement.
Vali	Monkey King in the Hindu epic Ramayana who is killed by prince Rama.
Vanaprastha sannyas	
	The third stage of life according to the *vedic* tradition, where the wife and husband lead the rest of their married life in spiritual activities in pursuit of the ultimate Truth.
Vasana	Mindset.
Vasudeva Kutumbaha	
	Statement of Krishna meaning 'The world is my family.'

Vatha	One of the three *doshas* or attributes of the body in Ayurveda. Energy conceptually made up of the elements ether and air. The proportions of ether and air determine how active *vatha* is.
Vatsalya bhava	Master disciple relationship in which the disciple sees the master as a child, as with mother Yashoda and child Krishna.
Vedas	Ancient scriptural texts explaining the deep spiritual Truths. There are four main Vedas – Rigveda, Yajurveda, Samaveda and Atharvaveda. These texts explain about the performance of sacrifice and consist of stories and chants. The Vedas are considered to be revelations of the Truths that happened to the mystics and seers.
Vedic	Referring to Veda or ancient scriptures.
Veera	Bravery.
Vijnanamaya kosha	Visualization sheath, the fourth *kosha* or energy sheath.
Vipassana	Teaching of enlightened master Buddha to look inwards by observing breath.
Vishnu	Sustainer in the Hindu Trinity of gods.
Vishuddhi chakra	*Chakra* or subtle energy center in the throat region. Locked by comparing ourselves with others.
Vivekachoodamani	Enlightened master Adi Shankara's philosophical work.
Vivekananda	Primary disciple of Ramakrishna Paramahamsa and Founder of the Ramakrishna Order. 19th century Eastern mystic considered a key figure in spreading awareness of Hinduism and Yoga in Europe and America.
Warren Bennis	Management and leadership consultant.
Yaksha	Demigod who according to Hindu mythology guards wealth.
Yama	Hindu god of death and justice.
yama	The first limb of Ashtanga Yoga comprising observance of the five principles of *satya*(truth), *ahimsa*(non-violence), *asteya*(non-stealing), *aparigraha* (minimal possessions) and *brahmacharya* (celibacy).
Yamuna	A holy Indian river associated with enlightened master Krishna.
Yantra	A device, usually a metal plate that is energized, used in spiritual practices.

Yashoda	Foster mother of enlightened master Krishna.
Yoga	Literally means 'uniting' of body-mind-spirit.
Yoga Sutras	The book on yoga authored by enlightened master Patanjali.
Yogaha chitta vritti nirodhaha	
	The second verse of Yoga Sutra: Yoga is stopping of the mind.
Yudhishtra	The eldest of the five princes of the Pandava family in the Indian epic Mahabharata.
Yukti	Clarity to know what needs to change and what needs to be accepted.
Zazen	Sitting meditation in Zen.
Zen	Japanese Buddhist practice. Derived from *dhyana*, meditation.
Zen *koans*	Riddles given as techniques in Zen to aid Self Realization.